Third Workshop on Insights from Negative Results in NLP (Insights 2022)

Dublin, Ireland
26 May 2022

ISBN: 978-1-7138-6741-8

Printed from e-media with permission by:

Curran Associates, Inc.
57 Morehouse Lane
Red Hook, NY 12571

Printed with permission by Curran Associates, Inc. (2023)

For permission requests, please contact the Association for Computational Linguistics at the address below.

Association for Computational Linguistics
209 N. Eighth Street
Stroudsburg, Pennsylvania 18360

Phone: 1-570-476-8006
Fax: 1-570-476-0860

acl@aclweb.org

Additional copies of this publication are available from:

Curran Associates, Inc.
57 Morehouse Lane
Red Hook, NY 12571 USA
Phone: 845-758-0400
Fax: 845-758-2633
Email: curran@proceedings.com
Web: www.proceedings.com

Insights 2022

The Third Workshop on Insights from Negative Results in NLP

Proceedings of the Workshop

May 26, 2022

The Insights organizers gratefully acknowledge the support from the following sponsors.

Silver

Google

Introduction

Publication of negative results is difficult in most fields, and the current focus on benchmark-driven performance improvement exacerbates this situation and implicitly discourages hypothesis-driven research. As a result, the development of NLP models often devolves into a product of tinkering and tweaking, rather than science. Furthermore, it increases the time, effort, and carbon emissions spent on developing and tuning models, as the researchers have little opportunity to learn from what has already been tried and failed.

Historically, this tendency is hard to combat. ACL 2010 invited negative results as a special type of research paper submissions[1], but received too few submissions and did not continue with it. *The Journal for Interesting Negative Results in NLP and ML*[2] has only produced one issue in 2008.

However, the tide may be turning. Despite the pandemic, the third iteration of the *Workshop on Insights from Negative Results* attracted 43 submissions and 1 from ACL Rolling Reviews.

The workshop maintained roughly the same focus, welcoming many kinds of negative results with the hope that they could yield useful insights and provide a much-needed reality check on the successes of deep learning models in NLP. In particular, we solicited the following types of contributions:

- broadly applicable recommendations for training/fine-tuning, especially if X that didn't work is something that many practitioners would think reasonable to try, and if the demonstration of X's failure is accompanied by some explanation/hypothesis;
- ablation studies of components in previously proposed models, showing that their contributions are different from what was initially reported;
- datasets or probing tasks showing that previous approaches do not generalize to other domains or language phenomena;
- trivial baselines that work suspiciously well for a given task/dataset;
- cross-lingual studies showing that a technique X is only successful for a certain language or language family;
- experiments on (in)stability of the previously published results due to hardware, random initializations, preprocessing pipeline components, etc;
- theoretical arguments and/or proofs for why X should not be expected to work.

In terms of topics/themes, 16 papers from our accepted proceedings discussed "lessons learned in pre-training/training neural architectures/large language models"; 10 discussed "great ideas that didn't work"; 10 papers performed probing tasks and datasets to draw deeper insights or understand reasons for success/failure; 9 dealt with issues of robustness, generalizability, compositionality, and few-shot performance; 2 were on the topic of "analyzing biases, errors, spurious correlations in data/model"; 1 paper focused on issues in replication of research results and 1 paper on the impact of data augmentation. Some submissions fit in more than one category.

We accepted 24 short papers (55.8% acceptance rate) and one paper from ACL Rolling Reviews.

We hope the workshop will continue to contribute to the many reality-check discussions on progress in NLP. If we do not talk about things that do not work, it is harder to see what the biggest problems are and where the community effort is the most needed.

[1] `https://mirror.aclweb.org/acl2010/papers.html`

[2] `http://jinr.site.uottawa.ca/`

Organizing Committee

Organizers

Shabnam Tafreshi, University of Maryland: ARLIS, USA
João Sedoc, New York University, USA
Anna Rogers, University of Copenhagen, Denmark
Aleksandr Drozd, RIKEN, Japan
Arjun Reddy Akula, Google AI, USA
Anna Rumshisky, University of Massachusetts Lowell / Amazon Alexa, USA

Program Committee

Program Committee

Ali Seyfi, George Washington University
Alicia Sagae, Amazon
Anil Kumar Nelakanti, Amazon
Arijit Adhikari, Amazon
Ashutosh Modi, IIT Kanpur
Chanjun Park, Korea University
Chen-Yu Lee, Google
Constantine Lignos, Brandeis University
Daniel Cer, Google
Deepika Jindal, Amazon
Djamé Seddah, University Paris-Sorbonne
Edison Marrese-Taylor, National Institute of Advanced Industrial Science and Technology (AIST)
Efsun Kayi, SiteRx
Ekaterina Vylomova, University of Melbourne
Ellie Pavlick, Brown University
Emiel Krahmer, Tilburg University
Emil Vatai, RIKEN
Huda Khayrallah, Microsoft
Machel Reid, The University of Tokyo
Indraneil Paul, Amazon
Jessica Ouyang, University of Texas at Dallas
Joel Mackenzie, University of Queensland
John P. Lalor, University of Notre Dame
Jordan Rodu, University of Virginia, Charlottesville
Kyle Lo, Allen Institute for Artificial Intelligence
Lingjia Deng, Bloomberg
Mahesh Goud Tandarpally, Amazon
Marco Basaldella, Amazon
Maximilian Spliethöver, Universität Paderborn
Michael Gamon, Microsoft Research
Montse Cuadros Oller, Vicomtech
Nada Almarwani, Taibah University
Neha Nayak Kennard, University of Massachusetts, Amherst
Olha Kaminska, Universiteit Gent
Pedro Rodriguez, Facebook
Phu Mon Htut, New York University
Prasanna Parasurama, New York University
Qingqing Cao, University of Washington, Seattle
Raphael Shu, RIKEN
Salvatore Giorgi, University of Pennsylvania
Sawsan Alqahtani, Princess Nourah Bint Abdulrahman University
Shubham Chatterjee, University of New Hampshire, Durham
Sotiris Lamprinidis, Corti
Sven Buechel, Friedrich-Schiller-Universität Jena
Tristan Naumann, Microsoft Research
Udita Patel, Amazon

Valentin Barriere, Joint Research Center
Wasi Uddin Ahmad, Amazon
Wazir Ali, ILMA University Karachi
Xutan Peng, University of Sheffield
Yash Parag Butala, Indian Institute of Technology Kharagpur
Yev V Perevodchikov, Amazon

Invited Speakers

Barbara Plank, IT University of Copenhagen
Tal Linzen, New York University

Keynote Talk: Power, Uncertainty and the Null

Tal Linzen
IT University of Copenhagen, Denmark

Bio: Tal Linzen is an Assistant Professor of Linguistics and Data Science at New York University and a Research Scientist at Google. Before moving to NYU in 2020, he was a faculty member at Johns Hopkins University, a postdoctoral researcher at the École Normale Supérieure in Paris, and a PhD student at NYU. At NYU, Tal directs the Computational Psycholinguistics Lab, which develops computational models of human language comprehension and acquisition, as well as methods for interpreting and evaluating neural network models for language technologies.

Keynote Talk: Off the Beaten Track: To Turn "Failures" into Signal and Insights

Barbara Plank
IT University of Copenhagen, Denmark

Bio: Barbara Plank is Chair (Professor) of AI and Computational Linguistics at LMU Munich, with a part-time affiliation at the IT University of Copenhagen. Her research focuses on various aspects of NLP and include learning under sample selection bias (domain adaptation, transfer learning), annotation bias (human disagreements and human uncertainty), learning from beyond the text, and in general learning under limited supervision. Barbara is the recipient of a 2019 Sapere Aude Research Leader grant and an Amazon Research Award. Barbara is on the advisory board of the European Association for Computational Linguistics, publicity director of the Association for Computational Linguistics and since 2022 president of the Northern European Association for Language Technology.

Table of Contents

Program

Thursday, May 26, 2022

08:45 - 09:00 *Opening Remarks*

09:00 - 10:00 *Invited Talk: Barbara Plank*

10:30 - 11:00 *Coffee Break*

11:00 - 11:30 *Thematic Session 1: Linguistically Informed Analysis*

Do Dependency Relations Help in the Task of Stance Detection?
Alessandra Teresa Cignarella, Cristina Bosco and Paolo Rosso

BPE beyond Word Boundary: How NOT to use Multi Word Expressions in Neural Machine Translation
Dipesh Kumar and Avijit Thawani

Challenges in including extra-linguistic context in pre-trained language models
Ionut Teodor Sorodoc, Laura Aina and Gemma Boleda

11:30 - 12:00 *Thematic Session 2: Transformers*

How Much Do Modifications to Transformer Language Models Affect Their Ability to Learn Linguistic Knowledge?
Simeng Sun, Brian Dillon and Mohit Iyyer

Pathologies of Pre-trained Language Models in Few-shot Fine-tuning
Hanjie Chen, Guoqing Zheng, Ahmed Hassan Awadallah and Yangfeng Ji

On Isotropy Calibration of Transformer Models
Yue Ding, Karolis Martinkus, Damian Pascual, Simon Clematide and Roger Wattenhofer

12:00 - 12:30 *Thematic Session 3: Towards Better Data*

Do Data-based Curricula Work?
Maxim K. Surkov, Vladislav D. Mosin and Ivan P. Yamshchikov

Clustering Examples in Multi-Dataset Benchmarks with Item Response Theory
Pedro Rodriguez, Phu Mon Htut, John P. Lalor and João Sedoc

Thursday, May 26, 2022 (continued)

	On the Impact of Data Augmentation on Downstream Performance in Natural Language Processing Itsuki Okimura, Machel Reid, Makoto Kawano and Yutaka Matsuo
12:30 - 14:00	*Lunch*
14:00 - 15:00	*Panel Discussion*
15:00 - 15:30	*Coffee Break*
10:00 - 10:30	*Thematic Session 4: Improving Evaluation Practices*
	Replicability under Near-Perfect Conditions – A Case-Study from Automatic Summarization Margot Mieskes
	On the Limits of Evaluating Embodied Agent Model Generalization Using Validation Sets Hyounghun Kim, Aishwarya Padmakumar, Di Jin, Mohit Bansal and Dilek Hakkani-Tur
16:00 - 17:00	*Invited Talk: Tal Linzen*
17:00 - 18:00	*Poster Session*
18:00 - 18:10	*Closing Remarks*

On Isotropy Calibration of Transformers

Yue Ding[*2], **Karolis Martinkus**[*1], **Damián Pascual**[*1],
Simon Clematide[2], **Roger Wattenhofer**[1]
[1]ETH Zürich [2]University of Zürich
yue.ding@uzh.ch damianp@ethz.ch martinkus@ethz.ch
siclemat@cl.uzh.ch wattenhofer@ethz.ch

Abstract

Different studies of the embedding space of transformer models suggest that the distribution of contextual representations is highly anisotropic — the embeddings are distributed in a narrow cone. Meanwhile, static word representations (e.g., Word2Vec or GloVe) have been shown to benefit from isotropic spaces. Therefore, previous work has developed methods to calibrate the embedding space of transformers in order to ensure isotropy. However, a recent study (Cai et al., 2021) shows that the embedding space of transformers is locally isotropic, which suggests that these models are already capable of exploiting the expressive capacity of their embedding space. In this work, we conduct an empirical evaluation of state-of-the-art methods for isotropy calibration on transformers and find that they do not provide consistent improvements across models and tasks. These results support the thesis that, given the local isotropy, transformers do not benefit from additional isotropy calibration.

1 Introduction

The impressive performance of transformer models (Vaswani et al., 2017) across almost all areas of Natural Language Processing (NLP) has sparked in-depth investigations of these models. A remarkable finding is that the contextual representations computed by transformers are strongly anistropic (Ethayarajh, 2019), i.e., they are unevenly distributed and localized in a narrow cone of the embedding space. This discovery, labeled as the *representation degeneration problem* by Gao et al. (2019) is surprising since it suggests that most of the expressive capacity of these high-dimensional spaces is neglected by transformers.

Furthermore, previous work on static word representations, e.g., GloVE (Pennington et al., 2014) or Word2Vec (Mikolov et al., 2013), established that isotropy is a desirable property in non-contextual embedding spaces (Mu and Viswanath, 2018). Indeed, Mu and Viswanath (2018) and Liu et al. (2019a) showed that post-processing static word embeddings in order to increase isotropy improves their performance in downstream tasks. Based on these results, recent work has developed methods to correct the anisotropy of the contextual representations generated by transformers (Gao et al., 2019; Wang et al., 2019b; Li et al., 2020). These isotropy calibration methods have been reported to produce small gains in performance on some NLP tasks.

However, in a recent study, Cai et al. (2021) show that the space of contextual embeddings of transformers is locally isotropic. By analyzing low dimensional sub-spaces the authors identify isolated clusters and manifolds and argue that isotropy does exist in these manifolds. In the same line, Luo et al. (2021) and Kovaleva et al. (2021) find that in BERT (Devlin et al., 2019) almost all of the embeddings present large values in the same two components of the embedding vector. These large components distort our understanding of the embedding spaces by making all the representations have high cosine similarity. In this work, we perform an extensive empirical evaluation of isotropy calibration methods across different tasks and models to determine if they provide consistent improvements. Our results question the utility of isotropy calibration in transformers, implicitly supporting the argument that transformers do already benefit from local isotropy (Cai et al., 2021).

2 Related Work

Since the appearance of the transformer architecture and its multiple variants, of which BERT (Devlin et al., 2019) stands out as the most researched model, a lot of effort has been devoted to understanding their inner workings (Rogers et al., 2020). Unlike static word embeddings such as GloVE or Word2Vec, transformers build contextual embed-

*First three authors in alphabetic order

Proceedings of the Third Workshop on Insights from Negative Results in NLP, pages 1 - 9
May 26, 2022 ©2022 Association for Computational Linguistics

dings, i.e., dynamic representations that aggregate information from other context words. These representations have sparked a lot of research interest. Wu et al. (2020) showed that different transformer architectures produce similar contextual representations. Chronis and Erk (2020) studied the similarity and relatedness of contextual representations in the embedding spaces of BERT, while Brunner et al. (2019) studied how identifiable the intermediate representations of BERT are with respect to the input. Zhao et al. (2020) quantified the contextual knowledge of BERT and Zhao et al. (2021) analyzed the embedding spaces of BERT in order to quantify the non-linearity of its layers.

Following the discovery of anisotropy in transformers (Gao et al., 2019; Ethayarajh, 2019), different isotropy calibration methods have been developed to correct this phenomenon. Gao et al. (2019) and Zhang et al. (2020) introduced regularization objectives that affect the embedding distances. Zhou et al. (2021) presented a module inspired by batch-norm that regularizes the embeddings towards isotropic representations. Wang et al. (2019b) proposed to control the singular value decay of the output layer of transformers and Li et al. (2020) used normalizing flows to map transformer embeddings to an isotropic space. However, Cai et al. (2021) show that contextual representations are locally isotropic and suggest that this property allows transformers to exploit their full expressive capacity, questioning the utility of isotropy calibration.

3 Isotropy Calibration Methods

The output distribution of transformers is typically parameterized as a softmax function:

$$P(\boldsymbol{Y}_i = \boldsymbol{y}_i|\boldsymbol{h}_i) = \frac{\exp(\boldsymbol{h}_i^T \boldsymbol{W}_{\mathcal{I}(\boldsymbol{y}_i)})}{\sum_{j=1}^{N} \exp(\boldsymbol{h}_i^T \boldsymbol{W}_j)} ,$$

where $\boldsymbol{W} \in \mathcal{R}^{N \times d}$ is the output weight matrix, d is the embedding dimension, N is the output size, $\boldsymbol{y}_i$ is the i-th output, $\mathcal{I}(\boldsymbol{y}_i)$ is the index of $\boldsymbol{y}_i$ and $\boldsymbol{h}$ is the contextual embedding produced by the model. Since this constitutes a shared space between model embeddings $\boldsymbol{h} \in \boldsymbol{H}$ and output embeddings, isotropy at the output distribution can be enforced by calibrating either $\boldsymbol{H}$ or $\boldsymbol{W}$.

We experiment with three prominent methods for isotropy calibration on transformers:

Cosine Regularization. Gao et al. (2019) introduce a simple regularization term that minimizes the cosine similarity between any two output embeddings in order to increase the aperture of the cone that contains the embeddings. This regularization term is given by:

$$\mathcal{R}_{cos} = \lambda_c \frac{1}{|\mathcal{V}|^2} \sum_{i}^{n} \sum_{j \neq i}^{n} \hat{\boldsymbol{w}}_i^T \hat{\boldsymbol{w}}_j ,$$

where $\boldsymbol{w}_i$ is the embedding of the i-th token in the vocabulary $\mathcal{V}$, $\hat{\boldsymbol{w}} = \frac{\boldsymbol{w}}{||\boldsymbol{w}||}$ and λ_c is the regularization constant.

Spectrum Control. Wang et al. (2019b) increase isotropy by mitigating the fast decay of the singular value distribution of the output matrix $\boldsymbol{W}$. They decompose $\boldsymbol{W}$ using Singular Value Decomposition (SVD), such that $\boldsymbol{W} = \boldsymbol{U}\boldsymbol{\Sigma}\boldsymbol{V}^T$, where $\boldsymbol{\Sigma} \in \mathcal{R}^{d \times d}$ is the diagonal matrix of singular values. Then, they add a regularization term to guide the singular value distribution towards a pre-specified slow-decaying prior distribution. This term spreads the variance away from the first few dominating singular values, increasing the isotropy of the space. They propose the following two regularization terms:

$$\mathcal{R}_{pol}(\boldsymbol{\Sigma}) = \lambda_p \sum_{k=1}^{d} (\sigma_k - c_1 k^{\gamma})^2 ,$$

for polynomial singular value decay; and

$$\mathcal{R}_{exp}(\boldsymbol{\Sigma}) = \lambda_e \sum_{k=1}^{d} (\sigma_k - c_1 \exp(-c_2 k^{\gamma}))^2 ,$$

for exponential decay, where λ_e, λ_p, c_1 and c_2 are regularization constants, σ_k is the k-th largest singular value and γ is a parameter which controls the rate of singular value decay.

Flow Model. Li et al. (2020) propose a method that leverages normalizing flows to learn an invertible mapping f_ϕ^{-1} between the embedding space of the transformer model and an isotropic (Gaussian) space $\mathcal{Z}$. First, an invertible flow model (Kingma and Dhariwal, 2018) f_ϕ is trained to generate transformer embedding vectors $\boldsymbol{h}$ from Gaussian noise $\boldsymbol{z}$:

$$\boldsymbol{z} \sim p_{\mathcal{Z}}(\boldsymbol{z}), \ \boldsymbol{h} = f_\phi(\boldsymbol{z}) .$$

Then, the model f_ϕ is inverted to map transformer embeddings $\boldsymbol{h}$ to the new (and isotropic) output embedding space $\mathcal{Z}$.

	SST-2	MRPC	CoLA	RTE	WNLI	STS-B	QNLI	MNLI		QQP
Model	Accuracy	F1	Mat. corr.	Accuracy	Accuracy	Pearson corr.	Accuracy	Match acc.	Mismatch acc.	Accuracy
BERT	**91.44 ±0.52**	**88.80±0.99**	**53.16±1.82**	**58.97±1.82**	53.52±4.88	**80.86 ±2.11**	88.78±0.57	81.02±0.17	81.78±0.40	89.31±0.06
+Cosreg	90.71 ±1.00	88.17 ±0.38	46.94 ±4.29	56.43 ±5.16	50.23 ±4.95	78.23 ±2.19	**89.58 ±0.19**	**81.20 ±0.41**	**82.04 ±0.21**	89.26 ±0.10
+Spectrum-Pol	90.86 ±1.35	81.22 ±0	0	49.58 ±3.62	**56.34 ±0**	NaN	81.24 ±4.45	64.33 ±27.80	64.76 ±27.48	87.15 ±2.23
+Spectrum-Exp	91.21 ±0.37	81.22 ±0	0	50.90 ±3.45	**56.34 ±0**	NaN	86.42 ±0.42	62.43 ±24.97	63.12 ±25.20	89.16 ±0.45
+Flow	91.09 ±0.54	86.99 ±0.89	51.19 ±1.81	54.27 ±1.46	48.36 ±5.86	78.88 ±3.46	86.21 ±3.38	80.65 ±0.46	81.15 ±0.21	**89.36 ±0.10**
RoBERTa	**92.97 ±0.63**	85.35 ±8.52	**53.67 ±3.32**	53.19 ±0.55	54.46 ±0.81	**83.10 ±2.87**	**91.00 ±0.46**	85.16 ±0.28	85.19 ±0.15	89.85 ±0.13
+Cosreg	92.66 ±0.23	**89.17 ±2.28**	48.99 ±5.61	**53.67 ±1.16**	53.52 ±1.41	28.44 ±44.84	90.89 ±0.19	**85.41 ±0.09**	**85.64 ±0.22** *	**89.87 ±0.12**
+Spectrum-Pol	88.08 ±0.99	81.22 ±0	0	52.71 ±0	**57.28 ±1.62** *	NaN	83.89 ±2.46	50.63 ±29.72	51.14 ±29.29	81.76 ±12.76
+Spectrum-Exp	90.71 ±1.09	81.22 ±0	0	52.95 ±0.42	56.34 ±0	NaN	82.25 ±3.14	84.46 ±0.51	84.77 0.41	80.95 ±13.89
DistilBERT	88.23 ±1.79	**87.97 ±1.02**	44.11 ±2.09	56.68 ±0.62	51.17 ±5.69	**23.63 ±41.08**	**87.53 ±0.13**	**78.84 ±0.27**	**79.50 ±0.32**	88.28 ±0.25
+Cosreg	88.53 ±1.55	87.88 ±1.36	**43.13 ±0.85**	**58.24 ±1.78**	52.11 ±2.44	-0.50 ±2.08	87.15 ±0.84	78.69 ±0.17	79.42 ±0.28	88.38 ±0.05
+Spectrum-Pol	88.80 ±0.37	81.22 ±0	0	54.15 ±2.50	**55.87 ±0.81**	NaN	85.47 ±0.96	78.39 ±0.17	79.13 ±0.05	**88.41 ±0.43**
+Spectrum-Exp	**88.92 ±0.67**	81.22 ±0	0	54.27 ±2.71	**55.87 ±0.81**	NaN	86.25 ±0.80	78.38 ±1.34	79.03 ±0.34	88.12 ±0.58

Table 1: Performance for different models and calibration methods on GLUE; * denotes significantly better performance than the corresponding uncalibrated model ($p < 0.05$, two-sample t-test). The NaN and 0 scores are caused by the model always predicting the same class.

4 Experiments

We evaluate the impact of each of these calibration methods on state-of-the-art transformer models in three prominent areas of Natural Language Processing: language understanding, machine translation, and summarization. For all of the models, we use the implementation and fine-tuning parameters from HuggingFace (Wolf et al., 2020) (cf. Appendix B). We run each experiment three times and report the mean and standard deviation. Fine-tuning time is reported on a Nvidia Titan RTX GPU.

To characterize the isotropy of the output embedding space we adopt the I_1 and I_2 isotropy measures from (Wang et al., 2019b), with $I_1(\boldsymbol{W}) \in [0, 1]$ and $I_2(\boldsymbol{W}) \geq 0$. Larger $I_1(\boldsymbol{W})$ and smaller $I_2(\boldsymbol{W})$ indicate more isotropic embeddings (cf. App. A for details).

4.1 Language Understanding

We consider three representative transformer models with different sizes, BERT-base (Devlin et al., 2019), RoBERTa (Liu et al., 2019b), and DistilBERT (Sanh et al., 2020). We evaluate these models on the development set of GLUE (Wang et al., 2019a), a well-known benchmark for language understanding that consists of nine different tasks. Due to the high computational cost of flow calibration and the large number of tasks, we apply this method only on BERT to save resources.

In Table 1 we report the performance per task of the calibrated and uncalibrated models. We observe the same pattern for all three models. In the overwhelming majority of cases, the calibrated models perform comparably to or worse than the uncalibrated ones, with calibration improving performance with statistical significance ($p < 0.05$, two-sample t-test) only in RoBERTa for WNLI with exponential decay and MNLI mismatched with cosine regularization. More specifically, cosine regularization and flow calibration (in BERT) do not affect performance much, while spectrum control in some cases produces severe performance degradation or even prevents learning, e.g., CoLA and STS-B. Furthermore, flow calibration adds a large training overhead, requiring on average 4.2 times more time per training epoch.

These results reveal that no isotropy calibration method yields consistently better performance than the uncalibrated models in language understanding tasks.

4.2 Machine Translation

We test multilingual BART (M-BART) (Liu et al., 2020) on English-Romanian and German-English WMT16 (Bojar et al., 2016) translation datasets. In Table 2 we report BLUE scores, compute time, and the isotropy metrics, for the uncalibrated and calibrated models. To reduce the high computational cost of flow calibration, we apply this method only on a reduced version of 50 000 samples for both tasks, English-Romanian and German-English translation. As a reference, we also provide the scores of the uncalibrated model on the small datasets. We find, that while cosine regularization does not significantly affect either BLEU scores or isotropy metrics, both variants of spectrum control improve isotropy but produce a performance degradation of over 3 and 5 BLEU points in the English-Romanian and German-English tasks respectively, while requiring 25% to 50% more computation

	EN-RO				DE-EN			
Model	BLEU (↑)	I_1(↑)	I_2(↓)	Time (min)	BLEU (↑)	I_1(↑)	I_2(↓)	Time (min)
M-BART	**26.15 ±0.08**	0.88 ±0.01	0.60 ±0	108 ±0	22.81 ±0.35	0.89 ±0.01	0.60 ±0	176 ±0
+*Cosreg*	26.07 ±0.10	0.88 ±0.01	0.60 ±0	110 ±0	**23.03 ±0.27**	0.89 ±0.01	0.60 ±0	188 ±1
+*Spectrum-Pol*	22.94 ±0.18	**1.00 ±0**	**0.02 ±0**	176 ±2	16.27 ±0.06	**1.00 ±0**	**0.02 ±0**	265 ±0
+*Spectrum-Exp*	22.92 ±0.05	**1.00 ±0**	**0.02 ±0**	170 ±1	16.24 ±0.12	**1.00 ±0**	**0.02 ±0**	230 ±18
M-BART (small dataset)	**9.09 ±1.02**	0.88 ±0	**0.60 ±0**	9 ±0	**11.61 ±2.25**	**0.88 ±0**	**0.60 ±0**	9 ±0
+*Flow*	8.57 ±2.52	**0.89 ±0**	**0.60 ±0**	95 ±0	10.93 ±0.70	**0.88 ±0**	**0.60 ±0**	96 ±1

Table 2: Multilingual BART performance, isotropy (I_1 and I_2) and fine-tuning time per epoch with different calibration methods for English - Romanian and German - English translation. Due to computational cost, the flow method was tested only on a smaller version of the EN-RO dataset with 50 000 sentences.

time. On the other hand, flow calibration yields comparable BLEU score to the uncalibrated model but requires on average 10.5 times more computation per epoch. These results suggest a negative and counter-intuitive relation between isotropy and downstream performance: when isotropy increases, performance decreases. We observe a similar trend for language understanding in Appendix C.

Overall, and in line with the results in the previous section, isotropy calibration in machine translation tends to degrade performance and increase the computational budget.

4.3 Summarization

We evaluate BART (Lewis et al., 2020) on the CNN/DM summarization task (Hermann et al., 2015); again we use a reduced dataset (20 000 articles) for flow calibration. The results in Table 3 show that none of the calibrated models performs significantly better than their uncalibrated counterparts in terms of ROUGE score (Lin, 2004) (cf. Appendix D). Cosine regularization does not affect performance nor isotropy, while spectrum control improves isotropy (I_1 and I_2) at the cost of a small performance drop. The flow model performs comparably to uncalibrated BART but requires 5.5 times more computation. Overall, we find no evidence that isotropy calibration provides gains in summarization.

	CNN / Daily Mail			
Model	R-1 (↑)	I_1(↑)	I_2(↓)	Time (min)
BART	**38.21 ±0.05**	0.95 ±0.01	0.25 ±0	246 ±8
+*Cosreg*	**38.21 ±0.05**	0.95 ±0.01	0.25 ±0	240 ±8
+*Spectrum-Pol*	37.36 ±0.08	**0.99 ±0**	**0.04 ±0**	245 ±20
+*Spectrum-Exp*	37.43 ±0.08	**0.99 ±0**	**0.04 ±0**	230 ±18
BART (small d.)	**36.56 ±0.25**	**0.94 ±0**	**0.25 ±0**	17 ±0
+*Flow*	36.15 ±0.30	**0.94 ±0**	**0.25 ±0**	95 ±2

Table 3: ROUGE-1 score, isotropy (I_1 and I_2), and fine-tuning time per epoch with different calibration methods on BART for summarization. Due to computational cost, the flow calibration method was tested on a smaller version of the dataset.

metrics as well as the most significant performance drop. On the other hand, the effect of cosine regularization and flow calibration is small in both, isotropy and performance.

According to Cai et al. (2021), the local isotropy of the embedding space of transformers may enable them to exploit their full expressive capacity. Furthermore, concurrent findings by Luo et al. (2021) and Kovaleva et al. (2021) reveal that certain components of the contextual embeddings consistently present very large magnitudes, which distort the cosine distances in the embedding space and questions their anisotropy. This could explain why additional isotropy calibration does not consistently improve the performance of transformers in downstream tasks.

5 Discussion

Our extensive evaluation shows that none of the considered isotropy calibration methods produce consistent improvements over the uncalibrated models across tasks, domains and architectures. In fact, we observe a negative relation between isotropy calibration and downstream performance. The most aggressive method, i.e., spectrum control, produces the largest improvement in isotropy

In light of our results, we discourage isotropy calibration of transformers as a means of improving downstream performance. However, we believe that further investigation of the embedding space of transformers may be beneficial to increase our ability to interpret these models and improve their architecture.

References

Sanjeev Arora, Yuanzhi Li, Yingyu Liang, Tengyu Ma, and Andrej Risteski. 2016. A latent variable model approach to pmi-based word embeddings. *Transactions of the Association for Computational Linguistics*, 4:385–399.

Ondrej Bojar, Rajen Chatterjee, Christian Federmann, Yvette Graham, Barry Haddow, Matthias Huck, Antonio Jimeno Yepes, Philipp Koehn, Varvara Logacheva, Christof Monz, Matteo Negri, Aurelie Neveol, Mariana Neves, Martin Popel, Matt Post, Raphael Rubino, Carolina Scarton, Lucia Specia, Marco Turchi, Karin Verspoor, and Marcos Zampieri. 2016. Findings of the 2016 conference on machine translation. In *Proceedings of the First Conference on Machine Translation*, pages 131–198, Berlin, Germany. Association for Computational Linguistics.

Gino Brunner, Yang Liu, Damian Pascual, Oliver Richter, Massimiliano Ciaramita, and Roger Wattenhofer. 2019. On identifiability in transformers. In *International Conference on Learning Representations*.

Xingyu Cai, Jiaji Huang, Yuchen Bian, and Kenneth Church. 2021. Isotropy in the contextual embedding space: Clusters and manifolds. In *International Conference on Learning Representations*.

Gabriella Chronis and Katrin Erk. 2020. When is a bishop not like a rook? when it's like a rabbi! multi-prototype bert embeddings for estimating semantic relationships. In *Proceedings of the 24th Conference on Computational Natural Language Learning*, pages 227–244.

Jacob Devlin, Ming-Wei Chang, Kenton Lee, and Kristina Toutanova. 2019. Bert: Pre-training of deep bidirectional transformers for language understanding. In *Proceedings of the 2019 Conference of the North American Chapter of the Association for Computational Linguistics: Human Language Technologies, Volume 1 (Long and Short Papers)*, pages 4171–4186.

Kawin Ethayarajh. 2019. How contextual are contextualized word representations? Comparing the geometry of BERT, ELMo, and GPT-2 embeddings. In *Proceedings of the 2019 Conference on Empirical Methods in Natural Language Processing and the 9th International Joint Conference on Natural Language Processing (EMNLP-IJCNLP)*, pages 55–65, Hong Kong, China. Association for Computational Linguistics.

Jun Gao, Di He, Xu Tan, Tao Qin, Liwei Wang, and Tieyan Liu. 2019. Representation degeneration problem in training natural language generation models. In *International Conference on Learning Representations*.

Karl Moritz Hermann, Tomás Kociský, Edward Grefenstette, Lasse Espeholt, Will Kay, Mustafa Suleyman, and Phil Blunsom. 2015. Teaching machines to read and comprehend. In *NIPS*, pages 1693–1701.

Durk P Kingma and Prafulla Dhariwal. 2018. Glow: Generative flow with invertible 1x1 convolutions. In *Advances in Neural Information Processing Systems*, volume 31. Curran Associates, Inc.

Olga Kovaleva, Saurabh Kulshreshtha, Anna Rogers, and Anna Rumshisky. 2021. BERT busters: Outlier dimensions that disrupt transformers. In *Findings of the Association for Computational Linguistics: ACL-IJCNLP 2021*, pages 3392–3405, Online. Association for Computational Linguistics.

Mike Lewis, Yinhan Liu, Naman Goyal, Marjan Ghazvininejad, Abdelrahman Mohamed, Omer Levy, Veselin Stoyanov, and Luke Zettlemoyer. 2020. Bart: Denoising sequence-to-sequence pre-training for natural language generation, translation, and comprehension. In *Proceedings of the 58th Annual Meeting of the Association for Computational Linguistics*, pages 7871–7880.

Bohan Li, Hao Zhou, Junxian He, Mingxuan Wang, Yiming Yang, and Lei Li. 2020. On the sentence embeddings from pre-trained language models. In *Proceedings of the 2020 Conference on Empirical Methods in Natural Language Processing (EMNLP)*, pages 9119–9130, Online. Association for Computational Linguistics.

Chin-Yew Lin. 2004. Rouge: A package for automatic evaluation of summaries. In *Text summarization branches out*, pages 74–81.

Tianlin Liu, Lyle Ungar, and Joao Sedoc. 2019a. Unsupervised post-processing of word vectors via conceptor negation. In *Proceedings of the AAAI Conference on Artificial Intelligence*, volume 33, pages 6778–6785.

Yinhan Liu, Jiatao Gu, Naman Goyal, Xian Li, Sergey Edunov, Marjan Ghazvininejad, Mike Lewis, and Luke Zettlemoyer. 2020. Multilingual denoising pre-training for neural machine translation. *Transactions of the Association for Computational Linguistics*, 8:726–742.

Yinhan Liu, Myle Ott, Naman Goyal, Jingfei Du, Mandar Joshi, Danqi Chen, Omer Levy, Mike Lewis, Luke Zettlemoyer, and Veselin Stoyanov. 2019b. Roberta: A robustly optimized bert pretraining approach. *arXiv preprint arXiv:1907.11692*.

Ziyang Luo, Artur Kulmizev, and Xiao-Xi Mao. 2021. Positional artefacts propagate through masked language model embeddings. In *ACL*.

Tomas Mikolov, Kai Chen, Gregory S. Corrado, and Jeffrey Dean. 2013. Efficient estimation of word representations in vector space. In *ICLR*.

Jiaqi Mu and Pramod Viswanath. 2018. All-but-the-top: Simple and effective postprocessing for word representations. In *International Conference on Learning Representations*.

Jeffrey Pennington, Richard Socher, and Christopher D Manning. 2014. Glove: Global vectors for word representation. In *Proceedings of the 2014 conference on empirical methods in natural language processing (EMNLP)*, pages 1532–1543.

Anna Rogers, Olga Kovaleva, and Anna Rumshisky. 2020. A primer in bertology: What we know about how bert works. *Transactions of the Association for Computational Linguistics*, 8:842–866.

Victor Sanh, Lysandre Debut, Julien Chaumond, and Thomas Wolf. 2020. Distilbert, a distilled version of bert: smaller, faster, cheaper and lighter.

Ashish Vaswani, Noam Shazeer, Niki Parmar, Jakob Uszkoreit, Llion Jones, Aidan N Gomez, Łukasz Kaiser, and Illia Polosukhin. 2017. Attention is all you need. In *Proceedings of the 31st International Conference on Neural Information Processing Systems*, pages 6000–6010.

Alex Wang, Amanpreet Singh, Julian Michael, Felix Hill, Omer Levy, and Samuel R Bowman. 2019a. Glue: A multi-task benchmark and analysis platform for natural language understanding. In *7th International Conference on Learning Representations, ICLR 2019*.

Lingxiao Wang, Jing Huang, Kevin Huang, Ziniu Hu, Guangtao Wang, and Quanquan Gu. 2019b. Improving neural language generation with spectrum control. In *International Conference on Learning Representations*.

Thomas Wolf, Lysandre Debut, Victor Sanh, Julien Chaumond, Clement Delangue, Anthony Moi, Pierric Cistac, Tim Rault, Remi Louf, Morgan Funtowicz, Joe Davison, Sam Shleifer, Patrick von Platen, Clara Ma, Yacine Jernite, Julien Plu, Canwen Xu, Teven Le Scao, Sylvain Gugger, Mariama Drame, Quentin Lhoest, and Alexander Rush. 2020. Transformers: State-of-the-art natural language processing. In *Proceedings of the 2020 Conference on Empirical Methods in Natural Language Processing: System Demonstrations*, pages 38–45, Online. Association for Computational Linguistics.

John Wu, Yonatan Belinkov, Hassan Sajjad, Nadir Durrani, Fahim Dalvi, and James Glass. 2020. Similarity analysis of contextual word representation models. In *Proceedings of the 58th Annual Meeting of the Association for Computational Linguistics*, pages 4638–4655.

Zhong Zhang, Chongming Gao, Cong Xu, Rui Miao, Qinli Yang, and Junming Shao. 2020. Revisiting representation degeneration problem in language modeling. In *Proceedings of the 2020 Conference on Empirical Methods in Natural Language Processing: Findings*, pages 518–527.

Mengjie Zhao, Philipp Dufter, Yadollah Yaghoobzadeh, and Hinrich Schütze. 2020. Quantifying the contextualization of word representations with semantic class probing. In *Proceedings of the 2020 Conference on Empirical Methods in Natural Language Processing: Findings*, pages 1219–1234.

Sumu Zhao, Damián Pascual, Gino Brunner, and Roger Wattenhofer. 2021. Of non-linearity and commutativity in bert. In *2021 International Joint Conference on Neural Networks (IJCNN)*, pages 1–8.

Wenxuan Zhou, Bill Yuchen Lin, and Xiang Ren. 2021. Isobn: Fine-tuning bert with isotropic batch normalization. *Proceedings of the AAAI Conference on Artificial Intelligence*, 35(16):14621–14629.

A Isotropy Metrics

To characterize the isotropy of the output embedding space we adopt the I_1 and I_2 isotropy measures from (Wang et al., 2019b).

$$I_1(\boldsymbol{W}) = \frac{\min_{\boldsymbol{v} \in \boldsymbol{V}} Z(\boldsymbol{v})}{\max_{\boldsymbol{v} \in \boldsymbol{V}} Z(\boldsymbol{v})},$$

is based on the observation by (Arora et al., 2016), that the partition function $Z(\boldsymbol{v}) = \sum_{i=1}^{n} \exp(\boldsymbol{v}^T \boldsymbol{w}_i)$ should be close to a constant for any unit vector $\boldsymbol{v}$ if the embedding matrix $\boldsymbol{W}$ is isotropic. Here, we abuse notation and $\boldsymbol{w}_i \in \boldsymbol{W}$ is the i-th row of the embedding matrix $\boldsymbol{W}$. Following (Mu and Viswanath, 2018) we use the set of eigenvectors of $\boldsymbol{W}^T \boldsymbol{W}$ as $\boldsymbol{V}$. The second measure

$$I_2(\boldsymbol{W}) = \sqrt{\frac{\sum_{\boldsymbol{v} \in \boldsymbol{V}} (Z(\boldsymbol{v}) - \bar{Z}(\boldsymbol{v}))^2}{|V| \bar{Z}(\boldsymbol{v})^2}},$$

is the sample standard deviation of the partition function $Z(\boldsymbol{v})$ normalized by its average $\bar{Z}(\boldsymbol{v})$. This way, $I_1(\boldsymbol{W}) \in [0, 1]$ and $I_2(\boldsymbol{W}) \geq 0$. Larger $I_1(\boldsymbol{W})$ and smaller $I_2(\boldsymbol{W})$ indicate more isotropic embeddings.

B Model Hyperparameter Configuration

For all the models used in his work we use the implementation from HuggingFace and follow their instructions for the hyperparameters. In particular, we use the following configurations:

BERT and DistilBERT. Learning rate $2e^{-5}$ without scheduling, batch size 32, 3 training epochs for all GLUE tasks except for MRPC and WNLI, for which we train during 5 epochs.

RoBERTa. Learning rate of $1e^{-5}$ for all GLUE tasks except for SST-2 and STS-B, for which the learning rate is set to $1e^{-5}$, same number of epochs as for BERT and DistilBERT, batch size of 32.

M-BART and BART. Learning rate of $3e^{-5}$ with polynomial decay, batch size 48, and 5 training epochs.

C Isotropy Scores on GLUE

Here, in Table 4, we present the isotropy scores obtained in our evaluation of GLUE with BERT, RoBERTa, and DistilBERT, which were not included in the main text due to lack of space.

The isotropy metrics I_1 and I_2 show the opposite trend to the performance metrics. An improvement in isotropy reflects a decrease in downstream performance. This way, we see that across models and tasks, cosine regularization and flow calibration (for BERT) have a small impact on isotropy and that the performance of the models calibrated with these techniques is close to the that of the uncalibrated models. On the other hand, spectrum control produces a very significant increase in isotropy, with many tasks reaching a I_1 of 1.00; while in Table 1 we see how it produces strong performance degradation. This, further suggests a negative relation between isotropy and the downstream performance of transformers.

Model	SST-2		MRPC		CoLA	
	$I_1(\uparrow)$	$I_2(\downarrow)$	$I_1(\uparrow)$	$I_2(\downarrow)$	$I_1(\uparrow)$	$I_2(\downarrow)$
BERT	0.91 ±0.01	0.4 ±0	0.91 ±0.01	0.38 ±0.01	0.91 ±0.01	0.39 ±0.01
+*Cosreg*	0.91 ±0.2	0.39 ±0.02	0.92 ±0.01	0.39 ±0.2	0.91 ±0.01	0.39 ±0.01
+*Spectrum-Pol*	**1.00 ±0**	**0.007 ±0.003**	**1.00 ±0**	$7e^{-4} \pm 3e^{-4}$	**1.00 ±0**	**$6e^{-4} \pm 1e^{-4}$**
+*Spectrum-Exp*	0.99 ±0.01	0.02 ±0.02	**1.00 ±0**	**$6e^{-4} \pm 2e^{-4}$**	**1.00 ±0**	$7e^{-4} \pm 3e^{-4}$
+*Flow*	0.92 ±0.01	0.40 ±0	0.91 ±0.01	0.40 ±0	0.91 ±0.01	0.39 ±0.01
RoBERTa	0.91 ±0.01	0.39 ±0.01	0.92 ±0.01	0.39 ±0.01	0.91 ±0.01	0.40 ±0.01
+*Cosreg*	0.92 ±0.01	0.40 ±0.01	0.91 ±0.01	0.39 ±0.01	0.91 ±0.01	0.40 ±0.01
+*Spectrum-Pol*	**1.00 ±0**	0.008 ±0.002	**1.00 ±0**	$5e^{-4} \pm 4e^{-4}$	**1.00 ±0**	**$5e^{-4} \pm 2e^{-4}$**
+*Spectrum-Exp*	**1.00 ±0**	**0.005 ±0.004**	**1.00 ±0**	$1e^{-4} \pm 2e^{-4}$	**1.00 ±0**	$6e^{-4} \pm 4e^{-4}$
DistilBERT	0.91 ±0.01	0.38 ±0.01	0.92 ±0.01	0.39 ±0.01	0.92 ±0.01	0.38 ±0.01
+*Cosreg*	0.91 ±0.01	0.39 ±0.01	0.92 ±0.01	0.38 ±0.01	0.92 ±0.01	0.38 ±0.01
+*Spectrum-Pol*	**1.00 ±0.01**	0.012 ±0.016	**1.00 ±0**	**$7e^{-4} \pm 5e^{-4}$**	**1.00 ±0**	**$11e^{-4} \pm 9e^{-4}$**
+*Spectrum-Exp*	**1.00 ±0.01**	**0.009 ±0.010**	**1.00 ±0**	**$7e^{-4} \pm 5e^{-4}$**	**1.00 ±0**	**$11e^{-4} \pm 9e^{-4}$**

Model	RTE		WNLI		STS-B	
	$I_1(\uparrow)$	$I_2(\downarrow)$	$I_1(\uparrow)$	$I_2(\downarrow)$	$I_1(\uparrow)$	$I_2(\downarrow)$
BERT	0.92 ±0.01	0.39 ±0.02	0.91 ±0.01	0.39 ±0.02	0.95 ±0	0.22 ±0.01
+*Cosreg*	0.92 ±0.01	0.40 ±0.03	0.91 ±0.01	0.40 ±0.01	0.95 ±0.01	0.23 ±0.01
+*Spectrum-Pol*	**1.00 ±0**	**$2e^{-4} \pm 1e^{-4}$**	**1.00 ±0**	$1e^{-4} \pm 2e^{-4}$	**1.00 ±0**	0.002 ±0
+*Spectrum-Exp*	**1.00 ±0**	$3e^{-4} \pm 2e^{-4}$	**1.00 ±0**	$2e^{-4} \pm 3e^{-4}$	**1.00 ±0**	**$13e^{-4} \pm 6e^{-4}$**
+*Flow*	0.92 ±0.01	0.39 ±0.01	0.92 ±0.01	0.39 ±0.02	0.95 ±0.01	0.23 ±0.01
RoBERTa	0.91 ±0.01	0.40 ±0.01	0.91 ±0.01	0.39 ±0.01	0.95 ±0.01	0.23 ±0.01
+*Cosreg*	0.91 ±0	0.41 ±0	0.91 ±0.01	0.40 ±0.01	0.95 ±0	0.23 ±0.01
+*Spectrum-Pol*	**1.00 ±0**	**$3e^{-4} \pm 2e^{-4}$**	**1.00 ±0**	**$3e^{-4} \pm 1e^{-4}$**	**1.00 ±0**	**$7e^{-4} \pm 3e^{-4}$**
+*Spectrum-Exp*	**1.00 ±0**	**$3e^{-4} \pm 2e^{-4}$**	**1.00 ±0**	**$3e^{-4} \pm 1e^{-4}$**	**1.00 ±0**	$15e^{-4} \pm 13e^{-4}$
DistilBERT	0.92 ±0.01	0.38 ±0.01	0.92 ±0	0.39 ±0.01	0.95 ±0	0.22 ±0.01
+*Cosreg*	0.92 ±0	0.38 ±0.01	0.92 ±0.01	0.38 ±0.01	0.95 ±0	0.22 ±0.01
+*Spectrum-Pol*	**1.00 ±0**	**$2e^{-4} \pm 3e^{-4}$**	**1.00 ±0**	$1e^{-4} \pm 2e^{-4}$	**1.00 ±0**	**$9e^{-4} \pm 1e^{-4}$**
+*Spectrum-Exp*	**1.00 ±0**	**$2e^{-4} \pm 3e^{-4}$**	**1.00 ±0**	$1e^{-4} \pm 2e^{-4}$	**1.00 ±0**	**$9e^{-4} \pm 1e^{-4}$**

Model	QNLI		MNLI		QQP	
	$I_1(\uparrow)$	$I_2(\downarrow)$	$I_1(\uparrow)$	$I_2(\downarrow)$	$I_1(\uparrow)$	$I_2(\downarrow)$
BERT	0.92 ±0.01	0.39 ±0.01	0.93 ±0.01	0.32 ±0	0.92 ±0.01	0.39 ±0.01
+*Cosreg*	0.92 ±0.01	0.39 ±0.01	0.93 ±0.01	0.32 ±0.01	0.9 ±0	0.39 ±0.01
+*Spectrum-Pol*	0.99 ±0.01	0.06 ±0.02	0.95 ±0.01	0.21 ±0.04	0.92 ±0.02	0.39 ±0.06
+*Spectrum-Exp*	**1.00 ±0**	**$5e^{-4} \pm 1e^{-4}$**	**0.98 ±0.01**	**0.08 ±0.03**	**0.97 ±0.03**	**0.12 ±0.12**
+*Flow*	0.92 ±0.01	0.39 ±0.01	0.93 ±0	0.31 ±0	0.92 ±0.01	0.39 ±0.01
RoBERTa	0.91 ±0.01	0.40 ±0.01	0.93 ±0.01	0.32 ±0	0.92 ±0.01	0.39 ±0
+*Cosreg*	0.92 ±0.01	0.40 ±0.01	0.93 ±0.01	0.93 ±0.01	0.32 ±0.01	0.39 ±0
+*Spectrum-Pol*	**1.00 ±0**	**0.005 ±0.003**	0.96 ±0.03	0.15 ±0.13	**0.99 ±0.2**	**0.04 ±0.07**
+*Spectrum-Exp*	**1.0 ±0.01**	0.012 ±0.015	**0.98 ±0.01**	**0.10 ±0.04**	**0.99 ±0.01**	**0.04 ±0.06**
DistilBERT	0.92 ±0	0.38 ±0.01	0.93 ±0.01	0.32 ±0	0.92 ±0.1	0.38 ±0.01
+*Cosreg*	0.92 ±0.01	0.39 ±0.01	0.93 ±0	0.32 ±0	0.992 ±0.01	0.39 ±0.01
+*Spectrum-Pol*	0.99 ±0.01	0.03 ±0.04	0.93 ±0.01	0.29 ±0.01	0.93 ±0.03	0.36 ±0.17
+*Spectrum-Exp*	**1.00 ±0.01**	**0.02 ±0.03**	**0.97 ±0.1**	**0.13 ±0.01**	**0.95 ±0.01**	**0.25 ±0.01**

Table 4: Isotropy of the embedding space of the different transformer model and calibration method combinations on GLUE tasks.

D Complete Summarization Results

Here we report the complete summarization results, including the ROUGE-2 and ROUGE-L metrics, omitted in the main text.

	CNN / Daily Mail					
Model	R-1 (↑)	R-2 (↑)	R-L (↑)	$I_2(\uparrow)$	$I_2(\downarrow)$	Time (min)
BART	**38.21 ±0.05**	**17.62 ±0.03**	**27.06 ±0.08**	0.95 ±0.01	0.25 ±0	246 ±8
+*Cosreg*	**38.21 ±0.05**	**17.62 ±0.03**	**27.06 ±0.08**	0.95 ±0.01	0.25 ±0	240 ±8
+*Spectrum-Pol*	37.36 ±0.08	16.60 ±0.08	25.26 ±0.09	**0.99 ±0**	**0.04 ±0**	245 ±20
+*Spectrum-Exp*	37.43 ±0.08	16.62 ±0.01	26.30 ±0.05	**0.99 ±0**	**0.04 ±0**	230 ±18
BART (small dataset)	**36.56 ±0.25**	**15.62 ±0.07**	**25.05 ±0.07**	**0.94 ±0**	**0.25 ±0**	17 ±0
+*Flow*	36.15 ±0.30	15.40 ±0.23	24.79 ±0.19	**0.94 ±0**	**0.25 ±0**	95 ±2

Table 5: Complete BART summariation performance, embedding space isotropy and fine-tuning time per epoch using different calibration methods on the CNN / DailyMail dataset. Due to computational cost, the flow calibration method was tested on a smaller version of the dataset with 20 000 articles.

The performance in terms of ROUGE-2 and ROUGE-L scores follows the same patterns as ROUGE-1. Similar to language understanding and machine translation, increasing isotropy does not improve performance.

Do Dependency Relations Help in the Task of Stance Detection?

Alessandra Teresa Cignarella[1], **Cristina Bosco**[1] **and Paolo Rosso**[2]
1. Dipartimento di Informatica, Università degli Studi di Torino, Italy
2. PRHLT Research Center, Universitat Politècnica de València, Spain
alessandrateresa.cignarella@unito.it
cristina.bosco@unito.it
prosso@dsic.upv.es

Abstract

In this paper we present a set of multilingual experiments tackling the task of *Stance Detection* in five different languages: English, Spanish, Catalan, French and Italian. Furthermore, we study the phenomenon of stance with respect to six different targets – one per language, and two different for Italian – employing a variety of machine learning algorithms that primarily exploit morphological and syntactic knowledge as features, represented throughout the format of Universal Dependencies. Results seem to suggest that the methodology employed is not beneficial *per se*, but might be useful to exploit the same features with a different methodology.

1 Introduction and Related Work

The task of monitoring people's opinion towards particular targets in political topics or public life debates has grown in the last decade, thus leading to the creation of a specific area of investigation in NLP named *Stance Detection* (SD). Research on this topic, indeed, might have an impact on different aspects of everyone's life such as public administration, policy-making, advertisement, marketing strategies and security. In fact, through the constant monitoring of people's opinion, desires, complaints and beliefs on political agenda or public services, administrators could better meet population's needs (Küçük and Can, 2020).

SD, as a task, shares various similarities with Sentiment Analysis (SA), and, exactly like Sentiment Analysis, also SD has been applied in several domains. For instance, to discover the reputation of an enterprise, what is the general public thought regarding a political reform, if costumers of a fashion brand are happy about the customer service, etc... Nevertheless, whereas the aim of SA is categorizing texts according to a notion of polarity (positive, negative or neutral), the aim of SD consists in classifying texts according to the attitude they express towards a given target of interest (Mohammad et al., 2017).

The first shared task entirely dedicated to SD was held for English at SemEval in 2016, i.e., *Task 6 "Detecting Stance in Tweets"* (Mohammad et al., 2016). In the following years, many more shared tasks followed tackling the same issue in different languages and regarding different targets: Chinese (Xu et al., 2016), Spanish and Catalan (Taulé et al., 2017, 2018), Italian (Cignarella et al., 2020b), and lastly Spanish and Basque (Agerri et al., 2021).

Provided that several approaches based on different types of linguistic knowledge have been applied to address the SD task, in this paper we investigate the contribution of syntactic information and in particular that provided by dependency relations. Therefore, we exploit some of the datasets made available in the above-mentioned evaluation campaigns in different languages. In particular, we aimed at answering the following research question:

RQ: *Do features derived from morphology and syntax help automatic systems to address the task of stance detection?*

Indeed, some research already explored different kinds of syntactic features and their interaction in several NLP tasks, showing their effectiveness. For example, Sidorov et al. (2012) exploited syntactic dependency-based n-grams for general-purpose classification tasks, Socher et al. (2013) investigated sentiment and syntax with to the development of a sentiment treebank, and Kanayama and Iwamoto (2020) showed a pipeline method that makes the most of syntactic structures based on *Universal Dependencies* (UD[1]), achieving high precision in sentiment analysis for 17 languages. Morphology and syntax have also been proved useful in a number of other tasks, such as rumour detection (Ghanem et al., 2019), authorship attribution (Posadas-Duran et al., 2014; Sidorov et al.,

[1] https://universaldependencies.org/.

Proceedings of the Third Workshop on Insights from Negative Results in NLP, pages 10 - 17
May 26, 2022 ©2022 Association for Computational Linguistics

language	target and source	train				test			
		AGAINST	FAVOUR	NONE	TOTAL	AGAINST	FAVOUR	NONE	TOTAL
English	Hillary Clinton (Mohammad et al., 2016)	393	118	178	689	172	45	78	295
Spanish	Independence Referendum (Taulé et al., 2017)	335	1,446	2,538	4,319	84	361	636	1,081
Catalan	Independence Referendum (Taulé et al., 2017)	131	2,648	1,540	4,319	32	663	386	1,081
French	Emmanuel Macron (Lai et al., 2020)	244	71	109	424	64	20	22	106
Italian	Constitutional Referendum (Lai et al., 2020)	389	129	148	666	97	34	36	167
Italian	Sardines Movement (Cignarella et al., 2020b)	1,028	589	515	2,132	742	196	172	1,110

Table 1: Benchmark datasets used for target-specific SD.

2014) and humor recognition (Liu et al., 2018). To the best of our knowledge there is no prior work exploiting dependency-based syntactic features for addressing the task of Stance Detection.

2 Methodology

The main goal of the experiments presented in this work consists in evaluating the contribution of syntax-based linguistic features extracted from the datasets described above to the task of SD. Therefore, we performed a set of experiments where several models were implemented exploiting classical machine learning algorithms and state-of-the-art language models implemented with the Python libraries *scikit-learn* and *keras*. The methodology we propose here, in which a multilingual setting is proposed and neural models are evaluated together with dependency-based features, recalls the idea that dependency based syntax might be useful in a variety of language scenarios for the task of SD and with a manifold of algorithms and architectures.

2.1 Datasets and pre-processing

Mirroring our previous work regarding irony detection in (Cignarella et al., 2020a), from which we replicate the methods and techniques used, we propose here to address SD as a multi-class classification task, testing an automatic system on five languages: English, Spanish, Catalan, French and Italian. Furthermore, with respect to Italian, we were able to test the approach on two different datasets with two different targets of interest, namely: the *Constitutional Referendum* (Lai et al., 2020) and the *Sardines Movement* (Cignarella et al., 2020b). In the multilingual experimental setting, we took advantage of three benchmark datasets made available during the last few years within evaluation campaigns, i.e., *SemEval 2016 - Task 6* (Mohammad et al., 2016), *StanceCat at IberEval 2017* (Taulé et al., 2017) and *SardiStance at EVALITA 2020* (Cignarella et al., 2020b), and two datasets created *ad hoc* in the research group where we work, for previous studies on SD (with target Emmanuel Macron and Constitutional Referendum (Lai et al., 2020) and are freely available online.[2]

In Table 1, for each dataset, we report the language, the target of interest, the name of the shared task (or research) in which it was released through their paper reference, the number of tweets for each class (AGAINST, FAVOUR, NONE) and the total number of instances, for both training set and test set. The aim of our task is, thus, to determine the stance expressed by the user with respect to a given target.

In order to extract the information that is crucial for performing the experiments, we needed to apply also a layer of morpho-syntactic annotation to the corpora that are annotated only for SD. For this purpose, we selected the *standard de facto* Universal Dependencies and we benefited from the UDPipe[3] tool. Considering that all the datasets used consist of Twitter data, whenever possible, we used resources where this genre, or at least user-generated content of some kind was included as training data for parsing. More precisely, the model for English has been trained on the EWT treebank (Silveira et al., 2014), that for Spanish on both GSD-Spanish corpus (McDonald et al., 2013) and the ANCORA corpus (Taulé et al., 2008). Also the model for Catalan was trained on the ANCORA corpus, while that for French on the GSD-French corpus (McDonald et al., 2013). Finally, the model for Italian was trained on the POSTWITA-UD corpus (Sanguinetti et al., 2018), on the ISTD treebank (Simi et al., 2014) and on the TWITTIRÒ-UD corpus (Cignarella et al., 2019).

The precision in this phase of the work can be a bottleneck for what concerns the accuracy of the

[2] https://github.com/mirkolai/MultilingualStanceDetection/tree/master/dataset.

[3] https://ufal.mff.cuni.cz/udpipe.

experiments that we will describe in the following sections. In fact, the approach is entirely based on dependency syntax and the results strictly depend upon the quality of parsed data. The performance of UDpipe's parsing is close to the state-of-the-art ones, therefore, we considered the annotation obtained automatically reasonably acceptable for the present study. However there always is margin for some error, we assumed precision and error were similarly distributed in each language setting.

2.2 Features and Models

Firstly, tweets were stripped from URLs and characters were normalized to lowercase. Later, thanks to the application of the UDPipe pipeline we were able to generate dependency-based syntactic trees for all the tweets taken into consideration in each language (e.g., Figure 1).

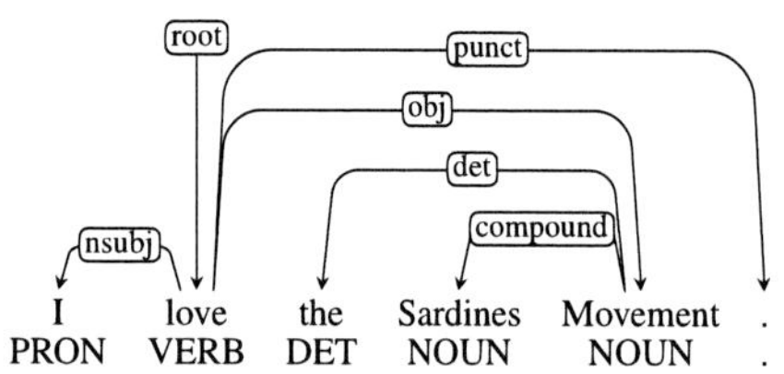

Figure 1: Example of a dependency tree in UD format.

On the basis of texts encoded in UD format, we engineered and tested the following features:

- ngrams,
  chargrams;
- deprelneg,
  deprel;
- relationformVERB,
  relationformNOUN,
  relationformADJ;
- Sidorovbigramsform,
  Sidorovbigramsupostag,
  Sidorovbigramsdeprel.

A detailed description for each feature is available in the Appendix and is inspired by our previous work (Cignarella et al., 2020a; Cignarella, 2021).

Having as primary goal the exploration of the features listed in the previous paragraph and testing their effectiveness in the task of SD, we fed them into a variety of models, including the following: Support Vector Machine (SVM), Logistic Regression (LR), Random Forest (RF), Multilayer Perceptron (MLP) an Multilingual BERT (M-BERT). The results obtained by combining all the features with all the models listed above resulted in a very big amount of numbers, which most of the time were neither informative nor conclusive. Because of this we reported only the best scoring models in the section below.

3 Experiments and Results

We propose two different experimental settings. The first one aims at exploring the dependency-based features listed above paired with classical machine learning (ML) algorithms, in order to perform a feature selection and discover the best combination. In the second setting, we experiment with the Multilingual Bidirectional Encoder Representations from Transformers (M-BERT) and different additions of the features explored in the first setting.

3.1 Selection of best features

In order to identify the most relevant features, we tested different combinations of features and the models mentioned in Section 2.2 and we evaluated them according to the averaged macro F1-score.[4]

From the observation of Table 2 a vastly heterogeneous scenario emerges. There seems not to be any regular pattern among language scenarios, regarding the same features exploited for SD. On the contrary, the Multilayer Perceptron is proven to be the best performing classical ML algorithm across all languages, aside from the setting regarding the Constitutional Referendum in Italian. This has an explanation, that was already found out in precedent work (Lai et al., 2020) and a special clarification regarding the nature of the dataset is due. Indeed, the Italian dataset on the Constitutional Referendum seems to be particularly *sui generis* when compared with the other five. Within the dataset the exploitation of hashtags is wide and coherent in the whole corpus. For instance the hashtags #iovotosì (#Ivoteyes) and #iovotono (#Ivoteno) have been exploited almost in each tweet that we took into consideration, and we believe that just their presence (as boolean value) already is a clear manifestation of stance. For this reason, only two features are already sufficient to reach an extremely high F1-score (0.967): ngrams and Sidorovbigramsupostag. The same reasoning applies to Support Vector Machines as they are sufficiently

[4]The average value obtained between the F1-score of the AGAINST class and the F1-score of the FAVOUR class as it was done in (Mohammad et al., 2016).

features	English Clinton	French Macron	Spanish Independencia	Catalan Independencia	Italian Referendum	Italian Sardines
model	MLP	MLP	MLP	MLP	SVM	MLP
macro F1-score	.673	.596	.493	.497	.967	.651
ngrams			✓		✓	✓
chargrams	✓	✓	✓	✓		✓
deprel	✓		✓	✓		✓
deprelneg	✓	✓		✓		
relationformVERB	✓	✓	✓			
relationformNOUN		✓				
relationformADJ			✓			
Sidorovbigramsform		✓		✓		
Sidorovbigramsdeprel	✓			✓		✓
Sidorovbigramsupostag		✓	✓		✓	✓

Table 2: Features exploited in the best runs with classical ML algorithms in each language scenario.

language	target	best run (report and score)		*SVM*	M-BERT		
				+unigrams	—	+syntax	+best_feats
English	H. Clinton	Zarrella and Marsh (2016)	.671	.570	.650	.562 (↓ .088)	.636 (↓ .014)
French	E. Macron	Lai et al. (2020)	.687	.526	.511	.511 (= .000)	.533 (↑ .022)
Spanish	Independencia	Lai et al. (2017)	.489	.420	.467	.443 (↓ .024)	.463 (↓ .004)
Catalan	Independencia	Lai et al. (2017)	.490	.468	.478	.462 (↓ .016)	.476 (↓ .002)
Italian	Referendum	Lai et al. (2020)	.971	.951	.959	.960 (↑ .001)	.960 (↑ .001)
Italian	Sardines	Giorgioni et al. (2020)	.685	.578	.586	.599 (↑ .013)	.563 (↓ .023)

Table 3: Results obtained combining M-BERT and dependency-based syntactic features. Green values and arrows pointing up show an increment in performance with respect to results obtained by the bare architecture. Red values and arrows pointing down indicate a performance reduction, with respect to results obtained by the bare architecture. Orange values show no change.

good to perform textual classification where the only presence such a textual feature (a polarized hashtag) is so blatant in indicating stance.

From Table 2 it also emerges how in all the configurations used for achieving the best score at least one dependency-based syntactic feature was exploited and in particular those based on Sidorov et al.'s work, i.e., the last three rows of the table. This provides evidence for giving a partial answer to our research question (*Do features derived from morphology and syntax help automatic systems address the task of stance detection?*), since those are the features where the structure from root to branches of syntactic trees is encoded.

3.2 Syntactically-informed M-BERT

In the second setting, we performed experiments where, for each language scenario, we ran the straightforward M-BERT model. We also implemented the base architecture by adding the dependency-based syntactic features detailed in previous sections in two different ways, in order to have a clear-cut evidence on the actual contribution derived from dependency syntax to SD.

In Table 3 we report the results of the best system exploiting these datasets. Furthermore, we added the baseline results achieved with a SVM and a bag of words of unigrams, as it is the most common baseline proposed in most SD shared tasks. Each of the experiments with M-BERT has been performed 5 times with fixed hyper-parameters[5] in order to take into account the differences of random initialization, and the average macro F1 score of such number of runs is reported.

Firstly, it is interesting to see how, the M-BERT base architecture never surpasses the results obtained with more complex architectures such as those proposed by the participants of shared tasks, confirming the complexity of the task.

Moreover, by having a look at the colorful right-hand side of Table 3, it can be seen how the addition of syntactic knowledge (M-BERT+syntax) determined a widely varied spectrum of outcomes. By the predominance of the colours orange and red (indicating stasis or loss in terms of performance), it is obvious to state that morphosyntactic information, taken alone and encoded into the M-BERT

[5] BatchSize = 8, LearningRate = $1e-5$, EarlyStop = 5.

architecture does not provide strong nor consistent beneficial contribution to the task of SD. Not only the results obtained by the models *M-BERT+syntax* and *M-BERT+best_feats* obtain results lower than the state of the art approaches, but in most cases, they result in being also lower than the results obtained with the base architecture (M-BERT). Lastly, it is furthermore arguable that results show low (almost to none) statistical significance. In order to verify that, we applied the *t-test* with the Bonferroni correction and the outcomes have shown indeed not to be statistically significant. It might be worth it to explore new ways of encoding such features and integrating them into BERT, and also to perform new experiments with other BERT-based architectures that are language specific, rather than using the multilingual version (AlBERTo for Italian (Polignano et al., 2019), BETO for Spanish (Cañete et al., 2020), CamemBERT for French (Martin et al., 2019), etc...).

4 Discussion and insights

The outcomes obtained in the investigation are slightly disappointing, but they do not come as a total surprise. When we were formulating the research question regarding SD, we had anticipated that there were no linguistic theories nor research work pointing towards the fact that morphosyntax might prove useful in this task. Furthermore, a clear explanation could be seen by observing how two simple sentences having opposite stance, present identical syntactic structure:

Ex.1 I **love** the Sardines Movement.

Ex.2 I **hate** the Sardines Movement.

we had already anticipated that taking morphology and syntax as only features to detect stance might indeed be calling a long shot.

With the experience matured with this research, we can state that – even if we are not obtaining the new state-of-the-art results – the outcomes lead in the direction of further investigation, pointing mainly towards a better understanding of features' behaviour when stacked in a pre-trained language model such as M-BERT.

Finally, even though the results obtained with M-BERT turned out to be not statistically significant, this research was oriented in studying whether some features derived from morphology and syntax could help automatic systems to address the task of stance detection. It would be unfair not mentioning the fact that in the first experimental setting, that was mainly dedicated to the selection of the best features to be later fed as linguistic input into M-BERT, we actually obtained better results with respect to state-of-the-art models in four languages out of six and in the remaining two we obtained close results that are definitely comparable (see the macro F1-score of the best ML systems in Table 2 and compare it with the best results from shared tasks reported in Table 3).

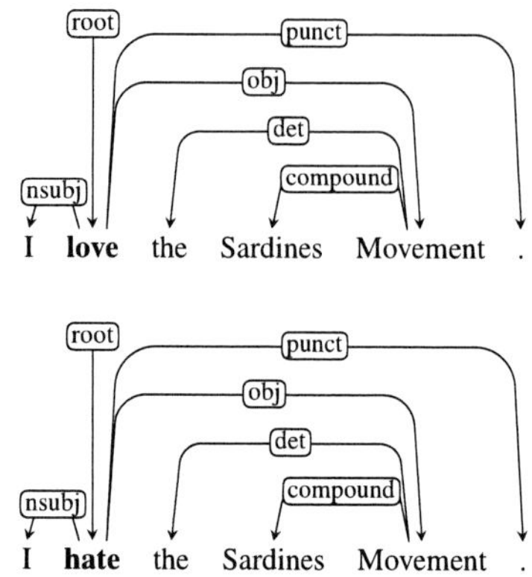

Figure 2: Dependency trees of Ex.1 and Ex.2.

5 Conclusion

The lesson learned form this work suggests that morphosyntactic cues combine well as features in classical machine learning algorithms, but they do not seem to provide an increment in terms of performance in the neural architecture of M-BERT in the case study of multilingual Stance Detection. Indeed, as shown in linguistics, the expression of one's stance is frequently a phenomenon that seems to depend more often on semantics rather than on syntactic patterns or constructions.

Acknowledgements

This work has been partially funded by "Be Positive!" (under the 2019 "Google.org Impact Challenge on Safety" call) and also partially supported by the European project "STERHEOTYPES - STudying European Racial Hoaxes and sterEOTYPES" funded by Compagnia di San Paolo and VolksWagen Stiftung under the "Challenges for Europe" call for Project (CUP: B99C20000640007). The work of the last author was partially funded by the Generalitat Valenciana under DeepPattern (PROMETEO/2019/121).

References

Rodrigo Agerri, Roberto Centeno, María Espinosa, Joseba Fernandez de Landa, and Alvaro Rodrigo. 2021. VaxxStance @ IberLEF 2021: Overview of the Task on Going Beyond Text in Cross-Lingual Stance Detection. *Procesamiento del Lenguaje Natural*, 67:173–181.

José Cañete, Gabriel Chaperon, Rodrigo Fuentes, and Jorge Pérez. 2020. Spanish Pre-Trained BERT Model and Evaluation Data. In *to appear in PML4DC at ICLR 2020*.

Alessandra Teresa Cignarella. 2021. *Dependency Syntax in the Automatic Detection of Irony and Stance*. Ph.D. thesis, Università degli studi di Torino and Universitat Politècnica de València.

Alessandra Teresa Cignarella, Valerio Basile, Manuela Sanguinetti, Cristina Bosco, Farah Benamara, and Paolo Rosso. 2020a. Multilingual Irony Detection with Dependency Syntax and Neural Models. In *Proceedings of the 28th International Conference on Computational Linguistics (COLING 2020)*. ACL.

Alessandra Teresa Cignarella, Cristina Bosco, and Paolo Rosso. 2019. Presenting TWITTIRO-UD: An Italian Twitter Treebank in Universal Dependencies. In *Proceedings of the 5th International Conference on Dependency Linguistics (Depling, SyntaxFest 2019)*. ACL.

Alessandra Teresa Cignarella, Mirko Lai, Cristina Bosco, Viviana Patti, and Paolo Rosso. 2020b. SardiStance@EVALITA2020: Overview of the Stance Detection in Italian Tweets. In *Proceedings of the 7th Evaluation Campaign of Natural Language Processing and Speech Tools for Italian (EVALITA 2020)*.

Bilal Ghanem, Alessandra Teresa Cignarella, Cristina Bosco, Paolo Rosso, and Francisco Manuel Rangel Pardo. 2019. UPV-28-UNITO at SemEval-2019 Task 7: Exploiting Post's Nesting and Syntax Information for Rumor Stance Classification. In *Proceedings of the 12th International Workshop on Semantic Evaluation (SemEval 2019)*. ACL.

Simone Giorgioni, Marcello Politi, Samir Salman, Danilo Croce, and Roberto Basili. 2020. UNITOR@Sardistance2020: Combining Transformer-based architectures and Transfer Learning for robust Stance Detection. In *Proceedings of the 7th Evaluation Campaign of Natural Language Processing and Speech Tools for Italian (EVALITA 2020)*. CEUR-WS.org.

Hiroshi Kanayama and Ran Iwamoto. 2020. How Universal are Universal Dependencies? Exploiting Syntax for Multilingual Clause-level Sentiment Detection. In *Proceedings of the 12th Language Resources and Evaluation Conference (LREC 2020)*. ELRA.

Dilek Küçük and Fazli Can. 2020. Stance detection: A survey. *ACM Computing Surveys (CSUR)*, 53(1):1–37.

Mirko Lai, Alessandra Teresa Cignarella, Delia Irazú Hernández Farías, Cristina Bosco, Viviana Patti, and Paolo Rosso. 2020. Multilingual stance detection in social media political debates. *Computer Speech & Language*, 63(101075).

Mirko Lai, Alessandra Teresa Cignarella, and Delia Irazú Hernandez Fariás. 2017. iTACOS at IberEval2017: Detecting Stance in Catalan and Spanish Tweets. In *Proceedings of the 2nd Workshop on Evaluation of Human Language Technologies for Iberian Languages (IberEval 2017)*. CEUR-WS.org.

Lizhen Liu, Donghai Zhang, and Wei Song. 2018. Exploiting syntactic structures for humor recognition. In *Proceedings of the 27th International Conference on Computational Linguistics*. Association for Computational Linguistics (ACL).

Louis Martin, Benjamin Muller, Pedro Javier Ortiz Suárez, Yoann Dupont, Laurent Romary, Éric Villemonte de la Clergerie, Djamé Seddah, and Benoît Sagot. 2019. CamemBERT: a Tasty French Language Model. *arXiv preprint arXiv:1911.03894*.

Ryan McDonald, Joakim Nivre, Yvonne Quirmbach-Brundage, Yoav Goldberg, Dipanjan Das, Kuzman Ganchev, Keith Hall, Slav Petrov, Hao Zhang, Oscar Täckström, et al. 2013. Universal dependency annotation for multilingual parsing. In *Proceedings of the 51st Annual Meeting of the Association for Computational Linguistics (ACL 2013)*. ACL.

Saif Mohammad, Svetlana Kiritchenko, Parinaz Sobhani, Xiaodan Zhu, and Colin Cherry. 2016. SemEval-2016 Task 6: Detecting Stance in Tweets. In *Proceedings of the 10th International Workshop on Semantic Evaluation (SemEval 2016)*. ACL.

Saif M. Mohammad, Parinaz Sobhani, and Svetlana Kiritchenko. 2017. Stance and sentiment in tweets. *ACM Transactions on Internet Technology (TOIT)*, 17(3):1–23.

Marco Polignano, Pierpaolo Basile, Marco de Gemmis, Giovanni Semeraro, and Valerio Basile. 2019. ALBERTO: Italian BERT Language Understanding Model for NLP Challenging Tasks Based on Tweets. In *Proceedings of the 6th Italian Conference on Computational Linguistics (CLiC-it 2019)*. CEUR-WS.org.

Juan-Pablo Posadas-Duran, Grigori Sidorov, and Ildar Batyrshin. 2014. Complete syntactic n-grams as style markers for authorship attribution. In *Proceedings of the Mexican International Conference on Artificial Intelligence (MICAI 2014)*. Springer.

Manuela Sanguinetti, Cristina Bosco, Alberto Lavelli, Alessandro Mazzei, Oronzo Antonelli, and Fabio Tamburini. 2018. PoSTWITA-UD: an Italian Twitter Treebank in Universal Dependencies. In *Proceedings of the 11th International Conference on Language Resources and Evaluation (LREC-2018)*. ELRA.

Grigori Sidorov. 2014. Should Syntactic N-grams Contain Names of Syntactic Relations? *International Journal of Computational Linguistics Applications*, 5(2):25–47.

Grigori Sidorov, Francisco Velasquez, Efstathios Stamatatos, Alexander Gelbukh, and Liliana Chanona-Hernández. 2012. Syntactic dependency-based n-grams as classification features. In *Proceedings of the Mexican International Conference on Artificial Intelligence (MICAI 2012)*. Springer.

Grigori Sidorov, Francisco Velasquez, Efstathios Stamatatos, Alexander Gelbukh, and Liliana Chanona-Hernández. 2013. Syntactic dependency-based n-grams: More evidence of usefulness in classification. In *International Conference on Intelligent Text Processing and Computational Linguistics (CICLing 2013)*. Springer.

Grigori Sidorov, Francisco Velasquez, Efstathios Stamatatos, Alexander Gelbukh, and Liliana Chanona-Hernández. 2014. Syntactic n-grams as Machine Learning Features for Natural Language Processing. *Expert Systems with Applications*, 41(3):853–860.

Natalia Silveira, Timothy Dozat, Marie-Catherine De Marneffe, Samuel R Bowman, Miriam Connor, John Bauer, and Christopher D Manning. 2014. A gold standard dependency corpus for English. In *Proceedings of the 9th International Conference on Language Resources and Evaluation (LREC 2014)*. ELRA.

Maria Simi, Cristina Bosco, and Simonetta Montemagni. 2014. Less is More? Towards a Reduced Inventory of Categories for Training a Parser for the Italian Stanford Dependencies. In *Proceedings of the 9th International Conference on Language Resources and Evaluation (LREC 2014)*. ELRA.

Richard Socher, Alex Perelygin, Jean Y. Wu, Jason Chuang, Christopher D. Manning, Andrew Y. Ng, and Christopher Potts. 2013. Recursive Deep Models for Semantic Compositionality Over a Sentiment Treebank. In *Proceedings of the 2013 Conference on Empirical Methods in Natural Language Processing (EMNLP 2013)*. ACL.

Mariona Taulé, Maria Antònia Martí, Francisco M. Rangel Pardo, Paolo Rosso, Cristina Bosco, and Viviana Patti. 2017. Overview of the Task on Stance and Gender Detection in Tweets on Catalan Independence. In *Proceedings of the 2nd Workshop on Evaluation of Human Language Technologies for Iberian Languages (IberEval 2017) co-located with 33th Conference of the Spanish Society for Natural Language Processing (SEPLN 2017)*. CEUR-WS.org.

Mariona Taulé, Maria Antònia Martí, and Marta Recasens. 2008. AnCora: Multilevel Annotated Corpora for Catalan and Spanish. In *Proceedings of the 6th Language Resources and Evaluation Conference (LREC 2008)*. ELRA.

Mariona Taulé, Francisco M. Rangel Pardo, M. Antònia Martí, and Paolo Rosso. 2018. Overview of the Task on Multimodal Stance Detection in Tweets on Catalan #1Oct Referendum. In *Proceedings of the 3rd Workshop on Evaluation of Human Language Technologies for Iberian Languages (IberEval 2018) co-located with 34th Conference of the Spanish Society for Natural Language Processing (SEPLN 2018)*. CEUR-WS.org.

Ruifeng Xu, Yu Zhou, Dongyin Wu, Lin Gui, Jiachen Du, and Yun Xue. 2016. Overview of NLPCC shared task 4: Stance detection in chinese microblogs. In *Natural Language Understanding and Intelligent Applications*. Springer.

Guido Zarrella and Amy Marsh. 2016. MITRE at SemEval-2016 Task 6: Transfer Learning for Stance Detection. In *Proceedings of the 10th International Workshop on Semantic Evaluation (SemEval 2016)*. ACL.

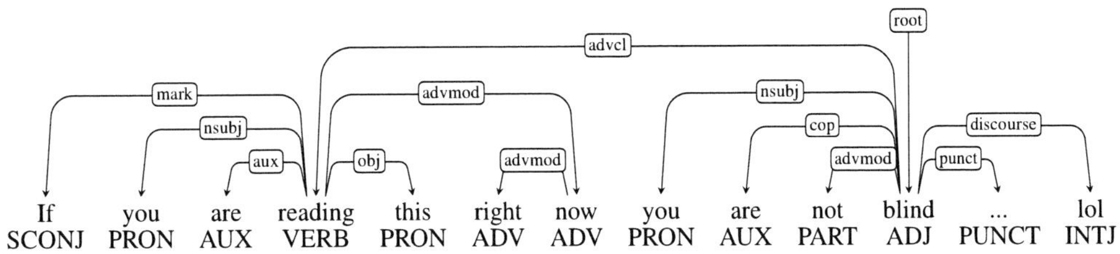

Figure 3: Dependency-based syntactic tree of an English tweet.

Appendix

The description of features as well as the content of the vectors for the syntactic features we developed, referring to the tweet in Figure 3, are as follows:

• n-grams: We extracted unigrams, bigrams and trigrams of tokens; e.g., *[If, you, are, reading, ..., If you, you are, are reading, ..., If you are, you are reading, are reading this, ...]*;

• char-grams: We considered the sequence of char-grams in a range from 2 to 5 characters; eg *[If, fy, yo, ou, ..., Ifyou, fyoua, youar, ouare, uarer, ...]*;

• deprelneg: We considered the presence of negation in the text, relying on the morphosyntactic cues present in the UD format. When a negation was present, we appended the correspondent dependency relation in the feature vector. For instance in Figure 3, we spot a negation in *[... are **not** blind ...]*, the dependency relation of "not" is `advmod`, therefore, we append it in the feature vector;

• deprel: We built a bag of words of 5-grams, 6-grams and 7-grams of dependency relations as occurring in the linear order of the sentence from left to right; e.g., *[mark nsubj aux obj advmod, nsubj aux obj advmod advmod, ..., advmod advmod nsubj cop advmod root punct, advmod nsubj cop advmod root punct discourse]*;

• relationformVERB: We create a feature vector with all the tuples of tokens that are connected with a dependency distance $= 1$, by starting from a verb and at the same time we blank the verb itself. For instance, in the example the first verb is "*reading*" and some of the tuples of tokens connected through this verb are, e.g., *[IfVERBthis, youVERBthis, areVERBthis, IfVERBnow, youVERBnow, ...]*;

• relationformNOUN: We applied the same procedure of the feature above but considering nouns as starting points for collecting tuples;

• relationformADJ: in the same fashion of the two features above, we repeated the same procedure for adjectives too;

• Sidorovbigramsform: We created a bag of word-forms (tokens), considering the bigrams that can be collected following the syntactic tree structure (rather than the bigrams that can be collected reading the sentence from left to right).[6] Such that: e.g., *[blind reading, blind you, blind are, blind not, reading if, reading you, ...]*;

• Sidorovbigramsupostag: as the feature above, we created a bag of part-of-speech tags;

• Sidorovbigramsdeprel: as the two features above, we created a bag of words based on dependency relations (*deprels*).

[6]Please refer to (Sidorov et al., 2013) and (Sidorov, 2014) for more details on this regard.

Evaluating the Practical Utility of Confidence-score based Techniques for Unsupervised Open-world Intent Classification

Sopan Khosla
AWS AI Labs, Amazon
sopankh@amazon.com

Rashmi Gangadharaiah
AWS AI Labs, Amazon
rgangad@amazon.com

Abstract

Open-world classification in dialog systems require models to detect open intents, while ensuring the quality of in-domain (ID) intent classification. In this work, we revisit methods that leverage distance-based statistics for *unsupervised* out-of-domain (OOD) detection. We show that despite their superior performance on threshold-independent metrics like AUROC on test-set, threshold values chosen based on the performance on a validation-set do not generalize well to the test-set, thus resulting in substantially lower performance on ID or OOD detection accuracy and F1-scores. Our analysis shows that this lack of generalizability can be successfully mitigated by setting aside a *hold-out* set from validation data for threshold selection (sometimes achieving relative gains as high as 100%). Extensive experiments on seven benchmark datasets show that this fix puts the performance of these methods at par with, or sometimes even better than, the current state-of-the-art OOD detection techniques.

1 Introduction

Open intent detection is of significant importance in practical dialog systems. Prior art (Zhang et al., 2021a) has shown that an intent classifier's performance degrades when it encounters examples of an unseen intent. Open-world classification (Fei and Liu, 2016) tries to mitigate this by not only correctly classifying data that appeared in training (ID), but also detecting examples that are not a part of any existing class (OOD). Schölkopf et al. (2001) and Tax and Duin (2004) use SVMs to find the decision boundary of each positive class (ID). Bendale and Boult (2016) leverage deep neural networks to learn representations that capture high-level semantic concepts. To detect OOD samples, Hendrycks and Gimpel (2017) use the softmax probability as the confidence score, where some negative samples are used for confidence threshold discovery. Other works (Zhou et al., 2021; Ren et al., 2021; Podolskiy et al., 2021; Zhan et al., 2021) use the distance between a new sample and the ID distributions to define their confidence scores. Whereas, Zhang et al. (2021a) learn an adaptive decision boundary (ADB) of each positive class by only using ID data and thus removing the dependence on a confidence-score completely.

Threshold-based OOD detection allows for more control, especially in scenarios where correctly predicting ID intents takes priority over detecting negatives or vice-versa. This has motivated researchers to evaluate confidence-based methods on threshold-independent metrics like Area Under ROC curve (AUROC) or Area Under PR curve (AUPR) on test-sets for an unbiased comparison. This is especially true for works on distance-based (e.g. Mahalanobis distance, Cosine similarity) confidence-scores (Zhan et al., 2021; Ren et al., 2021; Zhou et al., 2021), which seldom comment on the threshold selection criteria or the threshold-dependent performance of the underlying method and thus fail to reveal much about their practical utility.

In this work, we evaluate state-of-the-art approaches that use **d**istance-**b**ased **s**tatistics (DBS) to arrive at confidence-scores for Open-World Classification. Unlike previous works, we specifically focus on their performance on threshold-dependent metrics. We show that threshold values (δ) chosen based on the performance on the validation-set, used to tune the classifier, do not generalize well on the test-set. This results in poor test-set ID/OOD Accuracy and F1-scores as compared to confidence-score-independent techniques like ADB on multiple benchmark datasets. We analyse this lack of generalizability and propose the use of a hold-out set of ID samples from validation data for threshold selection. This fix improves the threshold-dependent performance of DBS approaches putting their test accuracy and F1-scores on ID/OOD detection at par with, or sometimes even better, than previously proposed open-classification techniques.

Proceedings of the Third Workshop on Insights from Negative Results in NLP, pages 18 - 23
May 26, 2022 ©2022 Association for Computational Linguistics

2 Methodology

We explore multiple state-of-the-art strategies for unsupervised open-world intent classification. The term *unsupervised* here refers to the absence of open-intent samples during training. We consider two approaches that leverage **l**ogit-**b**ased **s**tatistics (LBS) as their confidence-score (i.e. Maximum Softmax Probability and Energy), two DBS approaches (i.e. Mahalanobis distance and Cosine similarity), and Adaptive Decision Boundary (ADB) that does not rely on confidence-scores.

Maximum Softmax Probability (MSP). Several prior works adopt this method as a baseline for OOD detection (Hendrycks and Gimpel, 2017; Hsu et al., 2020; Hendrycks et al., 2020). MSP uses the maximum class probability $1 - max_{j=1}^{C}(p_j)$ among C training classes as its OOD indicator. p_j denotes the probability of jth class.

Energy. Liu et al. (2020) show that energy scores not only better distinguish ID and OOD samples than softmax scores, but also align with the probability density of the inputs. A higher energy score indicates a higher likelihood of OODness.

Mahalanobis Distance (Maha) can be used to calculate the distance of an input sample to a distribution of samples from class c. We follow (Lee et al., 2018; Zhou et al., 2021) to compute the Mahalanobis distance from the penultimate layer of the transformer model by fitting a class-conditional multivariate Gaussian distribution. Finally, the OOD score for an instance is calculated as the minimum Mahalanobis distance among the C classes.

Cosine Similarity (Zhou et al., 2021). The OOD score is calculated as the negative of the maximum cosine similarity between an instance at inference time and samples in the validation set.

Adaptive Decision Boundary (ADB) (Zhang et al., 2021a) does not rely on an OOD score for open-world classification. This approach aims to learn the euclidean distance decision boundaries for every seen class using the representations extracted from the pre-trained multi-class classification model trained on labeled ID training data. These spherical decision boundaries act as the distinction between ID and OOD samples.

Dataset	TRAIN-ID	VAL-ID	VAL-OOD	TEST-ID	TEST-OOD
CLINC	15,000	3,000	100	4,500	1,000
ROSTD	30,000	4,000	1,500	8,600	3,000
BANK77OOS	5,905	1,506	730	2,000	2,080
OOSBANK	500	500	600	500	1,350
OOSCREDIT	500	500	600	500	1,350
BANK	9,003	1,000	-	3,080	-
SO	12,000	2,000	-	6,000	-

Table 1: Data Statistics (SO = STACKOVERFLOW). -ID and -OOD refer to the in-domain and out-of-domain utterances present in each split.

3 Experimental Setup

3.1 Data

We evaluate the open-world intent classification strategies on six challenging benchmark datasets. Table 1 provides details on dataset statistics.

CLINC contains 150 intents, 22,500 ID queries and 1,200 OOD queries (Larson et al., 2019).

BANK includes 13,083 customer service queries across 77 intents in the banking domain (Casanueva et al., 2020).

STACKOVERFLOW (Xu et al., 2015) contains 20 different classes of technical question titles. BANK and STACKOVERFLOW do not contain explicit OOD utterances, so we follow (Shu et al., 2017; Zhang et al., 2021a) and only consider 75% samples from all the classes as seen classes.

ROSTD extends the English part of multilingual dialog dataset (Schuster et al., 2019) with OOD utterances. Following Gangal et al. (2020), we evaluate the different techniques on the variant with 12 fine-grained ID classes.

Zhang et al. (2021b) proposed two datasets. The first contains utterances from two domains, i.e., the "Banking" (**OOSBANK**) and "Credit cards" domain (**OOSCREDIT**) with both (1) out-of-domain and out-of-scope (OOD-OOS) queries and (2) in-domain but out-of-scope (ID-OOS) queries. The second dataset (**BANK77OOS**) extends BANK to include ID-OOS queries based on 27 held-out semantically similar in-scope intents. We combine both OOD-OOS and ID-OOS into a common OOD class.

3.2 Evaluation Metrics

We evaluate the performance of different open-world classification techniques on threshold-independent metrics like $AUROC$ and $AUPR_{out}$. Following previous work (Shu et al., 2017; Lin and Xu, 2019), we also evaluate the overall performance on accuracy (*Acc*) and macro F1-score on

	Performance on VAL (Pipeline 1) / VAL-HOLD (Pipeline 2)						Performance on TEST set (Pipeline 1 / Pipeline 2)					
	$AUROC\uparrow$	$AUPR_{out}\uparrow$	$F1_{All}\uparrow$	$F1_{In}\uparrow$	$F1_{Out}\uparrow$	$Acc\uparrow$	$AUROC\uparrow$	$AUPR_{out}\uparrow$	$F1_{All}\uparrow$	$F1_{In}\uparrow$	$F1_{Out}\uparrow$	$Acc\uparrow$
CLINC												
MSP	96.2 / 96.4	62.2 / 82.6	96.4 / 95.0	96.7 / 95.2	60.7 / 74.5	95.4 / 93.6	96.5 / 96.7	87.4 / 87.8	93.0 / 93.6	93.2 / 93.7	75.3 / 77.6	90.1 / 90.9
Energy	96.8 / 97.1	68.9 / 87.3	96.5 / 95.4	96.7 / 95.5	66.3 / 79.5	95.8 / 94.2	97.0 / 97.1	89.8 / 90.2	93.2 / 94.0	93.3 / 94.1	77.5 / 80.9	90.6 / 91.8
Cosine	100.0 / 98.1	100.0 / 88.7	97.2 / 95.4	97.2 / 95.5	100.0 / 80.9	97.0 / 94.5	97.4 / 97.4	90.1 / 90.1	53.8 / 94.1	53.9 / 94.2	43.9 / 81.5	52.3 / 91.8
Maha	99.7 / 98.3	98.2 / 89.6	97.4 / 95.6	97.6 / 95.7	80.8 / 83.3	97.0 / 94.8	97.6 / 97.6	90.9 / 90.8	87.9 / **94.2**	88.0 / 94.3	69.2 / 82.1	83.7 / **92.1**
ROSTD												
MSP	89.8 / 91.1	82.0 / 92.5	91.4 / 88.7	93.2 / 89.9	69.9 / 73.6	87.1 / 78.0	89.1 / 90.2	81.6 / 82.4	91.1 / 90.5	93.0 / 92.2	68.7 / 69.8	87.0 / 87.1
Energy	89.7 / 91.5	83.9 / 93.4	92.2 / 89.0	94.0 / 90.4	69.8 / 72.9	87.4 / 77.9	89.0 / 90.7	83.1 / 85.0	91.9 / 91.3	93.8 / 93.1	68.7 / 69.7	87.2 / 87.3
Cosine	100.0 / 99.5	100.0 / 99.6	97.8 / 96.7	97.6 / 96.7	100.0 / 96.7	99.0 / 96.5	99.5 / 99.4	98.5 / 98.4	59.2 / 95.6	58.7 / 95.7	64.4 / 94.2	69.3 / 96.8
Maha	99.9 / 99.6	99.8 / 99.6	97.8 / 97.1	97.7 / 97.1	99.5 / 97.1	99.0 / 96.9	99.6 / 99.5	98.8 / 98.7	86.7 / **95.7**	86.4 / 95.8	90.1 / 94.8	94.2 / **96.9**
BANK77OOS												
MSP	87.9 / 87.6	79.8 / 91.5	82.2 / 74.4	82.4 / 74.3	72.1 / 80.7	79.0 / 76.8	90.6 / 89.8	91.6 / 91.2	78.3 / 77.8	78.3 / 77.7	82.1 / 82.1	79.7 / 79.5
Energy	90.0 / 89.8	84.0 / 93.3	83.1 / 76.1	83.2 / 75.9	75.6 / 84.2	80.5 / 79.9	92.3 / 91.7	93.5 / 93.1	79.5 / 79.5	79.4 / 79.4	84.5 / 85.0	81.5 / 82.0
Cosine	100.0 / 91.8	100.0 / 94.2	89.9 / 77.5	89.7 / 77.3	100.0 / 86.7	93.0 / 82.3	93.5 / 93.6	94.1 / 94.1	7.3 / 80.0	6.0 / 79.9	68.3 / 86.7	52.5 / 83.1
Maha	99.3 / 92.3	99.3 / 94.7	89.5 / 77.7	89.4 / 77.5	96.5 / 87.4	91.6 / 82.9	94.2 / 94.1	94.9 / 94.7	57.8 / **80.1**	57.4 / 79.9	78.7 / 87.3	71.6 / **83.4**
OOSBANK												
MSP	90.0 / 90.0	92.3 / 95.6	85.9 / 81.9	86.5 / 81.6	80.4 / 84.8	81.0 / 80.8	93.5 / 93.8	97.2 / 97.3	83.3 / 83.5	82.6 / 82.7	90.6 / 91.9	86.8 / 88.2
Energy	88.6 / 88.8	92.0 / 95.4	85.7 / 79.5	86.4 / 79.2	78.9 / 82.7	80.1 / 78.5	93.3 / 93.9	97.5 / 97.7	83.4 / 82.0	82.7 / 81.1	90.3 / 91.2	86.4 / 87.5
Cosine	100.0 / 94.4	100.0 / 97.2	99.1 / 84.0	99.0 / 83.4	100.0 / 90.3	99.7 / 86.8	96.0 / 96.2	98.3 / 98.3	31.5 / **84.2**	25.9 / 83.2	86.8 / 93.7	77.7 / 90.7
Maha	100.0 / 94.6	100.0 / 97.4	99.1 / 84.7	99.0 / 84.1	100.0 / 91.0	99.7 / 87.8	96.6 / 96.6	98.6 / 98.6	20.7 / **84.2**	14.3 / 83.2	85.6 / 93.9	75.4 / **91.0**
OOSCREDIT												
softmax	89.1 / 90.8	90.6 / 95.4	83.1 / 80.3	83.4 / 79.7	80.4 / 86.3	80.9 / 82.3	93.4 / 94.1	97.0 / 97.2	81.2 / 82.7	80.3 / 81.8	90.0 / 91.9	86.4 / 88.7
energy	87.9 / 89.6	90.7 / 95.2	82.2 / 77.5	82.7 / 77.1	76.8 / 81.7	78.5 / 77.6	93.2 / 93.9	97.2 / 97.5	80.5 / 81.5	79.7 / 80.6	88.4 / 90.2	84.6 / 86.7
cosine	100.0 / 94.9	100.0 / 97.0	98.4 / 86.7	98.3 / 86.2	100.0 / 92.5	99.1 / 89.7	96.4 / 96.5	98.2 / 98.2	44.3 / 88.4	39.8 / 87.7	88.7 / 95.4	81.3 / 93.2
maha	100.0 / 95.4	100.0 / 97.4	98.4 / 87.6	98.3 / 87.0	100.0 / 93.3	99.1 / 90.7	97.2 / 97.1	98.7 / 98.7	61.1 / **88.8**	58.1 / 88.1	91.1 / 95.6	85.6 / **93.7**
BANK-75%												
MSP	88.2 / 89.2	71.3 / 74.8	88.6 / 88.0	89.0 / 88.3	66.0 / 66.0	83.1 / 83.1	86.7 / 87.1	69.7 / 69.9	87.8 / 87.5	88.2 / 87.9	64.5 / 63.1	82.2 / 81.6
Energy	88.2 / 89.4	73.5 / 78.0	88.9 / 88.1	89.3 / 88.5	66.5 / 69.6	83.4 / 84.0	86.5 / 86.8	71.5 / 71.5	87.9 / 87.2	88.3 / 87.6	65.8 / 66.7	82.5 / 82.4
Cosine	100.0 / 91.7	100.0 / 79.4	95.6 / 89.0	95.5 / 89.3	100.0 / 73.4	96.6 / 85.6	89.9 / 89.5	74.8 / 74.2	23.7 / **88.4**	23.3 / 88.7	43.6 / 69.9	36.3 / 83.6
Maha	100.0 / 92.2	100.0 / 80.1	95.6 / 89.4	95.5 / 89.6	100.0 / 77.3	96.6 / 86.5	90.6 / 90.4	74.8 / 74.9	37.8 / 87.9	37.7 / 88.2	47.1 / 72.1	44.3 / **83.7**
STACKOVERFLOW-75%												
MSP	90.0 / 90.1	68.5 / 68.3	86.7 / 85.9	87.7 / 86.8	71.8 / 71.3	83.1 / 82.8	90.0 / 90.5	68.5 / 69.3	86.7 / 86.8	87.7 / 87.8	71.5 / 71.8	83.1 / 83.4
Energy	90.7 / 90.8	69.6 / 69.2	87.3 / 86.5	88.2 / 87.4	73.4 / 72.8	84.0 / 83.5	90.6 / 91.2	69.6 / 70.4	87.1 / 87.2	88.1 / 88.2	72.9 / 73.3	83.7 / 84.0
Cosine	100.0 / 91.5	100.0 / 69.2	91.4 / 87.0	90.8 / 87.8	100.0 / 75.0	93.1 / 84.4	91.9 / 92.0	70.6 / 71.6	28.2 / **87.9**	27.1 / 88.7	45.9 / 75.7	39.9 / **84.9**
Maha	99.7 / 91.6	99.6 / 69.7	91.3 / 87.1	91.0 / 87.9	96.0 / 75.4	92.4 / 84.4	91.9 / 92.2	69.7 / 71.5	74.7 / **87.8**	75.4 / 88.6	63.9 / 75.7	71.8 / **84.9**

Table 2: OOD detection performance of confidence-score based techniques on different benchmark datasets (↑: higher is better). Test $F1_{All}$ and Acc scores for the best performing pipeline are underlined. Highest scores on the datasets are in **bold**.[1,2] Models that leverage distance-based scores (DBS; *Maha* and *Cosine*) and are trained using Pipeline 1 consistently perform poorly on threshold-depenedent metrics on the test-set. Furthermore DBS models that use Pipeline 2 substantially outperform their Pipeline 1 counterparts on all datasets (Columns 10-13; green).

known classes ($F1_{In}$), open class ($F1_{Out}$), and all classes combined ($F1_{All}$). The latter four metrics can only be calculated once a threshold is chosen.

3.3 Hyperparameters

We leverage the RoBERTa-base model implemented in the HuggingFace library for classification and use most of the default hyperparameters.[3] We experiment with training batch sizes $\{32, 64, 128\}$. Model with batch size 64 performs the best across all datasets. The learning rate for ID classifier training is set to 2e-5. [4]

3.4 Holdout set for threshold selection

Prior open-world classification research (Lin and Xu, 2019; Zhang et al., 2021a,b) uses the ID (VAL-ID) and OOD (VAL-OOD) samples in the validation data for threshold (δ) selection (**Pipeline 1**). We also experiment with a second setup that splits VAL-ID into two parts. VAL-TUNE-ID is used to tune the in-domain classifier, whereas the other (VAL-HOLD-ID), along with VAL-OOD[5], helps in deciding δ (**Pipeline 2**). For each dataset, we randomly sample one-third of VAL-ID as our VAL-HOLD-ID.

Following prior art (Zhang et al., 2020, 2021b), we tune δ to maximize $(A_{in} + R_{oos})$. A_{in} and R_{oos} represent the ID accuracy and the out-of-scope recall respectively on VAL / VAL-HOLD set.

4 Results and Analysis

Table 2 shows the performance of all compared methods on both pipelines. We report the averaged scores on 10 random seeds.[6]

[1] Each result is an average of 10 runs with different seeds.

[2] Scores on VAL cannot be compared to VAL-HOLD (columns 2-7).

[3] https://huggingface.co/roberta-base

[4] All experiments are run on a Tesla V100 16GB GPU.

[5] VAL-HOLD = VAL-HOLD-ID + VAL-OOD

[6] We exclude the std. dev. values due to lack of space.

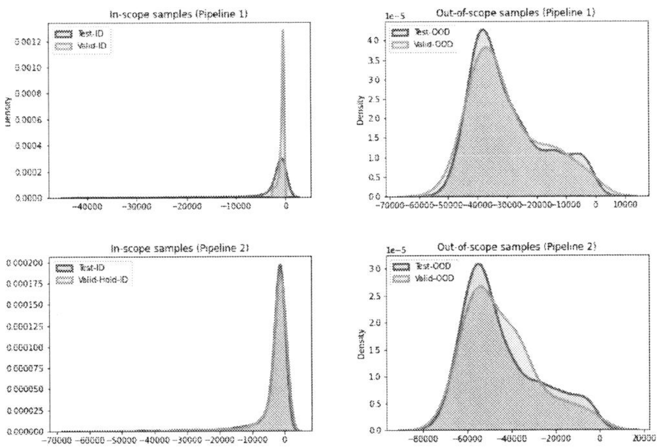

Figure 1: Maha distance (score) density plots for ID and OOD samples in CLINC dataset (VAL-OOD = VAL-HOLD-OOD). Top two charts show the density distribution for the model trained using Pipeline 1, whereas the bottom two focus on the model that uses Pipeline 2. We note that for Pipeline 1, the curve for VAL-ID looks substantially different from TEST-ID (top-left), suggesting that the thresholds selected using VAL-ID (Pipeline 1) might not generalize to the test set. Compare this to Pipeline 2 in-scope curve (bottom-left), where VAL-HOLD-ID almost exactly mimics the distribution of TEST-ID scores.

Dataset		$F1_{All}$	$F1_{In}$	$F1_{Out}$	Acc
CLINC	Maha	**94.2**	94.3	82.1	**92.1**
	ADB	93.3	93.4	79.3	90.6
	ADB-R	**94.3**	94.4	81.7	92.0
ROSTD	Maha	**95.7**	95.8	94.8	**96.9**
	ADB	95.0	95.7	86.5	93.3
	ADB-R	95.1	95.8	86.3	93.3
BANK77OOS	Maha	80.1	79.9	87.3	83.4
	ADB	78.6	78.5	84.7	81.6
	ADB-R	**81.1**	81.0	87.1	**83.9**
OOSBANK	Maha	**84.2**	83.2	93.9	**91.0**
	ADB	81.4	80.5	90.0	86.0
	ADB-R	81.9	81.1	89.5	85.5
OOSCREDIT	Maha	**88.8**	88.1	95.6	**93.7**
	ADB	82.8	82.0	90.8	87.2
	ADB-R	79.4	78.7	86.8	82.8
BANK-75%	Maha	87.9	88.2	72.1	**83.7**
	ADB*	86.0	86.3	66.5	81.1
	ADB-R	**88.4**	88.7	69.5	83.4
SO-75%	Maha	**87.8**	88.6	75.7	**84.9**
	ADB*	86.0	86.8	73.9	82.8
	ADB-R	87.6	88.5	74.5	84.3

Table 3: Test-set OOD detection performance of Cosine and Maha (Pipeline 2), and ADB variants on Accuracy and different F1-measures. ADB* denotes the official scores from (Zhang et al., 2021a). Maha (Pipeline 2) significantly outperforms ($p < 0.01$) ADB variants on ROSTD, OOSBANK, OOSCREDIT, and STACKOVERFLOW-75% datasets.

Models trained using Pipeline 1. In line with prior work (Zhou et al., 2021; Podolskiy et al., 2021), we find that Maha and Cosine perform better on the threshold-independent metrics ($AUROC$ and $AUPR_{out}$) across all datasets. This suggests that they are better at distinguishing ID instances from those considered to be OOD.[7]

Evaluation on threshold-dependent metrics (Acc and $F1$ scores) shows that the results obtained by MSP and Energy (LBS) on the test set do not differ much from the valid set, suggesting that the chosen δ generalizes well to unseen data. Compare this to Cosine and Maha (DBS) whose performance sees a drastic drop on the test set, despite achieving better scores on the valid set. This suggests that thresholds selected using Pipeline 1 for DBS might not transfer well to data in the wild, making them less useful in practice for OOD detection.

Models trained using Pipeline 2. On most datasets, the performance of these models on the test set mirrors that on the VAL-HOLD set. Furthermore, we see a consistent improvement in test Acc and $F1$ scores of all confidence-score methods as compared to their Pipeline 1 counterparts. Cosine and Maha see the highest gains, witnessing relative boosts as high as 100% on BANK-75% and STACKOVERFLOW-75%. Overall, thresholds chosen using Pipeline 2 seem to hold up better on unseen samples across the board, with Maha outperforming all other strategies on most datasets.

The top two plots in Figure 1 show the density plot of Mahalanobis distance values over CLINC ID and OOD data on VAL and test sets. We observe that although the distributions of TEST-OOD and VAL-OOD are quite similar, there are significant differences between the graphs for ID data (VAL-ID vs TEST-ID). There seem to be no VAL-ID samples with Maha score below -3000, whereas for TEST-ID, a substantial number of instances lie below -3000. This discrepancy might be a result of the slight overfitting of the trained ID classifier on VAL-ID samples as it leverages them for tuning. Compare this to the bottom two curves (in Figure 2) which plot Test vs VAL-HOLD instances. The density plots for both ID and OOD samples are almost identical. [8] Therefore, thresholds selected using VAL-HOLD are more likely to generalize to the unseen test set.

Comparison against ADB. ADB is the current state-of-the-art approach for unsupervised OOD detection. In Table 3, we report the performance of ADB (Zhang et al., 2021a)[9] and ADB-R where we replace the BERT encoder with RoBERTa-base

[7]Threshold-independent metrics cannot be calculated for ADB as it does not use a confidence-score for OOD detection.

[8]We see similar patterns across all datasets, but leave those figures out for brevity.

[9]https://github.com/thuiar/Adaptive-Decision-Boundary

and train the entire encoder during training. Maha (Pipeline 2) significantly outperforms ($p < 0.01$)[10] ADB and ADB-R on ROSTD, OOSBANK, OOS-CREDIT, and STACKOVERFLOW-75% while being competitive with the best performing ADB variant on the other three datasets.

5 Discussion and Conclusion

In this work, evaluate four confidence-score based unsupervised OOD detection techniques on seven state-of-the-art datasets. Most prior research (Zhou et al., 2021; Podolskiy et al., 2021) on methods that leverage distance-based statistics like Mahalanobis distance (Maha) or Cosine similarity (Cosine) only reports results on threshold-independent metrics like AUROC or AUPR. However, we show that despite their superior performance on AUROC, these techniques observe substantially lower scores on test ID and OOD detection Accuracy and F1-scores, when the entire validation-set (used to tune the ID classifier) is leveraged for threshold selection. This severely limits their practical utility.

Our analysis suggests that this discrepancy might be a result of the inadvertent overfitting of the trained classifier on VAL-ID samples. We show that this issue can be mitigated by leveraging a different evaluation setup that sets aside a hold-out set (not used during ID classifier tuning) from validation data for threshold selection. We observe that this new setup yields generalizable threshold values thus substantially improving the performance of Maha and Cosine on threshold-dependent metrics and making them more useful in real-world applications. Going forward, based on these findings, we would like to implore other researchers to also report the performance of their open-world classification approaches on threshold-dependent evaluation metrics, if applicable.

References

Abhijit Bendale and Terrance E Boult. 2016. Towards open set deep networks. In *Proceedings of the IEEE conference on computer vision and pattern recognition*, pages 1563–1572.

Iñigo Casanueva, Tadas Temčinas, Daniela Gerz, Matthew Henderson, and Ivan Vulić. 2020. Efficient intent detection with dual sentence encoders. In *Proceedings of the 2nd Workshop on Natural Language Processing for Conversational AI*, pages 38–45.

[10]We performed a one-tailed t-test to evaluate significance.

Geli Fei and Bing Liu. 2016. Breaking the closed world assumption in text classification. In *Proceedings of the 2016 Conference of the North American Chapter of the Association for Computational Linguistics: Human Language Technologies*, pages 506–514.

Varun Gangal, Abhinav Arora, Arash Einolghozati, and Sonal Gupta. 2020. Likelihood ratios and generative classifiers for unsupervised out-of-domain detection in task oriented dialog. In *Proceedings of the AAAI Conference on Artificial Intelligence*, volume 34, pages 7764–7771.

Dan Hendrycks and Kevin Gimpel. 2017. A baseline for detecting misclassified and out-of-distribution examples in neural networks. *Proceedings of ICLR*.

Dan Hendrycks, Xiaoyuan Liu, Eric Wallace, Adam Dziedzic, Rishabh Krishnan, and Dawn Song. 2020. Pretrained transformers improve out-of-distribution robustness. In *Proceedings of the 58th Annual Meeting of the Association for Computational Linguistics*, pages 2744–2751.

Yen-Chang Hsu, Yilin Shen, Hongxia Jin, and Zsolt Kira. 2020. Generalized odin: Detecting out-of-distribution image without learning from out-of-distribution data. In *Proceedings of the IEEE/CVF Conference on Computer Vision and Pattern Recognition*, pages 10951–10960.

Stefan Larson, Anish Mahendran, Joseph J. Peper, Christopher Clarke, Andrew Lee, Parker Hill, Jonathan K. Kummerfeld, Kevin Leach, Michael A. Laurenzano, Lingjia Tang, and Jason Mars. 2019. An evaluation dataset for intent classification and out-of-scope prediction. In *Proceedings of the 2019 Conference on Empirical Methods in Natural Language Processing and the 9th International Joint Conference on Natural Language Processing (EMNLP-IJCNLP)*, pages 1311–1316, Hong Kong, China. Association for Computational Linguistics.

Kimin Lee, Kibok Lee, Honglak Lee, and Jinwoo Shin. 2018. A simple unified framework for detecting out-of-distribution samples and adversarial attacks. *Advances in neural information processing systems*, 31.

Ting-En Lin and Hua Xu. 2019. Deep unknown intent detection with margin loss. In *Proceedings of the 57th Annual Meeting of the Association for Computational Linguistics*, pages 5491–5496.

Weitang Liu, Xiaoyun Wang, John Owens, and Yixuan Li. 2020. Energy-based out-of-distribution detection. *Advances in Neural Information Processing Systems*, 33:21464–21475.

Alexander Podolskiy, Dmitry Lipin, Andrey Bout, Ekaterina Artemova, and Irina Piontkovskaya. 2021. Revisiting mahalanobis distance for transformer-based out-of-domain detection. In *Proceedings of the AAAI Conference on Artificial Intelligence*, volume 35, pages 13675–13682.

Jie Ren, Stanislav Fort, Jeremiah Liu, Abhijit Guha Roy, Shreyas Padhy, and Balaji Lakshminarayanan. 2021. A simple fix to mahalanobis distance for improving near-ood detection. *Proceedings of ICML.*

Bernhard Schölkopf, John C Platt, John Shawe-Taylor, Alex J Smola, and Robert C Williamson. 2001. Estimating the support of a high-dimensional distribution. *Neural computation*, 13(7):1443–1471.

Sebastian Schuster, Sonal Gupta, Rushin Shah, and Mike Lewis. 2019. Cross-lingual transfer learning for multilingual task oriented dialog. In *Proceedings of the 2019 Conference of the North American Chapter of the Association for Computational Linguistics: Human Language Technologies, Volume 1 (Long and Short Papers)*, pages 3795–3805.

Lei Shu, Hu Xu, and Bing Liu. 2017. Doc: Deep open classification of text documents. In *Proceedings of the 2017 Conference on Empirical Methods in Natural Language Processing*, pages 2911–2916.

David MJ Tax and Robert PW Duin. 2004. Support vector data description. *Machine learning*, 54(1):45–66.

Jiaming Xu, Peng Wang, Guanhua Tian, Bo Xu, Jun Zhao, Fangyuan Wang, and Hongwei Hao. 2015. Short text clustering via convolutional neural networks. In *Proceedings of the 1st Workshop on Vector Space Modeling for Natural Language Processing*, pages 62–69.

Li-Ming Zhan, Haowen Liang, Bo Liu, Lu Fan, Xiao-Ming Wu, and Albert YS Lam. 2021. Out-of-scope intent detection with self-supervision and discriminative training. In *Proceedings of the 59th Annual Meeting of the Association for Computational Linguistics and the 11th International Joint Conference on Natural Language Processing (Volume 1: Long Papers)*, pages 3521–3532.

Hanlei Zhang, Hua Xu, and Ting-En Lin. 2021a. Deep open intent classification with adaptive decision boundary. In *Proceedings of the AAAI Conference on Artificial Intelligence*, volume 35, pages 14374–14382.

Jian-Guo Zhang, Kazuma Hashimoto, Yao Wan, Ye Liu, Caiming Xiong, and Philip S Yu. 2021b. Are pre-trained transformers robust in intent classification? a missing ingredient in evaluation of out-of-scope intent detection. *arXiv preprint arXiv:2106.04564*.

Jianguo Zhang, Kazuma Hashimoto, Wenhao Liu, Chien-Sheng Wu, Yao Wan, S Yu Philip, Richard Socher, and Caiming Xiong. 2020. Discriminative nearest neighbor few-shot intent detection by transferring natural language inference. In *Proceedings of the 2020 Conference on Empirical Methods in Natural Language Processing (EMNLP)*, pages 5064–5082.

Wenxuan Zhou, Fangyu Liu, and Muhao Chen. 2021. Contrastive out-of-distribution detection for pre-trained transformers. In *Proceedings of the 2021 Conference on Empirical Methods in Natural Language Processing*, pages 1100–1111.

Extending the Scope of Out-of-Domain: Examining QA models in multiple subdomains

Chenyang Lyu[†] **Jennifer Foster**[†] **Yvette Graham**[¶]
[†] School of Computing, Dublin City University, Dublin, Ireland
[¶] School of Computer Science and Statistics, Trinity College Dublin, Dublin, Ireland
chenyang.lyu2@mail.dcu.ie, jennifer.foster@dcu.ie, ygraham@tcd.ie

Abstract

Past work that investigates out-of-domain performance of QA systems has mainly focused on *general domains* (e.g. news domain, wikipedia domain), underestimating the importance of *subdomains* defined by the internal characteristics of QA datasets. In this paper, we extend the scope of "out-of-domain" by splitting QA examples into different subdomains according to their internal characteristics including *question type, text length, answer position*. We then examine the performance of QA systems trained on the data from different subdomains. Experimental results show that the performance of QA systems can be significantly reduced when the train data and test data come from different subdomains. These results question the generalizability of current QA systems in multiple subdomains, suggesting the need to combat the bias introduced by the internal characteristics of QA datasets.

1 Introduction

Examining the out-of-domain performance of QA systems is an important focus of the research community due to its direct connection to the generalizability and robustness of QA systems especially in production environments (Jia and Liang, 2017; Chen et al., 2017; Talmor and Berant, 2019; Fisch et al., 2019; Shakeri et al., 2020). Even though previous studies mostly focus on coarse-grained *general domains* (Ruder and Sil, 2021), the importance of finer-grained *subdomains* defined by the internal characteristics of QA datasets cannot be neglected. For example, several studies exploring specific internal characteristics of QA datasets have been carried out, including Ko et al. (2020), who reveal that the sentence-level answer position is a source of bias for QA models, and Sen and Saffari (2020) who investigate the effect of word-level question-context overlap. Building on this prior work as well as the definition and discussion of *subdomain* in Plank and Sima'an (2008); Plank (2016); Varis and Bojar (2021), we extend the scope of out-of-domain with a view to assessing the generalizability and robustness of QA systems by investigating their *out-of-subdomain* performance. As shown in Figure 1, we split the QA dataset into different *subdomains* based on its internal characteristics. Then we use the QA examples in each subdomain to train corresponding QA systems and evaluate their performance on all subdomains.

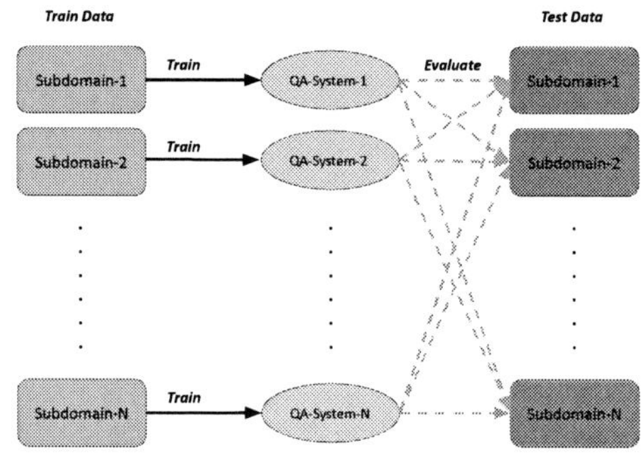

Figure 1: We train QA systems on each subdomain and evaluate each system on all subdomains

We focus on extractive QA as it is not only an important task in itself (Zhang et al., 2020) but also the crucial *reader* component in the retriever-reader model for Open-domain QA (Chen et al., 2017; Chen and Yih, 2020). In experiments with SQuAD 1.1 (Rajpurkar et al., 2016) and NewsQA (Trischler et al., 2017), we split the data into subdomains based on *question type, text length (context, question* and *answer)* and *answer position*. We then train QA systems on each subdomain and examine their performance on each subdomain. Results show that QA systems tend to perform worse when train and test data come from different subdomains, particularly those defined by *question type, answer length* and *answer position*.

Proceedings of the Third Workshop on Insights from Negative Results in NLP, pages 24 - 37
May 26, 2022

2 Experiments

We employ the QA datasets, SQuAD1.1 (Rajpurkar et al., 2016) and NewsQA (Trischler et al., 2017). For SQuAD1.1 we use the official dataset released by Rajpurkar et al. (2016) and for NewsQA we use the data from MRQA (Fisch et al., 2019). For question classification, we use the dataset from Li and Roth (2002). We use the BERT-base-uncased model from Huggingface (Wolf et al., 2019) for both question classification and QA.[1]

We adopt the following setup for training and evaluation: We split the original training set D into several disjoint subdomains $D_a, D_b, D_c, \ldots$; Then we sample subsets from each subdomain using sample sizes $n_1, n_2, n_3, \ldots$ in ascending order. The resulting subsets are denoted $D_a^{n_1}, D_a^{n_2}, \ldots, D_b^{n_1}, D_b^{n_2}, \ldots$. We train QA systems on each subset $D_a^{n_1}, D_a^{n_2}, \ldots$. The QA system trained on $D_a^{n_1}$ is denoted $QA_a^{n_1}$. We evaluate each QA system on the test data T which is also split into disjoint subdomains $T_a, T_b, T_c, \ldots$ similar to the training data D.

2.1 Question Type

In this experiment we investigate how QA models learn from QA examples with different question types. We adopt question classification data (Li and Roth, 2002) to train a question classifier that categorizes questions into the following five classes: *HUM, LOC, ENTY, DESC, NUM* (Zhang and Lee, 2003). The definitions and examples of each question type are shown in Table 1.

The training data is then partitioned into five categories according to their question type. Question type proportions for SQuAD1.1 and NewsQA are shown in Table 2, with a high proportion of *ENTY* and *NUM* questions in SQuAD1.1, while NewsQA has more *HUM* and *DESC* questions. We use QA examples of each question type to train a QA system, increasing the training set size in intervals of 500 from 500 to 8000. We evaluate it on the test data, which is also divided into five categories according to question type.

The F-1 scores of the QA systems trained on each question type *subdomain* are shown in Figure 2, for both SQuAD1.1 and NewsQA. The x-axis represents the training set size, the y-axis is the F-1 score. The results show that a QA system learns to answer a certain type of question mainly from the examples of the same question

[1]Hyperparameter settings are provided in Appendix A.1.

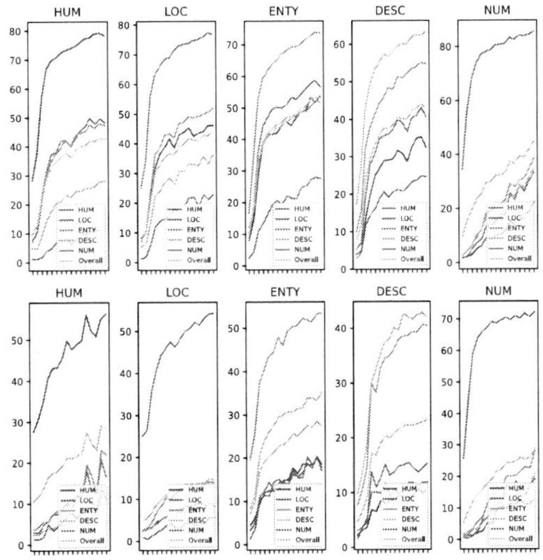

Figure 2: Visualization of F-1 learning curves for the QA systems trained on the *subdomains* of five question types (*HUM,LOC,ENTY,DESC,NUM*), tested on the *subdomains* for each question type and the original dev set of SQuAD1.1 (top) and NewsQA (bottom).

type – this is particularly true for *HUM* and *NUM* questions in SQuAD1.1 and *HUM, LOC* and *NUM* questions in NewsQA. Taking *NUM* questions as an example, the rightmost plots in Figure 2 show that performance on other question types results in only minor improvements as the training set size increases compared to the improvements on the *NUM* question type. The QA system gets most of the knowledge it needs to answer *NUM* questions from the *NUM* training examples and a similar pattern is present for other question types.

The results in Figure 2 show that the subdomain defined by *question type* is a source of bias when training and employing QA systems. We suspect that word use and narrative style vary over question types, injecting bias into QA systems when learning from QA examples with different question types. Therefore, we need to improve the diversity of question types when constructing and organising QA data.

2.2 Text Length

The effect of text length on the performance and generalizability of neural models has been discussed in text classification and machine translation (Amplayo et al., 2019; Varis and Bojar, 2021). As for QA, there are three components in a QA example: *context, question, answer*. The length of each component could potentially introduce addi-

Question type	Definition	Examples
HUM	people, individual, group, title	*What contemptible scoundrel stole the cork from my lunch ?* *Which professor sent the first wireless message in the USA ?* *Who was sentenced to death in February ?*
LOC	location, city, country, mountain, state	*Where is the Kalahari desert ?* *Where is the theology library at Notre Dame ?* *Where was Cretan when he heard screams ?*
ENTY	animal, body, color, creation, currency, disease/medical, event, food, instrument, language, plant, product, religion, sport, symbol, technique, term, vehicle	*What relative of the racoon is sometimes known as the cat-bear ?* *What is the world's oldest monographic music competition ?* *What was the name of the film about Jack Kevorkian ?*
DESC	definition, description, manner, reason	*What is Eagle 's syndrome styloid process ?* *How did Beyonce describe herself as a feminist ?* *What are suspects blamed for ?*
NUM	code, count, date, distance, money, order, other, percent, period, speed, temperature, size, weight	*How many calories are there in a Big Mac ?* *What year did Nintendo announce a new Legend of Zelda was in the works for Gamecube ?* *How many tons of cereal did Kelloggs donate ?*

Table 1: Definition of each question type and corresponding examples in SQuAD1.1 and NewsQA.

		LOC	ENTY	HUM	NUM	DESC
SQuAD1.1	Train set	11.4	27.6	20.7	24.5	15.5
	Dev set	10.5	27.6	21.0	23.0	17.4
NewsQA	Train set	11.4	16.9	30.0	18.8	22.6
	Dev set	12.3	16.9	32.2	17.8	20.5

Table 2: The percentage (%) of question types in the SQuAD1.1 and NewsQA train and dev sets.

tional bias and affect how QA systems learn from QA data. For example, a short context could be *easy* since a shorter context could reduce the search space for QA models to locate the answer; on the other hand, a short context could be *hard* as it could contain less information Therefore, the following question arises naturally: are *short* and *long* contexts/questions/answers equivalent?

To answer this question, we split the QA datasets into *short* and *long* groups according to the median of the length of *contexts/questions/answers*.[2] Then we train QA systems on the QA examples sampled from *short* ($QA_{S,context}$, $QA_{S,question}$, $QA_{S,answer}$) and *long* ($QA_{L,context}$, $QA_{L,question}$, $QA_{L,answer}$) groups respectively, increasing the training set size in intervals of 500 from 500 to 25000.

The results are shown in Figure 3, where the x-axis is the training set size and the y-axis is the ratio of the performance (EM and F-1 score) of the QA_S and corresponding QA_L systems on the *text length* subdomains of *context/question/answer*. If QA_L and QA_S have no obvious difference in terms of performance on *long* and *short* groups respectively, the ratio of their performance should be close to 1.

The results show that the performance of QA_L and QA_S trained on the subdomains of *context* and *question* length have no obvious difference as all the three curves converge to 1, although there are fluctuations when the sample sizes are small. In contrast, QA_L and QA_S trained on the subdomain of *answer* length behave differently – see the subplots in the two rightmost columns of Figure 3. QA_L performs much better than QA_S on the test examples with *long* answers and much worse than QA_S on the test examples with *short* answers.

The results in Figure 3 show that the length of the answer introduces strong bias to QA systems. We think this stems from the fact that QA_L tends to predict longer answers, whereas QA_S tends to pre-

[2]See the Appendix for more statistics.

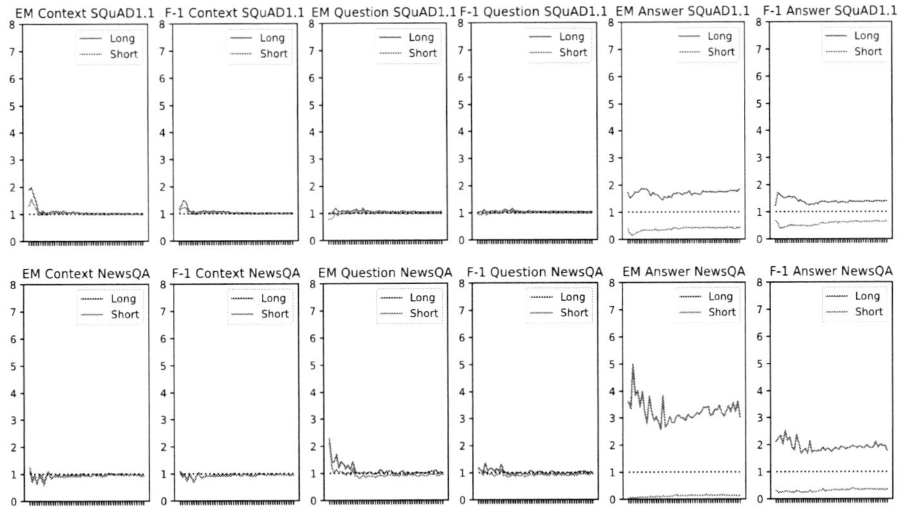

Figure 3: Visualization of performance (EM and F-1 score) ratio curves over *long* and *short* context, question and answer (from left to right) on SQuAD1.1 (top) and NewsQA (bottom). The *green, red* lines represent the ratio of the performance on the *long* and *short* groups. The dashed line is 1, indicating that two QA systems have the same performance. When the sample size increases, curves in *context* and *question* length converge to the dashed line, whereas there are substantial differences in the performance of QA_L and QA_S on the *answer length* subdomain.

	Context		Question		Answer	
	Long	Short	Long	Short	Long	Short
SQuAD1.1	4.03	4.13	4.00	4.23	6.41	2.78
NewsQA	5.46	5.33	5.16	5.87	9.57	3.51

Table 3: The average length of predicted answers of QA systems trained on *long* and *short* subdomains of *context, question* and *answer* on SQuAD1.1 and NewsQA.

dict shorter answers, and they thus underperform in the counterpart subdomain. We show the average length of the predicted answers of QA_L and QA_S in Table 3. Therefore, it is important to control the length distribution of answers when constructing and organising QA datasets, especially using NER tools in the answer extraction phase since they tend to find shorter answers.

2.3 Answer Position

Ko et al. (2020) study the effect of sentence-level answer position. Building on their analysis, we study the effect of two more types of answer position: character-level position and word-level position. We split the training set into *front* and *back* groups based on the median of the answer start positions at the character, word and sentence level.[3] Then we train QA systems on the examples sampled from the *front* ($QA_{F,char}, QA_{F,word}, QA_{F,sent}$) and *back* ($QA_{B,char}, QA_{B,word}, QA_{B,sent}$) groups respectively, increasing the training set size in intervals of 500 from 500 to 25000.

The results are shown in Figure 4, where the x-axis is the training set size and the y-axis is the ratio of the performance (EM and F-1 score) of QA_F and QA_B on the *answer position* subdomains at the character, word and sentence level. The results show that *answer position* is a source of bias at all three levels. QA_F performs much better than QA_B on test instances with answer positions in the *front*, whereas QA_B performs much better than QA_F on test instances with answer positions at the *back*. The effect of bias is more serious at the character and word level. We think this answer position bias is happening because words in different positions have different position embeddings, which could also affect word semantics in transformer architectures (Vaswani et al., 2017; Wang et al., 2020). This suggests the need to make sure answer position distribution is balanced as well as the need to develop QA systems that are more robust to answer position variation.

3 Conclusion

We presented a series of experiments investigating the *out-of-subdomain* performance of QA systems

[3]See the Appendix for more statistics.

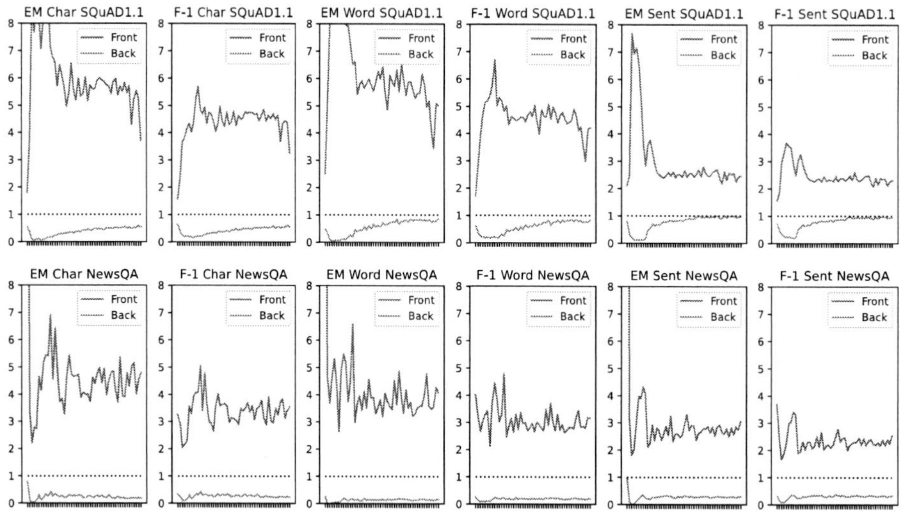

Figure 4: Visualization of performance (EM and F-1 score) ratio curves over *front* and *back* answer positions (char-level, word-level and sentence-level from left to right) on SQuAD1.1 (top) and NewsQA (bottom). The *green, red* lines represent the ratio of the performance on the *front* and *back* groups. The dashed line is 1, indicating that two QA systems have the same performance. The curves show that there are substantial differences in the performance of QA_F and QA_B in *answer position* subdomains, especially for character-level and word-level answer positions.

on two popular English extractive QA datasets: SQuAD1.1 and NewsQA. The experimental results show that the *subdomains* defined by *question type, answer length* and *answer position* inject strong bias into QA systems, with the result that the performance of QA systems is negatively impacted when train and test data come from different *subdomains*. The experiments provide useful information on how to control question diversity, answer length distribution as well as answer positions when constructing QA datasets and employing QA systems. In future work, we aim to apply our analysis to multilingual data to explore how QA models behave across different languages and we plan to investigate other types of QA beyond extractive.

Acknowledgements

This work was funded by Science Foundation Ireland through the SFI Centre for Research Training in Machine Learning (18/CRT/6183). We thank James Barry for his proofreading and helpful comments. We also thank the reviewers for their useful feedback.

References

Reinald Kim Amplayo, Seonjae Lim, and Seung-won Hwang. 2019. Text length adaptation in sentiment classification. In *Asian Conference on Machine Learning*, pages 646–661. PMLR.

Danqi Chen, Adam Fisch, Jason Weston, and Antoine Bordes. 2017. Reading Wikipedia to answer open-domain questions. In *Proceedings of the 55th Annual Meeting of the Association for Computational Linguistics (Volume 1: Long Papers)*, pages 1870–1879, Vancouver, Canada. Association for Computational Linguistics.

Danqi Chen and Wen-tau Yih. 2020. Open-domain question answering. In *Proceedings of the 58th Annual Meeting of the Association for Computational Linguistics: Tutorial Abstracts*, pages 34–37, Online. Association for Computational Linguistics.

Adam Fisch, Alon Talmor, Robin Jia, Minjoon Seo, Eunsol Choi, and Danqi Chen. 2019. MRQA 2019 shared task: Evaluating generalization in reading comprehension. In *Proceedings of the 2nd Workshop on Machine Reading for Question Answering*, pages 1–13, Hong Kong, China. Association for Computational Linguistics.

Robin Jia and Percy Liang. 2017. Adversarial examples for evaluating reading comprehension systems. In *Proceedings of the 2017 Conference on Empirical Methods in Natural Language Processing*, pages 2021–2031, Copenhagen, Denmark. Association for Computational Linguistics.

Miyoung Ko, Jinhyuk Lee, Hyunjae Kim, Gangwoo Kim, and Jaewoo Kang. 2020. Look at the first sentence: Position bias in question answering. In *Proceedings of the 2020 Conference on Empirical Methods in Natural Language Processing (EMNLP)*, pages 1109–1121, Online. Association for Computational Linguistics.

Xin Li and Dan Roth. 2002. Learning question classifiers. In *COLING 2002: The 19th International Conference on Computational Linguistics*.

Barbara Plank. 2016. What to do about non-standard (or non-canonical) language in NLP. In *Proceedings of the 13th Conference on Natural Language Processing, KONVENS 2016, Bochum, Germany, September 19-21, 2016*, volume 16 of *Bochumer Linguistische Arbeitsberichte*.

Barbara Plank and Khalil Sima'an. 2008. Subdomain sensitive statistical parsing using raw corpora. In *Proceedings of the International Conference on Language Resources and Evaluation, LREC 2008, 26 May - 1 June 2008, Marrakech, Morocco*. European Language Resources Association.

Pranav Rajpurkar, Jian Zhang, Konstantin Lopyrev, and Percy Liang. 2016. SQuAD: 100,000+ questions for machine comprehension of text. In *Proceedings of the 2016 Conference on Empirical Methods in Natural Language Processing*, pages 2383–2392, Austin, Texas. Association for Computational Linguistics.

Sebastian Ruder and Avi Sil. 2021. Multi-domain multilingual question answering. In *Proceedings of the 2021 Conference on Empirical Methods in Natural Language Processing: Tutorial Abstracts*, pages 17–21, Punta Cana, Dominican Republic & Online. Association for Computational Linguistics.

Priyanka Sen and Amir Saffari. 2020. What do models learn from question answering datasets? In *Proceedings of the 2020 Conference on Empirical Methods in Natural Language Processing (EMNLP)*, pages 2429–2438, Online. Association for Computational Linguistics.

Siamak Shakeri, Cicero Nogueira dos Santos, Henghui Zhu, Patrick Ng, Feng Nan, Zhiguo Wang, Ramesh Nallapati, and Bing Xiang. 2020. End-to-end synthetic data generation for domain adaptation of question answering systems. In *Proceedings of the 2020 Conference on Empirical Methods in Natural Language Processing (EMNLP)*, pages 5445–5460, Online. Association for Computational Linguistics.

Alon Talmor and Jonathan Berant. 2019. MultiQA: An empirical investigation of generalization and transfer in reading comprehension. In *Proceedings of the 57th Annual Meeting of the Association for Computational Linguistics*, pages 4911–4921, Florence, Italy. Association for Computational Linguistics.

Adam Trischler, Tong Wang, Xingdi Yuan, Justin Harris, Alessandro Sordoni, Philip Bachman, and Kaheer Suleman. 2017. NewsQA: A machine comprehension dataset. In *Proceedings of the 2nd Workshop on Representation Learning for NLP*, pages 191–200, Vancouver, Canada. Association for Computational Linguistics.

Dusan Varis and Ondřej Bojar. 2021. Sequence length is a domain: Length-based overfitting in transformer models. In *Proceedings of the 2021 Conference on Empirical Methods in Natural Language Processing*, pages 8246–8257, Online and Punta Cana, Dominican Republic. Association for Computational Linguistics.

Ashish Vaswani, Noam Shazeer, Niki Parmar, Jakob Uszkoreit, Llion Jones, Aidan N. Gomez, Lukasz Kaiser, and Illia Polosukhin. 2017. Attention is all you need. *CoRR*, abs/1706.03762.

Benyou Wang, Lifeng Shang, Christina Lioma, Xin Jiang, Hao Yang, Qun Liu, and Jakob Grue Simonsen. 2020. On position embeddings in bert. In *International Conference on Learning Representations*.

Thomas Wolf, Lysandre Debut, Victor Sanh, Julien Chaumond, Clement Delangue, Anthony Moi, Pierric Cistac, Tim Rault, R'emi Louf, Morgan Funtowicz, and Jamie Brew. 2019. Huggingface's transformers: State-of-the-art natural language processing. *ArXiv*, abs/1910.03771.

Dell Zhang and Wee Sun Lee. 2003. Question classification using support vector machines. In *Proceedings of the 26th annual international ACM SIGIR conference on Research and development in informaion retrieval*, pages 26–32.

Zhuosheng Zhang, Hai Zhao, and Rui Wang. 2020. Machine reading comprehension: The role of contextualized language models and beyond.

A Appendix

A.1 Experimental Setup

We use bert-based-uncased as our QA model. The learning rate is set to 3e-5, the maximum sequence length is set to 384, and the doc stride length is set to 128. We run the training process for 2 epochs. The training batch size is 48. The training was conducted on one GeForce GTX 3090 GPU.

A.2 Average Text Length and Answer Position for All Question Types

We show the average text length of *context, question and answer* as well as the average answer position on character-level, word-level and sentence-level for QA examples in all question types in SQuAD1.1 and NewsQA in Table 4 and Table 5.

A.3 Question Type Proportions, Average Text Length and Average Answer Position for *Long* and *Short* Text Length

The median of the *context, question, answer* is shown in Table 6. We show the question type proportion, average text length for *context, question*

		Context	Question	Answer
SQuAD1.1	HUM	123.20	9.79	2.82
	LOC	117.18	9.62	2.78
	DESC	119.32	9.91	5.82
	ENTY	117.43	10.54	3.04
	NUM	121.09	10.11	2.08
NewsQA	HUM	495.79	6.55	2.82
	LOC	478.84	6.34	2.87
	DESC	513.00	6.25	7.62
	ENTY	505.94	6.76	4.27
	NUM	476.23	7.20	2.07

Table 4: The average text length of context, question and answer in QA examples of each question type in the SQuAD1.1 and NewsQA training data.

		Char-Level	Word-Level	Sent-Level
SQuAD1.1	HUM	317.85	54.90	1.61
	LOC	308.81	53.71	1.53
	DESC	342.97	60.00	1.79
	ENTY	317.75	55.16	1.63
	NUM	315.78	56.19	1.67
NewsQA	HUM	532.11	101.02	3.71
	LOC	566.02	107.99	3.95
	DESC	844.13	160.05	5.98
	ENTY	751.48	143.90	5.49
	NUM	763.73	145.26	5.47

Table 5: The average answer position of character-level, word-level and sentence-level in QA examples of each question type in the SQuAD1.1 and NewsQA training data.

	Context	Question	Answer
SQuAD1.1	110	10	2
NewsQA	534	6	2

Table 6: The median of the *context, question, answer* length used to partition *long* and *short* subdomains.

		LOC	ENTY	HUM	NUM	DESC
SQuAD1.1	Long	11.11	26.68	21.65	24.8	15.43
	Short	11.73	28.42	19.68	24.2	15.52
NewsQA	Long	10.4	18.08	29.94	16.81	24.71
	Short	12.38	15.86	30.24	20.9	20.55

Table 7: The percentage of each question type in *long context* and *short context* groups.

		LOC	ENTY	HUM	NUM	DESC
SQuAD1.1	Long	10.36	28.59	20.37	24.73	15.63
	Short	12.11	26.90	20.84	24.35	15.37
NewsQA	Long	9.45	18.29	29.70	23.66	18.90
	Short	12.96	15.91	30.40	14.98	25.63

Table 8: The percentage of each question type in *long question* and *short question* groups.

		LOC	ENTY	HUM	NUM	DESC
SQuAD1.1	Long	10.87	27.32	19.69	21.8	19.86
	Short	11.79	27.72	21.29	26.29	12.55
NewsQA	Long	9.37	19.87	23.16	9.31	38.17
	Short	13.13	14.48	36.03	27.05	9.29

Table 9: The percentage of each question type in *long answer* and *short answer* groups.

		Context	Question	Answer
SQuAD1.1	Long	84.53	9.99	3.09
	Short	155.88	10.14	3.23
NewsQA	Long	350.44	6.54	3.79
	Short	641.35	6.69	4.25

Table 10: The average answer position on character-level, word-level and sentence-level in QA examples of *long context* and *short context* groups.

		Context	Question	Answer
SQuAD1.1	Long	119.12	7.8	3.25
	Short	120.76	13.57	3.03
NewsQA	Long	491.15	4.96	4.45
	Short	501.55	8.66	3.49

Table 11: The average answer position on character-level, word-level and sentence-level in QA examples of *long question* and *short question* groups.

		Context	Question	Answer
SQuAD1.1	Long	119.08	10.18	1.42
	Short	120.79	9.88	5.77
NewsQA	Long	489.32	6.82	1.5
	Short	503.34	6.37	6.95

Table 12: The average answer position on character-level, word-level and sentence-level in QA examples of *long answer* and *short answer* groups.

		Char	Word	Sent
SQuAD1.1	Long	402.02	70.36	2.14
	Short	239.75	41.78	1.17
NewsQA	Long	864.85	165.73	6.40
	Short	510.58	95.94	3.37

Table 13: The average answer position on character-level, word-level and sentence-level in QA examples of *long context* and *short context* groups.

		Char	Word	Sent
SQuAD1.1	Long	342.02	59.70	1.74
	Short	305.65	53.45	1.58
NewsQA	Long	726.78	138.64	5.22
	Short	655.98	124.50	4.61

Table 14: The average answer position on character-level, word-level and sentence-level in QA examples of *long question* and *short question* groups.

		Char	Word	Sent
SQuAD1.1	Long	324.65	57.77	1.71
	Short	316.70	54.65	1.60
NewsQA	Long	795.46	150.20	5.61
	Short	595.00	114.17	4.26

Table 15: The average answer position on character-level, word-level and sentence-level in QA examples of *long answer* and *short answer* groups.

	Char	Word	Sent
SQuAD1.1	262	46	1
NewsQA	358	67	2

Table 16: The median of the answer position on character-level, word-level and sentence-level used to partition *front* and *back* subdomains.

and answer as well as the average answer position on character-level, word-level and sentence-level for QA examples in *long* and *short* groups of *context, question, answer* in SQuAD1.1 and NewsQA in Table 7, Table 8, Table 9, Table 10 Table 11, Table 12, Table 13, Table 14, Table 15.

A.4 Question Type Proportions, Average Text Length and Average Answer Position for QA examples with *Front* and *Back* Answer Positions

The median of the answer position at the character, word and sentence levels is shown in Table 16. We show the question type proportion, average text length for *context, question and answer* as well as the average answer position at the character, word and sentence levels for QA examples in the *front* and *back* groups of answer positions at the character, word and sentence levels for SQuAD1.1 and NewsQA in Table 17, Table 18, Table 19, Table 20, Table 21, Table 22, Table 23, Table 24, Table 25.

A.5 QA examples with *long* and *short* answers

We give some QA examples with *long* and *short* answers in Table 26 and Table 27.

		LOC	ENTY	HUM	NUM	DESC
SQuAD1.1	Front	11.74	27.8	20.25	24.97	14.81
	Back	11.11	27.32	21.06	24.02	16.14
NewsQA	Front	13.07	15.59	37.2	15.61	18.46
	Back	9.71	18.36	22.97	22.1	26.8

Table 17: The percentage of each question type in *front* and *back* groups on character-level answer position

		LOC	ENTY	HUM	NUM	DESC
SQuAD1.1	Front	11.76	28.05	20.28	24.49	14.99
	Back	11.16	27.08	21.00	24.45	15.94
NewsQA	Front	13.02	15.59	37.20	15.64	18.48
	Back	9.74	18.43	22.85	22.11	26.81

Table 18: The percentage of each question type in *front* and *back* groups on word-level answer position

		LOC	ENTY	HUM	NUM	DESC
SQuAD1.1	Front	11.72	27.83	20.60	24.48	14.95
	Back	11.04	27.18	20.71	24.56	16.15
NewsQA	Front	13.19	15.76	36.08	16.36	18.54
	Back	9.56	18.54	23.11	22.06	26.67

Table 19: The percentage of each question type in *front* and *back* groups on sentence-level answer position

		Char	Word	Sent
SQuAD1.1	Front	116.25	20.6	0.44
	Back	524.15	91.3	2.85
NewsQA	Front	145.24	28.72	0.61
	Back	1230.24	232.96	9.15

Table 20: The average answer position on character-level, word-level and sentence-level in QA examples of *front* and *back* groups of character-level answer position.

		Char	Word	Sent
SQuAD1.1	Front	127.4	19.34	0.44
	Back	515.71	93.09	2.88
NewsQA	Front	151.46	28.04	0.65
	Back	1229.77	234.74	9.17

Table 21: The average answer position on character-level, word-level and sentence-level in QA examples of *front* and *back* groups of word-level answer position.

		Char	Word	Sent
SQuAD1.1	Front	158.46	26.12	0.4
	Back	532.52	95.11	3.28
NewsQA	Front	183.56	35.56	0.63
	Back	1280.56	242.86	9.89

Table 22: The average answer position on character-level, word-level and sentence-level in QA examples of *front* and *back* groups of sentence-level answer position.

		Context	Question	Answer
SQuAD1.1	Front	108.80	9.83	3.06
	Back	130.77	10.30	3.26
NewsQA	Front	473.52	6.50	3.28
	Back	518.08	6.72	4.75

Table 23: The average text length of context, question and answer in QA examples of *front* and *back* groups of character-level answer position

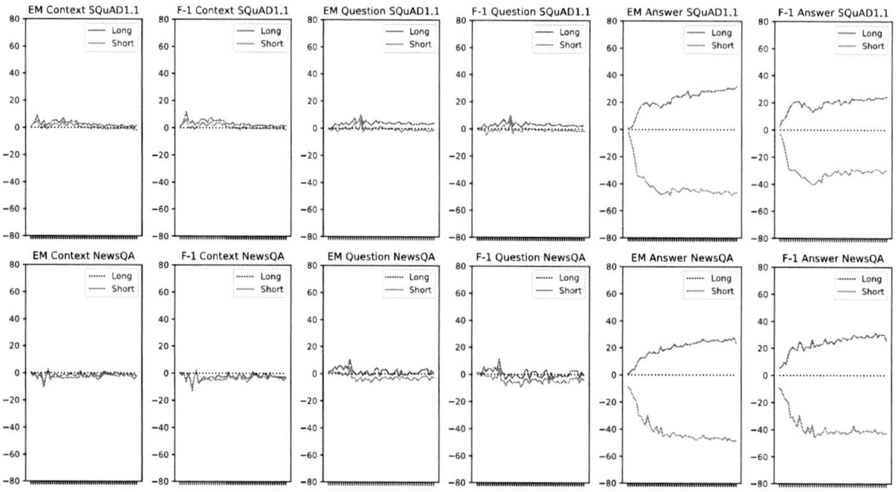

Figure 5: Visualization of performance (EM and F-1 score) difference curves over *short* and *long* context, question and answer (from left to right) on SQuAD1.1 (top) and NewsQA (bottom). The *green, red* lines represent the difference of the performance on the *long* and *short* groups. The dashed line is 0, indicating that two QA systems have the same performance. When the sample size increases, curves in *context* and *question* length converge to the dashed line, whereas there are substantial differences in the performance of QA_L and QA_S in the *answer length* subdomain.

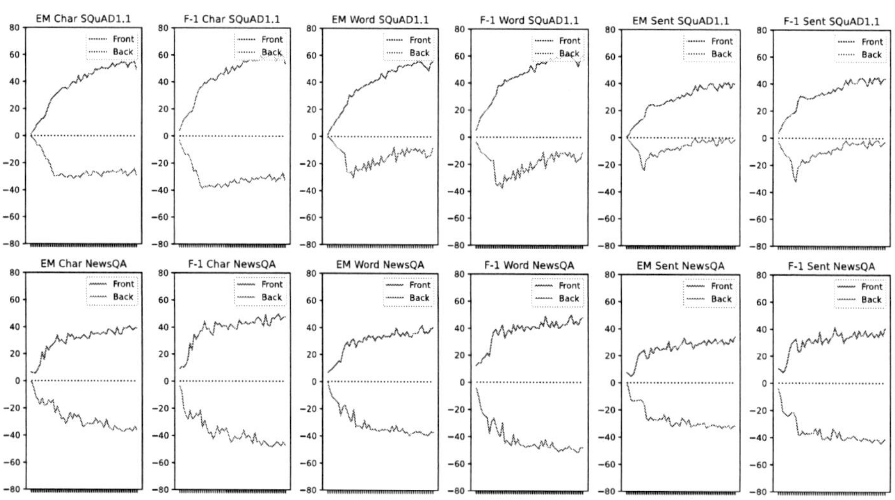

Figure 6: Visualization of performance (EM and F-1 score) difference curves over *front* and *back* answer positions (char-level, word-level and sentence-level from left to right) on SQuAD1.1 (top) and NewsQA (bottom). The *green, red* lines represent the difference of the performance on the *front* and *back* groups. The dashed line is 0, indicating that two QA systems have the same performance. The curves show that there are substantial differences in the performance of QA_F and QA_B in *answer position* subdomains especially for character-level and word-level answer positions.

		Context	Question	Answer
SQuAD1.1	Front	109.21	9.84	3.03
	Back	130.50	10.28	3.30
NewsQA	Front	473.13	6.50	3.32
	Back	518.72	6.72	4.72

Table 24: The average text length of context, question and answer in QA examples of *front* and *back* groups of word-level answer position

		Context	Question	Answer
SQuAD1.1	Front	110.14	9.93	3.04
	Back	132.44	10.23	3.33
NewsQA	Front	474.28	6.52	3.58
	Back	521.11	6.73	4.54

Table 25: The average text length of context, question and answer in QA examples of *front* and *back* groups of sentence-level answer position

A.6 QA examples with *front* and *back* answers

We give some QA examples with character-level answer positions in the *front* and *back* groups in Table 28 and Table 29.

A.7 Performance Difference for Text Length and Answer Position Experiments

We also show the difference in performance (EM and F-1 score) between QA systems ($QA_L - QA_S$ and $QA_F - QA_B$) on subdomains of *text length* and *answer position* in Figure 5 and Figure 6.

Answer Length	Question	Context
Long	Where was the main focus of Pan-Slavism?	Pan-Slavism, a movement which came into prominence in the mid-19th century, emphasized the common heritage and unity of all the Slavic peoples. The main focus was in the Balkans where the South Slavs had been ruled for centuries by other empires: ***the Byzantine Empire, Austria-Hungary, the Ottoman Empire, and Venice***. The Russian Empire used Pan-Slavism as a political tool; as did the Soviet Union, which gained political-military influence and control over most Slavic-majority nations between 1945 and 1948 and retained a hegemonic role until the period 1989–1991.
Long	What is one reason for homologs to appear?	Genes with a most recent common ancestor, and thus a shared evolutionary ancestry, are known as homologs. These genes appear either from ***gene duplication within an organism's genome***, where they are known as paralogous genes, or are the result of divergence of the genes after a speciation event, where they are known as orthologous genes,:7.6 and often perform the same or similar functions in related organisms. It is often assumed that the functions of orthologous genes are more similar than those of paralogous genes, although the difference is minimal.
Long	How does the water vapor that rises in warm air turn into clouds?	Solar radiation is absorbed by the Earth's land surface, oceans – which cover about 71% of the globe – and atmosphere. Warm air containing evaporated water from the oceans rises, causing atmospheric circulation or convection. ***When the air reaches a high altitude, where the temperature is low, water vapor condenses into clouds***, which rain onto the Earth's surface, completing the water cycle. The latent heat of water condensation amplifies convection, producing atmospheric phenomena such as wind, cyclones and anti-cyclones. Sunlight absorbed by the oceans and land masses keeps the surface at an average temperature of 14 °C. By photosynthesis green plants convert solar energy into chemically stored energy, which produces food, wood and the biomass from which fossil fuels are derived.

Table 26: Examples of QA examples with *long* answers where answers are highlighted.

Answer Length	Question	Context
Short	Who led the Exodus?	According to the Hebrew Bible narrative, Jewish ancestry is traced back to the Biblical patriarchs such as Abraham, Isaac and Jacob, and the Biblical matriarchs Sarah, Rebecca, Leah, and Rachel, who lived in Canaan around the 18th century BCE. Jacob and his family migrated to Ancient Egypt after being invited to live with Jacob's son Joseph by the Pharaoh himself. The patriarchs' descendants were later enslaved until the Exodus led by ***Moses***, traditionally dated to the 13th century BCE, after which the Israelites conquered Canaan.
Short	When did the Duke of Kent die?	Victoria was the daughter of Prince Edward, Duke of Kent and Strathearn, the fourth son of King George III. Both the Duke of Kent and King George III died in ***1820***, and Victoria was raised under close supervision by her German-born mother Princess Victoria of Saxe-Coburg-Saalfeld. She inherited the throne aged 18, after her father's three elder brothers had all died, leaving no surviving legitimate children. The United Kingdom was already an established constitutional monarchy, in which the sovereign held relatively little direct political power. Privately, Victoria attempted to influence government policy and ministerial appointments; publicly, she became a national icon who was identified with strict standards of personal morality.
Short	What is the evaluator called in a breed show?	In conformation shows, also referred to as breed shows, ***a judge*** familiar with the specific dog breed evaluates individual purebred dogs for conformity with their established breed type as described in the breed standard. As the breed standard only deals with the externally observable qualities of the dog (such as appearance, movement, and temperament), separately tested qualities (such as ability or health) are not part of the judging in conformation shows.

Table 27: Examples of QA examples with *short* answers where answers are highlighted.

Answer Position	Question	Context
Front	What are the first names of the men that invented youtube?	According to a story that has often been repeated in the media, ***Hurley and Chen*** developed the idea for YouTube during the early months of 2005, after they had experienced difficulty sharing videos that had been shot at a dinner party at Chen's apartment in San Francisco. Karim did not attend the party and denied that it had occurred, but Chen commented that the idea that YouTube was founded after a dinner party was probably very strengthened by marketing ideas around creating a story that was very digestible.
Front	Who became Chairman of the Council of Ministers in 1985?	In the fall of 1985, Gorbachev continued to bring younger and more energetic men into government. On September 27, ***Nikolai Ryzhkov*** replaced 79-year-old Nikolai Tikhonov as Chairman of the Council of Ministers, effectively the Soviet prime minister, and on October 14, Nikolai Talyzin replaced Nikolai Baibakov as chairman of the State Planning Committee (GOSPLAN). At the next Central Committee meeting on October 15, Tikhonov retired from the Politburo and Talyzin became a candidate. Finally, on December 23, 1985, Gorbachev appointed Yeltsin First Secretary of the Moscow Communist Party replacing Viktor Grishin.
Front	During what seasons is fog common in Boston?	Fog is fairly common, particularly in ***spring and early summer***, and the occasional tropical storm or hurricane can threaten the region, especially in late summer and early autumn. Due to its situation along the North Atlantic, the city often receives sea breezes, especially in the late spring, when water temperatures are still quite cold and temperatures at the coast can be more than 20 °F (11 °C) colder than a few miles inland, sometimes dropping by that amount near midday. Thunderstorms occur from May to September, that are occasionally severe with large hail, damaging winds and heavy downpours. Although downtown Boston has never been struck by a violent tornado, the city itself has experienced many tornado warnings. Damaging storms are more common to areas north, west, and northwest of the city. Boston has a relatively sunny climate for a coastal city at its latitude, averaging over 2,600 hours of sunshine per annum.

Table 28: Examples of QA examples with answers in *front* group where answers are highlighted.

Answer Position	Question	Context
Back	How many murders did Detroit have in 2015?	Detroit has struggled with high crime for decades. Detroit held the title of murder capital between 1985-1987 with a murder rate around 58 per 100,000. Crime has since decreased and, in 2014, the murder rate was 43.4 per 100,000, lower than in St. Louis, Missouri. Although the murder rate increased by 6% during the first half of 2015, it was surpassed by St Louis and Baltimore which saw much greater spikes in violence. At year-end 2015, Detroit had ***295*** criminal homicides, down slightly from 299 in 2014.
Back	Who was leading the Conservatives at this time?	Despite being a persistent critic of some of the government's policies, the paper supported Labour in both subsequent elections the party won. For the 2005 general election, The Sun backed Blair and Labour for a third consecutive election win and vowed to give him öne last chanceẗo fulfil his promises, despite berating him for several weaknesses including a failure to control immigration. However, it did speak of its hope that the Conservatives (led by ***Michael Howard***) would one day be fit for a return to government. This election (Blair had declared it would be his last as prime minister) resulted in Labour's third successive win but with a much reduced majority.
Back	Who lost the 2015 Nigerian presidential election?	Nigeria is a Federal Republic modelled after the United States, with executive power exercised by the president. It is influenced by the Westminster System model[citation needed] in the composition and management of the upper and lower houses of the bicameral legislature. The president presides as both Head of State and head of the national executive; the leader is elected by popular vote to a maximum of two 4-year terms. In the March 28, 2015 presidential election, General Muhammadu Buhari emerged victorious to become the Federal President of Nigeria, defeating then incumbent ***Goodluck Jonathan***.

Table 29: Examples of QA examples with answers in *back* group where answers are highlighted.

What Do You Get When You Cross Beam Search with Nucleus Sampling?

Uri Shaham **Omer Levy**
The Blavatnik School of Computer Science
Tel Aviv University

Abstract

We combine beam search with the probabilistic pruning technique of nucleus sampling to create two deterministic *nucleus search* algorithms for natural language generation. The first algorithm, p-exact search, locally prunes the next-token distribution and performs an exact search over the remaining space. The second algorithm, dynamic beam search, shrinks and expands the beam size according to the entropy of the candidate's probability distribution. Despite the probabilistic intuition behind nucleus search, experiments on machine translation and summarization benchmarks show that both algorithms reach the same performance levels as standard beam search.

1 Introduction

The standard approach to natural language generation uses a search algorithm, guided by an autoregressive (conditional) language model, to search through the space of possible strings. Since this search space is immense, pruning techniques have been introduced to facilitate tractable text generation. Beam search (Reddy, 1977) is a deterministic algorithm that prunes the search space according to the relative *rank* of each prefix, keeping only the top b prefixes at every step. Although rank-based pruning has no probabilistic justification – it is mainly motivated by its ability to limit memory consumption – beam search is an effective approach for generation tasks such as machine translation and summarization. Nucleus sampling (Holtzman et al., 2020), on the other hand, is a stochastic algorithm, which prunes the bottom *percentile* of the model's next-token distribution, thus eliminating bad candidates while retaining some degree of randomness, which is important for free-form generation. What if we were to replace beam search's rank-based pruning mechanism (top k) with the probabilistic mechanism of nucleus sampling (top p)?

We experiment with two variants of this hypothetical *nucleus search*. The first algorithm, *p-exact search*, locally prunes the search space by retaining only the top p of every next-token distribution that the underlying language model produces. It then performs an exact search over the remaining space, guaranteeing the most probable sequence under the local pruning assumption. The second algorithm, *dynamic beam search*, selects the top p *beams* at each step, according to their normalized probabilities (rather than top k, by rank). This method can shrink or enhance the number of beams to match the current step's low or high entropy, respectively.

We evaluate both algorithms on three conditional generation benchmarks: subword-level translation (WMT'14 EN-FR), character-level translation (IWSLT'14 DE-EN), and summarization (XSUM). While we observe that both nucleus search algorithms produce competitive results with standard beam search, we do not find any empirical advantage to our probabilistically-motivated approach.

We further analyze the algorithms by isolating the impact of dynamically expanding or shrinking the number of candidates. Experiments show that expanding the beam, even when entropy is high, tends to decrease performance. Pruning candidates, on the other hand, appears to have no adverse effects, and may even have a marginal positive effect in certain cases, which possibly cancels out with the negative effects of beam expansion.

2 Background

Natural language generation can be defined as a search problem in the space of possible sequences over a token vocabulary V, where the goal is to find an optimal sequence $Y = (y_1, ..., y_n) \in V^*$ according to some cost function. Typical search algorithms explore this infinite space via sequence prefixes, starting with the empty sequence, and

Proceedings of the Third Workshop on Insights from Negative Results in NLP, pages 38 - 45
May 26, 2022 ©2022 Association for Computational Linguistics

appending one potential token y_t at a time. Search terminates by returning a sequence (or a sequences set) that ends with a special token that indicates the end of the sequence (`EOS`).

The cost function is based on an underlying language model that, given a prefix $Y_{<t}$, induces a probability distribution over V, which we denote $P(y_t|Y_{<t})$.[1] The probability of a sequence (or prefix) Y is computed as the product of its tokens probabilities:

$$P(Y) = \prod_t P(y_t|Y_{<t}) \quad (1)$$

In practice, it is common to use the negative log probability instead:

$$-\log P(Y) = \sum_t -\log P(y_t|Y_{<t}) \quad (2)$$

This defines a monotonic additive cost function, where appending each token y_t adds a positive cost $-\log P(y_t|Y_{<t})$ to the total cost of the sequence.

2.1 Beam Search

In many natural language generation tasks, *beam search* (Reddy, 1977) is the algorithm of choice. It extends the simple greedy algorithm by considering k possible prefixes $\{Y^i_{\leq t}\}^k_{i=1}$ at each timestep. The beam size k is constant throughout the search, guaranteeing a limit on memory consumption.

At every step t, beam search ranks all the possible single-token extensions of the current k prefixes, and then keeps only the best k extensions according to their total cost (Equation 2). Once a prefix is appended with `EOS`, it is considered a complete sequence, and remains fixed as long as its cost is among the best k prefixes; if k (or more) better prefixes are found, it is discarded. The algorithm terminates when either the final token of all top k sequences is `EOS`, or when t exceeds the predefined maximum number of steps. In both cases, it returns all sequences in the beam that end with `EOS`.[2]

Assuming the models are tuned, results should improve as the beam size k increases. However, this assumption does *not* hold for contemporary models; in practice, text quality deteriorates when using large values of k (Koehn and Knowles, 2017). Furthermore, decoding with exact search (Dijkstra, 1959) reveals that translation models often rank the empty string as the most probable sequence (Stahlberg and Byrne, 2019). Perhaps unintentionally, searching with small beam sizes mitigates this flaw.[3]

2.2 Nucleus Sampling

Deterministic search algorithms, such as beam search, try to generate the most probable sequence. This is a desirable property when we have many constraints regarding the target output, as in translation or question answering. However, tasks that require more creativity and diversity in language may benefit from *stochastic* algorithms.

Holtzman et al. (2020) show that sampling from a language model's raw distribution P produces degenerate text, and instead, suggest to sample only from the *nucleus*, S_p: the smallest set of tokens whose sum of probabilities is larger than some hyperparameter p. Specifically, nucleus sampling prunes P by assigning zero probability to every token outside of S_p, and renormalizes the probabilities to get a new distribution P_p:

$$P_p(y|Y_{<t}) = \begin{cases} \frac{P(y|Y_{<t})}{\sum_{y' \in S_p} P(y'|Y_{<t})} & y \in S_p \\ 0 & y \notin S_p \end{cases}$$

Here, we refer to this mechanism as *tail pruning*. Sampling from P_p results in less degenerate and more human-like text than both full-distribution sampling and top-k sampling (Fan et al., 2018), which do not account for the distribution's entropy.

3 Nucleus Search

We combine beam search with tail pruning, producing two variants of *nucleus search*: *p-exact search* and *dynamic beam search*.

3.1 p-Exact Search

Stahlberg and Byrne (2019) show that exact search (Dijkstra, 1959) often produces extremely short and even empty sequences because the underlying model assigns a non-zero probability to the `EOS` token at each step. We use tail pruning (Section 2.2)

[1]The underlying model is often a *conditional* language model $P(y_t|Y_{<t}, X)$, which takes an additional sequence X as part of its input. For brevity, we omit X from our notation.

[2]Typically, the system selects the top sequence in the set, or chooses an alternative sequence via some reranking criterion.

[3]a.k.a. the "blessing" of beam search (Meister et al., 2020).

to round all near-zero probabilities (whether belonging to EOS or any other token) to zero. We apply exact search over the pruned space, guaranteeing the most probable sequence that contains only top-p tokens at each step.

Given a hyperparameter p, we apply tail pruning to the model's predicted token distribution $P(y_t|Y_{<t})$. The pruned distribution $P_p(y_t|Y_{<t})$ assigns zero probability to all tokens in the bottom $1-p$ of the original distribution, and remonrmalized probabilities for the rest. This procedure prunes the EOS token when it is unlikely, preventing empty sequences and reducing the brevity bias.

3.2 Dynamic Beam Search

Beam search keeps a fixed number (k) of prefixes according to their *rank*. When entropy is high, the difference between the k-th most probable prefix and the one ranked $k+1$ might be minuscule, and we may want the search algorithm to consider such candidate prefixes as well. Conversely, when entropy is low, the best prefix dominates the alternatives, making them redundant.

Dynamic beam search provides a mechanism for increasing the beam size when entropy is high, and pruning the number of prefixes when entropy is low. Let k_t be the number of viable prefixes at step t. The model predicts the next-token distribution for each prefix, creating $k_t \cdot |V|$ candidates. Each candidate Y^i is scored according to its *cumulative* probability $P(Y^i)$ (Equation 1). To determine the beam size, we first normalize the probability scores within the set of candidates, and then apply tail pruning on the normalized probability:

$$\hat{P}(Y^i) = \frac{P(Y^i)}{\sum_{j=1}^{k_t \cdot |V|} P(Y^j)}$$

As in p-exact search (Section 3.1), we use a hyperparameter p to determine the nucleus of $\hat{P}$, and thus the size of the next step's beam k_{t+1}. The normalized probability $\hat{P}(Y^i)$ is only used to compute the dynamic beam; we keep the original probability $P(Y^i)$ as each prefix's cumulative score.

4 Experiments

We compare our search algorithms to beam search on a variety of tasks, and use the same model across all settings, for each task.

4.1 Tasks

Machine Translation We evaluate on the WMT'14 EN-FR dataset (Bojar et al., 2014), using the model of Ott et al. (2018), a large Transformer (Vaswani et al., 2017) with 6 encoder and decoder layers, trained on 36M bilingual sentences, tokenized with BPE. We evaluate the generated sequences using SacreBLEU (Post, 2018), case-sensitive, with the 13a tokenizer.

Character-Level Machine Translation We train a character-level model on the IWSLT'14 DE-EN dataset (Cettolo et al., 2014), which contains approximately 172k bilingual sentences in its training set. We use the recommended settings in Fairseq (Ott et al., 2019) for a 6-layer encoder-decoder transformer. As with the subword-level dataset, performance is measured via SacreBLEU.

Summarization We evaluate on the XSUM dataset (Narayan et al., 2018). To alleviate memory issues and improve data quality, we remove examples where the source document is longer than 800 tokens (1,663 examples), or when the target is longer than one quarter of the source document (698 examples). Our cleaned version of the XSUM test set contains 8,972 document-summarization pairs. We use the large fine-tuned BART model (Lewis et al., 2020), and compute ROUGE-L (Lin and Hovy, 2003) via compare-mt (Neubig et al., 2019).

4.2 Implementation

Although both nucleus search algorithms can theoretically consume an unbounded amount of memory, our implementation caps the number of candidate prefixes by a large constant: 320 for WMT'14 and XSUM, and 160 for character-level translation.

We explore p in increments of 0.1 for both nucleus search algorithms. For beam search, we experiment with all beam sizes from 1 to 5, as well as exponentially increasing beam sizes from 5 to 320. To present a complete picture of the algorithms' behaviors, we report results for all hyperparameter settings, rather than selecting the best configuration according to the validation set. This experiment design limits our ability to claim the superiority of one algorithm over another, but as we show in Section 5, the performance differences are so small that no such claim will be made.

Search Algo	Hyper-param (k or p)	WMT'14 EN-FR	IWSLT'14 DE-EN (Char)	XSUM
Beam	1	40.3	33.3	35.5
	2	40.7	33.6	36.2
	3	**40.8**	33.6	36.4
	4	**40.8**	33.6	36.5
	5	40.6	33.5	36.5
	10	40.5	33.5	**36.6**
	20	40.2	33.1	36.4
	40	39.6	27.4	36.1
	80	38.7	18.1	35.7
	160	32.2	5.3	34.3
	320	11.8	5.3	28.1
p-Exact	0.1	40.3	33.3	35.5
	0.2	40.3	33.3	35.7
	0.3	40.5	33.3	36.1
	0.4	40.5	33.4	36.5
	0.5	40.6	33.5	**36.6**
	0.6	40.6	33.5	**36.6**
	0.7	40.2	33.6	36.3
	0.8	39.2	33.6	35.9
	0.9	27.8	33.2	33.1
Dynamic	0.1	40.2	33.3	35.5
	0.2	40.3	33.3	35.6
	0.3	40.5	33.4	36.0
	0.4	40.6	33.4	36.2
	0.5	40.6	33.4	36.5
	0.6	40.6	**33.7**	36.5
	0.7	40.0	**33.7**	36.0
	0.8	38.9	33.6	35.4
	0.9	18.1	33.1	31.5

Table 1: Scores of different algorithms and settings on various generation tasks. **Bold** numbers indicate the highest result on the task, and underlined numbers indicate that the result is within 0.2 points of the top score.

5 Results

Main Result Table 1 shows the performance of each search algorithm across the different tasks.[4] In line with previously reported trends (Koehn and Knowles, 2017), we observe that increasing the beam size beyond $k = 10$ can severely degrade performance. On the other hand, the probabilistic search algorithms appear to be more stable, with most hyperparameter settings achieving relatively high performance metrics until $p = 0.9$, where substantial performance degradation is evident.

Despite their increased stability, there appears to be no significant advantage to either p-exact search or dynamic beam search over the original beam search. In fact, the performance differences between the best settings of each algorithm are always under 0.2 BLEU/ROUGE, and often zero.

[4]This table shows performance without reranking (length normalization), to study the core algorithm. Appendix A contains the results with reranking, showing similar trends.

Search Algorithm		$\max(i) \leq 5$	$\max(i) > 5$
Beam	$k = 5$	42.2	**32.9**
Dynamic Beam	$p = 0.6$	**42.3**	32.2
#Examples		*2618*	*385*

Table 2: Performance on two subsets of WMT'14 EN-FR: (1) examples where dynamic beam search only selects prefixes from the top-5 options ($\max(i) \leq 5$), and (2) examples where the output of dynamic beam search contains at least one prefix that ranked 6 or worse ($\max(i) > 5$).

We find this trend counter-intuitive, since we originally assumed that expanding and trimming the beam based on entropy would benefit language generation. We further test these assumptions individually.

Expanded Beams We compare the performance of static beam search ($k = 5$) and dynamic beam search ($p = 0.6$) on two subsets of the translation task's test set:[5] (1) examples where dynamic beam search always selects from its top 5 prefixes, and (2) the complement, where every generated output contains at least one prefix that was ranked 6th or worse. Table 2 shows that in those cases where dynamic beam search actually uses the expanded beam, i.e. it chooses prefixes that rank lower than 5, it performs *worse* than static top-5 beam search by 0.7 BLEU. This subset accounts for only 13% of examples – which are probably harder for the model, given the 10-point difference in BLEU – while the majority 87% of cases are always composed from the top 5 (or less) prefixes.

Trimmed Beams We isolate the effect of probabilistic trimming by applying a $k = 5$ cap on the number of active beams, for both nucleus search variations. Table 3 shows that p-exact and dynamic beam trimming strategies have no negative effects, and may have a marginal positive effect.

6 Related Work

As a standard decoding strategy, there is a significant body of literature on beam search. Recently, there has been more focus on the empty string problem (Stahlberg and Byrne, 2019), and the fact that increasing the beam size beyond a small constant typically hurts performance. Meister et al. (2020) show that beam search optimize for sequences that

[5]We select $p = 0.6$ since it is the maximal value that achieved the top score on the WMT'14 EN-FR benchmark.

Search Algo	Hyper-param (k or p)	WMT'14 EN-FR	IWSLT'14 DE-EN (Char)	XSUM
Beam	1	40.3	33.3	35.5
	2	40.7	33.6	36.2
	3	40.8	33.6	36.4
	4	40.8	33.6	36.5
	5	40.6	33.5	36.5
p-Exact ($k = 5$)	0.1	40.3	33.3	35.5
	0.2	40.3	33.3	35.7
	0.3	40.5	33.3	36.1
	0.4	40.6	33.4	36.4
	0.5	40.8	33.5	**36.6**
	0.6	**41.0**	33.6	**36.6**
	0.7	40.9	33.7	**36.6**
	0.8	40.9	**33.8**	36.5
	0.9	40.8	**33.8**	36.5
Dynamic ($k = 5$)	0.1	40.2	33.3	35.5
	0.2	40.3	33.3	35.6
	0.3	40.5	33.4	36.0
	0.4	40.6	33.4	36.2
	0.5	40.6	33.4	36.4
	0.6	40.8	33.7	36.5
	0.7	40.7	33.7	**36.6**
	0.8	40.7	33.6	**36.6**
	0.9	40.6	33.5	36.5

Table 3: Scores of different algorithms and settings on various generation tasks, *when limiting the beam size to a maximum of 5*. **Bold** numbers indicate the highest result on the task, and underlined numbers indicate that the result is within 0.2 points of the top score.

distribute information uniformly, and therefore, using small beam sizes allows it to overcome the empty string problem. Shi et al. (2020) train models with multiple different EOS tokens based on their positions, instead of a single universal EOS token. Peters and Martins (2021) replace the softmax function with the sparse entmax transformation (Peters et al., 2019) that *can* assign absolute zero probability to tokens. This method has a similar effect to our p-exact search, but requires training the model with entmax, while our contribution only modifies the search algorithm.

Massarelli et al. (2020) also propose a combination of beam search and sampling methods, but with a different method and a different goal. They focus on free-form text generation, addressing two problems – repetition and halucination – by sampling the first few tokens, and then switching over to beam search. Freitag and Al-Onaizan (2017) explore how using a small fixed beam size, pruned further according to the relative or absolute distance from the top scored candidate, can increase decoding speed. In this work, we focus on the quality of the generated text, comparing the use of a fixed beam size to tail pruning, an established method that keeps candidates according to the nucleus of the distribution.

7 Conclusion

Language models predict a distribution over their vocabulary, yet beam search only utilizes the rank of different candidates, not their actual probability scores. A natural assumption is that searching the space of prefixes with a constant number of options is not optimal. We hypothesize that using the probability scores to dynamically determine the number of candidates may benefit natural language generation. We test our hypothesis by introducing two nucleus search algorithms, which incorporate probabilistic tail pruning (Holtzman et al., 2020) with beam search, but find that they perform on par with the baseline beam search algorithm when its beam size is restricted to a small constant.

Acknowledgements

This work was supported by the Tel Aviv University Data Science Center, the Blavatnik Fund, the Alon Scholarship, and Intel Corporation. We would like to thank Ari Holtzman, Jonathan Berant, Ori Yoran, Lior Vassertail, and Yuval Kirstain for their valuable feedback.

References

Ondřej Bojar, Christian Buck, Christian Federmann, Barry Haddow, Philipp Koehn, Christof Monz, Matt Post, and Lucia Specia, editors. 2014. *Proceedings of the Ninth Workshop on Statistical Machine Translation*. Association for Computational Linguistics, Baltimore, Maryland, USA.

Mauro Cettolo, Jan Niehues, Sebastian Stüker, Luisa Bentivogli, and Marcello Federico. 2014. Report on the 11th iwslt evaluation campaign, iwslt 2014. In *Proceedings of the International Workshop on Spoken Language Translation, Hanoi, Vietnam*, volume 57.

Edsger W Dijkstra. 1959. A note on two problems in connexion with graphs. *Numerische mathematik*, 1(1):269–271.

Angela Fan, Mike Lewis, and Yann Dauphin. 2018. Hierarchical neural story generation. In *Proceedings of the 56th Annual Meeting of the Association for Computational Linguistics (Volume 1: Long Papers)*, pages 889–898, Melbourne, Australia. Association for Computational Linguistics.

Markus Freitag and Yaser Al-Onaizan. 2017. Beam search strategies for neural machine translation. In *Proceedings of the First Workshop on Neural Machine Translation*, pages 56–60, Vancouver. Association for Computational Linguistics.

Ari Holtzman, Jan Buys, Maxwell Forbes, and Yejin Choi. 2020. The curious case of neural text degeneration. *International Conference on Learning Representations*.

Sébastien Jean, Orhan Firat, Kyunghyun Cho, Roland Memisevic, and Yoshua Bengio. 2015. Montreal neural machine translation systems for WMT'15. In *Proceedings of the Tenth Workshop on Statistical Machine Translation*, pages 134–140, Lisbon, Portugal. Association for Computational Linguistics.

Philipp Koehn and Rebecca Knowles. 2017. Six challenges for neural machine translation. In *Proceedings of the First Workshop on Neural Machine Translation*, pages 28–39, Vancouver. Association for Computational Linguistics.

Mike Lewis, Yinhan Liu, Naman Goyal, Marjan Ghazvininejad, Abdelrahman Mohamed, Omer Levy, Veselin Stoyanov, and Luke Zettlemoyer. 2020. BART: Denoising sequence-to-sequence pretraining for natural language generation, translation, and comprehension. In *Proceedings of the 58th Annual Meeting of the Association for Computational Linguistics*, pages 7871–7880, Online. Association for Computational Linguistics.

Chin-Yew Lin and Eduard Hovy. 2003. Automatic evaluation of summaries using n-gram cooccurrence statistics. In *Proceedings of the 2003 Human Language Technology Conference of the North American Chapter of the Association for Computational Linguistics*, pages 150–157.

Luca Massarelli, Fabio Petroni, Aleksandra Piktus, Myle Ott, Tim Rocktäschel, Vassilis Plachouras, Fabrizio Silvestri, and Sebastian Riedel. 2020. How decoding strategies affect the verifiability of generated text. In *Findings of the Association for Computational Linguistics: EMNLP 2020*, pages 223–235, Online. Association for Computational Linguistics.

Clara Meister, Ryan Cotterell, and Tim Vieira. 2020. If beam search is the answer, what was the question? In *Proceedings of the 2020 Conference on Empirical Methods in Natural Language Processing (EMNLP)*, pages 2173–2185, Online. Association for Computational Linguistics.

Kenton Murray and David Chiang. 2018. Correcting length bias in neural machine translation. In *Proceedings of the Third Conference on Machine Translation: Research Papers*, pages 212–223, Brussels, Belgium. Association for Computational Linguistics.

Shashi Narayan, Shay B. Cohen, and Mirella Lapata. 2018. Don't give me the details, just the summary! topic-aware convolutional neural networks for extreme summarization. In *Proceedings of the 2018 Conference on Empirical Methods in Natural Language Processing*, pages 1797–1807, Brussels, Belgium. Association for Computational Linguistics.

Graham Neubig, Zi-Yi Dou, Junjie Hu, Paul Michel, Danish Pruthi, and Xinyi Wang. 2019. compare-mt: A tool for holistic comparison of language generation systems. In *Proceedings of the 2019 Conference of the North American Chapter of the Association for Computational Linguistics (Demonstrations)*, pages 35–41, Minneapolis, Minnesota. Association for Computational Linguistics.

Myle Ott, Sergey Edunov, Alexei Baevski, Angela Fan, Sam Gross, Nathan Ng, David Grangier, and Michael Auli. 2019. fairseq: A fast, extensible toolkit for sequence modeling. In *Proceedings of the 2019 Conference of the North American Chapter of the Association for Computational Linguistics (Demonstrations)*, pages 48–53, Minneapolis, Minnesota. Association for Computational Linguistics.

Myle Ott, Sergey Edunov, David Grangier, and Michael Auli. 2018. Scaling neural machine translation. In *Proceedings of the Third Conference on Machine Translation: Research Papers*, pages 1–9, Brussels, Belgium. Association for Computational Linguistics.

Ben Peters and André F. T. Martins. 2021. Smoothing and shrinking the sparse Seq2Seq search space. In *Proceedings of the 2021 Conference of the North American Chapter of the Association for Computational Linguistics: Human Language Technologies*, pages 2642–2654, Online. Association for Computational Linguistics.

Ben Peters, Vlad Niculae, and André F. T. Martins. 2019. Sparse sequence-to-sequence models. In *Proceedings of the 57th Annual Meeting of the Association for Computational Linguistics*, pages 1504–1519, Florence, Italy. Association for Computational Linguistics.

Matt Post. 2018. A call for clarity in reporting BLEU scores. In *Proceedings of the Third Conference on Machine Translation: Research Papers*, pages 186–191, Brussels, Belgium. Association for Computational Linguistics.

D. Raj Reddy. 1977. Speech understanding systems: A summary of results of the five-year research effort at carnegie-mellon university.

Xing Shi, Yijun Xiao, and Kevin Knight. 2020. Why neural machine translation prefers empty outputs.

Felix Stahlberg and Bill Byrne. 2019. On NMT search errors and model errors: Cat got your tongue? In *Proceedings of the 2019 Conference on Empirical Methods in Natural Language Processing and the 9th International Joint Conference on Natural Language Processing (EMNLP-IJCNLP)*, pages 3356–3362, Hong Kong, China. Association for Computational Linguistics.

Ashish Vaswani, Noam Shazeer, Niki Parmar, Jakob Uszkoreit, Llion Jones, Aidan N Gomez, Ł ukasz Kaiser, and Illia Polosukhin. 2017. Attention is all you need. In *Advances in Neural Information Processing Systems*, volume 30. Curran Associates, Inc.

A Results with Reranking

When presenting our main results (Section 5), we follow related work (Peters and Martins, 2021) and focus on the outputs generated using the algorithms themselves, without reranking. For completeness, we also present the results of applying length normalization (Jean et al., 2015; Murray and Chiang, 2018), i.e. reranking the set of sequences produced by beam search according to their average log-probability, rather than their cumulative log-probability:

$$\text{score}(Y) = \frac{1}{n}\sum_{t=1}^{n} -\log P(y_t|Y_{<t})$$

Table 4 shows that length normalization improves stability, and slightly increases performance overall. However, it does *not* increase the performance gap between the different algorithms, with respect to the results in Section 5 (without reranking); all three variants produce text that scores within 0.2 BLEU/ROUGE from the best performing setting in every task.

Search Algo	Hyper-param (k or p)	WMT'14 EN-FR	IWSLT'14 DE-EN (Char)	XSUM
Beam	1	40.3	33.3	35.5
	2	40.8	33.8	36.3
	3	**41.1**	<u>34.0</u>	<u>36.4</u>
	4	**41.1**	<u>34.1</u>	<u>36.5</u>
	5	<u>41.0</u>	<u>34.1</u>	**36.6**
	10	<u>41.0</u>	**34.2**	**36.6**
	20	<u>41.0</u>	**34.2**	<u>36.5</u>
	40	40.6	**34.2**	<u>36.4</u>
	80	40.1	**34.2**	36.3
	160	39.4	**34.2**	36.2
	320	38.3	**34.2**	36.2
p-Exact	0.1	40.3	33.3	35.5
	0.2	40.3	33.3	35.6
	0.3	40.5	33.4	36.0
	0.4	40.7	33.4	36.2
	0.5	<u>41.0</u>	33.6	<u>36.4</u>
	0.6	**41.1**	33.7	36.3
	0.7	<u>41.0</u>	<u>34.0</u>	36.3
	0.8	40.3	<u>34.1</u>	36.2
	0.9	38.8	<u>34.1</u>	36.1
Dynamic	0.1	40.2	33.3	35.5
	0.2	40.3	33.3	35.6
	0.3	40.5	33.4	36.0
	0.4	40.6	33.4	36.2
	0.5	40.8	33.4	<u>36.4</u>
	0.6	<u>41.0</u>	33.8	<u>36.5</u>
	0.7	<u>41.0</u>	<u>34.0</u>	36.3
	0.8	40.6	<u>34.1</u>	36.2
	0.9	38.6	**34.2**	36.2

Table 4: The performance of different decoding algorithms and hyperparameter settings on various conditional generation tasks with *length normalization (reranking)*. **Bold** numbers indicate the highest result on the task, and <u>underlined</u> numbers indicate that the result is within 0.2 points of the top score.

How Much Do Modifications to Transformer Language Models Affect Their Ability to Learn Linguistic Knowledge?

Simeng Sun[1] **Brian Dillon**[2] **Mohit Iyyer**[1]
[1]College of Information and Computer Sciences, University of Massachusetts Amherst
[2]Department of Linguistics, University of Massachusetts Amherst
{simengsun, bwdillon, miyyer}@umass.edu

Abstract

Recent progress in large pretrained language models (LMs) has led to a growth of analyses examining what kinds of linguistic knowledge are encoded by these models. Due to computational constraints, existing analyses are mostly conducted on publicly-released LM checkpoints, which makes it difficult to study how various factors during *training* affect the models' acquisition of linguistic knowledge. In this paper, we train a suite of small-scale Transformer LMs that differ from each other with respect to architectural decisions (e.g., self-attention configuration) or training objectives (e.g., multi-tasking, focal loss). We evaluate these LMs on BLiMP, a targeted evaluation benchmark of multiple English linguistic phenomena. Our experiments show that while none of these modifications yields significant improvements on aggregate, changes to the loss function result in promising improvements on several subcategories (e.g., detecting adjunct islands, correctly scoping negative polarity items). We hope our work offers useful insights for future research into designing Transformer LMs that more effectively learn linguistic knowledge.

1 Introduction

At the core of many natural language processing tasks are language models (LMs), which compute the probability distribution of the next token that follows a given input context. The Transformer (Vaswani et al., 2017), as one of the most popular architectures for language modeling, has been widely adopted for large-scale pre-training, such as in BERT (Devlin et al., 2019), GPT-2 (Radford et al., 2019) and GPT-3 (Brown et al., 2020). The success of large-scale LM pretraining has propelled a surge of analysis on the linguistic knowledge encoded by language models.

While prior works have uncovered many exciting facts regarding the linguistic capability of those pretrained LMs (Hewitt and Manning, 2019; Liu et al., 2019; Jawahar et al., 2019), most of these analyses are conducted on publicly-released model checkpoints, and thus the impact of various LM *training* configurations remains relatively unexplored, limited to LSTM LM configurations (Linzen et al., 2016) or varying training data size (Zhang et al., 2021).

In this work, we focus on Transformer LMs (Vaswani et al., 2017) instead of LSTMs, and we investigate two aspects of LM training distinct from previous works – (1) the LM training objective, for which we experiment with the focal loss and multi-task training; and (2) the Transformer's self-attention mechanism, which we restrict to a local window of tokens. We train a suite of Transformer LMs that minimally differ from each other in one of these two aspects, and evaluate the effect of these changes via non-parametric probing on BLiMP (Warstadt et al., 2020a), a targeted evaluation benchmark of multiple English linguistic phenomena (e.g., island effects, anaphor agreement). Experimental results demonstrate that *none* of these modifications yields significant gains on BLiMP *in aggregate*. However, we do observe that modified training objectives (e.g, using focal loss instead of standard cross entropy loss) result in improvements to specific *subtypes* of linguistic phenomena. Overall, our experiments suggest that it could be promising to scale up Transformer LMs with modified training objectives, as they may help improve syntactic generalization.

2 Method

Language models compute $p(w_i \mid w_{<i})$, the probability distribution of the next token w_i given the preceding context $w_{<i}$. The conventional training objective of an LM is to minimize the surprisal of tokens in a training set. The surprisal of a single token can be expressed as the negative log probability of that token given the preceding context

Proceedings of the Third Workshop on Insights from Negative Results in NLP, pages 46 - 53
May 26, 2022

(prefix):

$$l_i = -\log p(w_i \mid w_{<i})$$

While many models were proposed to compute $p(w_i \mid w_{<i})$, we focus on the Transformer architecture (Vaswani et al., 2017), which consists of a stack of alternated self-attention and feed-forward blocks and has become the mainstream architecture for large-scale LM pretraining.

Unlike prior work, which has focused on *fixed* Transformer language model checkpoints, we are curious to see how intervening in the training process would impact the resulting models. Specifically, we ask: **are there any training objectives or model design choices that would improve the models' acquisition of linguistic knowledge?**

2.1 Altered training process

To understand how varying training configurations affect the linguistic capacities of the final models, we narrow our focus to the LM training objective and the self-attention mechanism. We train a set of Transformer LMs, each differing from each other in only the changes described below:

Focal loss (FL) As shown by Zhang et al. (2021), language models learn different linguistic phenomena at different speeds and require different amounts of data. For instance, the learning curve for *subject-verb agreement* phenomena plateaus after training on more than 10M tokens, whereas *filler gap dependencies* display steadily increasing performance even up to 30B tokens of training data. This suggests that each phenomenon has an inherent "difficulty", with some requiring more data for an LM to master. In such a scenario, can we improve the acquisition of linguistic knowledge by forcing the model to pay more attention to the "difficult" tokens? To achieve this, one potential alternative to the standard log loss training objective is focal loss (Lin et al., 2018), which can be intuitively explained as reducing the penalty on "easy" well-predicted tokens and increasing the penalty on the "hard" tokens. Formally, the surprisal of each target token is negatively scaled by the predicted probability:

$$l_i^{FL} = -(1 - p(w_i \mid w_{<i}))^{\gamma} \log(p(w_i \mid w_{<i}))$$

Here, γ is a hyper-parameter controlling the relative importance between poorly-predicted and well-predicted tokens. Larger values of γ allocate more weight to tokens with high surprisal.

Masked loss (ML) In the focal loss setting, well-predicted tokens still receive a certain amount of penalty. As an extreme version of the focal loss setting, we simply zero out the loss (masked loss) for the tokens whose predicted probability exceeds a given threshold. Formally, given a threshold t, the masked loss is thus:

$$l_i^{ML} = -\Big(1 - \mathbb{I}(p(w_i \mid w_{<i}) \geq t)\Big) \log \Big(p(w_i \mid w_{<i})\Big)$$

Auxiliary loss (AL) Multitask training is commonly adopted to provide extra supervision signals to the language model (Winata et al., 2018; Zhou et al., 2019). To explicitly endow an LM with better understanding of syntactic knowledge, we add an auxiliary task where the model is trained to predict labels derived from an external constituency parser using the final layer's token-level representations. The loss of this prediction task is added to the original loss, weighted by a hyper-parameter α.

$$l_i^{AL} = -\alpha \log p(w_i \mid w_{<i}) - (1-\alpha) \log p(c_i \mid w_{<i})$$

c_i denotes the linguistic label for each token, which we obtain by associating a token with both the the smallest non-terminal constituent type containing that token and the depth of that constituent in the parse tree. For example, a noun phrase "`red apple`" having depth 3 in the parse tree will have "`NP3 NP3`" as the labels for the auxiliary task.

Local attention (LA) Besides the training objective, modifying the architecture is another way to change the inductive biases of the model. As there is a huge number of potential architectural modifications, we constrain our changes to only the attention mechanism as it does not change the total number of parameters and is thus easier to perform a fair comparison. Instead of using the standard self-attention, we adopt *local attention*, where the attention window is limited to only k tokens immediately preceding the target token (Child et al., 2019; Roy et al., 2021; Sun and Iyyer, 2021). We hope that these local attention variants can more easily pick up a recency bias previously shown to exist in RNN language models (Kuncoro et al., 2018). However, note that although the model only attends to the previous k tokens in each layer, the effective receptive field can still be large as the information is propagated through the stacked Transformer layers.

2.2 Evaluation on BLiMP

To measure the amount of linguistic knowledge captured by each language model variant, we use BLiMP (Warstadt et al., 2020a), a benchmark of English linguistic minimal pairs. It contains pairs of grammatical and ungrammatical sentences, the latter of which is minimally edited from the grammatical one. The sentence pairs fall into 67 paradigms spanning 12 common English grammar phenomena[1]. A language model makes the correct prediction on this task when it assigns the grammatical sentence higher probability than the ungrammatical one. Each paradigm contains 1K examples, and the accuracy of each paradigm can be treated as a proxy of the amount of specific linguistic knowledge encoded by the LM.

3 Experiments

Data: We use the same English Wikipedia data used by Gulordava et al. (2018) for our LM pretraining corpus. This corpus contains around 100M tokens in total (80M for training). The vocabulary includes 50K words and a special `<unk>` token substituted for infrequent words.

Models: We present four models each trained with slightly different setting. **(1) Focal Loss (FL)**: This model is trained with focal loss, the γ is set to 2.[2] **(2) Masked Loss (ML)**: This model is trained with masked loss, with the masking threshold set to 0.9.[3] **(3) Auxiliary Loss (AL):** This model is trained with auxiliary task of predicting the constituent label, where α is set to 0.5. **(4) Local Attention (LA)**: This is the Transformer in which all self-attentions are replaced with local attention on the preceding 5 tokens.[4]

Training: Following prior work on this dataset (Dai et al., 2019; Sun and Iyyer, 2021), we train 16-layer Transformer language models with embedding dimension size 410, hidden dimension 2100, and 10 attention heads per layer. The models are trained with the Adam optimizer $\beta_1 = 0.9, \beta_2 = 0.999$, learning rate 0.00025, and 2000 warmup steps for max 150K steps. Training is performed on GeForce GTX 1080 Ti GPUs and early stopped (average 26h training) when the validation loss stops decreasing for consecutive 10 checkpoints. All evaluations were conducted on model checkpoints with the lowest validation loss.

Phenomena	BASE	FL	ML	AL	LA
island	0.52	**0.55**	0.55	0.50	0.53
anaphor_agree	**0.97**	0.96	0.94	0.97	0.96
arg_struct	0.64	0.62	0.63	**0.64**	0.63
det_noun	0.84	**0.87**	0.85	0.85	0.86
subj_verb	**0.86**	0.85	0.85	0.85	0.84
ellipsis	0.76	0.79	0.77	0.76	**0.81**
ctrl_raising	0.72	**0.74**	0.71	0.72	0.72
quant	0.70	0.69	0.68	0.64	**0.71**
irregular_form	0.91	0.93	0.92	**0.95**	0.92
npi	0.64	0.66	0.67	0.63	**0.68**
binding	0.75	0.76	0.75	**0.77**	0.76
filler_gap	0.73	0.72	0.72	0.71	**0.74**
Average	0.75	0.76	0.75	0.75	**0.76**

Table 1: Performance of each LM variant on BLIMP, each phenomenon is averaged over subcategories within. **BASE** stands for baseline model, **FL** stands for the model trained with focal loss ($\gamma = 2$), **ML** stands for the model trained with masked loss ($t = 0.9$), **AL** stands for model trained with auxiliary loss, **LA** stands for the model trained with local attention.

4 Results & Analysis

Overall, we did not find a significant improvement on BLiMP after applying the aforementioned modifications. Table 1 contains the averaged score of each model evaluated on BLiMP. However, zooming in on each category, we notice significant changes in a subset of paradigms. We observe similar aggregate scores because better performance on certain paradigms are canceled out by worse performance on other paradigms within the same phenomena.[5] In this section, we delineate paradigms showing notable gains compared to the baseline model as shown in Table 2. While we present descriptive observations from the experimental results, more ideal analysis should include mechanistic explanation linking the modifications and the resulting inductive biases, such as those in (Lakretz et al., 2019), which we leave as future work.

[1] We refer the readers to (Warstadt et al., 2020a) for detailed description and the construction process of each paradigm.

[2] γ is picked from tuning validation perplexity over $\{0.5, 1, 2\}$

[3] t is picked from tuning over $\{0.85, 0.9, 0.95, 0.999\}$

[4] We tried local $\{2, 3, 5, 10\}$, and 5 yielded the lowest validation perplexity.

[5] Table 3 in Appendix contains results of all 67 paradigms of each model evaluated on BLiMP.

Paradigms	BASE	FL	ML	AL	LA
Adjunct island	0.69	0.81	0.89	0.85	0.69
Complex NP island	0.50	0.46	0.48	0.50	0.55
Complext left branch	0.42	0.39	0.38	0.33	0.33
Object extraction	0.74	0.78	0.77	0.67	0.80
Echo question	0.48	0.49	0.46	0.42	0.40
Simple question	0.34	0.41	0.37	0.31	0.41
Subject island	0.31	0.41	0.40	0.39	0.37
Wh. island	0.66	0.63	0.62	0.55	0.71
Det. noun agr. 1	0.93	0.93	0.94	0.94	0.93
Det. noun agr. 2	0.94	0.95	0.94	0.93	0.95
Det. noun agr. irregular 1	0.84	0.83	0.84	0.84	0.83
Det. noun agr. irregular 2	0.87	0.88	0.86	0.86	0.87
Det. noun agr. w/ adj. 2	0.81	0.88	0.84	0.84	0.86
Det. noun agr. w/ adj. 1	0.84	0.88	0.85	0.84	0.86
Det. noun agr. w/ adj. irregular 1	0.73	0.76	0.75	0.75	0.76
Det. noun agr. w/ adj. irregular 2	0.77	0.82	0.79	0.79	0.84
Ellipsis 1	0.70	0.73	0.75	0.69	0.78
Ellipsis 2	0.82	0.84	0.79	0.82	0.84
Matrix q. npi	0.14	0.17	0.26	0.15	0.22
NPI present 1	0.58	0.53	0.54	0.47	0.59
NPI present 2	0.69	0.60	0.63	0.57	0.61
Only NPI licensor present	0.88	0.91	0.87	0.94	0.90
Only NPI scope	0.66	0.79	0.82	0.77	0.84
Sent. neg. NPI	1.00	1.00	0.99	1.00	1.00
Sent. neg. NPI scope	0.50	0.60	0.56	0.49	0.58
Object gap	0.73	0.72	0.75	0.70	0.79
Subject gap	0.88	0.87	0.89	0.84	0.91
Subject gap long dist.	0.92	0.88	0.84	0.87	0.88
No gap vs. that	0.94	0.95	0.94	0.95	0.96
No gap long dist. vs. that	0.97	0.98	0.98	0.98	0.96
Gap vs. that	0.49	0.50	0.46	0.48	0.45
Gap long dist. vs. that	0.17	0.15	0.18	0.15	0.20

Table 2: Model performance on subset of BLiMP paradigms, each group of paradigms from top to bottom corresponds to island effect, determiner noun agreement, ellipsis, negative polarity item, and filler gap, respectively[1]. Those values below the baseline accuracy are marked in orange, those above in blue.

Island Effects An island is a constituent from which a word cannot be moved, e.g., in *"What was Bill thinking while arguing about news?"*, it is illegal to move *news* out of the island: *"What was Bill thinking news while arguing about?"*. The BLiMP benchmark breaks down island effects to eight paradigms based on the type of islands, and we find all our proposed modifications to the training objective lead to much better accuracy on the targeted pairs of adjunct island and sentential subject island. The model trained with masked loss improves identification accuracy of wrong adjunct island sentences from 0.69 (BASE) to 0.89. Smaller improvements are also observed for multiple other island effects when the model is trained with focal loss. Surprisingly, the model forced to predict the constituent labels does not perform well on island effects examples and the model trained with local attention outperforms the baseline by large margin on complex NP island and Wh island.

Determiner Noun Agreement Another notable change is within determiner noun agreement. This phenomenon tests whether a model recognizes incorrect noun after a determiner (e.g., *"that tables"* is unacceptable). The model trained with focal loss is better than the baseline model on multiple paradigms by large margins, especially on cases where adjective is inserted between the determiner and the noun. The accuracy of baseline model is improved from 81% to 88%. The second best modification is when the Transformer is trained with local attention, which consistently outperforms the baseline for all but two paradigms.

Ellipsis and Irregular Forms The model trained with local attention outperforms all other models on ellipsis, showing better ability to distinguish incorrectly omitted nouns (e.g. *"She took four heavy bags and he took five big"* has incorrectly omitted nouns at the end). Another consistent pattern arises in the irregular forms phenomenon, the model trained with auxiliary loss is better at recognizing incorrect past participle adjectives, suggesting the model assigns low probability to verbs when expecting a noun phrase, which could be a benefit from learning to predict the constituent labels.

Negative Polarity Item The last phenomenon we focus on is negative polarity items. We find that models trained with modified loss function outperform the baseline on identifying the correct scope of polarity item "ever" in the presence of the focus operator "only"(e.g., *"Those students who only Tim teaches ever pass the exam."* is incorrect as *ever* needs to be licensed by the word *only*, which should be in the main clause). The improvement is especially significant ($\sim$ 20 points) when evaluating the model trained with local attention. However, the baseline model is better at two other paradigms in the same phenomenon.

5 Related Work

Our work is closely related to recent analyses on the linguistic knowledge encoded within large pretrained LMs. One typical approach to probing the ingrained linguistic knowledge is through diagnostic classifiers, or probes (Alain and Bengio, 2017; Belinkov et al., 2017; Hewitt and Liang, 2019; Voita and Titov, 2020; Pimentel et al., 2020), a classifier trained with the intermediate representations of an LM. Previous works tend to evaluate the language models on set of multiple probing tasks (Liu et al., 2019; Conneau et al., 2018), each capturing a distinct linguistic phenomenon. Another type of probing relies on datasets constructed via linguistic rules that are specific to targeted linguistic phenomena (Jumelet and Hupkes, 2018; Marvin and Linzen, 2018; Warstadt et al., 2020b,a). Previous works have intervened at least two aspects of LM training: (1) the size of training data (van Schijndel et al., 2019; Zhang et al., 2021) and (2) the training task (Linzen et al., 2016; Ravfogel et al., 2019).

6 Conclusion

To complement recent analyses on the linguistic knowledge encoded by released Transformer LM checkpoints, we investigate four Transformer language models, each trained with slightly different settings. We evaluate these variants on BLiMP, a targeted evaluation set to probe the language models' capability of various linguistic phenomena. Our results show that although the averaged performance is similar after applying those changes, there are promising gains on local paradigms. We hope our work could shed light on future research into more effective learning of syntactic knowledge by Transformer language models.

References

Guillaume Alain and Yoshua Bengio. 2017. Understanding intermediate layers using linear classifier probes. *ArXiv*, abs/1610.01644.

Yonatan Belinkov, Nadir Durrani, Fahim Dalvi, Hassan Sajjad, and James Glass. 2017. What do neural machine translation models learn about morphology? In *Proceedings of the 55th Annual Meeting of the Association for Computational Linguistics (Volume 1: Long Papers)*, pages 861–872, Vancouver, Canada. Association for Computational Linguistics.

Tom Brown, Benjamin Mann, Nick Ryder, Melanie Subbiah, Jared D Kaplan, Prafulla Dhariwal, Arvind Neelakantan, Pranav Shyam, Girish Sastry, Amanda Askell, Sandhini Agarwal, Ariel Herbert-Voss, Gretchen Krueger, Tom Henighan, Rewon Child, Aditya Ramesh, Daniel Ziegler, Jeffrey Wu, Clemens Winter, Chris Hesse, Mark Chen, Eric Sigler, Mateusz Litwin, Scott Gray, Benjamin Chess, Jack Clark, Christopher Berner, Sam McCandlish, Alec Radford, Ilya Sutskever, and Dario Amodei. 2020. Language models are few-shot learners. In *Advances in Neural Information Processing Systems*, volume 33, pages 1877–1901. Curran Associates, Inc.

Rewon Child, Scott Gray, Alec Radford, and Ilya Sutskever. 2019. Generating long sequences with sparse transformers. *arXiv preprint arXiv:1904.10509*.

Alexis Conneau, German Kruszewski, Guillaume Lample, Loïc Barrault, and Marco Baroni. 2018. What you can cram into a single $&!#* vector: Probing sentence embeddings for linguistic properties. In *Proceedings of the 56th Annual Meeting of the Association for Computational Linguistics (Volume 1: Long Papers)*, pages 2126–2136, Melbourne, Australia. Association for Computational Linguistics.

Zihang Dai, Zhilin Yang, Yiming Yang, Jaime Carbonell, Quoc Le, and Ruslan Salakhutdinov. 2019. Transformer-XL: Attentive language models beyond a fixed-length context. In *Proceedings of the 57th Annual Meeting of the Association for Computational Linguistics*, pages 2978–2988, Florence, Italy. Association for Computational Linguistics.

Jacob Devlin, Ming-Wei Chang, Kenton Lee, and Kristina Toutanova. 2019. BERT: Pre-training of deep bidirectional transformers for language understanding. In *Proceedings of the 2019 Conference of the North American Chapter of the Association for Computational Linguistics: Human Language Technologies, Volume 1 (Long and Short Papers)*, pages 4171–4186, Minneapolis, Minnesota. Association for Computational Linguistics.

Kristina Gulordava, Piotr Bojanowski, Edouard Grave, Tal Linzen, and Marco Baroni. 2018. Colorless green recurrent networks dream hierarchically. In *Proceedings of the 2018 Conference of the North American Chapter of the Association for Computational Linguistics: Human Language Technologies, Volume 1 (Long Papers)*, pages 1195–1205, New Orleans, Louisiana. Association for Computational Linguistics.

John Hewitt and Percy Liang. 2019. Designing and interpreting probes with control tasks. In *Proceedings of the 2019 Conference on Empirical Methods in Natural Language Processing and the 9th International Joint Conference on Natural Language Processing (EMNLP-IJCNLP)*, pages 2733–2743, Hong Kong, China. Association for Computational Linguistics.

John Hewitt and Christopher D. Manning. 2019. A structural probe for finding syntax in word representations. In *Proceedings of the 2019 Conference of the North American Chapter of the Association for Computational Linguistics: Human Language Technologies, Volume 1 (Long and Short Papers)*, pages 4129–4138, Minneapolis, Minnesota. Association for Computational Linguistics.

Ganesh Jawahar, Benoît Sagot, and Djamé Seddah. 2019. What does BERT learn about the structure of language? In *Proceedings of the 57th Annual Meeting of the Association for Computational Linguistics*, pages 3651–3657, Florence, Italy. Association for Computational Linguistics.

Jaap Jumelet and Dieuwke Hupkes. 2018. Do language models understand anything? on the ability of LSTMs to understand negative polarity items. In *Proceedings of the 2018 EMNLP Workshop BlackboxNLP: Analyzing and Interpreting Neural Networks for NLP*, pages 222–231, Brussels, Belgium. Association for Computational Linguistics.

Adhiguna Kuncoro, Chris Dyer, John Hale, Dani Yogatama, Stephen Clark, and Phil Blunsom. 2018. LSTMs can learn syntax-sensitive dependencies well, but modeling structure makes them better. In *Proceedings of the 56th Annual Meeting of the Association for Computational Linguistics (Volume 1: Long Papers)*, pages 1426–1436, Melbourne, Australia. Association for Computational Linguistics.

Yair Lakretz, German Kruszewski, Theo Desbordes, Dieuwke Hupkes, Stanislas Dehaene, and Marco Baroni. 2019. The emergence of number and syntax units in LSTM language models. In *Proceedings of the 2019 Conference of the North American Chapter of the Association for Computational Linguistics: Human Language Technologies, Volume 1 (Long and Short Papers)*, pages 11–20, Minneapolis, Minnesota. Association for Computational Linguistics.

Tsung-Yi Lin, Priya Goyal, Ross Girshick, Kaiming He, and Piotr Dollár. 2018. Focal loss for dense object detection.

Tal Linzen, Emmanuel Dupoux, and Yoav Goldberg. 2016. Assessing the ability of LSTMs to learn syntax-sensitive dependencies. *Transactions of the Association for Computational Linguistics*, 4:521–535.

Nelson F. Liu, Matt Gardner, Yonatan Belinkov, Matthew E. Peters, and Noah A. Smith. 2019. Linguistic knowledge and transferability of contextual representations. In *Proceedings of the 2019 Conference of the North American Chapter of the Association for Computational Linguistics: Human Language Technologies, Volume 1 (Long and Short Papers)*, pages 1073–1094, Minneapolis, Minnesota. Association for Computational Linguistics.

Rebecca Marvin and Tal Linzen. 2018. Targeted syntactic evaluation of language models. In *Proceedings of the 2018 Conference on Empirical Methods in Natural Language Processing*, pages 1192–1202, Brussels, Belgium. Association for Computational Linguistics.

Tiago Pimentel, Josef Valvoda, Rowan Hall Maudslay, Ran Zmigrod, Adina Williams, and Ryan Cotterell. 2020. Information-theoretic probing for linguistic structure. In *Proceedings of the 58th Annual Meeting of the Association for Computational Linguistics*, pages 4609–4622, Online. Association for Computational Linguistics.

Alec Radford, Jeffrey Wu, Rewon Child, David Luan, Dario Amodei, and Ilya Sutskever. 2019. Language models are unsupervised multitask learners. *OpenAI blog*, 1(8):9.

Shauli Ravfogel, Yoav Goldberg, and Tal Linzen. 2019. Studying the inductive biases of RNNs with synthetic variations of natural languages. In *Proceedings of the 2019 Conference of the North American Chapter of the Association for Computational Linguistics: Human Language Technologies, Volume 1 (Long and Short Papers)*, pages 3532–3542, Minneapolis, Minnesota. Association for Computational Linguistics.

Aurko Roy, Mohammad Saffar, Ashish Vaswani, and David Grangier. 2021. Efficient content-based sparse attention with routing transformers. *Transactions of the Association for Computational Linguistics*, 9:53–68.

Simeng Sun and Mohit Iyyer. 2021. Revisiting simple neural probabilistic language models. In *Proceedings of the 2021 Conference of the North American Chapter of the Association for Computational Linguistics: Human Language Technologies*, pages 5181–5188, Online. Association for Computational Linguistics.

Marten van Schijndel, Aaron Mueller, and Tal Linzen. 2019. Quantity doesn't buy quality syntax with neural language models. In *Proceedings of the 2019 Conference on Empirical Methods in Natural Language Processing and the 9th International Joint Conference on Natural Language Processing (EMNLP-IJCNLP)*, pages 5831–5837, Hong Kong, China. Association for Computational Linguistics.

Ashish Vaswani, Noam Shazeer, Niki Parmar, Jakob Uszkoreit, Llion Jones, Aidan N Gomez, Łũkasz Kaiser, and Illia Polosukhin. 2017. Attention is all you need. In *Advances in Neural Information Processing Systems*, volume 30. Curran Associates, Inc.

Elena Voita and Ivan Titov. 2020. Information-theoretic probing with minimum description length. In *Proceedings of the 2020 Conference on Empirical Methods in Natural Language Processing (EMNLP)*, pages 183–196, Online. Association for Computational Linguistics.

Alex Warstadt, Alicia Parrish, Haokun Liu, Anhad Mohananey, Wei Peng, Sheng-Fu Wang, and Samuel R. Bowman. 2020a. BLiMP: A benchmark of linguistic minimal pairs for English. In *Proceedings of the Society for Computation in Linguistics 2020*, pages 409–410, New York, New York. Association for Computational Linguistics.

Alex Warstadt, Alicia Parrish, Haokun Liu, Anhad Mohananey, Wei Peng, Sheng-Fu Wang, and Samuel R. Bowman. 2020b. BLiMP: The benchmark of linguistic minimal pairs for English. *Transactions of the Association for Computational Linguistics*, 8:377–392.

Genta Indra Winata, Andrea Madotto, Chien-Sheng Wu, and Pascale Fung. 2018. Code-switching language modeling using syntax-aware multi-task learning. In *Proceedings of the Third Workshop on Computational Approaches to Linguistic Code-Switching*, pages 62–67, Melbourne, Australia. Association for Computational Linguistics.

Yian Zhang, Alex Warstadt, Xiaocheng Li, and Samuel R. Bowman. 2021. When do you need billions of words of pretraining data? In *Proceedings of the 59th Annual Meeting of the Association for Computational Linguistics and the 11th International Joint Conference on Natural Language Processing (Volume 1: Long Papers)*, pages 1112–1125, Online. Association for Computational Linguistics.

Wenjie Zhou, Minghua Zhang, and Yunfang Wu. 2019. Multi-task learning with language modeling for question generation. In *Proceedings of the 2019 Conference on Empirical Methods in Natural Language Processing and the 9th International Joint Conference on Natural Language Processing (EMNLP-IJCNLP)*, pages 3394–3399, Hong Kong, China. Association for Computational Linguistics.

A Evaluation on BLIMP

Phenomena	Paradigms	BASE	FL	ML	AL	LA
	adjunct_island	0.69	0.81	0.89	0.85	0.69
	complex_NP_island	0.50	0.46	0.48	0.50	0.55
	coordinate_structure_constraint_complex_left_branch	0.42	0.39	0.38	0.33	0.33
	coordinate_structure_constraint_object_extraction	0.74	0.78	0.77	0.67	0.80
	left_branch_island_echo_question	0.48	0.49	0.46	0.42	0.40
	left_branch_island_simple_question	0.34	0.41	0.37	0.31	0.41
	sentential_subject_island	0.31	0.41	0.40	0.39	0.37
Island Effects	wh_island	0.66	0.63	0.62	0.55	0.71
	anaphor_gender_agreement	0.96	0.95	0.91	0.96	0.95
Anaphor Agreement	anaphor_number_agreement	0.98	0.98	0.96	0.98	0.97
	animate_subject_passive	0.69	0.67	0.67	0.69	0.68
	animate_subject_trans	0.48	0.46	0.45	0.48	0.47
	causative	0.68	0.66	0.65	0.71	0.67
	drop_argument	0.52	0.49	0.51	0.48	0.51
	inchoative	0.64	0.64	0.64	0.62	0.66
	intransitive	0.57	0.57	0.58	0.58	0.57
	passive_1	0.72	0.71	0.72	0.73	0.74
	passive_2	0.72	0.72	0.71	0.72	0.70
Argument Structure	transitive	0.70	0.70	0.70	0.71	0.69
	determiner_noun_agreement_1	0.93	0.93	0.94	0.94	0.93
	determiner_noun_agreement_2	0.94	0.95	0.94	0.93	0.95
	determiner_noun_agreement_irregular_1	0.84	0.83	0.84	0.84	0.83
	determiner_noun_agreement_irregular_2	0.87	0.88	0.86	0.86	0.87
	determiner_noun_agreement_with_adj_2	0.81	0.88	0.84	0.84	0.86
	determiner_noun_agreement_with_adjective_1	0.84	0.88	0.85	0.84	0.86
	determiner_noun_agreement_with_adj_irregular_1	0.73	0.76	0.75	0.75	0.76
Determiner Noun Agreement	determiner_noun_agreement_with_adj_irregular_2	0.77	0.82	0.79	0.79	0.84
	distractor_agreement_relational_noun	0.85	0.82	0.81	0.86	0.82
	distractor_agreement_relative_clause	0.72	0.73	0.76	0.72	0.73
	irregular_plural_subject_verb_agreement_1	0.83	0.82	0.82	0.82	0.82
	irregular_plural_subject_verb_agreement_2	0.93	0.91	0.92	0.92	0.89
	regular_plural_subject_verb_agreement_1	0.93	0.92	0.92	0.92	0.91
Subject Verb Agreement	regular_plural_subject_verb_agreement_2	0.89	0.88	0.88	0.87	0.86
	ellipsis_n_bar_1	0.70	0.73	0.75	0.69	0.78
Ellipsis	ellipsis_n_bar_2	0.82	0.84	0.79	0.82	0.84
	existential_there_object_raising	0.75	0.72	0.69	0.72	0.68
	existential_there_subject_raising	0.82	0.85	0.81	0.81	0.84
	expletive_it_object_raising	0.74	0.78	0.69	0.75	0.70
	tough_vs_raising_1	0.44	0.45	0.49	0.43	0.53
Control & Raising	tough_vs_raising_2	0.87	0.91	0.86	0.89	0.86
	existential_there_quantifiers_1	0.97	0.97	0.95	0.96	0.95
	existential_there_quantifiers_2	0.16	0.24	0.12	0.16	0.16
	superlative_quantifiers_1	0.89	0.85	0.86	0.71	0.92
Quantifiers	superlative_quantifiers_2	0.80	0.71	0.78	0.74	0.80
	irregular_past_participle_adjectives	0.88	0.93	0.91	0.94	0.90
Irregular Forms	irregular_past_participle_verbs	0.94	0.93	0.93	0.95	0.93
	matrix_question_npi_licensor_present	0.14	0.17	0.26	0.15	0.22
	npi_present_1	0.58	0.53	0.54	0.47	0.59
	npi_present_2	0.69	0.60	0.63	0.57	0.61
	only_npi_licensor_present	0.88	0.91	0.87	0.94	0.90
	only_npi_scope	0.66	0.79	0.82	0.77	0.84
	sentential_negation_npi_licensor_present	1.00	1.00	0.99	1.00	1.00
NPI	sentential_negation_npi_scope	0.50	0.60	0.56	0.49	0.58
	principle_A_case_1	1.00	1.00	1.00	1.00	1.00
	principle_A_case_2	0.88	0.88	0.88	0.90	0.90
	principle_A_c_command	0.61	0.64	0.62	0.65	0.63
	principle_A_domain_1	0.98	0.99	0.98	0.98	0.98
	principle_A_domain_2	0.69	0.71	0.77	0.70	0.75
	principle_A_domain_3	0.60	0.57	0.56	0.60	0.63
Binding	principle_A_reconstruction	0.49	0.51	0.45	0.53	0.41
	wh_questions_object_gap	0.73	0.72	0.75	0.70	0.79
	wh_questions_subject_gap	0.88	0.87	0.89	0.84	0.91
	wh_questions_subject_gap_long_distance	0.92	0.88	0.84	0.87	0.88
	wh_vs_that_no_gap	0.94	0.95	0.94	0.95	0.96
	wh_vs_that_no_gap_long_distance	0.97	0.98	0.98	0.98	0.96
	wh_vs_that_with_gap	0.49	0.50	0.46	0.48	0.45
Filler Gap	wh_vs_that_with_gap_long_distance	0.17	0.15	0.18	0.15	0.20

Table 3: **BASE** stands for baseline model, **FL** stands for the model trained with focal loss ($\gamma = 2$), **ML** stands for the model trained with masked loss, the threshold $t = 0.9$, **AL** stands for model trained with auxiliary loss, the auxiliary task is to predict corresponding constituent label, **LA** stands for the model trained with local attention. The values below the baseline accuracy is marked in orange, above in blue.

Cross-lingual Inflection as a Data Augmentation Method for Parsing

Alberto Muñoz-Ortiz, Carlos Gómez-Rodríguez and David Vilares
Universidade da Coruña, CITIC
Departamento de Ciencias de la Computación y Tecnologías de la Información
Campus de Elviña s/n, 15071
A Coruña, Spain
{alberto.munoz.ortiz, carlos.gomez, david.vilares}@udc.es

Abstract

We propose a morphology-based method for low-resource (LR) dependency parsing. We train a morphological inflector for target LR languages, and apply it to related rich-resource (RR) treebanks to create cross-lingual (x-inflected) treebanks that resemble the target LR language. We use such inflected treebanks to train parsers in zero- (training on x-inflected treebanks) and few-shot (training on x-inflected and target language treebanks) setups. The results show that the method sometimes improves the baselines, but not consistently.

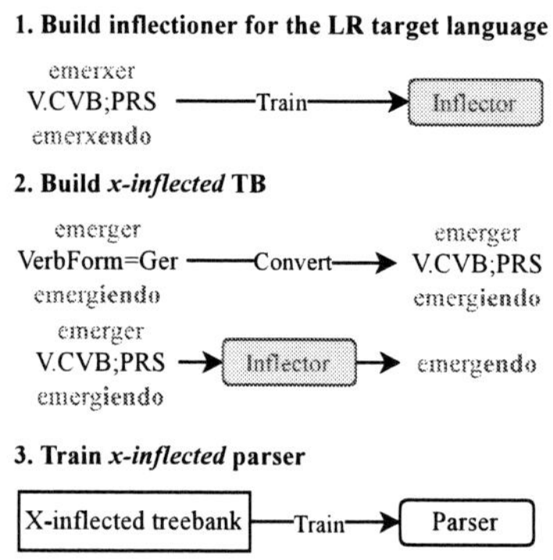

Figure 1: X-inflection process for a target LR language (Galician) using a source RR treebank (Spanish).

1 Introduction

Dependency parsers (Dozat et al., 2017; Ma et al., 2018; Strzyz et al., 2019) already achieve accurate results for certain setups (Berzak et al., 2016). Yet, they require large amounts of data to work, which hurts low-resource (LR) scenarios. In this line, authors have studied how to overcome this problem.

On data augmentation, recent approaches have replaced subtrees of sentences to generate new ones (Vania et al., 2019; Dehouck and Gómez-Rodríguez, 2020). On cross-lingual learning, authors have explored delexicalized approaches from rich-resource (RR) treebanks. (McDonald et al., 2011; Falenska and Çetinoğlu, 2017). Wang and Eisner (2018) permuted constituents of distant treebanks to generate synthetic ones that resembled the target language. Vilares et al. (2016); Ammar et al. (2016) merged treebanks to train multilingual parsers that sometimes could outperform the equivalent monolingual version, which has applications for less-resourced parsing. In the context of multilingual representations, Mulcaire et al. (2019) trained a zero-shot parser on top of a polyglot language model, relying on merged RR treebanks too.

In other matters, morphological inflection (Cotterell et al., 2016; Pimentel et al., 2021) generates words from lemmas and morphological feats (e.g. look → looking). Also, it is known that morphology helps parsing and that morphological complexity relates to the magnitude of the improvements (Dehouck and Denis, 2018). Yet, as far as we know, there is no work on cross-lingual morphological inflection as a data augmentation method for parsing. Here, we propose a technique that lies in the intersection between data augmentation, cross-lingual learning, and morphological inflection.

Contribution We introduce a method that uses cross-lingual morphological inflection to generate 'synthetic creole' treebanks, which we call *x-inflected* treebanks. To do so, we require a *source* language treebank from a closely-related language (for which lemmas and morphological feats are available), and a morphological inflection system trained for the *target* language. This way, we expect to generate x-inflected treebanks that should resemble *to a certain extent* the target language (see Figure 1). The goal is to improve the parser's performance for languages for which little or no annotated data are available, but for which we can train an accurate morphological inflection system that can be later applied to a related RR treebank and resemble the target language. The

Proceedings of the Third Workshop on Insights from Negative Results in NLP, pages 54 - 61
May 26, 2022 ©2022 Association for Computational Linguistics

code is available at `https://github.com/amunozo/x-inflection`.

2 Preliminaries

We now describe the basics of our work:

Datasets We use UniMorph (UM; McCarthy et al., 2020) for morphology and Universal Dependencies (UD; Zeman et al., 2020)

Key concepts We call *inflector* a morphological system that produces a word form from an input lemma and a set of morphological feats in a given language. We call *target UD treebank* each of the LR treebanks where we test our approach. We call *source UD treebanks* the RR treebanks related to a target LR treebank, used to create a cross-lingual inflected treebank, aka *x-inflected treebank*, which results from applying an inflector over the lemmas and feats of a source UD treebank.

3 X-inflection as data augmentation

Character-level models, such as the ones used for morphological inflection, identify shared morphemes across languages with overlapping alphabets (Lee et al., 2017; Vania, 2020). Thus, if two languages share a significant amount of lemmas, n-grams or inflections, an inflector for the first language could maybe produce noisy-but-useful inflected forms for lemmas and feats available for the second language. We hypothesize that this idea can be used for syntactic data augmentation in LR scenarios. Under the assumption that an inflector is available for our target LR language (easier than annotating syntactic data), we could use it to transform a related RR treebank, obtaining silver syntactic data that, despite lexical and grammatical imperfections, could help boost performance.

Our method consists of three steps: (i, §3.1) training an inflector for a given target language using UM data, (ii, §3.2) *x-inflecting* the source UD treebank, cross-lingually applying the inflector trained in (i), and (iii, §3.3) training the *x-inflected* parsers. We summarized the process in Figure 1.

3.1 Building the inflectors

We train the inflectors using the Wu et al. (2018) model, and leave all the hyperparameters at their default value. It is a seq2seq model that uses a hard monotonic attention mechanism to identify what parts of the input the model should focus on to generate the correct output string. It offers a good trade-off between speed and accuracy, compared with other alternatives that we tested in early experiments (Wu et al., 2021). We train the models on UM data, and for each language, we shuffle and split it 80-10-10 for the training, development and test sets (so lemmas are distributed)[1].

3.2 Building the *x-inflected* treebanks

This step requires to: (i) transform the feats column of the source UD treebank into a readable format by the inflector (i.e., UM format), to then (ii) apply the inflector to generate the x-inflected word forms, and (iii) format the output into an x-inflected treebank (i.e., going back to the UD format).

Transform UD feats into UM feats To x-inflect the source treebank, we first need to convert the morphological feats of the UD treebanks to the UM schema, using the converter by McCarthy et al. (2018).

In early experiments, we also trained inflectors directly on UD feats (following §3.1), but the results showed that x-inflected parsers trained this way performed worse, so we discarded it.

More specifically, the selected converter creates a mapping between both schemata. Yet, annotation errors and missing values in both schemata, together with disagreements between them, makes the process non-trivial. To counteract this, the approach introduces a language-dependent post-editing process, which consists in an iterative process that analyzes those forms and lemmas present both in UD and UM, comparing their annotations, and creating rules to refine the mappings between schemata. However, this extra refinement process is only available for some languages.

X-inflecting treebanks The lemmas and UM-transformed feats of the source UD treebank are sent to the target LR language inflector. The x-inflection is not applied to all elements, only to those lemmas of the source UD treebank whose part-of-speech is contained in the UM data of our target language (e.g., verbs or nouns, see details in Appendix A). Then, these x-inflected forms replace the original forms in the source UD treebank.

3.3 Training the *x-inflected* parsers

We train the parsers with a graph-based (GB) model (Dozat et al., 2017). It contextualizes words with

[1]For languages containing files for different dialects (e.g. Livvi), we concatenated all the forms prior to splitting.

Group	LR	ISO	RR
Iberian	Galician	glg	Spanish, Catalan, Portuguese
N. Germanic	Faroese	fao	Norwegian (nb), Norwegian (nn), Swedish, Icelandic, Danish
Finno-Ugric	Hungarian	hun	Finnish, Estonian
West Slavic	Czech	ces	Polish, Slovak
South Slavic	Slovenian	slv	Bulgarian, Croatian, Serbian
Romance	Latin	lat	Spanish, Romanian, French, Catalan, Italian
Baltic	Lithuanian	lit	Latvian
Celtic	Welsh	cym	Irish, Scottish Gaelic
Finnic	Livvi	olo	Finnish, Estonian
Finno-Permic	North Sami	sme	Finnish, Estonian

Table 1: LR and RR languages used in our experiments. Some LR treebanks come from RR languages (Czech, Latin) to have more samples.

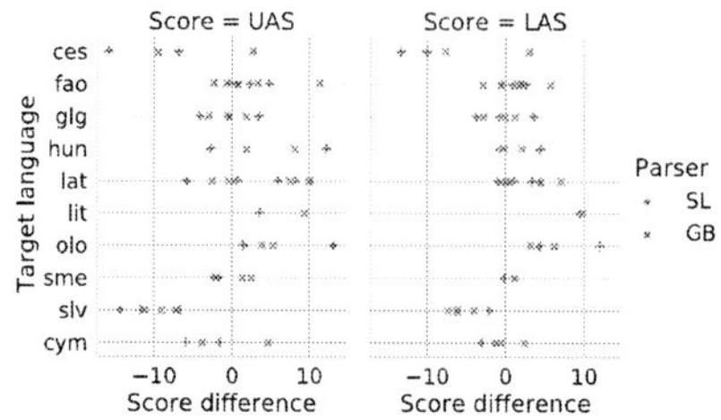

Figure 2: Score differences between x-inflected versions using different source treebanks and the baseline, for both sequence labeling (+) and graph-based (×) parsers.

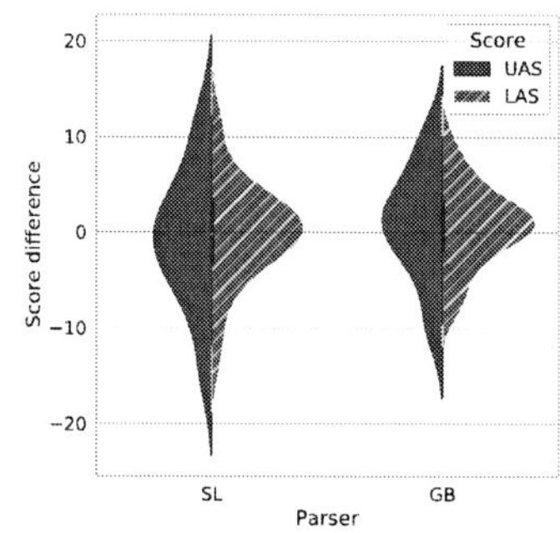

Figure 3: ΔUAS/LAS between the x-inflected models and the baseline for the sequence labeling (SL) and the graph-based (GB) parser.

bidirectional LSTMs (Hochreiter and Schmidhuber, 1997) and computes head and dependent representations for each word. Then, a biaffine transformation of such vectors is used to find the highest scoring parse tree. We also study a sequence labeling (SL) parser (Strzyz et al., 2019) as a lower bound. This parser can be seen as a vanilla biLSTM that only needs softmaxes (instead of a biaffine attention module) to predict syntactic labels, using 2-planar encodings (Strzyz et al., 2020), that are naturally decoded into to a dependency tree and work more robustly on low-resource setups (Muñoz-Ortiz et al., 2021).

4 Experiments

We test both (i, §4.1) zero-shot and (ii, §4.2) few-shot setups. For evaluation, we use unlabeled (UAS) and labeled attachment scores (LAS). Appendix E reports the hardware and costs.

Data We use 10 LR and 21 RR treebanks. Although our method can be applied to any pair of treebanks, the availability of UM and UD resources (in the sense of having LR languages in UM and related RR languages in UD) restricts our empirical analysis to Indo-European and Uralic languages (see Table 1). Yet, we have reasonable diversity and degrees of morphological inflection. For our empirical analysis, we use a relaxed definition of the concept LR for Czech and Latin (as the treebanks used are LR but there are RR treebanks for them in UD), and of the concept RR for Scottish Gaelic (as the treebank used is larger than the Welsh one but not RR). See Appendix B for the details.

4.1 Experiment 1: Zero-shot setup

We test if our method improves parsing accuracy under the assumption that there is no available training data in the target language, but there is an UD treebank for a related language, and enough UM data to train an inflector for the target language. Although the selected LR treebanks have a training set, we here do not use them, but we will in §4.2.

Setup For each target LR treebank, we first pair them with related source UD treebanks (from 1 to 5)[2], such that they all belong to the most restricted phylogenetic group for which UD data is available. We then train our x-inflected parsers and evaluate them on the corresponding target LR treebank. We compare the results against a baseline consisting in models trained on the source RR treebanks.

Results Figure 2 shows the results for the zero-shot setup (full results in Appendix C). The differences in performance are inconsistent: for some target LR treebanks the x-inflected models always obtain improvements, e.g. Livvi, for some others the models only obtain decreases, e.g. Slovenian, and for some others there is a mix, e.g. Faroese.

Figure 3 shows the distributions of LAS and UAS differences (Δ) against the baseline versions. For the SL parser, the distribution is centered in 0,

[2]Depending on the resource availability in UM and UD.

with the occurrence of some extreme results. For the GB parser, we see less extreme results and a distribution centered slightly above 0. This suggests that our method could be more effective for the GB approach, but we do not have clear evidence.

To shed light on what factors might affect the results, Table 2 shows the Pearson correlation coefficient (PCC) of the LAS and UAS differences between the x-inflected models and the baselines; *with respect to* features such as the number of forms and lemmas seen in UM training data, feature and lemma overlap between the target and source UD treebanks, or the number of UD training sentences. Although small, the results show some correlations e.g. for the number of forms and lemmas of the UM data ($0.3 - 0.5$).

	GB		SL	
	UAS	LAS	UAS	LAS
# UM target language forms	0.31	0.34	**0.49**	**0.47**
# UM target language lemmas	0.32	0.32	**0.50**	**0.42**
# UD source treebank training sents.	0.30	0.17	0.27	0.22
% Morph. feats shared between treebanks	-0.24	-0.24	-0.14	-0.06
% Lemmas shared between treebanks	-0.35	-0.32	-0.20	-0.18

Table 2: PCC of ΔLAS/UAS between the x-inflected models and the baselines vs different dimensions. Bold numbers represents p-values < 0.05.

4.2 Experiment 2: Few-shot setup

Experiment 1 did not show consistent improvements. However, we question whether the reason for our x-inflected models not consistently improving over the baseline could be that having some annotated data in the target language would help better guide the learning process, or that we are simply not taking advantage of x-inflecting more than one language treebank. In this line, previous studies have shown that training on harmonized treebanks, i.e. treebanks with the same annotation guidelines but coming from different languages, could improve performance over the corresponding monolingual model (Vilares et al., 2016), which has applications to less-resourced languages (Ammar et al., 2016).

Setup To test this, we train models on many x-inflected treebanks and evaluate them on the corresponding target LR test sets. Here, we also consider merging the available training data for the target LR language, to have a better understanding of how our approach behaves in few-shot setups. Particularly, we combine all the x-inflected treebanks from the phylogenetic groups described for the previous experiment (see again Table 1), instead of training separate models for each one. We compare the performance against two baselines: (i) models trained on the target LR language training set, and (ii) models trained on a merged training treebank composed of the training set of the target LR treebank and the original training sets of the source treebanks of the related languages (but without x-inflecting them).

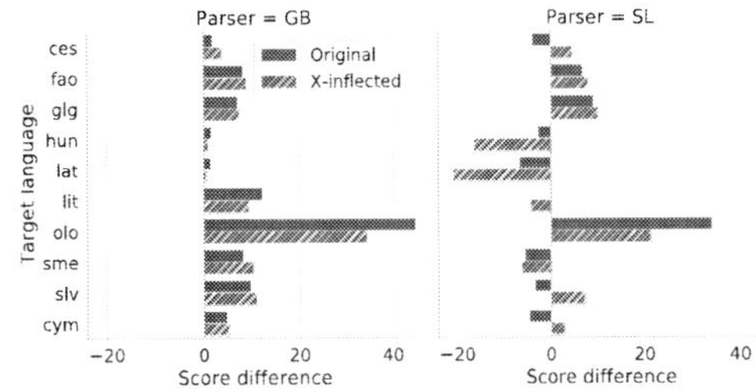

Figure 4: ΔLAS between the models trained on the original and x-inflected groups *with respect to* the model trained on the LR treebank, for both parsers. UAS shows the same tendency as seen in Appendix D.

Results Figure 4 shows the LAS differences between the merged original and x-inflected models *with respect to the* models that are only trained on data coming from the target LR language (UAS results in Appendix D). For the GB parser, all models trained on merged (original or x-inflected) treebanks perform better than their counterparts trained only on the LR treebank, suggesting that adding data from similar languages helps the parsers. However, merging non-x-inflected treebanks sometimes outperforms merging x-inflected treebanks (e.g. Livvi, Lithuanian, and Latin). For the SL parser merging treebanks is not always beneficial compared to training only on the LR training set. We see that the models trained on harmonized (original or x-inflected) treebanks improve only half of the times. Yet, we see some interesting patterns. For instance, when the x-inflection benefits a sequence-labeling model, it also benefits the graph-based one for the same merged treebank, and *vice versa*. Overall, merging x-inflected treebanks is the best option for 6 out of 10 models, although in many cases the differences are small.

5 Discussion

The results show that the proposed method is able to improve parsing results for some treebank pairs under both zero- and few-shot setups, but it also obtains decreases for other pairs. Due to the high number of factors involved, we were unable to clearly isolate those that are beneficial and those that are harmful. However, we identified some reasons that could partially explain the behaviour of the method:

- PCCs from Table 2 show that having more UM data is beneficial to obtain better parsing performance, so better inflectors create better x-inflected treebanks.
- Conversion between UM and UD schemata is non-trivial and dependent on the language pair (see McCarthy et al. (2018) for a detailed analysis), and thus incorrect feature conversions could express different morphological information and mislead the parser.
- Although both UD and UM aim to follow a universal annotation schema, not all languages are annotated exactly in the same way, expressing similar morphological phenomena with slightly different features or omitting some of them. Therefore, even when the conversion between schemata is correct, the annotation discrepancies between languages may confuse the inflector, which again, would output a word whose form would express different morphological information than the original form.

6 Conclusion

By cross-inflecting a rich-resource UD treebank using an inflector from a low-resource related language, we can obtain silver, syntactically annotated data to train dependency parsers. Although containing noise and grammatical imperfections, we aimed to test whether the approach could boost performance. The results show that it is possible to obtain improvements (but also decreases) both for zero- and few-shot setups.

About this, we could not clearly identify what aspects make the approach succeed or fail. Although we identified moderate correlations between scores and the amount of available UM data for the target language, we hypothesize that other aspects that are hard to measure could be playing a role: (i) incorrect/incomplete feature conversion from UM to UD schemata that might make the cross-lingual inflections carry different information that the inflections in the original language, or (ii) unknown input features for a given inflector due to differences in exhaustiveness between the UM and UD annotations.

Acknowledgements

This work is supported by a 2020 Leonardo Grant for Researchers and Cultural Creators from the FBBVA,[3] as well as by the European Research Council (ERC), under the European Union's Horizon 2020 research and innovation programme (FASTPARSE, grant agreement No 714150). The work is also supported by ERDF/MICINN-AEI (SCANNER-UDC, PID2020-113230RB-C21), by Xunta de Galicia (ED431C 2020/11), and by Centro de Investigación de Galicia "CITIC" which is funded by Xunta de Galicia, Spain and the European Union (ERDF - Galicia 2014–2020 Program), by grant ED431G 2019/01.

References

Waleed Ammar, George Mulcaire, Miguel Ballesteros, Chris Dyer, and Noah A. Smith. 2016. Many languages, one parser. *Transactions of the Association for Computational Linguistics*, 4:431–444.

Yevgeni Berzak, Yan Huang, Andrei Barbu, Anna Korhonen, and Boris Katz. 2016. Anchoring and agreement in syntactic annotations. In *Proceedings of the 2016 Conference on Empirical Methods in Natural Language Processing*, pages 2215–2224, Austin, Texas. Association for Computational Linguistics.

Ryan Cotterell, Christo Kirov, John Sylak-Glassman, David Yarowsky, Jason Eisner, and Mans Hulden. 2016. The sigmorphon 2016 shared task—morphological reinflection. In *Proceedings of the 14th SIGMORPHON Workshop on Computational Research in Phonetics, Phonology, and Morphology*, pages 10–22.

Mathieu Dehouck and Pascal Denis. 2018. A framework for understanding the role of morphology in Universal Dependency parsing. In *Proceedings of the 2018 Conference on Empirical Methods in Natural Language Processing*, pages 2864–2870, Brussels, Belgium. Association for Computational Linguistics.

Mathieu Dehouck and Carlos Gómez-Rodríguez. 2020. Data augmentation via subtree swapping for dependency parsing of low-resource languages. In *Proceedings of the 28th International Conference on Computational Linguistics*, pages 3818–3830, Barcelona, Spain (Online). International Committee on Computational Linguistics.

Timothy Dozat, Peng Qi, and Christopher D. Manning. 2017. Stanford's graph-based neural dependency parser at the CoNLL 2017 shared task. In *Proceedings of the CoNLL 2017 Shared Task: Multilingual*

[3]FBBVA accepts no responsibility for the opinions, statements and contents included in the project and/or the results thereof, which are entirely the responsibility of the authors.

Parsing from Raw Text to Universal Dependencies, pages 20–30, Vancouver, Canada. Association for Computational Linguistics.

Agnieszka Falenska and Özlem Çetinoğlu. 2017. Lexicalized vs. delexicalized parsing in low-resource scenarios. In *Proceedings of the 15th International Conference on Parsing Technologies*, pages 18–24, Pisa, Italy. Association for Computational Linguistics.

Sepp Hochreiter and Jürgen Schmidhuber. 1997. Long short-term memory. *Neural computation*, 9(8):1735–1780.

Jason Lee, Kyunghyun Cho, and Thomas Hofmann. 2017. Fully character-level neural machine translation without explicit segmentation. *Transactions of the Association for Computational Linguistics*, 5:365–378.

Xuezhe Ma, Zecong Hu, Jingzhou Liu, Nanyun Peng, Graham Neubig, and Eduard Hovy. 2018. Stack-pointer networks for dependency parsing. In *Proceedings of the 56th Annual Meeting of the Association for Computational Linguistics (Volume 1: Long Papers)*, pages 1403–1414, Melbourne, Australia. Association for Computational Linguistics.

Arya D. McCarthy, Christo Kirov, Matteo Grella, Amrit Nidhi, Patrick Xia, Kyle Gorman, Ekaterina Vylomova, Sabrina J. Mielke, Garrett Nicolai, Miikka Silfverberg, Timofey Arkhangelskiy, Nataly Krizhanovsky, Andrew Krizhanovsky, Elena Klyachko, Alexey Sorokin, John Mansfield, Valts Ernštreits, Yuval Pinter, Cassandra L. Jacobs, Ryan Cotterell, Mans Hulden, and David Yarowsky. 2020. UniMorph 3.0: Universal Morphology. In *Proceedings of the 12th Language Resources and Evaluation Conference*, pages 3922–3931, Marseille, France. European Language Resources Association.

Arya D. McCarthy, Miikka Silfverberg, Ryan Cotterell, Mans Hulden, and David Yarowsky. 2018. Marrying Universal Dependencies and Universal Morphology. In *Proceedings of the Second Workshop on Universal Dependencies (UDW 2018)*, pages 91–101. Association for Computational Linguistics.

Ryan McDonald, Slav Petrov, and Keith Hall. 2011. Multi-source transfer of delexicalized dependency parsers. In *Proceedings of the 2011 Conference on Empirical Methods in Natural Language Processing*, pages 62–72, Edinburgh, Scotland, UK. Association for Computational Linguistics.

Phoebe Mulcaire, Jungo Kasai, and Noah A. Smith. 2019. Low-resource parsing with crosslingual contextualized representations. In *Proceedings of the 23rd Conference on Computational Natural Language Learning (CoNLL)*, pages 304–315, Hong Kong, China. Association for Computational Linguistics.

Alberto Muñoz-Ortiz, Michalina Strzyz, and David Vilares. 2021. Not all linearizations are equally data-hungry in sequence labeling parsing. In *Proceedings of the International Conference on Recent Advances in Natural Language Processing (RANLP 2021)*, pages 978–988, Held Online. INCOMA Ltd.

Tiago Pimentel, Maria Ryskinaì, Sabrina MielkeZ, Shijie WuZ Eleanor Chodroff, Brian LeonardB, Garrett Nicolaiá, Yustinus Ghanggo AteÆ, Salam Khalifaè, Nizar Habashè, Charbel El-KhaissiS, et al. 2021. Sigmorphon 2021 shared task on morphological reinflection: Generalization across languages. *SIGMORPHON 2021*, page 154.

Michalina Strzyz, David Vilares, and Carlos Gómez-Rodríguez. 2019. Viable dependency parsing as sequence labeling. In *Proceedings of the 2019 Conference of the North American Chapter of the Association for Computational Linguistics: Human Language Technologies, Volume 1 (Long and Short Papers)*, pages 717–723, Minneapolis, Minnesota. Association for Computational Linguistics.

Michalina Strzyz, David Vilares, and Carlos Gómez-Rodríguez. 2020. Bracketing encodings for 2-planar dependency parsing. In *Proceedings of the 28th International Conference on Computational Linguistics*, pages 2472–2484, Barcelona, Spain (Online). International Committee on Computational Linguistics.

Clara Vania. 2020. *An examination of keystroke dynamics for continuous user authentication*. Ph.D. thesis, Queensland University of Technology.

Clara Vania, Yova Kementchedjhieva, Anders Søgaard, and Adam Lopez. 2019. A systematic comparison of methods for low-resource dependency parsing on genuinely low-resource languages. In *Proceedings of the 2019 Conference on Empirical Methods in Natural Language Processing and the 9th International Joint Conference on Natural Language Processing (EMNLP-IJCNLP)*, pages 1105–1116, Hong Kong, China. Association for Computational Linguistics.

David Vilares, Carlos Gómez-Rodríguez, and Miguel A. Alonso. 2016. One model, two languages: training bilingual parsers with harmonized treebanks. In *Proceedings of the 54th Annual Meeting of the Association for Computational Linguistics (Volume 2: Short Papers)*, pages 425–431, Berlin, Germany. Association for Computational Linguistics.

Dingquan Wang and Jason Eisner. 2018. Synthetic data made to order: The case of parsing. In *Proceedings of the 2018 Conference on Empirical Methods in Natural Language Processing*, pages 1325–1337, Brussels, Belgium. Association for Computational Linguistics.

Shijie Wu, Ryan Cotterell, and Mans Hulden. 2021. Applying the transformer to character-level transduction. In *Proceedings of the 16th Conference of the European Chapter of the Association for Computational Linguistics: Main Volume*, pages 1901–1907, Online. Association for Computational Linguistics.

Shijie Wu, Pamela Shapiro, and Ryan Cotterell. 2018. Hard non-monotonic attention for character-level transduction. In *Proceedings of the 2018 Conference on Empirical Methods in Natural Language Processing*, pages 4425–4438, Brussels, Belgium. Association for Computational Linguistics.

Daniel Zeman, Joakim Nivre, Mitchell Abrams, Elia Ackermann, Noëmi Aepli, Hamid Aghaei, Željko Agić, Amir Ahmadi, Lars Ahrenberg, Chika Kennedy Ajede, Gabrielė Aleksandravičiūtė, Ika Alfina, Lene Antonsen, Katya Aplonova, Angelina Aquino, Carolina Aragon, Maria Jesus Aranzabe, Hórunn Arnardóttir, Gashaw Arutie, Jessica Naraiswari Arwidarasti, Masayuki Asahara, Luma Ateyah, Furkan Atmaca, Mohammed Attia, Aitziber Atutxa, Liesbeth Augustinus, Elena Badmaeva, Keerthana Balasubramani, Miguel Ballesteros, Esha Banerjee, Sebastian Bank, Verginica Barbu Mititelu, Victoria Basmov, Colin Batchelor, John Bauer, Seyyit Talha Bedir, Kepa Bengoetxea, Gözde Berk, Yevgeni Berzak, Irshad Ahmad Bhat, Riyaz Ahmad Bhat, Erica Biagetti, Eckhard Bick, Agnė Bielinskienė, Kristín Bjarnadóttir, Rogier Blokland, Victoria Bobicev, Loïc Boizou, Emanuel Borges Völker, Carl Börstell, Cristina Bosco, Gosse Bouma, Sam Bowman, Adriane Boyd, Kristina Brokaitė, Aljoscha Burchardt, Marie Candito, Bernard Caron, Gauthier Caron, Tatiana Cavalcanti, Gülşen Cebiroğlu Eryiğit, Flavio Massimiliano Cecchini, Giuseppe G. A. Celano, Slavomír Čéplö, Savas Cetin, Özlem Çetinoğlu, Fabricio Chalub, Ethan Chi, Yongseok Cho, Jinho Choi, Jayeol Chun, Alessandra T. Cignarella, Silvie Cinková, Aurélie Collomb, Çağrı Çöltekin, Miriam Connor, Marine Courtin, Elizabeth Davidson, Marie-Catherine de Marneffe, Valeria de Paiva, Mehmet Oguz Derin, Elvis de Souza, Arantza Diaz de Ilarraza, Carly Dickerson, Arawinda Dinakaramani, Bamba Dione, Peter Dirix, Kaja Dobrovoljc, Timothy Dozat, Kira Droganova, Puneet Dwivedi, Hanne Eckhoff, Marhaba Eli, Ali Elkahky, Binyam Ephrem, Olga Erina, Tomaž Erjavec, Aline Etienne, Wograine Evelyn, Sidney Facundes, Richárd Farkas, Marília Fernanda, Hector Fernandez Alcalde, Jennifer Foster, Cláudia Freitas, Kazunori Fujita, Katarína Gajdošová, Daniel Galbraith, Marcos Garcia, Moa Gärdenfors, Sebastian Garza, Fabrício Ferraz Gerardi, Kim Gerdes, Filip Ginter, Iakes Goenaga, Koldo Gojenola, Memduh Gökırmak, Yoav Goldberg, Xavier Gómez Guinovart, Berta González Saavedra, Bernadeta Griciūtė, Matias Grioni, Loïc Grobol, Normunds Grūzītis, Bruno Guillaume, Céline Guillot-Barbance, Tunga Güngör, Nizar Habash, Hinrik Hafsteinsson, Jan Hajič, Jan Hajič jr., Mika Hämäläinen, Linh Hà Mỹ, Na-Rae Han, Muhammad Yudistira Hanifmuti, Sam Hardwick, Kim Harris, Dag Haug, Johannes Heinecke, Oliver Hellwig, Felix Hennig, Barbora Hladká, Jaroslava Hlaváčová, Florinel Hociung, Petter Hohle, Eva Huber, Jena Hwang, Takumi Ikeda, Anton Karl Ingason, Radu Ion, Elena Irimia, Ọlájídé Ishola, Tomáš Jelínek, Anders Johannsen, Hildur Jónsdóttir, Fredrik Jørgensen, Markus Juutinen, Sarveswaran K, Hüner Kaşıkara, Andre Kaasen, Nadezhda Kabaeva, Sylvain Kahane, Hiroshi Kanayama, Jenna Kanerva, Boris Katz, Tolga Kayadelen, Jessica Kenney, Václava Kettnerová, Jesse Kirchner, Elena Klementieva, Arne Köhn, Abdullatif Köksal, Kamil Kopacewicz, Timo Korkiakangas, Natalia Kotsyba, Jolanta Kovalevskaitė, Simon Krek, Parameswari Krishnamurthy, Sookyoung Kwak, Veronika Laippala, Lucia Lam, Lorenzo Lambertino, Tatiana Lando, Septina Dian Larasati, Alexei Lavrentiev, John Lee, Phng Lê Hồng, Alessandro Lenci, Saran Lertpradit, Herman Leung, Maria Levina, Cheuk Ying Li, Josie Li, Keying Li, Yuan Li, KyungTae Lim, Krister Lindén, Nikola Ljubešić, Olga Loginova, Andry Luthfi, Mikko Luukko, Olga Lyashevskaya, Teresa Lynn, Vivien Macketanz, Aibek Makazhanov, Michael Mandl, Christopher Manning, Ruli Manurung, Cătălina Mărănduc, David Mareček, Katrin Marheinecke, Héctor Martínez Alonso, André Martins, Jan Mašek, Hiroshi Matsuda, Yuji Matsumoto, Ryan McDonald, Sarah McGuinness, Gustavo Mendonça, Niko Miekka, Karina Mischenkova, Margarita Misirpashayeva, Anna Missilä, Cătălin Mititelu, Maria Mitrofan, Yusuke Miyao, AmirHossein Mojiri Foroushani, Amirsaeid Moloodi, Simonetta Montemagni, Amir More, Laura Moreno Romero, Keiko Sophie Mori, Shinsuke Mori, Tomohiko Morioka, Shigeki Moro, Bjartur Mortensen, Bohdan Moskalevskyi, Kadri Muischnek, Robert Munro, Yugo Murawaki, Kaili Müürisep, Pinkey Nainwani, Mariam Nakhlé, Juan Ignacio Navarro Horñiacek, Anna Nedoluzhko, Gunta Nešpore-Bērzkalne, Lng Nguyễn Thị, Huyền Nguyễn Thị Minh, Yoshihiro Nikaido, Vitaly Nikolaev, Rattima Nitisaroj, Alireza Nourian, Hanna Nurmi, Stina Ojala, Atul Kr. Ojha, Adédayọ Olúòkun, Mai Omura, Emeka Onwuegbuzia, Petya Osenova, Robert Östling, Lilja Øvrelid, Şaziye Betül Özateş, Arzucan Özgür, Balkız Öztürk Başaran, Niko Partanen, Elena Pascual, Marco Passarotti, Agnieszka Patejuk, Guilherme Paulino-Passos, Angelika Peljak-Łapińska, Siyao Peng, Cenel-Augusto Perez, Natalia Perkova, Guy Perrier, Slav Petrov, Daria Petrova, Jason Phelan, Jussi Piitulainen, Tommi A Pirinen, Emily Pitler, Barbara Plank, Thierry Poibeau, Larisa Ponomareva, Martin Popel, Lauma Pretkalniņa, Sophie Prévost, Prokopis Prokopidis, Adam Przepiórkowski, Tiina Puolakainen, Sampo Pyysalo, Peng Qi, Andriela Rääbis, Alexandre Rademaker, Taraka Rama, Loganathan Ramasamy, Carlos Ramisch, Fam Rashel, Mohammad Sadegh Rasooli, Vinit Ravishankar, Livy Real, Petru Rebeja, Siva Reddy, Georg Rehm, Ivan Riabov, Michael Rießler, Erika Rimkutė, Larissa Rinaldi, Laura Rituma, Luisa Rocha, Eiríkur Rögnvaldsson, Mykhailo Romanenko, Rudolf Rosa, Valentin Roșca, Davide Rovati, Olga Rudina, Jack Rueter, Kristján Rúnarsson, Shoval Sadde, Pegah Safari, Benoît Sagot, Aleksi Sahala, Shadi Saleh, Alessio Salomoni, Tanja Samardžić, Stephanie Samson, Manuela Sanguinetti, Dage Särg, Baiba Saulīte, Yanin Sawanakunanon, Kevin Scannell, Salvatore Scarlata, Nathan Schneider, Sebastian Schuster, Djamé Seddah, Wolfgang Seeker, Mojgan Seraji, Mo Shen, Atsuko Shimada, Hiroyuki Shirasu, Muh

Shohibussirri, Dmitry Sichinava, Einar Freyr Sigurðsson, Aline Silveira, Natalia Silveira, Maria Simi, Radu Simionescu, Katalin Simkó, Mária Šimková, Kiril Simov, Maria Skachedubova, Aaron Smith, Isabela Soares-Bastos, Carolyn Spadine, Steinhór Steingrímsson, Antonio Stella, Milan Straka, Emmett Strickland, Jana Strnadová, Alane Suhr, Yogi Lesmana Sulestio, Umut Sulubacak, Shingo Suzuki, Zsolt Szántó, Dima Taji, Yuta Takahashi, Fabio Tamburini, Mary Ann C. Tan, Takaaki Tanaka, Samson Tella, Isabelle Tellier, Guillaume Thomas, Liisi Torga, Marsida Toska, Trond Trosterud, Anna Trukhina, Reut Tsarfaty, Utku Türk, Francis Tyers, Sumire Uematsu, Roman Untilov, Zdeňka Urešová, Larraitz Uria, Hans Uszkoreit, Andrius Utka, Sowmya Vajjala, Daniel van Niekerk, Gertjan van Noord, Viktor Varga, Eric Villemonte de la Clergerie, Veronika Vincze, Aya Wakasa, Joel C. Wallenberg, Lars Wallin, Abigail Walsh, Jing Xian Wang, Jonathan North Washington, Maximilan Wendt, Paul Widmer, Seyi Williams, Mats Wirén, Christian Wittern, Tsegay Woldemariam, Tak-sum Wong, Alina Wróblewska, Mary Yako, Kayo Yamashita, Naoki Yamazaki, Chunxiao Yan, Koichi Yasuoka, Marat M. Yavrumyan, Zhuoran Yu, Zdeněk Žabokrtský, Shorouq Zahra, Amir Zeldes, Hanzhi Zhu, and Anna Zhuravleva. 2020. Universal dependencies 2.7. LINDAT/CLARIAH-CZ digital library at the Institute of Formal and Applied Linguistics (ÚFAL), Faculty of Mathematics and Physics, Charles University.

Is BERT Robust to Label Noise? A Study on Learning with Noisy Labels in Text Classification

Dawei Zhu, Michael A. Hedderich, Fangzhou Zhai,
David Ifeoluwa Adelani & Dietrich Klakow
Saarland University, Saarland Informatics Campus, Germany
{dzhu,mhedderich,didelani,dietrich.klakow}@lsv.uni-saarland.de
fzhai@coli.uni-saarland.de

Abstract

Incorrect labels in training data occur when human annotators make mistakes or when the data is generated via weak or distant supervision. It has been shown that complex noise-handling techniques - by modeling, cleaning or filtering the noisy instances - are required to prevent models from fitting this label noise. However, we show in this work that, for text classification tasks with modern NLP models like BERT, over a variety of noise types, existing noise-handling methods do not always improve its performance, and may even deteriorate it, suggesting the need for further investigation. We also back our observations with a comprehensive analysis.

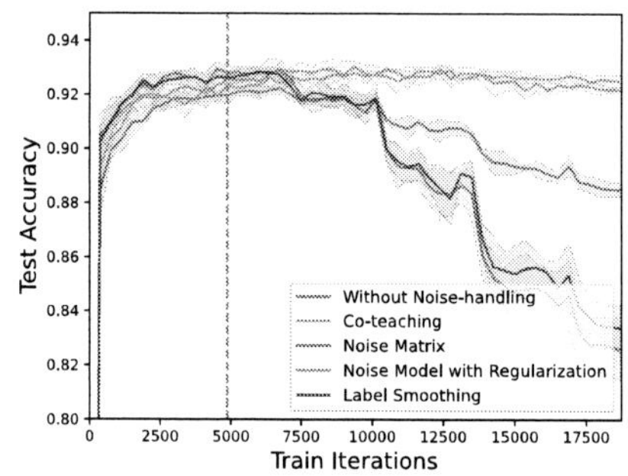

Figure 1: A typical training curve when learning with noise. Learning without noise-handling (blue) will reach a peak accuracy before memorizing the noise. Early-stopping on a noisy validation set (vertical grey line) is often sufficient to find such a peak. Injected uniform noise of 40% on AG-News dataset.

1 Introduction

For many languages, domains and tasks, large datasets with high-quality labels are not available. To tackle this issue, cheaper data acquisition methods have been suggested, such as crowdsourcing or automatic annotation methods like weak and distant supervision. Unfortunately, compared to gold-standard data, these approaches come with more labeling mistakes, which are known as noisy labels. Noise-handling has become an established approach to mitigate the negative impact of learning with noisy labels. A variety of methods have been proposed that model the noise, or clean and filter the noisy instances (Hedderich et al., 2021; Algan and Ulusoy, 2021). Jindal et al. (2019) show e.g. a 30% boost in performance after applying noise-handling techniques on a CNN-based text classifier.

In a recent work, Tänzer et al. (2021) showed that BERT (Devlin et al., 2019) has an inherent robustness against noisy labels. The generalization performance on the clean distribution drops only slowly with the increase of the mislabeled samples. Also, they show that early-stopping is crucial for learning with noisy labels as BERT will eventually memorize all wrong labels when trained long enough. However, their experiments only focus on a single type of noise and a limited range of noise levels. It remains unclear if BERT still performs robustly under a wider range of noise types and with higher fractions of mislabeled samples. Moreover, they perform early-stopping on a clean validation set, which may not be available under low resource settings. Last but not least, they do not compare to any noise-handling methods.

In this work, we investigate the behaviors of BERT on tasks with different noise types and noise levels. We also study the effect of noise-handling methods under these settings. Our main results include **(1)** BERT is robust against injected noise, but could be vulnerable to noise from weak supervision. In fact, the latter, even at a low level, can be more challenging than high injected noise. **(2)** Existing noise-handling methods do not improve the peak performance of BERT under any noise settings we investigated; as is shown with further analysis, noise-handling methods rarely render the correct labels more distinguishable from the incorrect ones. [1]

[1]Our implementation is available on: https://github.com/uds-lsv/BERT-LNL.

Proceedings of the Third Workshop on Insights from Negative Results in NLP, pages 62 - 67
May 26, 2022 ©2022 Association for Computational Linguistics

2 Learning with Noisy Labels

Problem Settings We consider a k-class classification problem. Let D denote the true data generation distribution over $\mathcal{X} \times \mathcal{Y}$ where $\mathcal{X}$ is the feature space and $\mathcal{Y} = \{1, ..., k\}$ is the label space. In a typical classification task, we are provided with a training dataset $S = \{(x_i, y_i)_{i=1}^n\}$ sampled from D. In learning with noisy labels, however, we have no access to D. Instead, a noisy training set $\hat{S} = \{(x_i, \hat{y}_i)_{i=1}^n\}$ sampled from a label-corrupted data distribution $\hat{D}$. The goal is to learn a classifier that generalizes well on the clean distribution by only exploiting $\hat{S}$.

Injected Label Noise To rigorously evaluate noise-handling methods at different noise levels, researchers in this area often construct noisy datasets from clean ones by injecting noise. This can, e.g., reflect annotation scenarios such as crowdsourcing, where some annotators answer randomly or prefer an early entry in a list of options. Modeling such noise is achieved by flipping the labels of the clean instances according to a pre-defined noise level $\varepsilon \in [0, 1)$ and a noise type. There are two commonly used noise types: the single-flip noise (Reed et al., 2015):

$$p_{\text{sflip}}(\hat{y} = j | y = i) = \begin{cases} 1 - \varepsilon, & \text{for } i = j \\ \varepsilon, & \text{for one } i \neq j \\ 0, & else \end{cases}$$

and uniform-flip (van Rooyen et al., 2015) noise

$$p_{\text{uni}}(\hat{y} = j | y = i) = \begin{cases} 1 - \varepsilon, & \text{for } i = j \\ \frac{\varepsilon}{k-1}, & \text{for } i \neq j \end{cases}.$$

These noise generation processes are feature-independent, i.e. $p(\cdot | y = i, x) = p(\cdot | y = i)$. Therefore, they can be described by a noise transition matrix T with $T_{ij} := p(\hat{y} = j | y = i)$. It is usually assumed that the noise is diagonally-dominant when generating the noisy labels, i.e. $\forall i, T_{ii} > max_{j \neq i} T_{ij}$.

Label Noise from Weak Supervision Distant and weak supervision (Mintz et al., 2009; Ratner et al., 2016) have become essential methods to acquire labeled data in low-resource scenarios. The resulting noise, unlike injected noise, is often feature-dependent (Lange et al., 2019). We evaluate our methods on two real-world datasets in Hausa and Yorùbá to cover this type of noise.

Dataset	Classes	Average Lengths	Train Samples	Validation Samples	Test Samples	Train Noise Level
IMDB	2	292	21246	3754	25000	various
AG-News	4	44	108000	12000	7600	various
Yorùbá	7	13	1340	189	379	33.28%
Hausa	5	10	2045	290	582	50.37%

Table 1: Statistics of the text classification datasets. The train noise level is the false discovery rate (i.e. 1-precision) of the noisy labels in the training set. The original AG-News has 120k training instances and no validation instances. We therefore held-out 10% of the training samples for validation.

3 Early-Stopping on Noisy Validation Set

When trainied on noisy data without noise-handling, BERT reaches a high generalization performance before it starts fitting the noise. Then it memorizes the noise and the performance on clean distribution drops dramatically (the blue curve in Figure 1). Hence, for models without noise-handling, it is crucial to stop training when the generalization performance reaches its maximum.

Tänzer et al. (2021) use a clean validation set to find this point. However, a clean validation set is often unavailable in realistic low-resource scenarios as it requires manual annotation. Therefore, we use a noisy validation set for early-stopping in all of our experiments and we attain models that generalize well on the clean distribution.

In our example in Figure 1, we see that while most noise-handling methods prevent BERT from fitting the noise in the long run, their peak performance is not significantly higher than a vanilla model without noise-handling.

4 Experiments

Dataset Construction We experiment with four text classification datasets: two benchmarks, AG-News (Zhang et al., 2015) and IMDB (Maas et al., 2011), injected with different levels of single-flip or uniform noise; for the weakly supervised noise, we make use of two news topics datasets in two low-resource languages: Hausa and Yorùbá (Hedderich et al., 2020). Hausa and Yorùbá are the second and the third most spoken indigenous language in Africa, with 40 and 35 million native speakers, respectively (Eberhard et al., 2019). The noisy labels were gazetteered. For example, to identify texts for the class "Africa", a labeling rule based on a list of African countries and their capitals is used. Note that while we can vary the noise levels of injected noise, the amount of weak supervision noise in Hausa and Yorùbá is fixed[2]. We summarize some basic statistics of the datasets in Table 1.

Implementation We use of-the-shelf BERT models for our tasks. Specifically, we apply the BERT-base model for AG-News and IMDB, and the mBERT-base for Yorùbá and Hausa. The fine-tuning approach follows (Devlin et al., 2019). In all settings, we apply early-stopping on a noisy validation set to mimic the realistic low-resource settings, while the test set remains clean. For more implementation details and a discussion on clean and noisy validation sets, see Appendix B and E.

4.1 Baselines

We compare learning without noise-handling with four popular noise-handling methods.[3]

Without Noise-handling Train BERT on the noisy training set as it was clean. A noisy validation set is used for early-stopping.

No Validation For the sake of comparison, we train the model without noise-handling and until the training loss converges.

Noise Matrix A noise transition matrix is appended after BERT's prediction to transform the clean label distribution to the noisy one. A variety of methods exists for estimating the noise matrix, i.e. Sukhbaatar et al. (2015); Bekker and Goldberger (2016); Patrini et al. (2017); Hendrycks et al. (2018); Yao et al. (2020). To exclude the effects of estimation errors in the evaluation, we use the ground truth transition matrix as it is the best possible estimation. This matrix is fixed after initialization.

Noise Matrix with Regularization The previous state-of-the-art for text classification with noisy labels (Jindal et al., 2019). Similar to *Noise Matrix*, it appends a noise matrix after BERT's output. During training, the matrix is learned with an $l2$ regularization and is not necessarily normalized to be a probability matrix. In the original implementation they use CNN-based models as backbone, we switch it to BERT for fair comparison.

Co-teaching Han et al. (2018) Train two networks to pick cleaner training subsets for each other. The Co-teaching framework requires an estimation of the noise level. Similarly to NMat, we use the ground truth noise level to exclude the performance drop caused by estimation error.

Label Smoothing Label smoothing (Szegedy et al., 2016) is a commonly used method to improve model's generalization and calibration. It mixes the one-hot label with a uniform vector, preventing the model from getting overconfident on the samples. Lukasik et al. (2020) further shows that it improves noise robustness.

4.2 Experimental Results

We evaluate our baselines on both injected noise (on AG-News and IMDB) and weak supervision noise (on Hausa and Yorùbá). The test accuracy is presented Figure 2. On injected noise, our results match and extend the findings by Tänzer et al. (2021) that BERT is noise robust. For example, the test accuracy drops only about 10% after injecting 70% wrong labels (Figure 2(a)). However, we find that BERT is vulnerable under weak supervision noise. The performance can drop up to 35% in a dataset like Hausa with 50% weak supervision noise compared to training with clean labels (Figure 2(c)). This indicates that the experience on injected noise may not be transferable to weak supervision noise.

We also observe that noise-handling methods are not always helpful. For injected noise, the benefits from noise-handling become obvious only under high noise levels. But even then, there is no clear winner, meaning that it is hard to decide beforehand which noise method to apply - with the risk that they may even perform worse than BERT without noise-handling. The same applies to weak supervision noise. The maximal performance gap between the best model and BERT without noise-handling is less than 4% and 1.5% under injected noise and weak supervision noise, respectively.

4.3 Analysis of Loss Distributions

To shed some light on why BERT is robust against injected noise but not weak supervision noise, we track the losses on correctly and wrongly labeled samples during training. Figure 4 depicts typical distributions of losses associated with correctly and incorrectly labeled samples, respectively, when early-stopping is triggered. We see that they have minimal overlap, thus different behaviors throughout the training, potentially allowing the model to distinguish correctly and incorrectly labeled sam-

[2] refer to Appendix A for detailed noise distribution.

[3] For a fair comparison, early-stopping on a noisy validation set is applied to all four noise-handling methods.

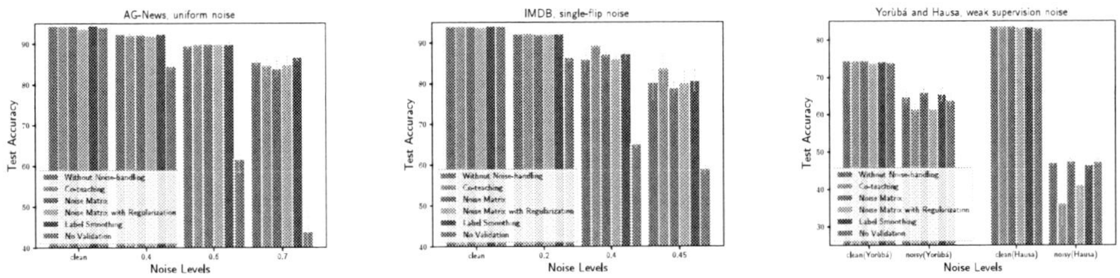

(a) AG-News, uniform noise (b) IMDB, single-flip noise (c) Yorùbá & Hausa, weak supervision noise

Figure 2: Test accuracy in different noise settings. a) & b) injected noise with different noise levels c) weak supervision noise, at noise levels of 33.28% and 50.37% in Yorùbá and Hausa, respectively. Noise-handling methods do not always improve peak performances. Further plots in Appendix C.

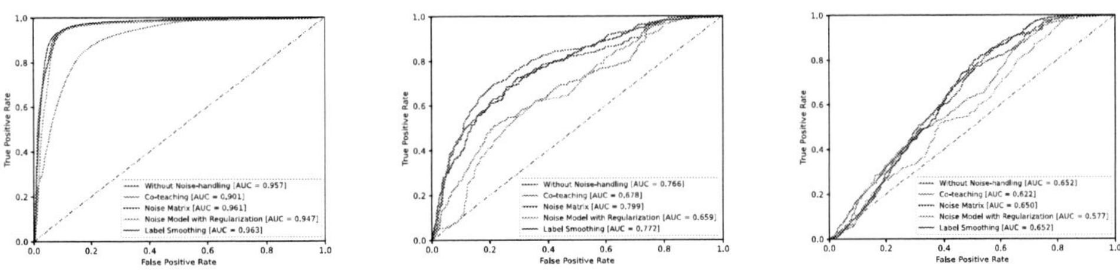

(a) AG-News - 70% uniform noise (b) Yorùbá - weak supervision noise (c) Hausa - weak supervision noise

Figure 3: ROC curves on wrong label detection (binary classification) using the losses. The losses are recorded at the training step when early-stopping is triggered. Noise-handling methods do not make the losses of correct and incorrect labels more distinguishable. Further plots in Appendix D.

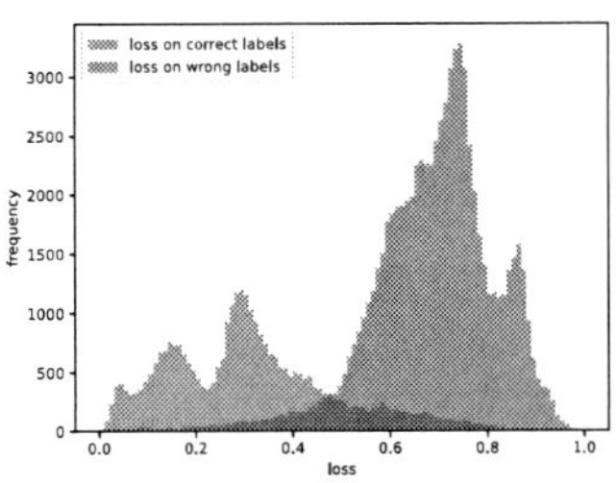

Figure 4: Loss histogram at the training iteration when the early-stopping is triggered. AG-News dataset with 70% uniform noise.

ples from each other. We could further quantify the difference by their separability. Figure 3 presents the receiver operating characteristic (ROC) curves of a thresholds-based classifier. We observe that **(1)** under injected noise, an area under curve (AUC) of more than 90 can be easily achieved without noise-handling (Figure 3(a)), supporting our observation that injected noise has rather a low impact on BERT. **(2)** Under weak-supervision noise, the AUC score is significantly lower, which means the correct and incorrect labels are less distinguishable. Therefore, BERT fits both labels at similar rates. One reason could be that the noise in weak supervision is often feature-dependent, it might become easier for BERT to fit them, which in turn deteriorates the generalization. **(3)** We do not observe a raise in AUC scores when applying noise-handling methods, indicating that noise-handling methods rarely enhance BERT's ability to further avoid the negative impact of wrong labels. This is consistent with the observation in Section 4.2 that noise-handling methods have little impact on BERT's generalization performance.

5 Conclusion

On several text classification datasets and for different noise types, we showed that BERT is noise resistant under injected noise, but not necessarily under weak supervision noise. In both cases, the improvement obtained by applying noise-handling methods are limited. Our analysis on the separability of losses corresponding to correct and incorrect labeled samples provides evidence to this argument. Our analysis offers both motivation and insights to further improve label noise-handling methods and make them useful on more realistic types of noise.

6 Broader Impact Statement and Ethics

Noisy labels are a cheaper source of supervision. This could make it easier to use machine learning for improper use cases. However, it also opens up NLP methods for low-resource settings such as under-resourced languages or applications developed by individuals or small organizations. It can, therefore, be a step towards the democratization of AI.

Acknowledgments

This work has been partially funded by the Deutsche Forschungsgemeinschaft (DFG, German Research Foundation) – Project-ID 232722074 – SFB 1102 and the EU Horizon 2020 projects ROXANNE under grant number 833635 and COMPRISE under grant agreement No. 3081705.

References

Görkem Algan and Ilkay Ulusoy. 2021. Image classification with deep learning in the presence of noisy labels: A survey. *Knowl. Based Syst.*, 215:106771.

Alan Joseph Bekker and Jacob Goldberger. 2016. Training deep neural-networks based on unreliable labels. In *2016 IEEE International Conference on Acoustics, Speech and Signal Processing, ICASSP 2016, Shanghai, China, March 20-25, 2016*, pages 2682–2686. IEEE.

Jacob Devlin, Ming-Wei Chang, Kenton Lee, and Kristina Toutanova. 2019. BERT: pre-training of deep bidirectional transformers for language understanding. In *Proceedings of the 2019 Conference of the North American Chapter of the Association for Computational Linguistics: Human Language Technologies, NAACL-HLT 2019, Minneapolis, MN, USA, June 2-7, 2019, Volume 1 (Long and Short Papers)*, pages 4171–4186. Association for Computational Linguistics.

David M. Eberhard, Gary F. Simons, and Charles D. Fennig (eds.). 2019. Ethnologue: Languages of the world. twenty-second edition.

Bo Han, Quanming Yao, Xingrui Yu, Gang Niu, Miao Xu, Weihua Hu, Ivor W. Tsang, and Masashi Sugiyama. 2018. Co-teaching: Robust training of deep neural networks with extremely noisy labels. In *Advances in Neural Information Processing Systems 31: Annual Conference on Neural Information Processing Systems 2018, NeurIPS 2018, December 3-8, 2018, Montréal, Canada*, pages 8536–8546.

Michael A. Hedderich, David Ifeoluwa Adelani, Dawei Zhu, Jesujoba O. Alabi, Udia Markus, and Dietrich Klakow. 2020. Transfer learning and distant supervision for multilingual transformer models: A study on african languages. In *Proceedings of the 2020 Conference on Empirical Methods in Natural Language Processing, EMNLP 2020, Online, November 16-20, 2020*, pages 2580–2591. Association for Computational Linguistics.

Michael A. Hedderich, Lukas Lange, Heike Adel, Jannik Strötgen, and Dietrich Klakow. 2021. A survey on recent approaches for natural language processing in low-resource scenarios. In *Proceedings of the 2021 Conference of the North American Chapter of the Association for Computational Linguistics: Human Language Technologies*, pages 2545–2568, Online. Association for Computational Linguistics.

Dan Hendrycks, Mantas Mazeika, Duncan Wilson, and Kevin Gimpel. 2018. Using trusted data to train deep networks on labels corrupted by severe noise. In *Advances in Neural Information Processing Systems 31: Annual Conference on Neural Information Processing Systems 2018, NeurIPS 2018, December 3-8, 2018, Montréal, Canada*, pages 10477–10486.

Ishan Jindal, Daniel Pressel, Brian Lester, and Matthew S. Nokleby. 2019. An effective label noise model for DNN text classification. In *Proceedings of the 2019 Conference of the North American Chapter of the Association for Computational Linguistics: Human Language Technologies, NAACL-HLT 2019, Minneapolis, MN, USA, June 2-7, 2019, Volume 1 (Long and Short Papers)*, pages 3246–3256. Association for Computational Linguistics.

Lukas Lange, Michael A. Hedderich, and Dietrich Klakow. 2019. Feature-dependent confusion matrices for low-resource NER labeling with noisy labels. In *Proceedings of the 2019 Conference on Empirical Methods in Natural Language Processing and the 9th International Joint Conference on Natural Language Processing (EMNLP-IJCNLP)*, pages 3554–3559, Hong Kong, China. Association for Computational Linguistics.

Michal Lukasik, Srinadh Bhojanapalli, Aditya Menon, and Sanjiv Kumar. 2020. Does label smoothing mitigate label noise? In *International Conference on Machine Learning*, pages 6448–6458. PMLR.

Andrew L. Maas, Raymond E. Daly, Peter T. Pham, Dan Huang, Andrew Y. Ng, and Christopher Potts. 2011. Learning word vectors for sentiment analysis. In *The 49th Annual Meeting of the Association for Computational Linguistics: Human Language Technologies, Proceedings of the Conference, 19-24 June, 2011, Portland, Oregon, USA*, pages 142–150. The Association for Computer Linguistics.

Mike Mintz, Steven Bills, Rion Snow, and Daniel Jurafsky. 2009. Distant supervision for relation extraction without labeled data. In *Proceedings of the Joint Conference of the 47th Annual Meeting of the ACL and the 4th International Joint Conference on Natural Language Processing of the AFNLP*, pages 1003–1011, Suntec, Singapore. Association for Computational Linguistics.

Giorgio Patrini, Alessandro Rozza, Aditya Krishna Menon, Richard Nock, and Lizhen Qu. 2017. Making deep neural networks robust to label noise: A loss correction approach. In *2017 IEEE Conference on Computer Vision and Pattern Recognition, CVPR 2017, Honolulu, HI, USA, July 21-26, 2017*, pages 2233–2241. IEEE Computer Society.

Alexander J Ratner, Christopher M De Sa, Sen Wu, Daniel Selsam, and Christopher Ré. 2016. Data programming: Creating large training sets, quickly. In *Advances in Neural Information Processing Systems*, volume 29. Curran Associates, Inc.

Scott E. Reed, Honglak Lee, Dragomir Anguelov, Christian Szegedy, Dumitru Erhan, and Andrew Rabinovich. 2015. Training deep neural networks on noisy labels with bootstrapping. In *3rd International Conference on Learning Representations, ICLR 2015, San Diego, CA, USA, May 7-9, 2015, Workshop Track Proceedings*.

Sainbayar Sukhbaatar, Joan Bruna, Manohar Paluri, Lubomir Bourdev, and Rob Fergus. 2015. Training convolutional networks with noisy labels. In *3rd International Conference on Learning Representations, ICLR 2015*.

Christian Szegedy, Vincent Vanhoucke, Sergey Ioffe, Jonathon Shlens, and Zbigniew Wojna. 2016. Rethinking the inception architecture for computer vision. *2016 IEEE Conference on Computer Vision and Pattern Recognition (CVPR)*, pages 2818–2826.

Michael Tänzer, Sebastian Ruder, and Marek Rei. 2021. BERT memorisation and pitfalls in low-resource scenarios. *CoRR*, abs/2105.00828.

Brendan van Rooyen, Aditya Krishna Menon, and Robert C. Williamson. 2015. Learning with symmetric label noise: The importance of being unhinged. In *Advances in Neural Information Processing Systems 28: Annual Conference on Neural Information Processing Systems 2015, December 7-12, 2015, Montreal, Quebec, Canada*, pages 10–18.

Yu Yao, Tongliang Liu, Bo Han, Mingming Gong, Jiankang Deng, Gang Niu, and Masashi Sugiyama. 2020. Dual T: reducing estimation error for transition matrix in label-noise learning. In *Advances in Neural Information Processing Systems 33: Annual Conference on Neural Information Processing Systems 2020, NeurIPS 2020, December 6-12, 2020, virtual*.

Xiang Zhang, Junbo Jake Zhao, and Yann LeCun. 2015. Character-level convolutional networks for text classification. In *Advances in Neural Information Processing Systems 28: Annual Conference on Neural Information Processing Systems 2015, December 7-12, 2015, Montreal, Quebec, Canada*, pages 649–657.

Ancestor-to-Creole Transfer is Not a Walk in the Park

Heather Lent Emanuele Bugliarello Anders Søgaard
University of Copenhagen, Denmark
{hcl, emanuele, soegaard}@di.ku.dk

Abstract

We aim to learn language models for Creole languages for which large volumes of data are not readily available, and therefore explore the potential transfer from ancestor languages (the 'Ancestry Transfer Hypothesis'). We find that standard transfer methods do not facilitate ancestry transfer. Surprisingly, different from other non-Creole languages, a very distinct two-phase pattern emerges for Creoles: As our training losses plateau, and language models begin to overfit on their source languages, perplexity on the Creoles *drop*. We explore if this *compression* phase can lead to practically useful language models (the 'Ancestry Bottleneck Hypothesis'), but also falsify this. Moreover, we show that Creoles even exhibit this two-phase pattern even when training on random, unrelated languages. Thus Creoles seem to be typological outliers and we speculate whether there is a link between the two observations.

1 Introduction

Creole languages refer to vernacular languages, many of which developed in colonial plantation settlements in the 17th and 18th centuries. Creoles most often emerged as a result of contact between social groups that spoke mutually unintelligible languages, i.e., from the interactions of speakers of nonstandard varieties of European languages and speakers of non-European languages (Lent et al., 2021). Some argue these languages have an exceptional status among the world's languages (McWhorter, 1998), while others counter that Creoles are not unique, and evolve in the typical manner as other languages (Aboh and DeGraff, 2016). In this paper, we will present experiments in evaluating language models trained on non-Creole languages for Creoles, as well as in various control settings. We first explore the following hypothesis:

R1: Language models trained on ancestor languages should transfer well to Creole languages.

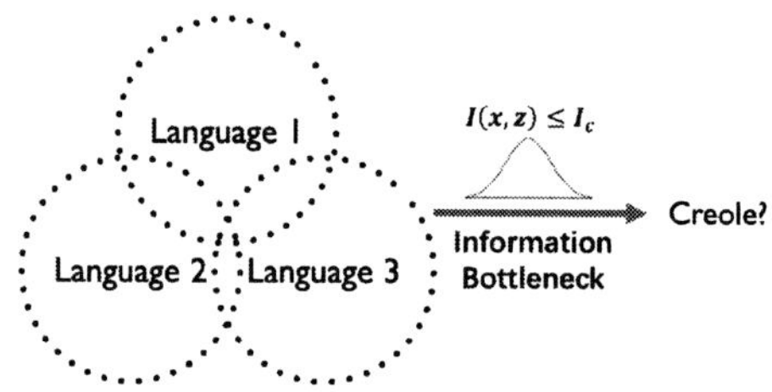

Figure 1: Does the Information Bottleneck principle capture some of the dynamics of Creole formation?

We call **R1** the 'Ancestry Transfer Hypothesis.' Our experiments, however, suggest that **R1** is *not* easily validated. We note, though, that ancestor-to-Creole training exhibits divergent behavior when training *for long*, leading to the following hypothesis:

R2: Language models trained on ancestor languages can, after a compression phase, transfer well to Creole languages.

We call **R2** the 'Ancestry Bottleneck Hypothesis.' While compression benefits transfer, performance never seems to reach useful levels. Furthermore, similar effects are observed with Creoles when training on non-ancestor languages. Our findings here are not relevant to applied NLP, but they shed light on cross-lingual training dynamics (Singh et al., 2019; Deshpande et al., 2021), and we believe they have potential implications for the linguistic study of Creoles (DeGraff, 2005b), as well as for information bottleneck theory (Tishby et al., 1999).

Our contributions We conduct a large set of experiments on cross-lingual zero-shot applications of language models to Creoles, primarily to test whether ancestor languages provide useful training data for Creoles (the 'Ancestry Transfer Hypothesis;' **R1**). Our results are a mix of negative and positive results: **First Negative Result:** Ordinary transfer methods do not enable ancestor-to-Creole transfer. **First Positive Result:** Regardless of the

Proceedings of the Third Workshop on Insights from Negative Results in NLP, pages 68 - 74
May 26, 2022 ©2022 Association for Computational Linguistics

Creole	Ancestors	Random Controls
Nigerian Pidgin	English, Hausa, Yoruba, Portuguese	Afrikaans, Cherokee, Hungarian, Quechua
Jamaican Patois	English, Hausa, Spanish, Igbo	Afrikaans, Cherokee, Hungarian, Quechua
Saint Lucian Creole	French, Hausa, Yoruba, Igbo	Afrikaans, Cherokee, Hungarian, Quechua
Haitian Creole	French, Fon, Spanish, Igbo	Afrikaans, Cherokee, Hungarian, Quechua
Non-Creole	**Relatives**	**Random Controls**
Spanish	French, Italian, Portuguese, Romanian	Afrikaans, Cherokee, Hungarian, Quechua
Danish	Norweigan, Icelandic, Swedish, German	Afrikaans, Cherokee, Hungarian, Quechua

Table 1: Transfer setups in our study. We aim to learn target Creoles and Non-Creoles by training on **1)** their Ancestors or Relatives, respectively; and **2)** languages unrelated to the target ones as a control (Random Controls).

source languages, when training for long periods of time, a compression phase takes places for Creoles: as the models overfit their training data, perplexity on Creoles begin to decrease. This pattern is unique to Creoles as it does not emerge for target non-Creole languages. **Second Negative Result:** The compression phase does not lead to better representations for downstream tasks in the target Creoles.

2 Background

Cross-lingual training dynamics Several multilingual language models have been presented and evaluated in recent years. Since Singh et al. (2019) showed that mBERT (Devlin et al., 2019) generalizes well across related languages, but compartmentalizes language families, several researchers have explored the training dynamics of training multilingual language models across related or distant language sets (Lauscher et al., 2020; Keung et al., 2020; Deshpande et al., 2021). Unlike most previous work on cross-lingual training, we focus on evaluation on unseen (Creole) languages. This set-up is also explored in previous work focusing on generalization to unseen scripts (Muller et al., 2021; Pfeiffer et al., 2021). Muller et al. (2021) argue that generalization to unseen languages is possible for seen scripts, but hard or impossible for unseen scripts, but this paper identifies a third category of unseen languages with seen scripts, which exhibit non-traditional learning curves in the zero-shot pre-training regime.

Linguistic theories of Creole Creolists have long debated whether Creole languages have an exceptional status among the world's languages (DeGraff, 2005a). McWhorter (1998) argue that Creoles are *simpler* than other languages, and defined by minimal usage of inflectional morphology, little or no use of tone encoding lexical or syntactic contrasts, and generally semantically transparent derivation. Others have argued that Creoles cannot be be unambiguously distinguished from non-Creoles on strictly structural, synchronic grounds (DeGraff, 2005a). On this view Creole grammars do not form a separate typological class, but exhibit many similarities with the grammars of their parent languages, e.g., the similarities in lexical case morphology between French and Haitian Creole. We do not take sides in this debate, but observe that the exceptionalist position would explain our results that zero-shot transfer to Creole languages is particularly difficult. Exceptionalism also aligns well with the heatmaps presented in §5.

Information Bottleneck The Information Bottleneck principle (Tishby et al., 1999) is an information-theoretic framework for extracting output-relevant representations of inputs, i.e., compressed, non-parametric and model-independent representations that are as informative as possible about the output. Compression is formalized by mutual information with input. A Lagrange multiplier controls the trade-off between these two quantities (informativity and compression). Being able to compute this trade-off assumes the joint input–output distribution is accessible. The trade-off is found by ignoring task-irrelevant factors and learning an invariant representation. The intuition behind the 'Ancestry Bottleneck Hypothesis' (**R2**) is that invariant representations are particularly useful for Creoles (see Figure 1 for an illustration).

3 Multilingual Training

This section sets out to evaluate the 'Ancestry Transfer Hypothesis' (**R1**). To this end, we evaluate multilingual language models – trained with a BERT architecture from scratch, but of smaller size and with less data (Dufter and Schütze, 2020) – on Creoles such as Nigerian Pidgin or Haitian Creole. We compare two scenarios: **1)** a scenario in which the training languages are languages that are

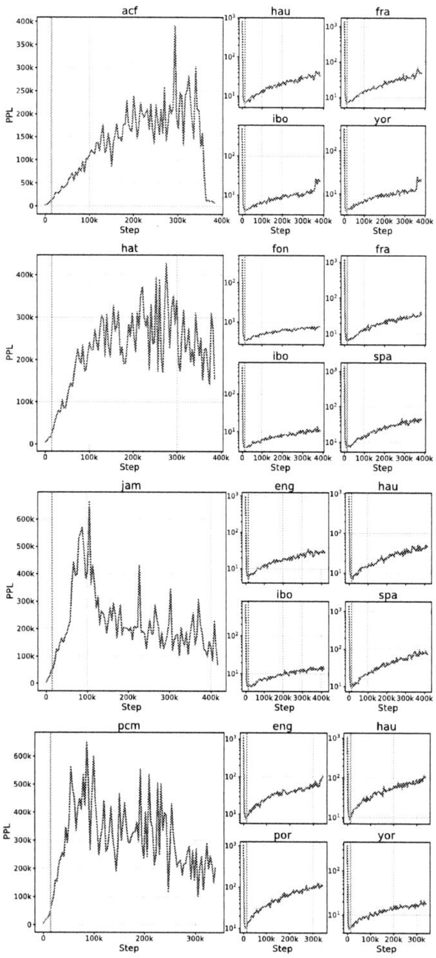

Figure 2: Four zero-shot transfer experiments for Creole languages. The left-hand side plot shows the (zero-shot) validation curve for checkpoints on Creole data; the small plots show the learning curves for the training languages. We see an initial increase in perplexity (disproving **R1**). The yellow vertical line denotes 100 epochs. We also see a subsequent decrease in perplexity.

said to be *parent* or *ancestor* languages of the Creole, such as French to Haitian, and **2)** a scenario in which *random*, unrelated training languages were selected. To compare against Creoles, we also explore these transfer scenarios for two target non-Creoles – Spanish and Danish – training on languages closely related to them (i.e., as typically done in cross-lingual learning). Table 1 lists all the transfer scenarios that we investigated. Our experimental protocol follows Dufter and Schütze (2020), and it is described in detail below.

We aim to learn language models for Creole languages for which large volumes of data are not readily available, and therefore explore the potential transfer from ancestor languages (the 'Ancestry Transfer Hypothesis'). We find that standard transfer methods do not facilitate ancestry transfer. Surprisingly, different from other non-Creole languages, a very distinct two-phase pattern emerges for Creoles: As our training losses plateau, and language models begin to overfit on their source languages, perplexity on the Creoles *drop*. We explore if this *compression* phase can lead to practically useful language models (the 'Ancestry Bottleneck Hypothesis'), but also falsify this. Moreover, we show that Creoles even exhibit this two-phase pattern even when training on random, unrelated languages. Thus Creoles seem to be typological outliers and we speculate whether there is a link between the two observations.

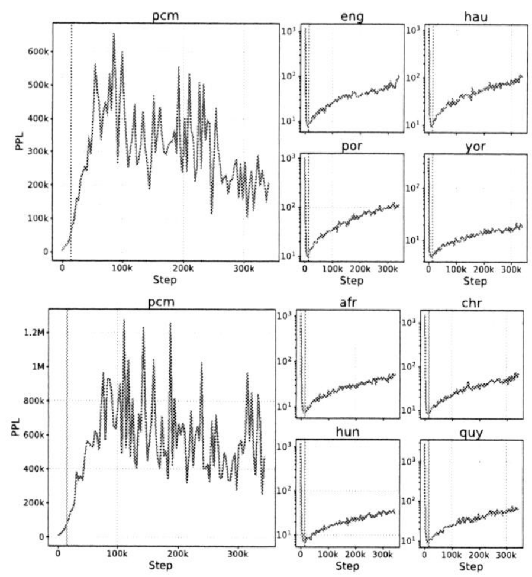

Figure 3: Learning curves for Nigerian Pidgin English when training on **ancestor** languages (top) and when training on **random** languages (bottom). No significant differences are observed. This disproves **R2**.

Experimental protocol We train BERT-smaller models (Dufter et al., 2020), consisting of a single attention head (shown to be sufficient for achieving multilinguality by K et al. 2020). Although training smaller models means our results are not directly comparable to larger models like mBERT or XLM-R (Conneau et al., 2019), there is evidence to support that smaller transformers can work better for smaller datasets (Susanto et al., 2019), and that the typical transformer architecture would likely be overparameterized for our small data (Kaplan et al., 2020). Thus, the BERT-smaller models appear to be the most appropriate match for our very small datasets. The models are trained on a multilingual dataset, consisting of an equal parts of each source

Hyperparameter	Creole	Non-Creole
Vocabulary size	10,240	10,240
Learning rate	1.00E-04	5.00E-05
Weight decay	1.00E-03	1.00E-03
Dropout	1.00E-01	1.00E-01
Batch size	256	256

Table 2: The hyperparameters used for target Creole and Non-Creole experiments. Vocab size, weight decay, and dropout were the same across Creole and Non-Creole experiments, however the Non-Creoles required a smaller learning rate, in order to successfully learn. All experiments were run on a TitanRTX GPU.

language, taken from the Bible Corpus (Mayer and Cysouw, 2014). We chose Bible data to train our models as it facilitates a controlled setup with parallel data in many languages whilst including our low-resource Creoles and ancestors. For each experiment, we learn a custom BERT tokenizer on source and target languages, with a vocabulary size of 10,240 word pieces (Wu et al., 2016).[1] Each model is trained for 100 epochs (see Table 2).

We also follow Dufter and Schütze (2020)'s approach of calculating the perplexity on 15% of randomly masked tokens (w), with probabilities (p), as $\exp(-1/n \sum_{k=1}^{n} \log(p_{w_k}))$. We calculate perplexity on held out development data for both source and target languages. Our code is available online.[2]

Results In Figure 2, by 100 epochs (indicated by a yellow vertical line), we observe two different patterns for Creoles and non-Creoles. For target Creole languages, the models are able to learn the ancestor languages, but perplexity on the held out Creoles consistently climbs. On the other hand, for target non-Creoles, we observe a slight initial drop in perplexity before it starts to increase as the models overfit the source languages.

4 Training For Longer

It seems linguistically plausible that training for longer on ancestor languages to learn more invariant representations should better facilitate zero-shot transfer to Creole languages. This is the essence of the 'Ancestry Bottleneck Hypothesis' (**R2**), which we explore in this section.

[1]We explored different vocabulary sizes (1,024, 2,048 and 10,240) as well as other tokenization techniques (grapheme-to-phoneme and byte-pair encodings Sennrich et al. 2016), which did not affect the overall findings discussed below.

[2]`https://github.com/hclent/ancestor-to-creole`

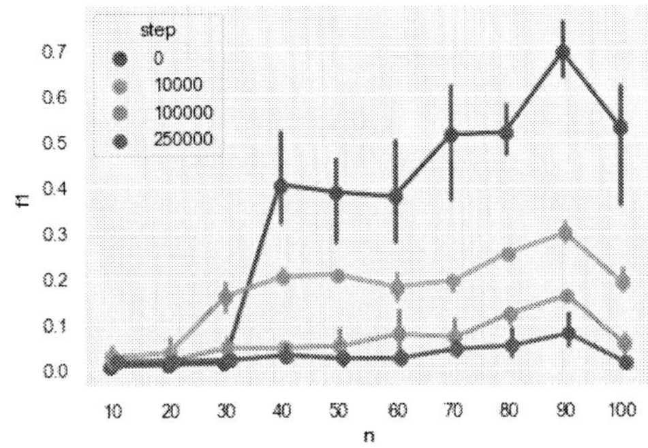

Figure 4: Results for downstream performance on Nigerian Pidgin NER, across 3 random seeds. The top row shows our model trained on ancestor of Nigerian Pidgin (pcm), while the bottom one shows results for mBERT. Step 0 in the legend refers to the pre-trained mBERT, without any further training on ancestor languages.

Creole compression We continue training our models for 5 days, for each Creole and non-Creole target language – which typically results in 300k–500k steps of training (and thus, extremely overfit). As the models overfit to the source languages, we observe a notable drop in perplexity for Creoles, which is true *regardless* of the training data (ancestors versus random controls), as shown in Figure 2 and Figure 3. On the other hand, these plots show that this compression does not emerge for non-Creole target languages, as their complexity steadily increases as the models overfit their training data more and more.

Downstream performance Next, in order to determine if this compression present for Creoles can be beneficial, we used MACHAMP (van der Goot et al., 2021) to check the ability of our Nigerian Pidgin models to fine-tune for downstream NER (Adelani et al., 2021). We evaluate the representations learned at different stages of pre-training by fine-tuning our checkpoints corresponding to early stage (10,000 steps), maximum perplexity, and post-compression (last checkpoint). Each model is fine-tuned for 10 epochs. Figure 4 shows that, across three random seeds, post-compression checkpoints consistently perform worse than pre-compression or max-complexity checkpoints. The results negate **R2**, i.e., that the compression effect observed during training would be useful for Creoles.[3]

Few-shot learning Finally, we assess the ability of our models to learn Creoles from few examples

[3]We also compared the results of a pre-trained mBERT, which, unsurprisingly, outperformed all of our checkpoints (corresponding to smaller models learned from tiny data).

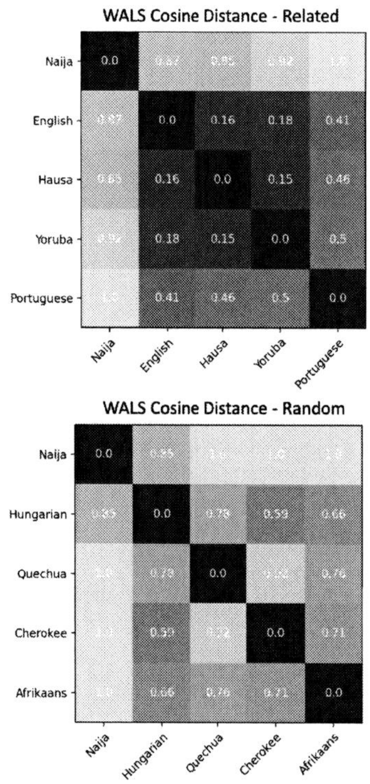

Figure 5: Heatmaps of WALS cosine distances between Nigerian Pidgin (Naija) and its parent and random training languages. We observe that Nigerian Pidgin is *less* related to any of these languages, than any of them internally (except Quechua and Cherokee).

(n=10, ..., 100) at different training stages. Once again, few-shot learning from post-compression checkpoints led to higher perplexity than training from maximum perplexity or early checkpoints.

5 Creoles through the Lens of WALS

We have observed unique patterns for Creoles. Namely, multilingual learning of the related languages did not lead to successful transfer to Creoles; and that Creoles exhibit a unique compression effect. Here, we speculate whether there is a link between these observations, and investigate whether typological features can shed lights into our results. To that effect, we use The World Atlas of Language Structures (WALS)[4], which has been used to study Creoles before (Daval-Markussen and Bakker, 2012). Here, we use the cosine distance between the normalized (full) WALS feature vectors as our distance metric.[5]

In Figure 5, we present an example heatmap for Nigerian Pidgin, which shows that Nigerian Pidgin is *less* related to ancestor and random languages than any of them internally (except Quechua and Cherokee). We found this pattern present for each of the Creoles. Thus, it would seem that Creoles' relatively large distance[6] from other languages may make cross-lingual transfer a particular challenge for learning Creoles.[7]

6 Conclusion

We have presented two hypotheses (**R1** and **R2**) about the possibility of zero-shot transfer to Creoles, both built on the idea that Creoles share characteristics with their ancestor languages. This is not exactly equivalent to the so-called superstratist view of Creole genesis, which maintains that Creoles are essentially regional varieties of their European ancestor languages, but if the superstratist view was correct, **R1** would very likely be easily validated (Singh et al., 2019). Our results show the opposite trend, however. Zero-shot transfer to Creole languages from their ancestor languages is hard. We do not claim that our results favor an exceptionalist position on Creoles. While we performed a first analysis of several segmentation approaches (i.e., BERT word piece, grapheme-to-phoneme, and byte-pair encodings) – which did not change the training dynamics – we believe that a rigorous comparison would be beneficial for future work in ancestor-to-Creole transfer. We hope that continued investigation in this direction can shed more light on cross-lingual transfer, especially with regards to Creoles, and that this work has demonstrated that not all transfer between related languages is trivial.

7 Acknowledgments

■ We would like to thank the reviewers for their feedback on this manuscript. This project has received funding from the European Union's Horizon 2020 research and innovation programme under the Marie Skłodowska-Curie grant agreement No 801199 (for Heather Lent and Emanuele Bugliarello) and the Google Research Award (for Heather Lent and Anders Søgaard).

[4] `wals.info`.

[5] `https://github.com/mayhewsw/wals`.

[6] We note that previous work has suggested that WALS features alone may be insufficient for typological comparison of Creoles to non-Creoles (Murawaki, 2016).

[7] We also note that cosine distance might not be meaningful here, as the normalized (full) space does not represent the feature geometry of the space that the linguists that developed the features in WALS were assuming.

References

Enoch Oladé Aboh and Michel DeGraff. 2016. A null theory of creole formation based on universal grammar.

David Ifeoluwa Adelani, Jade Abbott, Graham Neubig, Daniel D'souza, Julia Kreutzer, Constantine Lignos, Chester Palen-Michel, Happy Buzaaba, Shruti Rijhwani, Sebastian Ruder, Stephen Mayhew, Israel Abebe Azime, Shamsuddeen H. Muhammad, Chris Chinenye Emezue, Joyce Nakatumba-Nabende, Perez Ogayo, Aremu Anuoluwapo, Catherine Gitau, Derguene Mbaye, Jesujoba Alabi, Seid Muhie Yimam, Tajuddeen Rabiu Gwadabe, Ignatius Ezeani, Rubungo Andre Niyongabo, Jonathan Mukiibi, Verrah Otiende, Iroro Orife, Davis David, Samba Ngom, Tosin Adewumi, Paul Rayson, Mofetoluwa Adeyemi, Gerald Muriuki, Emmanuel Anebi, Chiamaka Chukwuneke, Nkiruka Odu, Eric Peter Wairagala, Samuel Oyerinde, Clemencia Siro, Tobius Saul Bateesa, Temilola Oloyede, Yvonne Wambui, Victor Akinode, Deborah Nabagereka, Maurice Katusiime, Ayodele Awokoya, Mouhamadane MBOUP, Dibora Gebreyohannes, Henok Tilaye, Kelechi Nwaike, Degaga Wolde, Abdoulaye Faye, Blessing Sibanda, Orevaoghene Ahia, Bonaventure F. P. Dossou, Kelechi Ogueji, Thierno Ibrahima DIOP, Abdoulaye Diallo, Adewale Akinfaderin, Tendai Marengereke, and Salomey Osei. 2021. MasakhaNER: Named entity recognition for African languages. *Transactions of the Association for Computational Linguistics*, 9:1116–1131.

Alexis Conneau, Kartikay Khandelwal, Naman Goyal, Vishrav Chaudhary, Guillaume Wenzek, Francisco Guzmán, Edouard Grave, Myle Ott, Luke Zettlemoyer, and Veselin Stoyanov. 2019. Unsupervised cross-lingual representation learning at scale. *CoRR*, abs/1911.02116.

Aymeric Daval-Markussen and Peter Bakker. 2012. Explorations in creole research with phylogenetic tools. In *EACL 2012*.

Michael DeGraff. 2005a. o creole languages constitute an exceptional typological class? *Revue française de linguistique appliquée*, 10(1):11–24.

Michel DeGraff. 2005b. Linguists' most dangerous myth: The fallacy of creole exceptionalism. *Language in Society*, 34:533 – 591.

Ameet Deshpande, Partha Talukdar, and Karthik Narasimhan. 2021. When is bert multilingual? isolating crucial ingredients for cross-lingual transfer.

Jacob Devlin, Ming-Wei Chang, Kenton Lee, and Kristina Toutanova. 2019. BERT: Pre-training of deep bidirectional transformers for language understanding. In *Proceedings of the 2019 Conference of the North American Chapter of the Association for Computational Linguistics: Human Language Technologies, Volume 1 (Long and Short Papers)*, pages 4171–4186, Minneapolis, Minnesota. Association for Computational Linguistics.

Philipp Dufter, Martin Schmitt, and Hinrich Schütze. 2020. Increasing learning efficiency of self-attention networks through direct position interactions, learnable temperature, and convoluted attention. In *Proceedings of the 28th International Conference on Computational Linguistics*, pages 3630–3636, Barcelona, Spain (Online). International Committee on Computational Linguistics.

Philipp Dufter and Hinrich Schütze. 2020. Identifying elements essential for BERT's multilinguality. In *Proceedings of the 2020 Conference on Empirical Methods in Natural Language Processing (EMNLP)*, pages 4423–4437, Online. Association for Computational Linguistics.

Karthikeyan K, Zihan Wang, Stephen Mayhew, and Dan Roth. 2020. Cross-lingual ability of multilingual bert: An empirical study. *ArXiv*, abs/1912.07840.

Jared Kaplan, Sam McCandlish, Tom Henighan, Tom B. Brown, Benjamin Chess, Rewon Child, Scott Gray, Alec Radford, Jeffrey Wu, and Dario Amodei. 2020. Scaling laws for neural language models. *CoRR*, abs/2001.08361.

Phillip Keung, Yichao Lu, Julian Salazar, and Vikas Bhardwaj. 2020. Don't use English dev: On the zero-shot cross-lingual evaluation of contextual embeddings. In *Proceedings of the 2020 Conference on Empirical Methods in Natural Language Processing (EMNLP)*, pages 549–554, Online. Association for Computational Linguistics.

Anne Lauscher, Vinit Ravishankar, Ivan Vulić, and Goran Glavaš. 2020. From zero to hero: On the limitations of zero-shot language transfer with multilingual Transformers. In *Proceedings of the 2020 Conference on Empirical Methods in Natural Language Processing (EMNLP)*, pages 4483–4499, Online. Association for Computational Linguistics.

Heather Lent, Emanuele Bugliarello, Miryam de Lhoneux, Chen Qiu, and Anders Søgaard. 2021. On language models for creoles. In *Proceedings of the 25th Conference on Computational Natural Language Learning (CoNLL)*, page (to appear), Punta Cana, Dominican Republic. Association for Computational Linguistics.

Thomas Mayer and Michael Cysouw. 2014. Creating a massively parallel Bible corpus. In *Proceedings of the Ninth International Conference on Language Resources and Evaluation (LREC'14)*, pages 3158–3163, Reykjavik, Iceland. European Language Resources Association (ELRA).

John H. McWhorter. 1998. Identifying the creole prototype: Vindicating a typological class. 74(4):788–818.

Benjamin Muller, Antonios Anastasopoulos, Benoît Sagot, and Djamé Seddah. 2021. When being unseen from mBERT is just the beginning: Handling new languages with multilingual language models.

In *Proceedings of the 2021 Conference of the North American Chapter of the Association for Computational Linguistics: Human Language Technologies*, pages 448–462, Online. Association for Computational Linguistics.

Yugo Murawaki. 2016. Statistical modeling of creole genesis. In *NAACL*.

Jonas Pfeiffer, Ivan Vulić, Iryna Gurevych, and Sebastian Ruder. 2021. UNKs everywhere: Adapting multilingual language models to new scripts. In *Proceedings of the 2021 Conference on Empirical Methods in Natural Language Processing*, pages 10186–10203, Online and Punta Cana, Dominican Republic. Association for Computational Linguistics.

Rico Sennrich, Barry Haddow, and Alexandra Birch. 2016. Neural machine translation of rare words with subword units. In *Proceedings of the 54th Annual Meeting of the Association for Computational Linguistics (Volume 1: Long Papers)*, pages 1715–1725, Berlin, Germany. Association for Computational Linguistics.

Jasdeep Singh, Bryan McCann, Richard Socher, and Caiming Xiong. 2019. BERT is not an interlingua and the bias of tokenization. In *Proceedings of the 2nd Workshop on Deep Learning Approaches for Low-Resource NLP (DeepLo 2019)*, pages 47–55, Hong Kong, China. Association for Computational Linguistics.

Raymond Hendy Susanto, Ohnmar Htun, and Liling Tan. 2019. Sarah's participation in WAT 2019. In *Proceedings of the 6th Workshop on Asian Translation*, pages 152–158, Hong Kong, China. Association for Computational Linguistics.

Naftali Tishby, Fernando C. Pereira, and William Bialek. 1999. The information bottleneck method. pages 368–377.

Rob van der Goot, Ahmet Üstün, Alan Ramponi, Ibrahim Sharaf, and Barbara Plank. 2021. Massive choice, ample tasks (machamp):a toolkit for multitask learning in nlp.

Yonghui Wu, Mike Schuster, Zhifeng Chen, Quoc V Le, Mohammad Norouzi, Wolfgang Macherey, Maxim Krikun, Yuan Cao, Qin Gao, Klaus Macherey, et al. 2016. Google's neural machine translation system: Bridging the gap between human and machine translation. *arXiv preprint arXiv:1609.08144*.

What GPT Knows About Who is Who

Xiaohan Yang, Eduardo Peynetti, Vasco Meerman and **Chris Tanner**
Institute for Applied Computational Science
Harvard University
xiaohan_yang@g.harvard.edu, eduardo.peynetti@gmail.com,
vmeerman@g.harvard.edu, christanner@g.harvard.edu

Abstract

Coreference resolution – which is a crucial task for understanding discourse and language at large – has yet to witness widespread benefits from large language models (LLMs). Moreover, coreference resolution systems largely rely on supervised labels, which are highly expensive and difficult to annotate, thus making it ripe for prompt engineering. In this paper, we introduce a QA-based prompt-engineering method and discern *generative*, pre-trained LLMs' abilities and limitations toward the task of coreference resolution. Our experiments show that GPT-2 and GPT-Neo can return valid answers, but that their capabilities to identify coreferent mentions are limited and prompt-sensitive, leading to inconsistent results.

1 Introduction

Coreference resolution (CR) aims to identify and cluster all words (i.e., mentions) that refer to the same entity or event. Solving this task is essential for natural language understanding, as mismatched references will lead to bias. Recent improvements in CR have been incremental (Lee et al., 2017; Joshi et al., 2020; Cattan et al., 2020), compared to other NLP tasks that have demonstrated more real-world impact. One reason is the limited training corpora. For example, one of the primary datasets, ECB+ (Cybulska and Vossen, 2014), contains only 984 documents, including 6,833 mentions and 2,741 clusters. Moreover, this dataset was built around 43 news topics ten years ago, potentially leading to generalization problems for the state-of-the-art (SOTA) models.

When dealing with low-resource tasks, there is an emerging trend to perform *prompt engineering* with pre-trained LMs. Unlike fine-tuning (Brown et al., 2020; Wei et al., 2021), prompt engineering does not update the pre-trained model's weights when completing the downstream task. Instead, one transforms the downstream task to match the original task of the pre-trained model (Liu et al., 2021). For example, for machine translation, one can create prompts such as "English: I love bread. French:" and input them to a generative LM (e.g., GPT-2). If the pre-trained model encountered similar patterns during training, it should be able to generate the translated French sentence. Nevertheless, to the best of our knowledge, there is scarce research on applying this approach to coreference resolution (Sanh et al., 2021).

To better understand if pre-trained LMs can help resolve coreferences, we construct a QA-based prompting method and experiment with both GPT-2 (Radford et al., 2019) and GPT-Neo (Gao et al., 2020). By using this prompting methodology, we measure if these models can predict whether two mentions are coreferent. For evaluation, we use the ECB+ dataset, which provides gold mentions and clustering labels. We compare the results with unsupervised and supervised coreference resolution models, including a classic rule-based system (Lee et al., 2011), the seminal end-to-end neural model (Lee et al., 2017), and a recent SOTA model (Cattan et al., 2020).

2 Related Work

Prompt-based learning Prompt-based learning is a fast-growing area in NLP, as it can reduce the need to fine-tune models and rely on supervised labels. According to the survey by Liu et al., over 120 papers have been published since 2019, which collectively demonstrates effectiveness toward many different tasks: text classification (Tam et al., 2021; Holtzman et al., 2021), factual probing (Perez et al., 2021), question-answering (Tsimpoukelli et al., 2021), and more. Nevertheless, to the best of our knowledge, only one prompt-based learning paper concerned CR. Specifically, Sanh et al. introduces T0, a zero-shot generalization of T5 (Raffel et al., 2019). The authors convert various supervised datasets into task-specific prompts,

Proceedings of the Third Workshop on Insights from Negative Results in NLP, pages 75 - 81
May 26, 2022 ©2022 Association for Computational Linguistics

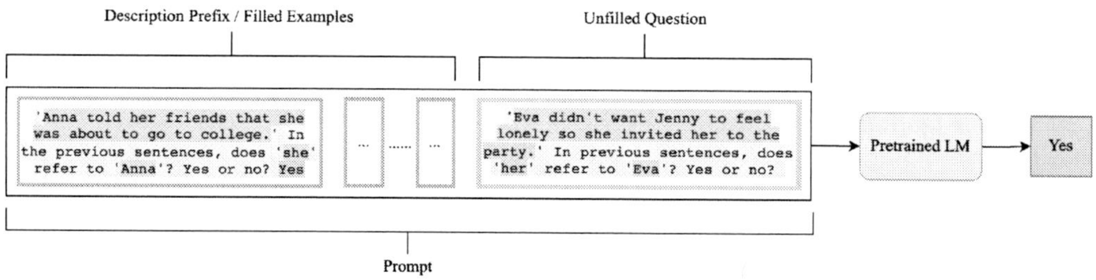

Figure 1: An example of prompt-based learning for CR. The green block represents the prefix, which serves as the description of the CR task and remains unchanged throughout an experiment for all inputs x. The purple block is the unfilled prompt, which changes for each input x and serves as the prediction. Moreover, in each block, the yellow part is the prompting function while the blue and red parts are the original data x and y, respectively.

including CR. Using the WSC dataset (Levesque et al., 2012), they achieve over 60% accuracy. Although this result is not comparable with supervised state-of-the-art (SOTA) models, it still offers compelling results and suggests the model might contain CR knowledge without requiring supervised training on the task. However, since the WSC dataset only focuses on highly ambiguous pronouns, it is not as complete as the standard CR task that involves named and nominal mentions.

Traditional CR Models Similar to other NLP tasks, most CR models can be categorized as being either unsupervised or supervised. A commonly used unsupervised model is the *Multi-Pass Sieve* model (Lee et al., 2011). This rule-based system extracts entity mentions and clusters them by applying 13 "filters" in successive manner. Amongst supervised models, *e2e-coref* (Lee et al., 2017) is the seminal end-to-end neural model. This model performs within-document CR and was trained on the OntoNotes (CoNLL-2012) dataset. Building on this architecture, Cattan et al. (2020) performs cross-document CR for entities and events by training on the ECB+ dataset and using RoBERTa (Liu et al., 2019) as an encoder. Although supervised models offer significant improvements over unsupervised models, they are expensive to train; most SOTA models have $O(n^4)$ complexity, where n is the length of each document.

3 Methodology

This section introduces our prompt-based learning method for CR. Typically, CR models can be broken down into three sub-tasks: (1) detecting mentions; (2) predicting whether two given mentions are coreferent or not; (3) and clustering mentions accordingly. The crux of CR research centers around the second part, which is also our focus.

Building on the approach introduced by Sanh et al. (2021), we define our input x as $[text, m_1, m_2]$ and output y as a binary label. Specifically, m_1 and m_2 are a pair of gold mentions in a document, and the $text$ are the sentences containing those mentions. For example, in Figure 1, within each green box, the successive blue parts are $text$, m_1, m_2, respectively. We define a prompting function f, which takes x as input and produces a question prompt q_x (Equation 1). Further details about f are in Appendix A.

$$q_x = f(x) \tag{1}$$

Moreover, to allow the model to understand the task, we use few-shot learning (Triantafillou et al., 2017) by constructing a filled prefix. In particular, we select k examples, A, from the training dataset and feed these examples into the same prompting function f. Then, we append the true label ('Yes' or 'No') to the outputs, yielding the filled prefix q_A (Equation 2). To be clear, each individual prefix $q_{i \in k}$ constitutes a single green box in Figure 1.

$$q_A = f(A) \tag{2}$$

Last, adding the unfilled prompt q_x to the filled prefix q_A will give us the full prompt for data point x. This allows us to get a prediction z without updating any parameters θ in the pre-trained LM.

$$z = P(q_A + q_x; \theta) \tag{3}$$

Since we use pre-trained LMs directly, without fine-tuning, we do not have control over its output; the model can generate invalid answers beyond our desired outputs, 'Yes' or 'No'. Therefore, we repeat the process m times to get a more robust prediction $\bar{z}$. To mitigate the bias of one specific f, we average the output of n different prompt formulas to get the final prediction (Equation 4).

$$y = \frac{\sum_{i=1}^{n} \bar{z}_i}{n} \tag{4}$$

4 Experimental Setup

Datasets We use the ECB+ dataset (Cybulska and Vossen, 2014) as our input source, which contains both within- and cross-document coreference information for both event and entity mentions. This dataset consists of 984 documents around 43 news topics, among which 196 documents are in the development set. After preprocessing the data, as described in Appendix B, our development set consists of 172 documents.

To generate a prefix x_0, we experiment with three data sources: the training sets of WSC (Levesque et al., 2012) and ECB+ (Cybulska and Vossen, 2014), and a simple dataset that we manually generated. The WSC dataset was used in the research most similar to ours, T0 (Sanh et al., 2021), which we compare against while using much smaller pretrained LMs (i.e., GPT-2 and GPT-Neo). As mentioned, ECB+ provides more natural and comprehensive references than WSC. Our manually generated dataset uses 10 very simple examples – allowing one to discern the impact on performance.

When using the ECB+ dataset, we only considered pairs of mentions that are within the same or successive sentences. When evaluating our model, we considered all mention-pair combinations, $[m_1, m_2]$, within said sentences. Relying on the gold mentions, we obtain a dataset with 17832 candidate mention pairs, among which 7.86% are positive samples. Finally, we apply 5 prompt functions from Sanh et al. to generate the full prompts.

Models We used three traditional CR models as baselines: *Multi-Pass Sieve* (Lee et al., 2011), the seminal end-to-end neural model (*e2e-coref*) (Lee et al., 2017), and a SOTA extension (the *Streamlining* model) (Cattan et al., 2020). Respectively, these models represent three categories: a rules-based model, a supervised model trained on a different dataset, and a supervised model trained on the same dataset. In terms of implementations, we use the CoreNLP toolkit for the *Multi-Pass Sieve* model (Manning et al., 2014) and AllenNLP (Gardner et al., 2018) for *e2e-coref*. Since there is no publicly available pre-trained *Streamlining* model (Cattan et al., 2020), we fully train the model from scratch using a V100 GPU on Google Colab. To fairly compare with other models, we set a 0.5 threshold for the pairwise scorer in the Streamlining model. We evaluate all models by their mention pairwise scorers, not their clustering decisions.

Limited by our computational resources, we choose GPT-2 and GPT-Neo-125M as our pretrained LMs [1]. During inference, the output token length is set to 1, since our expected output is one word (i.e., 'Yes' or 'No'). To generate more robust results, the repetition parameter m is set to 5. We ran our text generative models with multiple temperature settings ranging from 0 to 1, none of which produced significant changes. We settled on using a value of 0.7, to limit the greediness of the generated responses. In terms of few-shot learning, we experimented with $k \in \{0, 2, 4, 10\}$ and display the results from the 4-shot setting since it produces the best accuracy. To reduce bias introduced by prefixes, we ensure each prefix has equally-balanced samples. For example, for the 4-shot setting, the filled prefix will have 2 positive examples and 2 negative examples.

5 Results and Analysis

	Yes/No Predictions
0-shot	5%
2-shot	93.7%
4-shot	96.2%
10-shot	98%

Table 1: Percentage of Yes/No predictions by GPT-2

We first question if GPT-based models can produce valid answers. In Figure 1, we observe that GPT-2 predicts 'Yes' or 'No' for over 93.7% samples when at least 2 filled prefixes are provided.

However, although the answers are valid, they are inaccurate. In Figure 2, we plot the distribution of predicted labels for each model, where the red bars denote the distribution of positive examples (ground truth), and the blue bars denote negative ones (ground truth). Traditional CR models generally predict low values for negative examples, indicated by blue bars being concentrated at 0. As for positive examples, *e2e-coref* shows better precision since more positive examples are classified

[1]Our code can be found at `https://github.com/AwesomeCoref/prompt-coref`

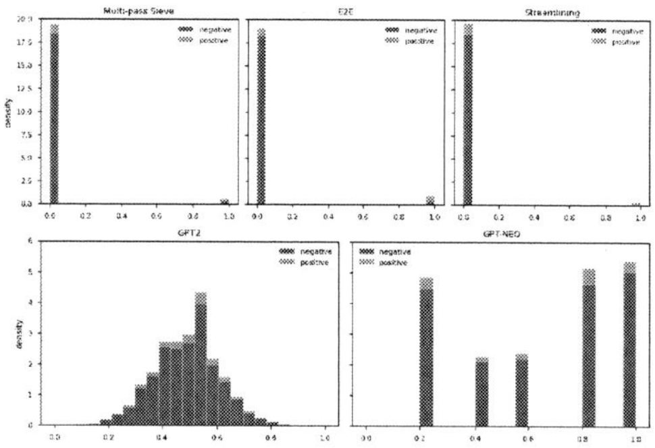

Figure 2: Distribution of predicted values

correctly at 1. Yet, GPT-2 seems to be both sensitive to prompts and unstable over the repetitions of each prompt. Furthermore, GPT-Neo's predictions are inaccurate and no better than random, even though it predicts consistent results for multiple runs with the same prompt.

Similar conclusions can be drawn from Table 2, where GPT-based models have the lowest AUC and F1 scores. Specifically, the extremely low precision causes the bad results. Since the ECB+ dataset is highly imbalanced, random predictions from GPT-based models will lead to a low precision, reflecting the proportion of positive samples. For completeness, we also perform an experiment on the WSC dataset (see GPT-2_{wsc}), which is a test dataset used by Sanh et al. (2021). GPT-2 also fails on this task, as its mean prediction averaged across different prompts is always "Yes" .

	Acc	Prec	Rec	F1	AUC
Multi Sieve	0.93	0.39	0.20	0.27	0.59
e2e-coref	0.95	0.62	0.46	0.53	0.72
Streamline	0.93	0.87	0.19	0.31	0.59
GPT-2	0.50	0.08	0.53	0.14	0.51
GPT-NEO	0.38	0.08	0.68	0.15	0.52
GPT-2_{wsc}	0.37	0.37	1.00	0.54	0.50

Table 2: Performance of different models.

POS and Entity Types While the overall performance indicates that GPT models are comparable to a random model, we hypothesize that for some subset of mention pairs, GPT might perform better. To investigate, we conducted experiments based on part-of-speech (POS) tags and named-entity types. Figure 3 shows that both GPT-2 and GPT-Neo can capture coreferent relationships relatively better when the second mention is a pronoun. Moreover, this trend is stronger when the first mention is a pronoun or a proper noun. Nonetheless, *e2e-coref* performs better than both GPT models across all POS tags, and the gap is widest when the second mention is a nominal noun phrase.

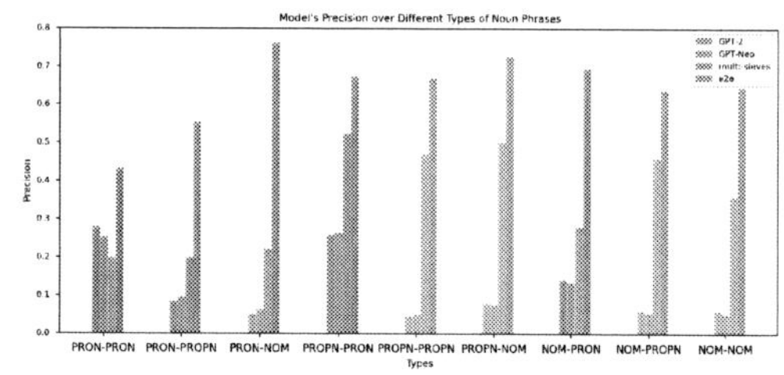

Figure 3: Model's precision over various types of noun phrases, including pronouns, proper nouns and nominal nouns. Each bar's hue intensity denotes the data density.

As for named entities, Figure 4 shows that both GPT-2 and GPT-Neo perform better in precision when one mention is of type PERSON. Moreover, GPT-Neo can identify coreferent relationships more precisely if the second mention is Non-GPE locations (i.e., LOC). However, their precision scores are far lower than the scores from classical CR models. In particular, both the multi-pass sieve model and e2e-coref model reach the highest precision when a mention is a PRODUCT object (e.g., vehicle, food) or a NORP object (e.g., nationality, religious or political group).

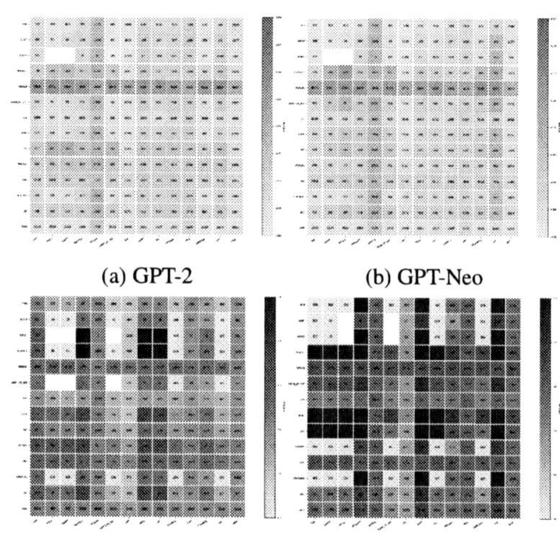

(a) GPT-2 (b) GPT-Neo (c) Multi-pass Sieve (d) e2e-coref

Figure 4: GPT-2's performance on different named-entity types. We use colors to denote performance and the text to show data density in each category.

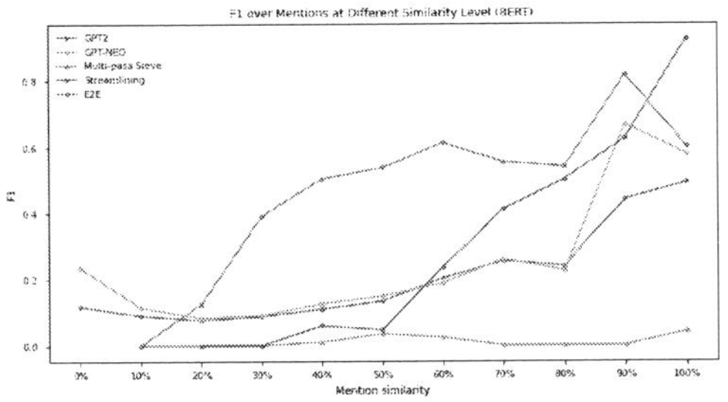

Figure 5: Different models' F1 score over various level of mention similarities based on BERT embedding.

Mention Similarity In addition to inspecting how performance varies with mention *types*, we also considered how performance is affected by mentions' similarity. Using pre-trained BERT (Devlin et al., 2018), we encode each mention into span representations by averaging its tokens' last hidden states. Then, we measure cosine similarity between mention pairs.

Figure 5 shows that F1 scores generally improve as the semantic similarity increases. Although, the multi-pass sieve model maintains a low F1 because it is a rule-based model that tends to predict False for most samples – which yields a high accuracy for unbalanced datasets. The e2e-coref model performs well on mentions that are not so similar, while the performance of Streamlining model improves drastically as similarity is greater than 50%. However, both GPT-2 and GPT-NEO yield low F1 (approximately 0.2) for mention pairs with less than 70% similarity. When considering mentions of higher similarity, GPT-based models can achieve over 0.4 F1 score.

6 Conclusion

In this paper, we rely on prompt-based learning to analyze how much GPT-like models know about coreference resolution. Despite the popularity of prompting in recent NLP research, we find that LLMs perform poorly on this task without fine-tuning. Nonetheless, these models achieve relatively better performance for specific types of mentions, including pronouns and person objects, and mention pairs with high similarity.

References

Tom B. Brown, Benjamin Mann, Nick Ryder, Melanie Subbiah, Jared Kaplan, Prafulla Dhariwal, Arvind Neelakantan, Pranav Shyam, Girish Sastry, Amanda Askell, Sandhini Agarwal, Ariel Herbert-Voss, Gretchen Krueger, Tom Henighan, Rewon Child, Aditya Ramesh, Daniel M. Ziegler, Jeffrey Wu, Clemens Winter, Christopher Hesse, Mark Chen, Eric Sigler, Mateusz Litwin, Scott Gray, Benjamin Chess, Jack Clark, Christopher Berner, Sam McCandlish, Alec Radford, Ilya Sutskever, and Dario Amodei. 2020. Language models are few-shot learners. *NeurIPS*.

Arie Cattan, Alon Eirew, Gabriel Stanovsky, Mandar Joshi, and Ido Dagan. 2020. Streamlining cross-document coreference resolution: Evaluation and modeling. *arXiv preprint arXiv:2009.11032*.

Agata Cybulska and Piek Vossen. 2014. Using a sledgehammer to crack a nut? lexical diversity and event coreference resolution. In *Proceedings of the Ninth International Conference on Language Resources and Evaluation (LREC'14)*, pages 4545–4552, Reykjavik, Iceland. European Language Resources Association (ELRA).

Jacob Devlin, Ming-Wei Chang, Kenton Lee, and Kristina Toutanova. 2018. Bert: Pre-training of deep bidirectional transformers for language understanding. *arXiv preprint arXiv:1810.04805*.

Leo Gao, Stella Biderman, Sid Black, Laurence Golding, Travis Hoppe, Charles Foster, Jason Phang, Horace He, Anish Thite, Noa Nabeshima, et al. 2020. The pile: An 800gb dataset of diverse text for language modeling. *arXiv preprint arXiv:2101.00027*.

Matt Gardner, Joel Grus, Mark Neumann, Oyvind Tafjord, Pradeep Dasigi, Nelson F. Liu, Matthew E. Peters, Michael Schmitz, and Luke Zettlemoyer. 2018. Allennlp: A deep semantic natural language processing platform. *CoRR*, abs/1803.07640.

Ari Holtzman, Peter West, Vered Schwartz, Yejin Choi, and Luke Zettlemoyer. 2021. Surface form competition: Why the highest probability answer isn't always right. *arXiv preprint arXiv:2104.08315*.

Mandar Joshi, Danqi Chen, Yinhan Liu, Daniel S. Weld, Luke Zettlemoyer, and Omer Levy. 2020. SpanBERT: Improving Pre-training by Representing and Predicting Spans. *Transactions of the Association for Computational Linguistics*, 8:64–77.

Heeyoung Lee, Yves Peirsman, Angel Chang, Nathanael Chambers, Mihai Surdeanu, and Dan Jurafsky. 2011. Stanford's multi-pass sieve coreference resolution system at the conll-2011 shared task. In *Proceedings of the 15th conference on computational natural language learning: Shared task*, pages 28–34. Association for Computational Linguistics.

Kenton Lee, Luheng He, Mike Lewis, and Luke Zettlemoyer. 2017. End-to-end neural coreference resolution.

Hector Levesque, Ernest Davis, and Leora Morgenstern. 2012. The winograd schema challenge. In *Thirteenth International Conference on the Principles of Knowledge Representation and Reasoning*.

Pengfei Liu, Weizhe Yuan, Jinlan Fu, Zhengbao Jiang, Hiroaki Hayashi, and Graham Neubig. 2021. Pre-train, prompt, and predict: A systematic survey of prompting methods in natural language processing. *ArXiv*, abs/2107.13586.

Yinhan Liu, Myle Ott, Naman Goyal, Jingfei Du, Mandar Joshi, Danqi Chen, Omer Levy, Mike Lewis, Luke Zettlemoyer, and Veselin Stoyanov. 2019. Roberta: A robustly optimized bert pretraining approach. *arXiv preprint arXiv:1907.11692*.

Christopher D Manning, Mihai Surdeanu, John Bauer, Jenny Rose Finkel, Steven Bethard, and David McClosky. 2014. The stanford corenlp natural language processing toolkit. In *Proceedings of 52nd annual meeting of the association for computational linguistics: system demonstrations*, pages 55–60.

Ethan Perez, Douwe Kiela, and Kyunghyun Cho. 2021. True few-shot learning with language models. *arXiv preprint arXiv:2105.11447*.

Alec Radford, Jeffrey Wu, Rewon Child, David Luan, Dario Amodei, Ilya Sutskever, et al. 2019. Language models are unsupervised multitask learners. *OpenAI blog*, 1(8):9.

Colin Raffel, Noam Shazeer, Adam Roberts, Katherine Lee, Sharan Narang, Michael Matena, Yanqi Zhou, Wei Li, and Peter J Liu. 2019. Exploring the limits of transfer learning with a unified text-to-text transformer. *arXiv preprint arXiv:1910.10683*.

Victor Sanh, Albert Webson, Colin Raffel, Stephen H. Bach, Lintang Sutawika, Zaid Alyafeai, Antoine Chaffin, Arnaud Stiegler, Teven Le Scao, Arun Raja, Manan Dey, M Saiful Bari, Canwen Xu, Urmish Thakker, Shanya Sharma Sharma, Eliza Szczechla, Taewoon Kim, Gunjan Chhablani, Nihal Nayak, Debajyoti Datta, Jonathan Chang, Mike Tian-Jian Jiang, Han Wang, Matteo Manica, Sheng Shen, Zheng Xin Yong, Harshit Pandey, Rachel Bawden, Thomas Wang, Trishala Neeraj, Jos Rozen, Abheesht Sharma, Andrea Santilli, Thibault Fevry, Jason Alan Fries, Ryan Teehan, Stella Biderman, Leo Gao, Tali Bers, Thomas Wolf, and Alexander M. Rush. 2021. Multitask prompted training enables zero-shot task generalization.

D Tam, RR Menon, M Bansal, S Srivastava, and C Raffel. 2021. Improving and simplifying pattern exploiting training 2021. *arXiv preprint arXiv:2103.11955*.

Eleni Triantafillou, Richard Zemel, and Raquel Urtasun. 2017. Few-shot learning through an information retrieval lens.

Maria Tsimpoukelli, Jacob Menick, Serkan Cabi, SM Ali Eslami, Oriol Vinyals, and Felix Hill. 2021. Multimodal few-shot learning with frozen language models. In *Thirty-Fifth Conference on Neural Information Processing Systems*.

Jason Wei, Maarten Bosma, Vincent Y Zhao, Kelvin Guu, Adams Wei Yu, Brian Lester, Nan Du, Andrew M Dai, and Quoc V Le. 2021. Finetuned language models are zero-shot learners. *arXiv preprint arXiv:2109.01652*.

A Prompt formulas

```
'[TEXT]' In the previous sentences, does '[MENTION2]' refer
to '[MENTION1]'? Yes or no?
```

```
'[TEXT]' Here, by '[MENTION2]' they mean '[MENTION1]'? Yes
or no?
```

```
'[TEXT]' Here, does '[MENTION2]' stand for '[MENTION1]'? Yes
or no?
```

```
'[TEXT]' In the passage above, can '[MENTION2]' be replaced
by '[MENTION1]'? Yes or no?
```

```
'[TEXT]' I think '[MENTION2]' means '[MENTION1]'. Yes or no?
```

Figure 6: Prompt Formulas. We experiment with these 5 prompt formulas mentioned in Sanh et al. (2021). Here, each block is one formula and the parts highlighted in blue are $[text, m_1, m_2]$ respectively.

B Data Preprocessing

The original ECB+ dataset is in XML format, where everything is tokenized. Moreover, the information about gold mentions and gold clusters is related to token ids. However, we cannot easily get the plain text by joining tokens with a space character. If we do so, we will get strange looking text as shown below.

> http : / / www . accesshollywood . com / lindsay - lohan - leaves - betty - ford - checks - into - malibu - rehab _ article _ 80744 Lindsay Lohan Leaves Betty Ford , Checks Into Malibu Rehab First Published : June 13 , 2013 4 : 59 PM EDT Lindsay Lohan has left the Betty Ford Center and is moving to a rehab facility in Malibu , Calif . , Access Hollywood has confirmed .

In this example, we can see objects like urls, datetime and punctuation are not in the right format. Since we are using the text as an input to the prompt function, we need to properly format them to align with normal text that GPTs are trained on. Moreover, as gold mention and gold clusters are based on original token ids in ECB+, when we parsed and re-formatted the data, we could match these ids again. Continuing with the previous example, our parsing algorithm cleans up the previous text to be something as follows.

> http://www.accesshollywood.com/lindsay-lohan-leaves-betty-ford-checks-into-malibu-rehab_article_80744 [EOS] Lindsay Lohan Leaves Betty Ford, Checks Into Malibu Rehab First Published: June 13, 2013 4: 59 PM EDT [EOS] Lindsay Lohan has left the Betty Ford Center and is moving to a rehab facility in Malibu, Calif., Access Hollywood has confirmed. [EOS]

C Additional Results

Here are additional results for our experiments.

Experiments on Prefix The aggregate results from few shot learning are displayed in Table 3. Our results show that 4-shots learning performs the best for both GPT-2 and GPT-NEO in terms of accuracy. Unexpectedly, as we increase the size of examples, the result does not improve accordingly. Given 10 examples in prefix, the model tend to predict "yes" more easily. One possible explanation might be that we have balanced examples in prefix while the actual querying data only have around 8% positive samples.

	Acc	Prec	Recall	F1	AUC
2-shots	0.39	0.08	0.64	0.14	0.50
4-shots	0.51	0.08	0.51	0.14	0.51
10-shots	0.19	0.08	0.90	0.15	0.51

Table 3: n-shot performance from the text generative models

	Acc	Prec	Recall	F1	AUC
simple	0.61	0.08	0.36	0.13	0.50
WSC	0.08	0.08	1.00	0.15	0.50
ecb+	0.54	0.08	0.48	0.14	0.51

Table 4: Average results from each dataset that is used for the experiments

Moreover, we experiment with various datasets for prefix as discussed in section 4. The results in Table 4 shows that prefix does have an impact on the results. The prefix generated from ECB+ dataset performs slightly better than others regarding to AUC. This is understandable because we evaluate on the ECB+ development set. Beyond our expectation, WSC-prefix result in a perfect recall and a super bad accuracy, which means that this prefix lead models to generate "yes" regardless of the context. This result further proves that GPT-2 is very sensitive to prompts.

Evaluating Biomedical Word Embeddings for Vocabulary Alignment at Scale in the UMLS Metathesaurus Using Siamese Networks

Goonmeet Bajaj[1], **Vinh Nguyen**[2], **Thilini Wijesiriwardene**[3], **Hong Yung Yip**[3], **Vishesh Javangula**[4], **Srinivasan Parthasarathy**[1], **Amit Sheth**[3], **Olivier Bodenreider**[2]
[1] The Ohio State University, [2] National Library of Medicine, [3] University of South Carolina, [4] George Washington University
{bajaj.32, parthasarathy.2}@osu.edu, vinh.nguyen@nih.gov, obodenreider@mail.nih.gov, {thilini, amit}@sc.edu, visheshj123@gwu.edu, hyip@email.sc.edu,

Abstract

Recent work uses a Siamese Network, initialized with BioWordVec embeddings (distributed word embeddings), for predicting synonymy among biomedical terms to automate a part of the UMLS (Unified Medical Language System) Metathesaurus construction process. We evaluate the use of contextualized word embeddings extracted from nine different biomedical BERT-based models for synonymy prediction in the UMLS by replacing BioWordVec embeddings with embeddings extracted from each biomedical BERT model using different feature extraction methods. Surprisingly, we find that Siamese Networks initialized with BioWordVec embeddings still outperform the Siamese Networks initialized with embedding extracted from biomedical BERT model.

1 Introduction

The UMLS (Bodenreider, 2004) is a biomedical terminology integration system that includes over 200 source vocabularies[1]. The UMLS Metathesaurus construction process organizes synonymous terms from these source vocabularies into *concepts*. The current Metathesaurus construction process uses a lexical similarity model and semantic preprocessing to determine synonymy, followed by a human review. The large scale and diversity of the Metathesaurus make the construction process very challenging, tedious, and error-prone. Therefore, to assist the UMLS Metathesaurus construction process, Nguyen et al. introduced the UMLS Vocabulary Alignment (UVA) task, or synonymy prediction task (Nguyen et al., 2021). They designed and train a Siamese Network to predict if two UMLS atoms are synonymous. The Siamese Network is initialized using BioWordVec embeddings, learned using fastText (Bojanowski et al., 2017). Given the recent successful use of contextualized word embeddings, extracted from Transformer models, for different downstream NLP tasks (Devlin et al., 2019; Vaswani et al., 2017; Peters et al., 2019), we explore the use of contextualized embeddings extracted from several distinct biomedical BERT-based language models.

Objectives. 1) Find which type of word embeddings, including contextualized embeddings, achieves the best performance when used with the Siamese Network for the synonymy prediction (or UVA) task. 2) Find which feature extraction method works best to extract word embeddings from the biomedical BERT models for optimal performance. 3) Find the best hyperparameters and optimization of the prediction task to train the Siamese Networks for the UVA task.

Approach. 1) We analyze the performance of the Siamese Networks initialized with embeddings from nine different biomedical BERT models for synonymy prediction. 2) We explore different feature extraction techniques to extract BERT embeddings. 3) We conduct a grid search and optimization of the prediction task to train the Siamese Networks.

Contributions. 1) We conduct an extensive analysis to extract embeddings from nine different biomedical BERT models using four feature extraction techniques. 2) Somewhat surprisingly, we find that Siamese Networks still achieve the highest performance for synonymy prediction when initialized with BioWordVec embeddings. 3) We find that no single feature extraction method works well across the different biomedical BERT models. 4) With a thorough grid search, we find substantial increases in F1-Score (e.g., 2.43%), when compared to the default hyperparameters. 5) Overall, our work contributes to defining best practices for the use of embeddings in Siamese Networks. See https://arxiv.org/abs/2109.13348 for an extension of this paper as it presents an extended analysis of the experiments and additional results.

2 UMLS - Knowledge Representation

The UMLS Metathesaurus links terms and codes between health records, pharmacy documents, and insurance documents (Bodenreider, 2004). The Metathesaurus consists of several building blocks, including atoms and concepts. All atoms in the UMLS Metathesaurus are assigned a unique identifier (AUI). Atoms that are synonymous are grouped into a single concept identified with a concept unique identifier (CUI). Table 1 contains examples of synonymous atoms and the identifiers assigned to each respective atom for a

[1] https://uts.nlm.nih.gov/uts/

Proceedings of the Third Workshop on Insights from Negative Results in NLP, pages 82 - 87
May 26, 2022

Tuple	Atom String	Source	AUI	CUI
t_1	Headache	MSH	A0066000	C0018681
t_2	Headaches	MSH	A0066008	C0018681
t_3	Cephalodynia	MSH	A26628141	C0018681
t_4	Cephalodynia	SNOMEDCT_US	A2957278	C0018681

Table 1: Examples tuples from UMLS consisting of an atom string, its source vocabulary name, its unique atom identifier (AUI), and its concept unique identifier (CUI). All tuples in the example table are synonymous and, hence, have the same CUI.

particular concept. For example, the term "Cephalodynia" appearing in both MSH and SNOMEDCT_US has different AUIs as shown in Table 1. Additionally, the strings "Headache" and "Headaches" have different AUIs because of the lexical variation (see Table 1). We use the 2020AA version of the UMLS, which contains 15.5 million atoms from 214 source vocabularies grouped into 4.28 million concepts.

3 Problem Formulation

An essential part of the UMLS construction process is identifying similar atoms across source vocabularies to integrate knowledge from different sources accurately. The UMLS Vocabulary Alignment (UVA) – or synonymy prediction – task is to identify synonymous atoms by measuring the similarity among pairs of atoms. A machine learning model should be able to identify the synonymous atoms are that lexically: *similar but are not synonymous* and *dissimilar but are synonymous*. Let (t_i, t_j) be a pair of input tuples, where $i \neq j$. Each tuple is initialized from a different source vocabulary in the form of (str, src, aui), where str is the atom string, src is the source vocabulary, and aui is the atom unique identifier (AUI). Let $f : T \times T \rightarrow 0, 1$ be a prediction function that maps a pair of input tuples to either 0 or 1. If $f(t_i, t_j) = 1$, then the atom strings (str_i, str_j) from t_i and t_j are synonymous and belong to the same concept (and hence, share same the CUI).

4 Dataset

We thank Nguyen et al. for sharing the dataset used in their work (Nguyen et al., 2021; Nguyen and Bodenreider, 2021). The dataset is created using the 2020AA release of the UMLS Metathesaurus. We use the ALL dataset for our study. The training and validation dataset contains a total of 192,400,462 examples, where 88.4% of the examples are negative examples. The testing dataset set contains a total of 173,035,862 examples, where 96.8% of the examples are negative examples. We refer the readers to Section 4.2 of (Nguyen et al., 2021) for a detailed description.

5 Related Work

We first describe the Siamese Networks for the UVA then describe the biomedical BERT variants.

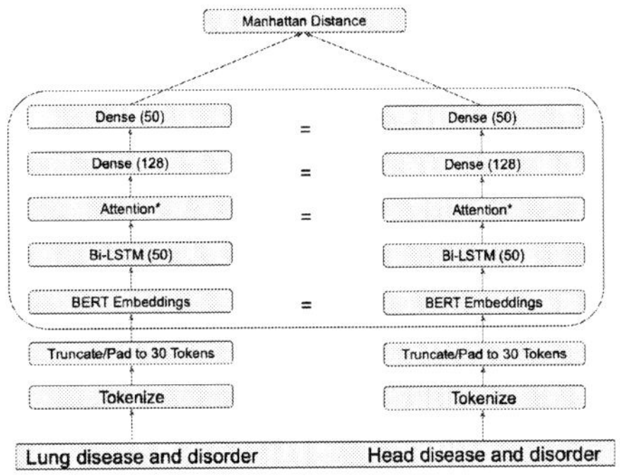

Figure 1: Siamese Network used for Synonymy Prediction. Nguyen et al. use BioWordVec embeddings, whereas we use contextualized word embeddings. "*" indicates optional attention layer.

Siamese Networks for the UVA Task

Nguyen et al. assess the similarity of atoms using lexical features of the atom strings (str). The authors design a Siamese Network that inputs a pair of atom strings, and outputs a similarity score between 0 and 1, $sim(str_i, str_j) \in [0, 1]$ (see Figure 1). The inputs are preprocessed, tokenized, and then sent through an initial embedding layer initialized with BioWordVec embeddings (Zhang et al., 2019). The word embeddings are then fed into Bidirectional Long Short Term Memory (Bi-LSTM) layers, followed by two dense layers. All atom pairs with a similarity > 0.5 are considered synonyms (using the Manhattan distance). Their deep learning model has a precision of 94.64%, recall of 94.96% and an F1-Score of 94.8% and outperforms a rule-based approach for synonymy prediction by 23% in recall, 2.4% in precision, and 14.1% in F1-Score. In their follow-up work, Nguyen et al. add an attention layer after the Bi-LSTM layers that improves the precision by +3.63% but decreases recall by 1.42%.

Biomedical BERT Models

In this section, we summarize the specific biomedical BERT variants used in this study. For brevity, we focus on biomedical BERT variants and omit the general presentation of BERT. We refer the interested reader to (Devlin et al., 2019) for details.

Table 2 compares the different biomedical BERT models used in this benchmarking study. To limit the scope of the biomedical BERT models, we only include models that have been pretrained with data from biomedical sources, such as biomedical terminologies (e.g., UMLS vocabularies), biomedical literature (e.g., PubMed), and clinical notes (e.g., MIMIC-III).

BioBERT: BioBERT is initialized from BERT and then pretrained on PubMed abstracts and PubMed Central (PMC) full-text articles (Lee et al., 2020). We use both BioBERT-Base and BioBERT-Large.

BlueBERT: BlueBERT is initialized with BERT weights provided by (Devlin et al., 2019) and further

Model Type	Embed. Dim.	Vocab Size	Token Size
BioWordVec	200	268,158,600	-
BioBERT (+ SapBERT)	768	28,996	13,230,336
BioBERT-Large (Cased)	1024	58,996	28,530,688
BlueBERT	1024	30,522	25,358,336
SapBERT	768	30,522	21,035,520
UMLSBERT (+ SapBERT)	768	28,996	13,230,336
BlueBERT+ SapBERT	768	30,522	19,018,752
VanillaBERT + SapBERT	768	30,522	19,018,752

Table 2: Comparison of different biomedical word embeddings in terms of the embedding dimension, vocabulary size, and the number of tokens.

pretrained with the PubMed Abstract and MIMIC-III datasets. We use BlueBERT-Large in our work.

SapBERT: SapBERT provides the current state-of-the-art (SOTA) results for six medical entity linking benchmarking datasets (Liu et al., 2021). SapBERT is trained on the UMLS with $4M$+ concepts and $10M$+ synonyms from over 150 vocabularies.

UMLSBERT: UMLSBERT is initialized with the pretrained Bio_ClinicalBERT model (Alsentzer et al., 2019) and pretrained with the MLM task on the MIMIC-III dataset with additional modifications.

{BioBERT, BlueBERT, UMLSBERT, VanillaBERT} + SapBERT: The SapBERT authors pretrain additional variants of SapBERT that are initialized using different BERT variants. We refer the reader to (Liu et al., 2021) for a detailed description.

6 Approach

To analyze the performance of the different embeddings extracted from the various BERT models, we train the Siamese Network end to end, similar to (Nguyen et al., 2021; Nguyen and Bodenreider, 2021). We investigate the use of the nine biomedical BERT models (mentioned in Section 5) as a source of word embeddings. Our experimental setup of consists of two primary steps for each of the Siamese Networks (with and without attention): 1) Feature extraction of word embeddings from biomedical BERT Models. 2) Grid search of optimal hyperparameters and optimization. Our code will be available at https://anonymous.4open.science/r/uva_embedding_benchmarking-8124/. For the training and testing data, we recommend reaching out to Nguyen et al. (Nguyen et al., 2021; Nguyen and Bodenreider, 2021).

Feature Extraction for the Siamese Network

BioWordVec has a fixed word embedding for each word or term (e.g., UMLS atom). For transformer models, word embedding extraction is not as straightforward because different layers of BERT capture different types of features (Jawahar et al., 2019; Liu et al., 2019; Reimers and Gurevych, 2017; Peters et al., 2018; van Aken et al., 2019; Devlin et al., 2019). We initialize Siamese Networks with token embeddings instead of word embeddings to use BERT models for the UVA task. To extract token embeddings for UMLS atoms from each BERT model, we: 1) Tokenize the atom strings using the model-specific vocabulary. 2) Create a token id tensor by mapping the token strings to their vocabulary indices. 3) Create a segment id tensor. 4) Feed the token id and segment id tensors in to the BERT model (in eval mode). 5) Create a separate token embedding matrix to initialize the Siamese Networks using each of the following methods:

- 1st token embedding and last layer
- 1st token embed. and avg. of last 4 layers
- Last token embedding and last layer
- Last token embed. and avg. of last 4 layers
- Avg. token embedding and last layer
- Avg. token embed. and avg. of last 4 layers

Of note, we do not use the "CLS" sentence representation as the word embedding for UMLS atoms because the Bi-LSTMs layers require a sequence as input. We only use the atom string to extract token embeddings because all vocabularies in the UMLS have this characteristic in common. In summary, we extract two sets of embeddings from each model (the 12th layer and average of the 9th to 12th layers) and use three different types of token embeddings (the first and last occurrence of the token in the dataset and the average embedding of each occurrence of the token in the dataset).

Grid Search and Optimization

The performance of deep learning models highly depends on the selection of hyperparameters (Hutter et al., 2014; Bergstra and Bengio, 2012; Reimers and Gurevych, 2017). Prior work by Nguyen et al. uses a fixed set of hyperparameters. Therefore, we conduct a grid search for the best-performing models to thoroughly investigate the performance of the Siamese Networks. Hyperparameters used in our experiment include optimizer (SGD, Adam) and learning rate (0.00001, 0.0001, 0.001, 0.01, 0.1). To limit computational cost, we conduct a grid search for the following Siamese Networks: BioWordVec (**BWV**), BioWordVec + Attention (**BWV + Att.**), SapBERT avg. token embedding extracted by averaging the last 4 layers (**SB Avg_Token + Avg_Last_4**), SapBERT avg. token embedding extracted from the last layer + Attention (**SB Avg_Token + Last_Lay + Att.**). Additionally, Nguyen et al. provide no rationale for the similarity threshold of 0.5 between the learned representations of two atoms. Therefore, we search for the best threshold for prediction based on the precision-recall curve to find a threshold that maximizes the F1-Score.

7 Results and Discussion

Table 3 presents the synonymy prediction results using embeddings extracted from BERT models and BioWordVec embeddings. The *Token Type* and *Extraction Method* columns indicate the feature extraction method that was used to initialize the model.

Performance with BERT Embeddings: We find that Siamese Networks initialized with BioWordVec still outperform all models initialized with embeddings ex-

	Siamese Network without Attention (Nguyen et al., 2021)								Siamese Network with Attention (Nguyen and Bodenreider, 2021)							
Embedding Type	**Token Type**	**Extraction Method**	**Threshold**	**Accuracy**	**Precision**	**Recall**	**F1-Score**	**AUC**	**Token Type**	**Extraction Method**	**Threshold**	**Accuracy**	**Precision**	**Recall**	**F1-Score**	**AUC**
BioWordVec	-	-	0.5612	0.9941	0.9075	0.9127	0.9101	0.9909	-	-	0.5490	0.9939	0.9056	0.9067	0.9061	0.9907
BioWordVec w. SGD, lr = 0.001	-	-	0.5587	0.9942	0.9087	0.9146	**0.9116**	0.9913	-	-	0.5507	0.9941	0.9078	0.9102	0.9090	0.9910
SapBERT	Avg.	Avg. Last 4	0.5802	0.9892	0.8496	0.8092	0.8289	0.9848	Avg.	Last Layer	0.5607	0.9902	0.8682	0.8247	0.8459	0.9855
SapBERT w. SGD, lr = 0.0001	-	-	-	-	-	-	-	-	Avg.	Last Layer	0.5979	0.9913	0.8824	0.8459	**0.8638**	0.9830
SapBERT w. Adam, lr = 0.0001	-	-	-	-	-	-	-	-	Avg.	Avg. Last 4	0.59	0.9912	0.8840	0.8372	0.8600	0.9830
BioBERT	First	Last Layer	0.5643	0.9853	0.7955	0.7380	0.7657	0.9758	Avg.	Avg. Last 4	0.5481	0.9862	0.81	0.7504	0.779	0.9774
BioBERT_Large	Avg.	Last Layer	0.5438	0.9881	0.8400	0.7810	0.8095	0.9807	Avg.	Last Layer	0.5438	0.9881	0.84	0.781	0.8095	0.9807
BlueBERT	First	Last Layer	0.5680	0.9859	0.8066	0.7424	0.7732	0.9765	Avg.	Last Layer	0.5500	0.9872	0.8247	0.7677	0.7952	0.9792
UMLSBERT	Avg.	Avg. Last 4	0.5755	0.9852	0.7921	0.7371	0.7636	0.9754	Avg.	Avg. Last 4	0.5501	0.9862	0.8151	0.7415	0.7765	0.9764
UMLSBERT + SapBERT	Avg.	Avg. Last 4	0.5543	0.9854	0.7948	0.7432	0.7681	0.9769	Avg.	Avg. Last 4	0.5452	0.9857	0.7992	0.7485	0.773	0.9771
BlueBERT + SapBERT	Avg.	Avg. Last 4	0.5810	0.9868	0.8154	0.7651	0.7895	0.9798	Avg.	Avg. Last 4	0.5596	0.9875	0.831	0.7701	0.7994	0.9797
BioBERT + SapBERT	Avg.	Avg. Last 4	0.5756	0.9851	0.7904	0.7348	0.7616	0.9756	Avg.	Avg. Last 4	0.5511	0.9861	0.81	0.7465	0.7769	0.9769
VanillaBERT + SapBERT	Avg.	Avg. Last 4	0.5614	0.9866	0.8125	0.7633	0.7872	0.9791	Avg.	Avg. Last 4	0.5467	0.9874	0.8268	0.772	0.7984	0.9801

Table 3: Results for Siamese Networks trained for 100 iterations initialized using different embeddings using the best prediction threshold (single run point estimates). Rows marked with "**w.**" contain the performance of the models after grid search.

tracted from biomedical BERT models. Though surprising, Schulz and Juric also find that current embeddings are limited in their ability to adequately encode medical terms when tested on large-scale datasets (Schulz and Juric, 2020).

Moreover, using a BERT model trained on more relevant domain-specific data and the right task yields more substantial gains. In particular, the SapBERT model, whose embeddings achieve the highest performance, is trained on PubMed and incorporates knowledge from the UMLS Metathesaurus by using semantic type embeddings and modifying the MLM task to indicate if which words belong to the same concept. These changes likely indicate why it outperforms the other biomedical BERT models for our task.

Feature Extraction for Biomedical BERT Models: Based on our experiments, no single feature extraction method provides the most useful embedding for all BERT models. However, results indicate that averaging all token embeddings and using the average of the last four hidden layers seems to work well for many of the models. The Siamese Network + Attention initialized with the average token embedding extracted from the last layer of SapBERT achieves the best F1-Score.

Performance after Grid Search: As mentioned in Section 6, we limit the grid search to the four best performing models: BWV, BWV + Att., SB Avg_Token + Avg_Last_4, and SB Avg_Token + Last_Lay + Att. Our grid search results indicate that the Siamese Network without attention outperforms the Siamese Network with attention when initialized with BioWordVec embeddings. Additionally, there is a 2.43% increase in F1-Score for the Siamese Network with attention and a 3.11% increase in F1-Score for the Siamese Network w.o. attention. Reducing the batch size leads to early stopping for all models but at the cost of performance (e.g, 4.67% drop in F1-Score for BWV + Att. w. SGD).

Optimizer. For the four best performing models, we see that SGD works better in three of the cases. For only one model, Adam performs similarly to SGD with a higher F1-Score by 0.16%. There is a 1% increase in F-1 Score for the Siamese Network with Attention initialized with SB + Avg_Token + Last_Lay embeddings. Using the SGD optimizer leads to earlier convergence for when using biomedical BERT embeddings.

Learning Rate. Regardless of the optimizer, increasing the learning rate (LR) to 0.01 and 0.1 leads to early stopping and results in poor F1-Scores. With a LR of 0.0001, the performance for the Siamese Networks initialized with SapBERT embeddings extracted using the average token and the last layer of the SapBERT model, F1-Score increases by about 0.6% for the model with attention and a 3.11% increase for the model without attention. Reducing the LR further decreases performance for Siamese Networks using BWV embeddings.

Threshold. The best performing thresholds range from 0.5438 to 0.581. On average using the best thresholds results in 0.0086% increase in F1-Score for the Siamese Networks without attention (results omitted due to space). Hence, 0.5 is an acceptable threshold.

8 Conclusion

We investigate if contextualized embeddings extracted from biomedical BERT-based language models can improve the performance of Siamese Networks, introduced by (Nguyen et al., 2021; Nguyen and Bodenreider, 2021), to predict synonymy in the UMLS Metathesaurus. Despite the excellent performance of BERT models on biomedical NLP tasks, BioWordVec embeddings still remain competitive for the UVA task. This confirms the importance of investigating the use of traditional distributed word embeddings. Among the biomedical BERT models, SapBERT trained on UMLS data performs best, suggesting the importance of using a model trained on datasets directly relevant to the task at hand. Finally, we demonstrate the importance of exploring different feature extraction methods and hyperparameter tuning for deep learning models.

9 Acknowledgments

The authors thank Liu et al. for providing the additional pretrained SapBERT models (Liu et al., 2021) and a cooperative AI Institute grant (AI-EDGE), from the National Science Foundation under CNS-2112471.

References

Emily Alsentzer, John Murphy, William Boag, Wei-Hung Weng, Di Jindi, Tristan Naumann, and Matthew McDermott. 2019. Publicly available clinical BERT embeddings. In *Proceedings of the 2nd Clinical Natural Language Processing Workshop*, pages 72–78, Minneapolis, Minnesota, USA. Association for Computational Linguistics.

James Bergstra and Yoshua Bengio. 2012. Random search for hyper-parameter optimization. *Journal of Machine Learning Research*, 13:281–305.

Olivier Bodenreider. 2004. The unified medical language system (UMLS): integrating biomedical terminology. *Nucleic acids research*, 32(suppl_1):D267–D270.

Piotr Bojanowski, Edouard Grave, Armand Joulin, and Tomas Mikolov. 2017. Enriching word vectors with subword information. *Transactions of the Association for Computational Linguistics*, 5:135–146.

Jacob Devlin, Ming-Wei Chang, Kenton Lee, and Kristina Toutanova. 2019. BERT: Pre-training of Deep Bidirectional Transformers for Language Understanding. In *Proceedings of NAACL-HLT*, pages 4171–4186.

Frank Hutter, Holger Hoos, and Kevin Leyton-Brown. 2014. An efficient approach for assessing hyperparameter importance. In *International conference on machine learning*, pages 754–762. PMLR.

Ganesh Jawahar, Benoît Sagot, and Djamé Seddah. 2019. What does BERT learn about the structure of language? In *ACL 2019-57th Annual Meeting of the Association for Computational Linguistics.*

Jinhyuk Lee, Wonjin Yoon, Sungdong Kim, Donghyeon Kim, Sunkyu Kim, Chan Ho So, and Jaewoo Kang. 2020. BioBERT: a pre-trained biomedical language representation model for biomedical text mining. *Bioinformatics*, 36(4):1234–1240.

Fangyu Liu, Ehsan Shareghi, Zaiqiao Meng, Marco Basaldella, and Nigel Collier. 2021. Self-alignment pretraining for biomedical entity representations. In *Proceedings of the 2021 Conference of the North American Chapter of the Association for Computational Linguistics: Human Language Technologies*, pages 4228–4238.

Nelson F. Liu, Matt Gardner, Yonatan Belinkov, Matthew E. Peters, and Noah A. Smith. 2019. Linguistic knowledge and transferability of contextual representations. In *Proceedings of the 2019 Conference of the North American Chapter of the Association for Computational Linguistics: Human Language Technologies, Volume 1 (Long and Short Papers)*, pages 1073–1094, Minneapolis, Minnesota. Association for Computational Linguistics.

Vinh Nguyen and Olivier Bodenreider. 2021. Adding an Attention Layer Improves the Performance of a Neural Network Architecture for Synonymy Prediction in the UMLS Metathesaurus. In *MedInfo*.

Vinh Nguyen, Hong Yung Yip, and Olivier Bodenreider. 2021. Biomedical Vocabulary Alignment at Scale in the UMLS Metathesaurus. In *Proceedings of the Web Conference 2021*, pages 2672–2683.

Matthew E. Peters, Mark Neumann, Mohit Iyyer, Matt Gardner, Christopher Clark, Kenton Lee, and Luke Zettlemoyer. 2018. Deep contextualized word representations. In *Proceedings of the 2018 Conference of the North American Chapter of the Association for Computational Linguistics: Human Language Technologies, Volume 1 (Long Papers)*, pages 2227–2237, New Orleans, Louisiana. Association for Computational Linguistics.

Matthew E Peters, Sebastian Ruder, and Noah A Smith. 2019. To tune or not to tune? adapting pretrained representations to diverse tasks. *ACL 2019*, page 7.

Nils Reimers and Iryna Gurevych. 2017. Reporting Score Distributions Makes a Difference: Performance Study of LSTM-networks for Sequence Tagging. In *Proceedings of the 2017 Conference on Empirical Methods in Natural Language Processing*, pages 338–348.

Claudia Schulz and Damir Juric. 2020. Can embeddings adequately represent medical terminology? new large-scale medical term similarity datasets have the answer! In *Proceedings of the AAAI Conference on Artificial Intelligence*, volume 34, pages 8775–8782.

Betty van Aken, Benjamin Winter, Alexander Löser, and Felix A Gers. 2019. How does bert answer questions? a layer-wise analysis of transformer representations. In *Proceedings of the 28th ACM International Conference on Information and Knowledge Management*, pages 1823–1832.

Ashish Vaswani, Noam Shazeer, Niki Parmar, Jakob Uszkoreit, Llion Jones, Aidan N Gomez, Łukasz Kaiser, and Illia Polosukhin. 2017. Attention is all you need. In *Advances in neural information processing systems*, pages 5998–6008.

Yijia Zhang, Qingyu Chen, Zhihao Yang, Hongfei Lin, and Zhiyong Lu. 2019. BioWordVec, improving biomedical word embeddings with subword information and MeSH. *Scientific data*, 6(1):1–9.

A Dataset

We thank Nguyen et al. for sharing the dataset used in their work (Nguyen et al., 2021; Nguyen and Bodenreider, 2021). To get a copy of the dataset, please sign the UMLS License Agreement and email Nguyen to receive the dataset.

B Experimental Details

We first train both Siamese Networks (with attention (Nguyen and Bodenreider, 2021) and without attention (Nguyen et al., 2021)) with the default hyperparameters for each biomedical BERT model with each of the different embedding extraction methods. The default hyperparameters rely on Adam as the optimizer with a learning rate of 0.001 and 8192 examples in batch. This results in 20 different Siamese Networks, each trained for 100 epochs. Next, we take the best performing Siamese models initialized with BERT embeddings and the two Siamese models initialized with BioWordVec embeddings and conduct a grid search to find the optimal hyperparameters. We conduct a grid search for a total of 4 Siamese Networks and evaluate each model using the following metrics: Accuracy, Precision, Recall, F1-Score, and AUC.

All experiments are run using a High Performance Computing cluster. The typical run time for a Siamese Network with BioWordVec embeddings is 48 hours for 100 iterations using a v100x NVIDIA GPU and requires about 220 GB of memory. A Siamese Network trained with BERT embeddings takes about 72 hours for 100 iterations using a v100x NVIDIA GPU and requires about 220 GB of memory. The training time is further increased to 88 hours for Siamese Networks trained with embeddings of dimensions 1024 (i.e., BioBERT-Large and BlueBERT embeddings).

C Limitations

Our work evaluates biomedical word embeddings extracted from BERT-based models for the Siamese Networks introduced by (Nguyen et al., 2021; Nguyen and Bodenreider, 2021). Our list of biomedical BERT models does not include all models; we consider the most recent biomedical BERT models that have achieved SOTA performance on NLP tasks. The narrow focus of our work allows us to conduct a thorough analysis of the embedding extraction methods and hyperparameters using nine different BERT models for two variants of the Siamese Network. However, our experimental setup is reproducible for similar NLP tasks.

As an additional exercise to test the usability of transformer based embeddings, we attempt to use the "CLS" sentence representation of the UMLS atoms. For a pair of UMLS atoms, we extract the "CLS" sentence representation of each UMLS atom and compute the similarity of the representation using both the Cosine and Manhattan distance functions. We find that this approach does not work well ($< 30\%$ accuracy). As future work, we can investigate if adding a deep neural net (different from a Siamese Network) can improve the performance.

On the Impact of Data Augmentation on Downstream Performance in Natural Language Processing

Itsuki Okimura, Machel Reid, Makoto Kawano, Yutaka Matsuo
The University of Tokyo
{okimura, machelreid, kawano, matsuo}@weblab.t.u-tokyo.ac.jp

Abstract

With in the broader scope of machine learning, data augmentation is a common strategy to improve generalization and robustness of machine learning models. While data augmentation has been widely used within computer vision, its use in the NLP has been comparably rather limited. The reason for this is that within NLP, the impact of proposed data augmentation methods on performance has not been evaluated in a unified manner, and effective data augmentation methods are unclear. In this paper, we look to tackle this by evaluating the impact of 12 data augmentation methods on multiple datasets when finetuning pre-trained language models. We find minimal improvements when data sizes are constrained to a few thousand, with performance degradation when data size is increased. We also use various methods to quantify the strength of data augmentations, and find that these values, though weakly correlate with downstream performance, correlate negatively or positively depending on the task. Furthermore, we find a glaring lack of consistently performant data augmentations. This all alludes to the difficulty of data augmentations for NLP tasks and we are inclined to believe that static data augmentations are not broadly applicable given these properties.

1 Introduction

Data augmentation may be useful in situations where the data size is insufficient for the number of parameters in the model, resulting in overtraining (Perez and Wang, 2017). It has been pointed out that data augmentation does not degrade the expressive power of the model and achieves an improvement in the generalization performance of the model without adjusting the hyperparameters (Hernández-García and König, 2018). While data augmentation is standard in the field of computer vision, it is not fully used in natural language processing. Two factors can be cited for this. The first reason is that there has been insufficient unified validation of data augmentation methods for a wide range of datasets and data sizes. Another reason is that it is still unclear what kind of data augmentation is effective for learning. In natural language processing, it is difficult to judge whether a data augmentation method is good or bad without relying on experiments, and it is necessary to search for effective data augmentations by trial and error (Feng et al., 2021). If it is possible to predict whether a data augmentation is effective for learning before training, it would be possible to search for data augmentations more efficiently.

This paper examines the performance impact of data augmentation methods that have been proposed for natural language processing on various datasets. Through this experiment, we will verify whether the data augmentation method can contribute to the improvement of performance on multiple datasets and problem settings. We also use various measures of the strength of a given data augmentation, and investigate its relationship with performance after learning. We find that although data augmentation strength (i.e. how significantly it perturbs the input) is correlated with the change in downstream performance to a given degree, its sign and degree often varies significantly. Based on this, we believe that static data augmentations are not a wise choice for NLP tasks with a reasonable amount of data, and may need to be combined with data-dependent modeling innovations to be broadly applicable to future work.

2 Related Work

Data Augmentation for NLP Data augmentation has been explored in NLP recently with EDA (Wei and Zou, 2019), as well as NL-augmenter (Dhole et al., 2021). Masked language modeling can be considered to be data augmentation (Devlin et al., 2019), while dictionary-derived augmentation methods have been employed recently for aug-

Proceedings of the Third Workshop on Insights from Negative Results in NLP, pages 88 - 93
May 26, 2022 ©2022 Association for Computational Linguistics

menting multilingual language models with large improvements (Chaudhary et al., 2020; Reid et al., 2021; Reid and Artetxe, 2022). However, Longpre et al. (2020) showed that two data augmentation methods in natural language processing had small effects on pre-trained language models. We further expand the scope of this study to examine the performance impact of 12 different data augmentation methods.

Evaluating Data Augmentation In the field of computer vision, researchers have been studying what kind of data augmentation contributes to the performance (Taylor and Nitschke, 2018; Perez and Wang, 2017). And some studies have been done to create metrics on data augmentation and evaluate the relationship with the performance of the model after training. Gontijo-Lopes et al. (2020) proposed two indices, affinity and diversity, to quantify how data augmentation improves the generalization of the model, and pointed out that data augmentation methods that are evaluated as having high affinity and diversity will lead to better performance in computer vision. Meanwhile, it is still unclear what characteristics of data augmentation methods are effective in the field of natural language processing.

3 Evaluation Metrics and Training Strategies

In this section, we briefly go over metrics we use to evaluate the strength of our data augmentations of a given task as well as strategies for training using data augmentations.

3.1 Training Strategy

In this subsection, we briefly discuss our two training strategies for incorporating data augmentation. Given an i.i.d. dataset $D = \{(x_1, y_1), (x_2, y_2), \ldots, (x_N, y_N)\}$ containing N examples where each x_i represents an input, and y_i represents the assigned label corresponding to x_i.

Oftentimes, we simply fit a given model on this dataset. However, given a data augmentation function $f(x_i) = \hat{x}_i$, where $\hat{x}_i$ represents an augmented input, we can also augment this dataset to improve the diversity of inputs which should hopefully lead to better model generalization and robustness. That is, we now have augmented dataset $\hat{D} = \{(\hat{x}_1, y_1), \ldots, (\hat{x}_N, \hat{y}_N)\}$.

We now explain the following finetuning methods:

Normal training Finetuning our models on D

1-step training Finetuning our models jointly on augmented dataset $\hat{D}$ and original dataset D—this method is commonly employed in computer vision.

2-step training To mitigate the distribution shift introduced by the augmentation, but still allowing the model to learn from the augmented dataset, we look at two-step finetuning where we first finetune on $\hat{D}$ and then finetune on D.

3.2 Data Augmentation Strength

We also look to analyse whether there are certain trends among the strength of augmentation methods and their impact on downstream performance. To do this, we measure the strength of augmentation methods using the following metrics:

Semantic Similarity We use semantic similarity (Cer et al., 2017) as a measure of strength of data augmentation. For example, if a given example is perturbed in a more significant manner, we assume that it's semantic similarity will decrease, therefore indicating a "stronger" data augmentation. We use SentenceBERT (Reimers and Gurevych, 2019) to measure the cosine similarity between sentence representation of the original example x_i and sentence representation of augmented example $\hat{x}_i$.

BLEU We use BLEU (Papineni et al., 2002; Post, 2018) as a metric that works on discrete tokens (therefore more sensitive to exact token matches), that is not model dependent as our semantic similarity measure is. That is, a lower BLEU score represents a stronger data augmentation.

BERTScore We also use text generation metric BERTScore (Zhang* et al., 2020), which measures cosine-similarity at a token-level, rather than on a sequence-level like our semantic similarity measure.

In our analyses (Sec. 5), we measure the correlation between these measures and the ± change in performance.

4 Experimental Setup

4.1 Data Augmentation Methods

In our experiments, we compared the performance of the model when trained with 12 typical data augmentation methods with that of the model trained without data augmentation. Our data augmentations methods are sourced from NL-Augmenter[1]

[1]https://github.com/GEM-benchmark/NL-Augmenter

(Dhole et al., 2021) and `nlpaug`[2] (Ma, 2019). We provide additional details in Appendix B.

4.2 Datasets

In experiments, we use three datasets for different language tasks, MRPC (Dolan and Brockett, 2005), SICK (Marelli et al., 2014), and SST-2 (Socher et al., 2013). MRPC is a dataset in which the task is to predict whether a sentence-pair is semantically equivalent. SICK is a dataset that contains a task to infer the connotation between a given premise and an explanation. In this experiment, it is a binary classification problem whether the meaning of the explanatory sentence is contained in the meaning of the premise sentence or not. SST-2 is a binary classification problem in which a dataset for sentiment analysis of sentences is created from movie reviews, are classified as positive or negative. For MRPC and SICK, we extended the data to the second sentence in the experiment, and the combination of the first sentence, the extended second sentence pair, and the original label was used as the augmented data set. For SST-2, the combination of the augmented sentence and the original label was used as the augmented data set.

4.3 Models

In this experiment, we used the GPT-2 (345M) (Radford et al., 2019) and BERT-large (Devlin et al., 2018) as pre-trained language models. We train models on a single NVIDIA V100 16GB GPU. We measured the performance of training on the original dataset as a *baseline*, and compared the performance of fine-tuning on the training dataset with the augmented data. We train models until convergence, and perform early stopping where we use a patience of 3 epochs for all models.

5 Results

Performance Changes Due to Data Augmentation Table 1 shows the scores for single-step and 2-step training on the data set with data augmentation (see Appendix D for per-task results). For both training strategies, we also measure the impact of data size, experimenting with various data sizes (10%, 50%, and 100% of the full dataset). When all data was used for training, we found that no data augmentation that improved scores on average for both the language model and the masked language model, except for the 2-step training with BERT with synonym substitution. This indicates that although data-augmentation has the tendency to help at a smaller scale, perhaps mitigating effects of (lack of) data diversity, as the data scale grows we notice that performance degrades where the augmentations most likely add more noise to the dataset.

Relationship between Data Augmentation Intensity and Post-training Performance The correlation coefficients measured by the difference in F1 scores between the data augmentation intensity obtained by the language model and the masked language model and the baseline for each model and learning method are shown in Table2. A positive value indicates that a weaker (i.e. more similar) data augmentation results in better performance. When we use 1-step training, this correlation is generally positive — this indicates that when using naive data combination, then a more similar (i.e. weaker augmentation) is generally more effective. This supports our hypothesis about distribution shift negatively impact augmentation. However, this finding varies significantly when switching to 2-step training depending on model and dataset. Given the relatively strong performance of 2-step training, this indicates that strength of data augmentation can have varying effects when using various training schedules/models.

6 Discussion

When all the original training data was used for training in the three datasets tested in this study, the effect of data augmentation on performance improvement was small, and the performance on the test data deteriorated in many cases. There are two possible reasons for this. The first is that the augmented data may have become noise. It is almost inevitable that data augmentation will result in the augmentation of sentences whose labels cannot be preserved. If some of the augmented sentences are incorrectly labeled, the quality of the dataset will deteriorate to some extent. Therefore, in a setting where a relatively large number of data can be prepared, such as using all the training data, the negative impact of the decrease in data quality is stronger than the positive impact of the increase in the number of data. The second reason is that the knowledge that can be obtained by data augmentation may have already been acquired through prior learning. This is also pointed out by Longpre et al. (2020). Therefore, for data

[2] `https://github.com/makcedward/nlpaug`

	1- step GPT2			1-step BERT			2-step GPT-2			2-step BERT		
	100%	50%	10%	100%	50%	10%	100%	50%	10%	100%	50%	10%
baseline	0.8997	0.8795	0.8567	0.9028	0.8866	0.8461	0.8997	0.8795	0.8567	0.9028	0.8866	0.8461
character substitution	0.8929	**0.8836**	0.8356	0.8982	0.8735	**0.8517**	0.8959	0.8768	0.8483	0.8954	0.8846	**0.8494**
W2V substitution	0.8902	0.8765	0.8311	0.8939	0.8595	0.8457	0.8886	0.8779	0.8501	0.9027	0.8862	0.8406
BERT-based substitution	0.8804	0.8728	0.8452	0.8780	0.8592	**0.8462**	0.8906	0.8790	0.8304	0.8957	0.8825	0.8292
synonym substitution	0.8946	**0.8846**	0.8338	0.8971	0.8710	**0.8535**	0.8920	0.8772	**0.8585**	**0.9032**	0.8826	**0.8462**
word paraphrase	0.8916	**0.8799**	0.8509	0.8980	0.8799	**0.8518**	0.8981	**0.8820**	0.8475	0.8972	**0.8871**	0.8424
LM-based substitution	0.8910	0.8745	0.8416	0.8928	0.8654	0.8368	0.8918	**0.8740**	0.8564	0.8941	0.8858	0.8420
subject-object switching	0.8958	**0.8875**	0.8362	0.8963	0.8780	0.8451	0.8932	**0.8875**	**0.8615**	0.8968	**0.8889**	**0.8476**
random word deletion	0.8889	**0.8857**	0.8544	0.8924	0.8782	**0.8568**	0.8910	**0.8765**	**0.8606**	0.8891	**0.8873**	0.8443
stammering insertion	0.8899	**0.8799**	0.8401	0.8990	0.8795	**0.8557**	0.8920	**0.8836**	**0.8604**	0.8974	**0.8902**	**0.8496**
EDA	0.8958	0.8774	0.8226	0.8995	0.8770	**0.8529**	0.8927	**0.8860**	**0.8571**	0.8967	0.8835	**0.8514**
back translation	0.8965	**0.8809**	0.8318	0.9003	0.8786	**0.8557**	0.8968	**0.8795**	**0.8607**	0.8924	**0.8867**	**0.8483**
summarization	0.8905	0.8770	0.8490	0.8901	0.8599	**0.8501**	0.8917	**0.8864**	**0.8600**	0.8896	0.8789	**0.8471**

Table 1: Table of average F1 scores in 1-step and 2-step training for each percentage of data used for training when data augmentation is used for MRPC, SICK and SST-2.

	Sentence similarity				BLEU				BERTScore			
	GPT-2		BERT		GPT-2		BERT		GPT-2		BERT	
	1-step	2-step	1-step	2-step	1-step	2-step	1-step	2-step	1-step	2-step	1-step	2-step
MRPC	0.2478	0.5813	0.5540	0.2011	0.3782	0.5150	0.6574	0.2712	0.2406	0.6119	0.4879	0.2064
SICK	0.5138	-0.1941	0.4790	-0.5216	0.2424	0.4192	0.0392	-0.5645	0.1085	0.1314	0.0483	-0.2592
SST-2	0.3251	0.3216	0.5897	-0.4152	0.2226	0.4876	0.2015	-0.2712	0.1686	0.3699	0.4524	-0.4342

Table 2: Correlation coefficient between data augmentation strength and difference in F1 score from baseline.

augmentation in a specific domain, it is possible that data augmentation based on knowledge about the domain, such as substitution based on a list of words that can be substituted in the domain, which cannot be obtained by pre-training with a general corpus, may be effective. On the other hand, when the number of data used for training was limited, we observed some cases where the performance improved even when using a pre-training model. Therefore, in domains where only a few hundred examples are available, performance improvement can be expected by augmenting the existing data.

In addition, in 1-step learning, the weaker the data augmentation, the better the performance. However, in 2-step learning, the relationship between the strength of consistent data augmentation and performance depended on the type of data set. This suggests that in 2-step learning, the effective strength of data augmentation may differ depending on the characteristics of the data set. For example, in MRPC, the difference between the data augmentation intensity and the F1 score of the baseline was negatively correlated because even trivial changes are likely to produce data that become noise in learning. In SICK and SST-2, even if some of the content changes, the labels of the sentences are retained as long as the words indicating relevance and emotion remain the same. In this case, the various sentences created by strong data reinforcement in two-stage learning contribute to the learning process, allowing clean data to be learned in the second half. This may be why the difference between the strength of the data reinforcement and the F1 score from the baseline may have been positively correlated in some cases. Therefore, by comparing the augmentation intensity determined by the proposed index, it may be possible to efficiently search for promising data augmentation methods before actual training. However, more work needs to be done to effectively use these methods in a practical setting.

7 Conclusion

In this paper, we observed that most of the data augmentation methods did not improve performance when training on datasets with thousands of examples, but some of them improved performance when training on datasets with hundreds of examples. This suggests that, depending on the task and the data size, data augmentation may be effective even when a pre-trained language model is used for training. We also defined data augmentation intensity, a measure to evaluate whether data augmentation produces sentences that are different from the original sentences, and evaluated the relationship between this measure and the performance after training. As a result, the data augmentation intensity showed different correlations with the change in performance after training depending on the target dataset. For tasks with enough data, this indicates the limited applicability and predictability of static data augmentations. In future work, we believe the NLP community should look at modeling or adaptive learning methods (Dery et al., 2022) to account for these differences in data.

References

Daniel Cer, Mona Diab, Eneko Agirre, Iñigo Lopez-Gazpio, and Lucia Specia. 2017. SemEval-2017 task 1: Semantic textual similarity multilingual and crosslingual focused evaluation. In *Proceedings of the 11th International Workshop on Semantic Evaluation (SemEval-2017)*, pages 1–14, Vancouver, Canada. Association for Computational Linguistics.

Aditi Chaudhary, Karthik Raman, Krishna Srinivasan, and Jiecao Chen. 2020. Dict-mlm: Improved multilingual pre-training using bilingual dictionaries.

Alexis Conneau, Kartikay Khandelwal, Naman Goyal, Vishrav Chaudhary, Guillaume Wenzek, Francisco Guzmán, Edouard Grave, Myle Ott, Luke Zettlemoyer, and Veselin Stoyanov. 2020. Unsupervised cross-lingual representation learning at scale. In *Proceedings of the 58th Annual Meeting of the Association for Computational Linguistics*, pages 8440–8451, Online. Association for Computational Linguistics.

Lucio M. Dery, Paul Michel, Ameet Talwalkar, and Graham Neubig. 2022. Should we be pre-training? an argument for end-task aware training as an alternative.

Jacob Devlin, Ming-Wei Chang, Kenton Lee, and Kristina Toutanova. 2018. Bert: Pre-training of deep bidirectional transformers for language understanding. *arXiv preprint arXiv:1810.04805*.

Jacob Devlin, Ming-Wei Chang, Kenton Lee, and Kristina Toutanova. 2019. BERT: Pre-training of deep bidirectional transformers for language understanding. In *Proceedings of the 2019 Conference of the North American Chapter of the Association for Computational Linguistics: Human Language Technologies, Volume 1 (Long and Short Papers)*, pages 4171–4186, Minneapolis, Minnesota. Association for Computational Linguistics.

Kaustubh D. Dhole, Varun Gangal, Sebastian Gehrmann, Aadesh Gupta, Zhenhao Li, Saad Mahamood, Abinaya Mahendiran, Simon Mille, Ashish Srivastava, Samson Tan, Tongshuang Wu, Jascha Sohl-Dickstein, Jinho D. Choi, Eduard Hovy, Ondrej Dusek, Sebastian Ruder, Sajant Anand, Nagender Aneja, Rabin Banjade, Lisa Barthe, Hanna Behnke, Ian Berlot-Attwell, Connor Boyle, Caroline Brun, Marco Antonio Sobrevilla Cabezudo, Samuel Cahyawijaya, Emile Chapuis, Wanxiang Che, Mukund Choudhary, Christian Clauss, Pierre Colombo, Filip Cornell, Gautier Dagan, Mayukh Das, Tanay Dixit, Thomas Dopierre, Paul-Alexis Dray, Suchitra Dubey, Tatiana Ekeinhor, Marco Di Giovanni, Rishabh Gupta, Rishabh Gupta, Louanes Hamla, Sang Han, Fabrice Harel-Canada, Antoine Honore, Ishan Jindal, Przemyslaw K. Joniak, Denis Kleyko, Venelin Kovatchev, Kalpesh Krishna, Ashutosh Kumar, Stefan Langer, Seungjae Ryan Lee, Corey James Levinson, Hualou Liang, Kaizhao Liang, Zhexiong Liu, Andrey Lukyanenko, Vukosi Marivate, Gerard de Melo, Simon Meoni, Maxime Meyer, Afnan Mir, Nafise Sadat Moosavi, Niklas Muennighoff, Timothy Sum Hon Mun, Kenton Murray, Marcin Namysl, Maria Obedkova, Priti Oli, Nivranshu Pasricha, Jan Pfister, Richard Plant, Vinay Prabhu, Vasile Pais, Libo Qin, Shahab Raji, Pawan Kumar Rajpoot, Vikas Raunak, Roy Rinberg, Nicolas Roberts, Juan Diego Rodriguez, Claude Roux, Vasconcellos P. H. S., Ananya B. Sai, Robin M. Schmidt, Thomas Scialom, Tshephisho Sefara, Saqib N. Shamsi, Xudong Shen, Haoyue Shi, Yiwen Shi, Anna Shvets, Nick Siegel, Damien Sileo, Jamie Simon, Chandan Singh, Roman Sitelew, Priyank Soni, Taylor Sorensen, William Soto, Aman Srivastava, KV Aditya Srivatsa, Tony Sun, Mukund Varma T, A Tabassum, Fiona Anting Tan, Ryan Teehan, Mo Tiwari, Marie Tolkiehn, Athena Wang, Zijian Wang, Gloria Wang, Zijie J. Wang, Fuxuan Wei, Bryan Wilie, Genta Indra Winata, Xinyi Wu, Witold Wydmański, Tianbao Xie, Usama Yaseen, M. Yee, Jing Zhang, and Yue Zhang. 2021. Nl-augmenter: A framework for task-sensitive natural language augmentation.

William B Dolan and Chris Brockett. 2005. Automatically constructing a corpus of sentential paraphrases. In *Proceedings of the Third International Workshop on Paraphrasing (IWP2005)*.

Christiane Fellbaum. 1998. *WordNet: An Electronic Lexical Database*. Bradford Books.

Steven Y. Feng, Varun Gangal, Jason Wei, Sarath Chandar, Soroush Vosoughi, Teruko Mitamura, and Eduard Hovy. 2021. A survey of data augmentation approaches for NLP. In *Findings of the Association for Computational Linguistics: ACL-IJCNLP 2021*, pages 968–988, Online. Association for Computational Linguistics.

Raphael Gontijo-Lopes, Sylvia J Smullin, Ekin D Cubuk, and Ethan Dyer. 2020. Affinity and diversity: Quantifying mechanisms of data augmentation. *arXiv preprint arXiv:2002.08973*.

Alex Hernández-García and Peter König. 2018. Data augmentation instead of explicit regularization. *arXiv preprint arXiv:1806.03852*.

Shayne Longpre, Yu Wang, and Christopher DuBois. 2020. How effective is task-agnostic data augmentation for pretrained transformers? *arXiv preprint arXiv:2010.01764*.

Edward Ma. 2019. Nlp augmentation. https://github.com/makcedward/nlpaug.

Marco Marelli, Luisa Bentivogli, Marco Baroni, Raffaella Bernardi, Stefano Menini, and Roberto Zamparelli. 2014. SemEval-2014 task 1: Evaluation of compositional distributional semantic models on full sentences through semantic relatedness and textual entailment. In *Proceedings of the 8th International Workshop on Semantic Evaluation (SemEval 2014)*, pages 1–8, Dublin, Ireland. Association for Computational Linguistics.

Tomas Mikolov, Ilya Sutskever, Kai Chen, Greg S Corrado, and Jeff Dean. 2013. Distributed representations of words and phrases and their compositionality. In *Advances in Neural Information Processing Systems*, pages 3111–3119.

Nathan Ng, Kyra Yee, Alexei Baevski, Myle Ott, Michael Auli, and Sergey Edunov. 2019. Facebook fair's wmt19 news translation task submission. In *Proc. of WMT*.

Kishore Papineni, Salim Roukos, Todd Ward, and Wei-Jing Zhu. 2002. Bleu: a method for automatic evaluation of machine translation. In *Proceedings of the 40th Annual Meeting of the Association for Computational Linguistics*, pages 311–318, Philadelphia, Pennsylvania, USA. Association for Computational Linguistics.

Luis Perez and Jason Wang. 2017. The effectiveness of data augmentation in image classification using deep learning. *arXiv preprint arXiv:1712.04621*.

Matt Post. 2018. A call for clarity in reporting BLEU scores. In *Proceedings of the Third Conference on Machine Translation: Research Papers*, pages 186–191, Brussels, Belgium. Association for Computational Linguistics.

Alec Radford, Jeffrey Wu, Rewon Child, David Luan, Dario Amodei, Ilya Sutskever, et al. 2019. Language models are unsupervised multitask learners. *OpenAI blog*, 1(8):9.

Machel Reid and Mikel Artetxe. 2022. PARADISE: Exploiting parallel data for multilingual sequence-to-sequence pretraining. In *Proceedings of the 2022 Conference of the North American Chapter of the Association for Computational Linguistics: Human Language Technologies*. Association for Computational Linguistics.

Machel Reid, Junjie Hu, Graham Neubig, and Yutaka Matsuo. 2021. AfroMT: Pretraining strategies and reproducible benchmarks for translation of 8 African languages. In *Proceedings of the 2021 Conference on Empirical Methods in Natural Language Processing*, pages 1306–1320, Online and Punta Cana, Dominican Republic. Association for Computational Linguistics.

Nils Reimers and Iryna Gurevych. 2019. Sentence-bert: Sentence embeddings using siamese bert-networks.

Richard Socher, Alex Perelygin, Jean Wu, Jason Chuang, Christopher D Manning, Andrew Y Ng, and Christopher Potts. 2013. Recursive deep models for semantic compositionality over a sentiment treebank. In *Proceedings of the 2013 conference on empirical methods in natural language processing*, pages 1631–1642.

Luke Taylor and Geoff Nitschke. 2018. Improving deep learning with generic data augmentation. In *2018 IEEE Symposium Series on Computational Intelligence (SSCI)*, pages 1542–1547. IEEE.

Jason Wei and Kai Zou. 2019. EDA: Easy data augmentation techniques for boosting performance on text classification tasks. In *Proceedings of the 2019 Conference on Empirical Methods in Natural Language Processing and the 9th International Joint Conference on Natural Language Processing (EMNLP-IJCNLP)*, pages 6382–6388, Hong Kong, China. Association for Computational Linguistics.

Thomas Wolf, Lysandre Debut, Victor Sanh, Julien Chaumond, Clement Delangue, Anthony Moi, Pierric Cistac, Tim Rault, Remi Louf, Morgan Funtowicz, Joe Davison, Sam Shleifer, Patrick von Platen, Clara Ma, Yacine Jernite, Julien Plu, Canwen Xu, Teven Le Scao, Sylvain Gugger, Mariama Drame, Quentin Lhoest, and Alexander Rush. 2020. Transformers: State-of-the-art natural language processing. In *Proceedings of the 2020 Conference on Empirical Methods in Natural Language Processing: System Demonstrations*, pages 38–45, Online. Association for Computational Linguistics.

Tianyi Zhang*, Varsha Kishore*, Felix Wu*, Kilian Q. Weinberger, and Yoav Artzi. 2020. Bertscore: Evaluating text generation with bert. In *International Conference on Learning Representations*.

Can Question Rewriting Help Conversational Question Answering?

Etsuko Ishii[*], **Yan Xu**[*], **Samuel Cahyawijaya**[*], **Bryan Wilie**
The Hong Kong University of Science and Technology
{eishii, yxucb, scahyawijaya, bwilie}@connect.ust.hk

Abstract

Question rewriting (QR) is a subtask of conversational question answering (CQA) aiming to ease the challenges of understanding dependencies among dialogue history by reformulating questions in a self-contained form. Despite seeming plausible, little evidence is available to justify QR as a mitigation method for CQA. To verify the effectiveness of QR in CQA, we investigate a reinforcement learning approach that integrates QR and CQA tasks and does not require corresponding QR datasets for targeted CQA. We find, however, that the RL method is on par with the end-to-end baseline. We provide an analysis of the failure and describe the difficulty of exploiting QR for CQA.

1 Introduction

The question rewriting (QR) task has been introduced as a mitigation method for conversational question answering (CQA). CQA asks a machine to answer a question based on the provided passage and a multi-turn dialogue (Reddy et al., 2019; Choi et al., 2018), which poses an additional challenge to comprehend the dialogue history. To ease the challenge, QR aims to teach a model to paraphrase a question into a self-contained format using its dialogue history (Elgohary et al., 2019a; Anantha et al., 2021a). Except for Kim et al. (2021), however, no one has provided evidence that QR is effective for CQA in practice. Existing works on QR often (i) depend on the existence of a QR dataset for every target CQA dataset, and (ii) focus more on generating high-quality rewrites than improving CQA performance, making them unsatisfactory for the justification of QR.

To verify the effectiveness of QR, we explore a reinforcement learning (RL) approach that integrates QR and CQA tasks without corresponding labeled QR datasets. In the RL framework, a QR model plays the role of "the agent" that receives

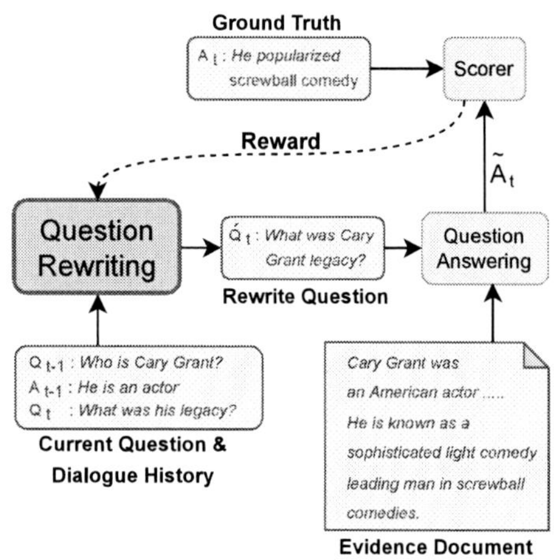

Figure 1: Overview of the RL approach. The current question Q_t and its dialogue history are reformulated into a self-contained question $\acute{Q}_t$ by the QR model. Then, $\acute{Q}_t$ is passed to the QA model to extract an answer span $\tilde{A}_t$ from the evidence document. We train the QR model by maximizing the reward obtained by comparing the predicted answer span $\tilde{A}_t$ with the gold span A_t.

rewards from a QA model that acts as "the environment." During training, the QR model aims to maximize the performance on the CQA task by generating better rewrites of the questions.

Despite the potential and plausibility of the RL approach, our experimental results suggest an upper bound of the performance, and it is on par with the baselines without QR. In this paper, we provide analysis to (i) understand the reason for the failure of the RL approach and (ii) reveal that QR cannot improve CQA performance even with the non-RL approaches. The code is available at https://github.com/HLTCHKUST/cqr4cqa.

2 Related Work

The CQA task aims to assist users in seeking information (Reddy et al., 2019; Choi et al., 2018; Campos et al., 2020). The key challenge is to re-

[*] Equal Contribution

Proceedings of the Third Workshop on Insights from Negative Results in NLP, pages 94 - 99
May 26, 2022 ©2022 Association for Computational Linguistics

Models		CoQA						QuAC		
		Overall F1	Child.	Liter.	M&H	News	Wiki.	F1	HEQ-Q	HEQ-D
	end-to-end	84.5	**84.4**	82.4	**82.9**	86.0	86.9	**67.8**	63.5	7.9
QReCC	pipeline	82.9	82.9	80.9	81.5	84.4	84.8	66.3	62.0	6.6
	ours	**84.7**	84.3	**83.1**	82.7	**86.3**	86.8	67.6	63.2	7.8
CANARD	pipeline	82.8	83.4	80.1	80.8	84.4	85.6	66.5	62.5	7.4
	EXCORD†	83.4 (+0.6)	**84.4 (1.9)**	81.2 (+1.0)	79.8 (-0.3)	84.6 (+0.3)	**87 (0.0)**	67.7 (+1.2)	**64.0 (+1.6)**	**9.3 (+2.1)**
	ours	84.4	84.1	82.7	82.6	86.0	86.7	67.4	62.7	8.1

Table 1: Evaluation results of our approach and baselines on the test set. EXCORD† follows the results reported by Kim et al. (2021) and (±x.x) indicate the improvement compared to their original baseline. **Bold** are the best results amongst all. Underlined represents the best score on each combination of the CQA and QR datasets.

solve the conversation history and understand a highly-contextualized question. Most prior works focus on model structures (Zhu et al., 2018; Yeh and Chen, 2019; Zhang et al., 2021b; Zhao et al., 2021) or training techniques (Ju et al., 2019; Xu et al., 2021) to improve the performance. QR tasks have been proposed to further improve CQA systems by paraphrase a question into a self-contained styles (Elgohary et al., 2019a; Petrén Bach Hansen and Søgaard, 2020; Anantha et al., 2021a). While many of the existing works on QR put more effort toward generating high-quality rewrites (Lin et al., 2020; Vakulenko et al., 2021), Kim et al. (2021) introduced a framework to leverage QR to finetune CQA models with a consistency-based regularization. QR has also been studied in single-turn QA and other information-seeking tasks (Nogueira and Cho, 2017; Buck et al., 2018).

3 Methodology

We denote a CQA dataset as $\{\mathcal{D}^n\}_{n=1}^N$ and the dialogue history at turn t as $\mathcal{D}_t = \{(Q_i, A_i)\}_{i=1}^t$, where Q_t is the question and A_t is the answer. Along with the QA pairs, the corresponding evidence documents Y_t are also given.

As depicted in Figure 1, our proposed RL framework involves a QA model as an environment and a QR model as an agent. Let $\acute{Q}_t = \{\acute{q}_l\}_{l=1}^L$ denote a generated rewritten question sequence of Q_t. The objective of the QR model is to rewrite the question Q_t at turn t into a self-contained version, based on the current question and the dialogue history $\mathcal{D}_{t-1}$. The agent takes an input state $X_t = (\mathcal{D}_{t-1}, Q_t)$ and generates a paraphrase $\acute{Q}_t$. Then, $\acute{X}_t = (\mathcal{D}_{t-1}, \acute{Q}_t)$ and an evidence document Y_t are provided to an environment, namely, the QA model f_ϕ, which extracts an answer span $\tilde{A}_t = f_\phi(\acute{X}_t, Y_t)$. We aim for the agent, a QR model π_θ, to learn to generate a high-quality paraphrase of the given question based on the reward received from the environment.

The policy, in our case the QR model, assigns probability

$$\pi_\theta(\acute{Q}_t|X_t) = \prod_{l=1}^{L} p(\acute{q}_l|\acute{q}_1, \dots, \acute{q}_{l-1}, X_t). \quad (1)$$

Our goal is to maximize the expected reward of the answer returned under the policy, namely,

$$\mathrm{E}_{\acute{q}_t \sim \pi_\theta(\cdot|q_t)}[r(f_\phi(\acute{X}_t))], \quad (2)$$

where r is a reward function. We apply the token-level F1-score between the predicted answer span $\tilde{A}_t$ and the gold span A_t as the reward r. We can directly optimize the expected reward in Eq. 2 using RL algorithms.

Prior to the training process, the QA model f_ϕ is fine-tuned on $\{\mathcal{D}^n\}$ and the QR model is initialized with $\pi_\theta = \pi_{\theta_0}$, where π_{θ_0} is a pretrained language model. We apply Proximal Policy Optimization (PPO) (Schulman et al., 2017; Ziegler et al., 2019) to train π_θ. PPO is a policy gradient method which alternates between sampling data through interaction with the environment and optimizing a surrogate objective function via stochastic gradient ascent. Following Ziegler et al. (2019), we apply a KL-penalty to the reward r so as to prevent the policy π_θ from drifting too far away from π_{θ_0}:

$$R_t = R(\acute{X}_t) = r(f_\phi(\acute{X}_t)) - \beta \mathrm{KL}(\pi_\theta, \pi_{\theta_0}),$$

where β represents a weight factor and R_t is the modified reward of r.

4 Experiments

4.1 Setup

We use a pretrained RoBERTa (Liu et al., 2019) model as the initial QA model and adapt it to the

	Question	F1 Score		Question	F1 Score
Q_t	What is the Vat the library of?	1.0	Q_t	Where did the band The Smashing Pumpkins put on display?	1.0
$\acute{Q}_t$	What is the Vat the Library of?	0.22	$\acute{Q}_t$	Where was the band The Smashing Pumpkins put on display?	0.0
Q_t	What was everybody doing?	0.91	Q_t	Which company produced the movie Island of Misfit Toys?	1.0
$\acute{Q}_t$	What was everyone doing?	0.0	$\acute{Q}_t$	Which company produced the movie, The Island of Misfit Toys?	0.0

Table 2: Minor modification of questions may cause a drastic change in CQA performance.

CQA tasks. For the QR models, we leverage pretrained GPT-2 (Radford et al., 2019) and first fine-tune them with QR datasets for better initialization. We attempt three settings: (a) directly fine-tune the QA model on the CQA datasets (end-to-end), (b) fine-tune the QA model with questions rewritten by the QR model (pipeline), and (c) train the QR model based on the reward obtained from the QA model. More details of the experiments can be found in Appendix A.

Datasets We conduct our experiments on two crowd-sourced CQA datasets, CoQA (Reddy et al., 2019) and QuAC (Choi et al., 2018). Since the test set is not publicly available for both CoQA and QuAC, following Kim et al. (2021), we randomly sample 5% of dialogues in the training set and adopt them as our validation set and report the test results on the original development set for the CoQA experiments. We apply the same split as Kim et al. (2021) for the QuAC experiments.

For the QR model pre-training, we use two QR datasets: QReCC (Anantha et al., 2021b) and CANARD (Elgohary et al., 2019b). CANARD is generated by rewriting a subset of the original questions in the QuAC datasets, and contains 40K questions in total. QReCC is built upon three publicly available datasets: QuAC, TREC Conversational Assistant Track (CAsT) (Dalton et al., 2020) and Natural Questions (NQ) (Kwiatkowski et al., 2019). QReCC contains 14K dialogues with 80K questions, and 9.3K dialogues are from QuAC.

Evaluation Metrics Following the leaderboards, we utilize the unigram F1 score to evaluate the QA performance. In CoQA evaluation, the QA models are also evaluated with the domain-wise F1 score. In QuAC evaluation, we incorporate the human equivalence score HEQ-Q and HEQ-D as well. HEQ-Q indicates the percentage of questions on which the model outperforms human beings and HEQ-D represents the percentage of dialogues on which the model outperforms human beings for all questions in the dialogue.

4.2 Results

We report our experimental results in Table 1. We see that our RL approach yields 0.9–1.6 F1 improvement over the pipeline setting regardless of the dataset combinations and performs almost as well as the end-to-end setting. This partially supports our expectation that RL lifts the CQA performance. However, we find it almost impossible to bring significant improvement over the end-to-end baseline despite our extensive trials. One reason why we cannot provide as much improvement as reported in Kim et al. (2021) would be related to the inputs of the QA model. Their EXCORD feeds the original questions together with the rewritten questions, whereas we only use the rewritten questions. It is also noteworthy that their results are consistently lower than ours, even lower than our end-to-end settings.

Our inspection of the questions generated by the QR models reveals that the models learn to copy the original questions by PPO training, and this is the direct reason that our method cannot outperform the end-to-end baselines. Indeed, on average, 89.6% of the questions are the same as the original questions after PPO training, although this value is 34.5% in the pipeline settings. We also discover a significant correlation between the performance and how much the QR models copy the original question (the correlation coefficient is 0.984 for CoQA and 0.967 for QuAC) and the edit distance from the original question (the correlation coefficient is -0.996 for CoQA and -0.989 for QuAC).

5 Discussion

In this section, we provide an analysis to (i) raise a sensitivity problem of the QA model to explain the failure of RL and (ii) disclose that there is no justification for QR, even in the non-RL approaches.

5.1 Sensitivity of the QA model

It appears that the QA models are more sensitive to trivial changes than the reward models in other successful language generation tasks, and this could

Perturb	Sentiment Analysis		CQA	
	Amazon	Yelp	CoQA	QuAC
Original	95.8	98.2	84.5	67.8
UPC	95.8 (-)	96.7 (**-1.5**)	74.8 (**-9.8**)	57.4 (**-10.5**)
SLW	91.9 (**-3.9**)	97.0 (**-1.1**)	83.0 (**-1.6**)	66.7 (**-1.1**)
WIF	94.3 (**-1.5**)	97.7 (**-0.5**)	82.6 (**-2.0**)	65.6 (**-2.2**)
SPP	94.8 (**-1.0**)	97.7 (**-0.5**)	78.3 (**-6.2**)	65.5 (**-2.4**)

Table 3: Robustness test on Sentiment Analysis and CQA tasks. We apply four perturbations: **UPC** (upper casing), **SLW** (slang word), **WIF** (word inflection), and **SPP** (sentence paraphrasing).

Datasets	QuAC Model		CANARD Model	
	F1	EM	F1	EM
QuAC	67.7	51.5	62.9	46.8
CANARD	65.1	49.9	63.3	46.9

Table 4: Results of the supervised learning approach. "XX Model" denotes the QA model trained on XX, and EM the percentage of the predictions the same as the gold.

account for our lower performance on CQA. As can be seen from the examples in Table 2, a subtle alteration such as uppercasing or replacement with synonyms can significantly change F1 scores.

To quantify the sensitivity of the reward models, we compare model robustness between our QA models and sentiment analysis models that have been reported in Ziegler et al. (2019) to be effective for stylistic language generation. We adopt publicly available models that are fine-tuned sentiment analysis datasets: BERT-based trained on Amazon polarity (McAuley and Leskovec, 2013)[1] and RoBERTa-base trained on Yelp polarity (Zhang et al., 2015)[2]. To test the robustness of the models, we introduce small perturbations to the samples in the test set using the NL-Augmenter toolkit (Dhole et al., 2021), and compare F1 scores on each task (experimental details in Appendix B).

Based on the robustness test given in Table 3, the QA models are shown to be significantly less robust against most perturbations compared to the sentiment analysis models. It is conceivable that this sensitivity of the QA model leads to a sparse reward problem for the agent, which causes instability for the model learning the optimal policy. An important direction for future studies is to ease the sparse reward problem by, for example, enhancing the robustness of the QA models.

[1]https://huggingface.co/fabriceyhc/bert-base-uncased-amazon_polarity

[2]https://huggingface.co/VictorSanh/roberta-base-finetuned-yelp-polarity

Datasets	CoQA		QuAC	
	F1	EM	F1	EM
end-to-end	**84.5**	**76.4**	**67.83**	51.47
QReCC	84.1	76.0	**67.83**	51.48
CANARD	83.7	75.8	67.81	**51.50**

Table 5: Results of the data augmentation approach. EM denotes the percentage of the predictions the same as the gold.

5.2 Can QR Help in Non-RL Approaches?

First, we evaluate with a simple supervised learning approach using rewrites provided by CANARD. Extracting the QuAC samples that have a CANARD annotation, we (i) evaluate the CANARD annotations with the QA model trained on QuAC (the model used in the main experiments) and (ii) train another QA model with the CANARD annotations. Training is under the same conditions of the QA model initialization as in the main experiments. As the results in Table 4 show, we can hardly observe the effectiveness of the CANARD annotations. This supports the claim in Buck et al. (2018) that better rewrites in the human eye are not necessarily better for machines and implies the difficulty of exploiting QR for CQA.

Moreover, we explore a data-augmentation approach to integrate QR and CQA. First, we generate ten possible rewrites using top-k sampling (Zhang et al., 2021a) for all the questions of the CQA datasets. To guarantee the quality of the rewrites, we select the best F1 scoring ones from every ten candidates and use them to teach another QR model how to reformulate questions (experimental details in Appendix C). As the results in Table 5 show, we consistently get worse scores compared to the end-to-end settings in CoQA, and almost the same scores for QuAC, not finding justification to apply QR in the manner of the data augmentation approach.

6 Conclusion

In this paper, we explore the RL approach to verify the effectiveness of QR in CQA, and report that the RL approach is on par with simple end-to-end baselines. We find the sensitivity of the QA models would disadvantage the RL training. Future work is needed to verify that QR is a promising mitigation method for CQA since even the non-RL approaches perform unsatisfactorily.

References

Raviteja Anantha, Svitlana Vakulenko, Zhucheng Tu, Shayne Longpre, Stephen Pulman, and Srinivas Chappidi. 2021a. Open-domain question answering goes conversational via question rewriting. In *Proceedings of the 2021 Conference of the North American Chapter of the Association for Computational Linguistics: Human Language Technologies*, pages 520–534, Online. Association for Computational Linguistics.

Raviteja Anantha, Svitlana Vakulenko, Zhucheng Tu, Shayne Longpre, Stephen Pulman, and Srinivas Chappidi. 2021b. Open-domain question answering goes conversational via question rewriting. In *Proceedings of the 2021 Conference of the North American Chapter of the Association for Computational Linguistics: Human Language Technologies*, pages 520–534.

Christian Buck, Jannis Bulian, Massimiliano Ciaramita, Wojciech Gajewski, Andrea Gesmundo, Neil Houlsby, and Wei Wang. 2018. Ask the right questions: Active question reformulation with reinforcement learning. In *International Conference on Learning Representations*.

Jon Ander Campos, Arantxa Otegi, Aitor Soroa, Jan Deriu, Mark Cieliebak, and Eneko Agirre. 2020. DoQA - accessing domain-specific FAQs via conversational QA. In *Proceedings of the 58th Annual Meeting of the Association for Computational Linguistics*, pages 7302–7314, Online. Association for Computational Linguistics.

Eunsol Choi, He He, Mohit Iyyer, Mark Yatskar, Wentau Yih, Yejin Choi, Percy Liang, and Luke Zettlemoyer. 2018. QuAC: Question answering in context. In *Proceedings of the 2018 Conference on Empirical Methods in Natural Language Processing*, pages 2174–2184, Brussels, Belgium. Association for Computational Linguistics.

Jeffrey Dalton, Chenyan Xiong, and Jamie Callan. 2020. Trec cast 2019: The conversational assistance track overview. *arXiv preprint arXiv:2003.13624*.

Kaustubh D. Dhole, Varun Gangal, Sebastian Gehrmann, Aadesh Gupta, Zhenhao Li, Saad Mahamood, Abinaya Mahendiran, Simon Mille, Ashish Srivastava, Samson Tan, Tongshuang Wu, Jascha Sohl-Dickstein, Jinho D. Choi, Eduard Hovy, Ondrej Dusek, Sebastian Ruder, Sajant Anand, Nagender Aneja, Rabin Banjade, Lisa Barthe, Hanna Behnke, Ian Berlot-Attwell, Connor Boyle, Caroline Brun, Marco Antonio Sobrevilla Cabezudo, Samuel Cahyawijaya, Emile Chapuis, Wanxiang Che, Mukund Choudhary, Christian Clauss, Pierre Colombo, Filip Cornell, Gautier Dagan, Mayukh Das, Tanay Dixit, Thomas Dopierre, Paul-Alexis Dray, Suchitra Dubey, Tatiana Ekeinhor, Marco Di Giovanni, Rishabh Gupta, Rishabh Gupta, Louanes Hamla, Sang Han, Fabrice Harel-Canada, Antoine Honore, Ishan Jindal, Przemyslaw K. Joniak, Denis Kleyko, Venelin Kovatchev, Kalpesh Krishna, Ashutosh Kumar, Stefan Langer, Seungjae Ryan Lee, Corey James Levinson, Hualou Liang, Kaizhao Liang, Zhexiong Liu, Andrey Lukyanenko, Vukosi Marivate, Gerard de Melo, Simon Meoni, Maxime Meyer, Afnan Mir, Nafise Sadat Moosavi, Niklas Muennighoff, Timothy Sum Hon Mun, Kenton Murray, Marcin Namysl, Maria Obedkova, Priti Oli, Nivranshu Pasricha, Jan Pfister, Richard Plant, Vinay Prabhu, Vasile Pais, Libo Qin, Shahab Raji, Pawan Kumar Rajpoot, Vikas Raunak, Roy Rinberg, Nicolas Roberts, Juan Diego Rodriguez, Claude Roux, Vasconcellos P. H. S., Ananya B. Sai, Robin M. Schmidt, Thomas Scialom, Tshephisho Sefara, Saqib N. Shamsi, Xudong Shen, Haoyue Shi, Yiwen Shi, Anna Shvets, Nick Siegel, Damien Sileo, Jamie Simon, Chandan Singh, Roman Sitelew, Priyank Soni, Taylor Sorensen, William Soto, Aman Srivastava, KV Aditya Srivatsa, Tony Sun, Mukund Varma T, A Tabassum, Fiona Anting Tan, Ryan Teehan, Mo Tiwari, Marie Tolkiehn, Athena Wang, Zijian Wang, Gloria Wang, Zijie J. Wang, Fuxuan Wei, Bryan Wilie, Genta Indra Winata, Xinyi Wu, Witold Wydmański, Tianbao Xie, Usama Yaseen, M. Yee, Jing Zhang, and Yue Zhang. 2021. Nl-augmenter: A framework for task-sensitive natural language augmentation.

Ahmed Elgohary, Denis Peskov, and Jordan Boyd-Graber. 2019a. Can you unpack that? learning to rewrite questions-in-context. In *Proceedings of the 2019 Conference on Empirical Methods in Natural Language Processing and the 9th International Joint Conference on Natural Language Processing (EMNLP-IJCNLP)*, pages 5918–5924, Hong Kong, China. Association for Computational Linguistics.

Ahmed Elgohary, Denis Peskov, and Jordan Boyd-Graber. 2019b. Can you unpack that? learning to rewrite questions-in-context. In *Proceedings of the 2019 Conference on Empirical Methods in Natural Language Processing and the 9th International Joint Conference on Natural Language Processing (EMNLP-IJCNLP)*, pages 5918–5924.

Ying Ju, Fubang Zhao, Shijie Chen, Bowen Zheng, Xuefeng Yang, and Yunfeng Liu. 2019. Technical report on conversational question answering. *arXiv preprint arXiv:1909.10772*.

Gangwoo Kim, Hyunjae Kim, Jungsoo Park, and Jaewoo Kang. 2021. Learn to resolve conversational dependency: A consistency training framework for conversational question answering. In *Proceedings of the 59th Annual Meeting of the Association for Computational Linguistics and the 11th International Joint Conference on Natural Language Processing (Volume 1: Long Papers)*, pages 6130–6141, Online. Association for Computational Linguistics.

Tom Kwiatkowski, Jennimaria Palomaki, Olivia Redfield, Michael Collins, Ankur Parikh, Chris Alberti, Danielle Epstein, Illia Polosukhin, Jacob Devlin, Kenton Lee, et al. 2019. Natural questions: A benchmark for question answering research. *Transactions of the*

Association for Computational Linguistics, 7:452–466.

Sheng-Chieh Lin, Jheng-Hong Yang, Rodrigo Nogueira, Ming-Feng Tsai, Chuan-Ju Wang, and Jimmy Lin. 2020. Conversational question reformulation via sequence-to-sequence architectures and pretrained language models. *arXiv preprint arXiv:2004.01909*.

Yinhan Liu, Myle Ott, Naman Goyal, Jingfei Du, Mandar Joshi, Danqi Chen, Omer Levy, Mike Lewis, Luke Zettlemoyer, and Veselin Stoyanov. 2019. Roberta: A robustly optimized bert pretraining approach. *arXiv preprint arXiv:1907.11692*.

Julian McAuley and Jure Leskovec. 2013. Hidden factors and hidden topics: Understanding rating dimensions with review text. In *Proceedings of the 7th ACM Conference on Recommender Systems*, RecSys '13, page 165–172, New York, NY, USA. Association for Computing Machinery.

Rodrigo Nogueira and Kyunghyun Cho. 2017. Task-oriented query reformulation with reinforcement learning. In *Proceedings of the 2017 Conference on Empirical Methods in Natural Language Processing*, pages 574–583, Copenhagen, Denmark. Association for Computational Linguistics.

Victor Petrén Bach Hansen and Anders Søgaard. 2020. What do you mean 'why?': Resolving sluices in conversations. *Proceedings of the AAAI Conference on Artificial Intelligence*, 34(05):7887–7894.

Alec Radford, Jeffrey Wu, Rewon Child, David Luan, Dario Amodei, Ilya Sutskever, et al. 2019. Language models are unsupervised multitask learners. *OpenAI blog*, 1(8):9.

Siva Reddy, Danqi Chen, and Christopher D. Manning. 2019. CoQA: A conversational question answering challenge. *Transactions of the Association for Computational Linguistics*, 7:249–266.

John Schulman, Filip Wolski, Prafulla Dhariwal, Alec Radford, and Oleg Klimov. 2017. Proximal policy optimization algorithms. *CoRR*, abs/1707.06347.

Svitlana Vakulenko, Shayne Longpre, Zhucheng Tu, and Raviteja Anantha. 2021. Question rewriting for conversational question answering. In *Proceedings of the 14th ACM International Conference on Web Search and Data Mining*, pages 355–363.

Yan Xu, Etsuko Ishii, Genta Indra Winata, Zhaojiang Lin, Andrea Madotto, Zihan Liu, Peng Xu, and Pascale Fung. 2021. Caire in dialdoc21: Data augmentation for information seeking dialogue system. In *Proceedings of the 1st Workshop on Document-grounded Dialogue and Conversational Question Answering (DialDoc 2021)*, pages 46–51.

Yi-Ting Yeh and Yun-Nung Chen. 2019. Flowdelta: Modeling flow information gain in reasoning for conversational machine comprehension. In *Proceedings of the 2nd Workshop on Machine Reading for Question Answering*, pages 86–90.

Hugh Zhang, Daniel Duckworth, Daphne Ippolito, and Arvind Neelakantan. 2021a. Trading off diversity and quality in natural language generation. In *Proceedings of the Workshop on Human Evaluation of NLP Systems (HumEval)*, pages 25–33, Online. Association for Computational Linguistics.

Xiang Zhang, Junbo Zhao, and Yann LeCun. 2015. Character-level Convolutional Networks for Text Classification . *arXiv:1509.01626 [cs]*.

Zhuosheng Zhang, Junjie Yang, and Hai Zhao. 2021b. Retrospective reader for machine reading comprehension. *Proceedings of the AAAI Conference on Artificial Intelligence*, 35(16):14506–14514.

Jing Zhao, Junwei Bao, Yifan Wang, Yongwei Zhou, Youzheng Wu, Xiaodong He, and Bowen Zhou. 2021. RoR: Read-over-read for long document machine reading comprehension. In *Findings of the Association for Computational Linguistics: EMNLP 2021*, pages 1862–1872, Punta Cana, Dominican Republic. Association for Computational Linguistics.

Chenguang Zhu, Michael Zeng, and Xuedong Huang. 2018. Sdnet: Contextualized attention-based deep network for conversational question answering. *arXiv preprint arXiv:1812.03593*.

Daniel M Ziegler, Nisan Stiennon, Jeffrey Wu, Tom B Brown, Alec Radford, Dario Amodei, Paul Christiano, and Geoffrey Irving. 2019. Fine-tuning language models from human preferences. *arXiv preprint arXiv:1909.08593*.

Clustering Examples in Multi-Dataset NLP Benchmarks with Item Response Theory

Pedro Rodriguez
me@pedro.ai

Phu Mon Htut
New York University
pmh330@nyu.edu

John P. Lalor
University of Notre Dame
john.lalor@nd.edu

Joao Sedoc
New York University
jsedoc@stern.nyu.edu

Abstract

In natural language processing, multi-dataset benchmarks for common tasks (e.g., SuperGLUE for natural language inference and MRQA for question answering) have risen in importance. Invariably, tasks and individual examples vary in difficulty. Recent analysis methods infer properties of examples such as difficulty. In particular, Item Response Theory (IRT) jointly infers example and model properties from the output of benchmark tasks (i.e., scores for each model-example pair). Therefore, it seems sensible that methods like IRT should be able to detect differences between datasets in a task. This work shows that current IRT models are not as good at identifying differences as we would expect, explain why this is difficult, and outline future directions that incorporate more (textual) signal from examples.

1 Introduction

Understanding and describing the data in natural language processing (NLP) benchmarks is crucial to ensuring their validity and reliability (Ferraro et al., 2015; Gebru et al., 2018; Bender and Friedman, 2018). This is even more important as multi-dataset task benchmarks have—for better or worse—become the norm (Raji et al., 2021). For example, SuperGLUE incorporates eight natural language inference (NLI) datasets (Wang et al., 2019), and MRQA incorporates twelve question answering (QA) datasets (Fisch et al., 2019). To better understand benchmark data, there are methods for analyzing examples in isolation (Lalor et al., 2018), characterizing a dataset's data distribution (Swayamdipta et al., 2020), using individual models to glean insight about datasets and examples (Feng et al., 2018), and using many models to do the same (Rodriguez et al., 2021; Vania et al., 2021). This paper investigates how effectively one method—Item Response Theory (IRT)—gives insight into multi-dataset benchmarks.

Outside of NLP, IRT provides insight into educational test questions (Lord et al., 1968; Baker, 2001) and political ideologies of legislators (Poole and Rosenthal, 2017). In NLP, IRT is used to identify helpful training examples (Lalor and Yu, 2020), detect errors in evaluation examples (Rodriguez et al., 2021), and estimate the future utility of examples in benchmarks (Vania et al., 2021). The goal of this paper is to identify the characteristics of multi-dataset benchmarks that IRT methods focus on. Are certain datasets easier than others? Can clustering highlight dataset or example properties?

We hypothesize that examples from similar datasets will cluster together as they should have similar IRT characteristics (such as difficulty level) compared to examples from other datasets. However, we do not see any distinct dataset-based clusters in our results. Instead, we find that IRT characteristics tend to group the examples of similar labels in the same clusters, suggesting that some label types are more difficult or more discriminating regardless of the datasets they belong to. In the rest of this paper, we describe IRT methods for benchmark analysis (§2), our clustering methods (§3), and our experimental results (§4).[1]

2 IRT for Benchmark Analysis

In this paper, we adapt IRT methods to explain *why* benchmarks examples are difficult, rather than solely assigning them difficulty values. This section describes the IRT models in our experiments and the test-bed we use in our experiments.

2.1 Item Response Theory Models

IRT is a probabilistic framework that models the likelihood that subject j (e.g., a model) answers test item i (e.g., a sentiment prediction) correctly.

[1] Code and data at www.pedro.ai/multidim-irt.

Proceedings of the Third Workshop on Insights from Negative Results in NLP, pages 100 - 112
May 26, 2022

Task	N	Datasets
Sentiment	24,620	Amazon reviews (Zhang et al., 2015), Yelp reviews,* SST-3 (Socher et al., 2013), and Dynasent Rounds 1 & 2 (Potts et al., 2021)
NLI	63,018	ANLI rounds one through three (Nie et al., 2020), HANS (McCoy et al., 2019), MNLI matched & MNLI mismatched (Williams et al., 2018), SNLI (Bowman et al., 2015), and Winogender (Rudinger et al., 2018)

*https://www.yelp.com/dataset

Table 1: Details of the datasets used in our experiments.

Likelihood of correct answer for subject j on item i.

$$p(y_{ij} = 1 | \gamma_i, \beta_i, \lambda_i, \theta_j) = \frac{\lambda_i}{1 + e^{-\gamma_i(\theta_j - \beta_i)}} \tag{1}$$

Discriminability of item i; Ability of subject j; Difficulty of item i

The likelihood of a correct response (Equation 1) is modeled as a relationship between the difficulty (β_i) of an item, its discriminability (γ_i), its feasibility (λ_i), and the subject's ability (θ_j). Typically, θ_j and β_i are unconstrained, λ_i is between zero and one, and γ_i is non-negative.

This model is a four parameter (4PL) IRT model (Equation 1) and while complex, easily simplifies to simpler models.[2] For example, when $\lambda_i = 1$ and $\gamma_i = 1$ this is a 1PL model. In this case, the difference between subject ability and item difficulty ($\theta_j - \beta_i$) determines the likelihood of a correct answer: as subject ability increases, the likelihood of a correct response increases. When only $\lambda_i = 1$, this is a 2PL model as in topic modeling experiments (§4.2). IRT parameters can also be multidimensional. In two experimental setups (§4.1 and §A), we use a 2PL model ($\lambda_i = 1$) where γ_i, β_i, and θ_j are multidimensional. We fit all models with `py-irt` (Lalor and Rodriguez, 2022).

2.2 Benchmark Data

Ideally, IRT methods should generalize across multiple datasets, tasks, and models. To accomplish this while minimizing engineering overhead, we use data from `dynabench.org` (Kiela et al., 2021)—a dynamic benchmark of multiple tasks, datasets, and model submissions (Table 1).[3] For each task, there are seven models: a majority baseline (always positive), ALBERT (Lan et al., 2020), BERT (Devlin et al., 2019), DeBERTa (He et al., 2020), FastText (Bojanowski et al., 2017; Joulin et al., 2017), RoBERTa (Liu et al., 2019), and T5 (Raffel et al., 2020). In experiments, IRT infers parameters from the subject-item (i.e., model-example) matrix where entries are one if the subject answered the item correctly and zero otherwise.

IRT analysis offers a way to assign properties like difficulty and discriminability to examples, but does little to explain why a particular example may be hard or easy. Next, we identify interpretable features that might explain IRT parameter values (e.g., label, topics, and embeddings).

3 Interpreting IRT Parameters

This section explains the methods that our experiments (§4) use to interpret IRT parameters. These methods fall into two categories: (1) methods that correlate examples' IRT parameters with dataset or label features and (2) methods that correlate derived textual information with IRT parameters (e.g., topic models or embeddings).

3.1 Multidimensional IRT Clustering

Intuitively, test instances—be they NLI examples or SAT questions—can be difficult along more than one dimension. An example might focus on testing commonsense reasoning instead of testing background knowledge. Therefore, it is sensible for IRT models to learn multidimensional parameters, but do different difficulty dimensions align with our intuitions on what might make examples easier or harder? To interpret evaluation data with multidimensional IRT, we: (1) train multidimensional IRT models,[4] (2) use t-SNE for dimensionality reduction (Poličar et al., 2019), (3) plot the resulting points in 2D space, and (4) color the points by

[2] 4PL models usually include a guessing parameter that indicates the likelihood of answering the item correctly by random guess. The guessing parameter is set to zero in our experiments.

[3] To avoid test set leakage, we use development set data.

[4] We set the dimension of the IRT model to the number of datasets per task (5 for sentiment and 8 for NLI), and the number of labels in each task (3 for both sentiment and NLI).

characteristics of each example such as the classification label or source dataset (§4.1).

3.2 Topic Models

Our next method is based on the intuition that textual information—in particular topical associations—affects example difficulty. If true, topical associations should correlate with IRT parameters. To test this, we fit a topic model to the five datasets in the Dynabench sentiment task (Table 1). To avoid having too many topics to interpret, we fit the model with five topics using the `mallet` software package (McCallum, 2002).[5] We obtain IRT parameters from a one dimensional, 2PL IRT model (Equation 1). As with multidimensional IRT, we jointly visualize an interpretable feature (topic assignment) and IRT parameter values (§4.2).

3.3 Using BERT to Predict IRT Parameters

If textual information is correlated item difficulty, then transformer models like BERT should also be able to predict IRT parameters given the item text. We test this idea by fine-tuning a BERT model (Devlin et al., 2019) with regression heads to predict the difficulty and discriminability parameters of a 4PL IRT model (Equation 1). As with the multidimensional clustering method, we also visualize embeddings from BERT-base (§4.3). The goal of our visualizations is to test: (1) how BERT embeddings change with IRT fine-tuning and (2) whether clusters correspond to interpretable instance features (e.g., label or source dataset).

4 Experiments

Next, we discuss what each interpretation method (§3) tells us about IRT parameter values.

4.1 Multidimensional IRT Clustering

Using the subject-item response matrix from Dynabench, we fit a multidimensional 2PL model, cluster with t-SNE, and color the datapoints by either dataset name or the example label.

When we run t-SNE on the difficulty parameters of a 5-dimensional 2PL model for sentiment datasets and color-code by dataset, we do not observe any distinct dataset-based clusters (Figure 1a). However, when we color-code by label, we observe more well-defined clusters, especially for the positive and negative labels (Figure 1b). This result suggests that some label types are more difficult for models to learn or more discriminating among the models regardless of which dataset they belong to. While the lack of dataset-based clustering is a negative result, label-based trends indicate consistency among items with the same label in terms of learned IRT parameters. However, the lack of breadth within a label suggests that each label can only accurately estimate a narrow range of ability levels in models.[6]

4.2 How Do Topics Relate to Item Difficulty?

We first validate that the topics inferred by the topic model (Table 2) are reasonable through manual inspection. The topic model successfully identifies at least five distinct review themes: media (e.g., movies, music), hotels, books, products, and food. Having verified that the topic model is at least reasonable, we next inspect the relationship between the highest scoring topic per example and its difficulty (Figure 3). We see that certain topics are more prevalent at different levels of difficulty; however, there is no clear delineation between topics and difficulties. This suggests that at least this topic model alone does not fully explain difficulty.[7]

4.3 How Does IRT Difficulty Influence BERT?

Figure 2 compares t-SNE visualizations of embeddings from a normal BERT model as opposed to a BERT model that is fine-tuned to predict 4PL difficulty and discriminability parameters from the sentiment task. When points are color coded by label, the embeddings of the IRT fine-tuned BERT model clearly form label-based clusters. In contrast, we do not observe clear patterns or clusters for the embeddings of the vanilla BERT model. This indicates separation of labels by IRT parameters.[8] This suggests that IRT parameters are correlated with dataset labels, and the BERT embeddings learned on IRT parameters encode label properties.

4.4 Discussion

It is generally agreed that some datasets are more challenging than others. Therefore, items in the

[5]For model training, we use an optimization interval of 10 with 3,000 iterations.

[6]We performed additional clustering analyses on the sentiment and NLI datasets, varying the IRT models learned and the IRT parameters used for clustering (Appendix A). In all cases we observed more well-defined label-based clusters than dataset-based clusters.

[7]We also replicate the plot with discriminability, but do not observe any visually discernible patterns.

[8]IRT-based distributions of examples (Figure 8 in the appendices) show that there are clearer patterns with respect to IRT when we group the examples by their dataset labels.

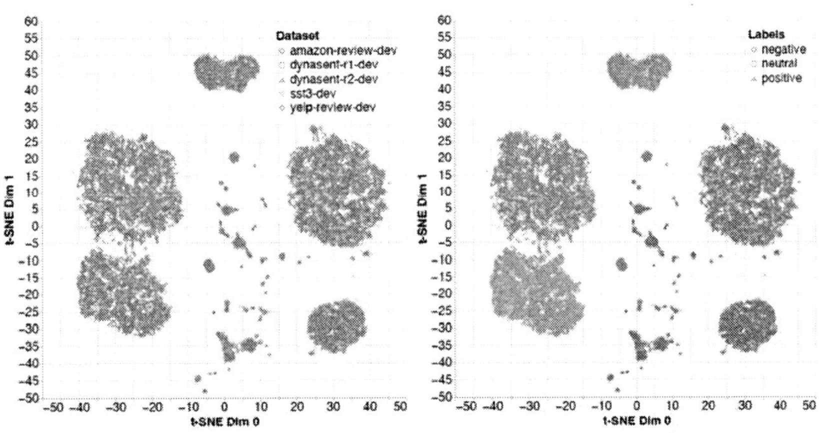

(a) (b)

Figure 1: t-SNE visualization of sentiment datasets on the 5-dimensional 2PL IRT difficulty parameter, colored by dataset (a) and by label (b). Coloring by dataset does not result in easily discernable clusters; coloring by label produces well separated clusters for positive and neutral labels. The negation cluster is distinct but has more intruders than other labels. This suggests example label is more correlated with difficulty than source dataset.

Topic ID	Topic Words in Dynabench Sentiment Datasets
0	movie num good album music great film songs love time
1	num place time room back service people hotel didn good
2	book read story good books num reading great time characters
3	num product great good bought work time buy back price
4	num food good place great service ordered back time restaurant

Table 2: We train a five-topic, topic model on the Dynabench sentiment data (Table 1). Topics correspond to five review themes: media, hotel, book, product, and food. Topic IDs and colors correspond to Figure 3.

same dataset should have similar IRT characteristics. However, our results indicate that benchmark datasets display more depth than breadth in terms of example IRT parameters. For a multi-dataset task such as NLI, examples clustered by IRT parameters group according to shared labels, not shared datasets. While learned latent topics show some variation across IRT difficulty, it is not clearly evident that certain topics are more difficult than others. While we cannot conclude that certain topics or datasets are more difficult than others, our results suggest that certain *labels* are.

5 Conclusion and Future Work

In this work, our expectation was that datasets would be separable by IRT-learned parameters. However, we found that clustering was more interpretable at the label level than the dataset level.

Future work in IRT should better jointly model the characteristics of NLP data as opposed to our methods that train these components in isolation. For example, it may be that the signal provided by dataset properties is second order to labels and our methods may not effectively model this (potential) multi-level relationship. Multidimensional IRT models that encode relationships between difficulty dimensions ought to better fit the data (e.g., predicting sentiment of restaurant reviews should overlap with hotel reviews, as they both involve service). If these models succeed, they should aid the interpretation of benchmarks. Lastly, as models provide more information through initiatives like Model Cards (Mitchell et al., 2019), IRT could jointly model these properties with latent ability parameters to glean insights into which differences in models yield empirical impacts.

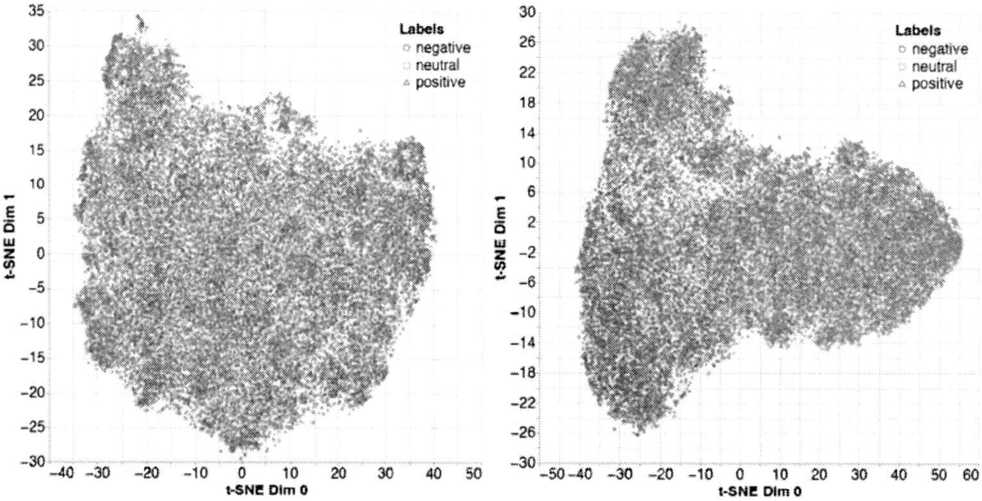

(a) (b)

Figure 2: Clustering results for the Dynasent datasets using a BERT embeddings from a BERT model used to predict IRT parameters. 2a: Cluster by labels using untrained BERT. 2b: Cluster by labels using trained BERT. Without fine-tuning, there are no clear patterns between BERT embeddings and label. However, fine-tuning to predict IRT parameters shows clear clustering patterns between embeddings and labels. This suggests that embeddings learned to predict IRT parameters can encode the properties of dataset labels.

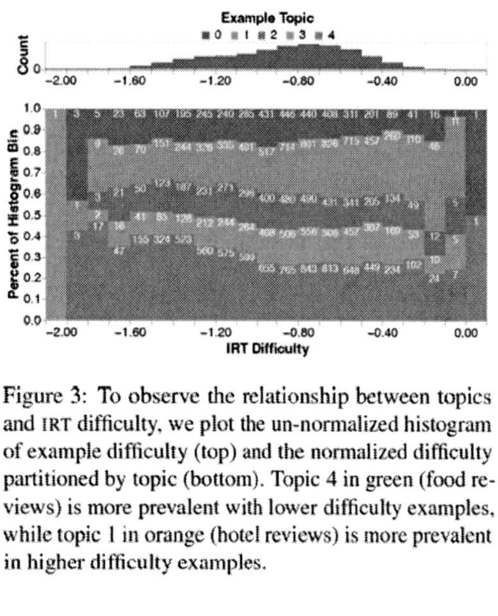

Figure 3: To observe the relationship between topics and IRT difficulty, we plot the un-normalized histogram of example difficulty (top) and the normalized difficulty partitioned by topic (bottom). Topic 4 in green (food reviews) is more prevalent with lower difficulty examples, while topic 1 in orange (hotel reviews) is more prevalent in higher difficulty examples.

References

Frank B Baker. 2001. *The Basics of Item Response Theory*. ERIC.

Emily M Bender and Batya Friedman. 2018. Data statements for natural language processing: Toward mitigating system bias and enabling better science. *Transactions of the Association for Computational Linguistics*, 6:587–604.

Piotr Bojanowski, Edouard Grave, Armand Joulin, and Tomas Mikolov. 2017. Enriching word vectors with subword information. *Transactions of the Association for Computational Linguistics*, 5:135–146.

Samuel R Bowman, Gabor Angeli, Christopher Potts, and Christopher D Manning. 2015. A large annotated corpus for learning natural language inference. In *Proceedings of Empirical Methods in Natural Language Processing*. Association for Computational Linguistics.

Jacob Devlin, Ming-Wei Chang, Kenton Lee, and Kristina Toutanova. 2019. BERT: Pre-training of deep bidirectional transformers for language understanding. In *Conference of the North American Chapter of the Association for Computational Linguistics*. Association for Computational Linguistics.

Shi Feng, Eric Wallace, Alvin Grissom II, Mohit Iyyer, Pedro Rodriguez, and Jordan Boyd-Graber. 2018. Pathologies of neural models make interpretations difficult. In *Proceedings of Empirical Methods in Natural Language Processing*. Association for Computational Linguistics.

Francis Ferraro, Nasrin Mostafazadeh, Ting-Hao Huang, Lucy Vanderwende, Jacob Devlin, Michel Galley, and Margaret Mitchell. 2015. A survey of current datasets for vision and language research. In *Proceedings of Empirical Methods in Natural Language Processing*. Association for Computational Linguistics.

Adam Fisch, Alon Talmor, Robin Jia, Minjoon Seo, Eunsol Choi, and Danqi Chen. 2019. MRQA 2019 shared task: Evaluating generalization in reading comprehension. In *Proceedings of the 2nd Workshop on Machine Reading for Question Answering*. Association for Computational Linguistics.

Timnit Gebru, Jamie Morgenstern, Briana Vecchione, Jennifer Wortman Vaughan, Hanna Wallach, Hal Daumé Iii, and Kate Crawford. 2018. Datasheets for datasets.

Pengcheng He, Xiaodong Liu, Jianfeng Gao, and Weizhu Chen. 2020. DeBERTa: Decoding-enhanced BERT with disentangled attention.

Armand Joulin, Edouard Grave, Piotr Bojanowski, and Tomas Mikolov. 2017. Bag of tricks for efficient text classification. In *Proceedings of the European Chapter of the Association for Computational Linguistics*.

Douwe Kiela, Max Bartolo, Yixin Nie, Divyansh Kaushik, Atticus Geiger, Zhengxuan Wu, Bertie Vidgen, Grusha Prasad, Amanpreet Singh, Pratik Ringshia, Zhiyi Ma, Tristan Thrush, Sebastian Riedel, Zeerak Waseem, Pontus Stenetorp, Robin Jia, Mohit Bansal, Christopher Potts, and Adina Williams. 2021. Dynabench: Rethinking benchmarking in NLP. In *Conference of the North American Chapter of the Association for Computational Linguistics*. Association for Computational Linguistics.

John P. Lalor and Pedro Rodriguez. 2022. py-irt: A scalable item response theory library for python. *arXiv preprint arXiv:2203.01282*.

John P Lalor, Hao Wu, Tsendsuren Munkhdalai, and Hong Yu. 2018. Understanding deep learning performance through an examination of test set difficulty: A psychometric case study. In *Proceedings of Empirical Methods in Natural Language Processing*. Association for Computational Linguistics.

John P Lalor and Hong Yu. 2020. Dynamic data selection for curriculum learning via ability estimation. In *Findings of the Association for Computational Linguistics: EMNLP*. Association for Computational Linguistics.

Zhenzhong Lan, Mingda Chen, Sebastian Goodman, Kevin Gimpel, Piyush Sharma, and Radu Soricut. 2020. ALBERT: A lite BERT for self-supervised learning of language representations. In *Proceedings of the International Conference on Learning Representations*.

Yinhan Liu, Myle Ott, Naman Goyal, Jingfei Du, Mandar Joshi, Danqi Chen, Omer Levy, Mike Lewis, Luke Zettlemoyer, and Veselin Stoyanov. 2019. RoBERTa: A robustly optimized BERT pretraining approach. *arXiv preprint arXiv:1907.11692*.

F M Lord, M R Novick, and Allan Birnbaum. 1968. Statistical theories of mental test scores.

Andrew Kachites McCallum. 2002. Mallet: A machine learning for language toolkit. http://mallet.cs.umass.edu.

Tom McCoy, Ellie Pavlick, and Tal Linzen. 2019. Right for the wrong reasons: Diagnosing syntactic heuristics in natural language inference. In *Proceedings of the Association for Computational Linguistics*. Association for Computational Linguistics.

Margaret Mitchell, Simone Wu, Andrew Zaldivar, Parker Barnes, Lucy Vasserman, Ben Hutchinson, Elena Spitzer, Inioluwa Deborah Raji, and Timnit Gebru. 2019. Model cards for model reporting. In *Proceedings of the Conference on Fairness, Accountability, and Transparency*. Association for Computing Machinery.

Yixin Nie, Adina Williams, Emily Dinan, Mohit Bansal, Jason Weston, and Douwe Kiela. 2020. Adversarial NLI: A new benchmark for natural language understanding. In *Proceedings of the Association for Computational Linguistics*. Association for Computational Linguistics.

Pavlin G. Poličar, Martin Stražar, and Blaž Zupan. 2019. openTSNE: a modular python library for t-sne dimensionality reduction and embedding.

Keith T Poole and Howard Rosenthal. 2017. *Ideology & congress: A political economic history of roll call voting*, 2 edition. Routledge, London, England.

Christopher Potts, Zhengxuan Wu, Atticus Geiger, and Douwe Kiela. 2021. DynaSent: A dynamic benchmark for sentiment analysis. In *Proceedings of the Association for Computational Linguistics*. Association for Computational Linguistics.

Colin Raffel, Noam Shazeer, Adam Roberts, Katherine Lee, Sharan Narang, Michael Matena, Yanqi Zhou, Wei Li, and Peter J Liu. 2020. Exploring the limits of transfer learning with a unified Text-to-Text transformer. *Journal of Machine Learning Research*, 21(140):1–67.

Inioluwa Deborah Raji, Emily M Bender, Amandalynne Paullada, Emily Denton, and Alex Hanna. 2021. AI and the everything in the whole wide world benchmark. In *NeurIPS: Datasets and Benchmarks Track*.

Pedro Rodriguez, Joe Barrow, Alexander Hoyle, John P. Lalor, Robin Jia, and Jordan Boyd-Graber. 2021. Evaluation examples are not equally informative: How should that change NLP leaderboards? In *Proceedings of the Association for Computational Linguistics*. Association for Computational Linguistics.

Rachel Rudinger, Jason Naradowsky, Brian Leonard, and Benjamin Van Durme. 2018. Gender bias in coreference resolution. In *Conference of the North American Chapter of the Association for Computational Linguistics*. Association for Computational Linguistics.

Richard Socher, Alex Perelygin, Jean Wu, Jason Chuang, Christopher D Manning, Andrew Ng, and Christopher Potts. 2013. Recursive deep models for semantic compositionality over a sentiment treebank.

In *Proceedings of Empirical Methods in Natural Language Processing*. Association for Computational Linguistics.

Swabha Swayamdipta, Roy Schwartz, Nicholas Lourie, Yizhong Wang, Hannaneh Hajishirzi, Noah A Smith, and Yejin Choi. 2020. Dataset cartography: Mapping and diagnosing datasets with training dynamics. In *Proceedings of Empirical Methods in Natural Language Processing*. Association for Computational Linguistics.

Clara Vania, Phu Mon Htut, William Huang, Dhara Mungra, Richard Yuanzhe Pang, Jason Phang, Haokun Liu, Kyunghyun Cho, and Samuel R. Bowman. 2021. Comparing test sets with item response theory. In *Proceedings of the Association for Computational Linguistics*. Association for Computational Linguistics.

Alex Wang, Yada Pruksachatkun, Nikita Nangia, Amanpreet Singh, Julian Michael, Felix Hill, Omer Levy, and Samuel Bowman. 2019. SuperGLUE: A stickier benchmark for General-Purpose language understanding systems. In *Proceedings of Advances in Neural Information Processing Systems*.

Adina Williams, Nikita Nangia, and Samuel Bowman. 2018. A Broad-Coverage challenge corpus for sentence understanding through inference. In *Conference of the North American Chapter of the Association for Computational Linguistics*. Association for Computational Linguistics.

Xiang Zhang, Junbo Zhao, and Yann LeCun. 2015. Character-level convolutional networks for text classification. *Proceedings of Advances in Neural Information Processing Systems*.

A Additional Visualizations

A.1 Dataset Based Clustering

In Figure 4a, we run t-SNE on the discriminability parameters of a 5-dimensional 2PL model learned for the Dynasent datasets and color-code by data set. We do not observe any distinct dataset-based clusters. We repeat the same visualizations using difficulty and discriminability parameters of a 3-dimensional 2PL model learned on Dynasent datasest (Figure 5a and 5c), a 3-dimensional 2PL model learned on NLI datasets (Figure 7a and 7c), and an 8-dimensional 2PL model learned on NLI datasets (Figure 6a and 6c). In all these experiments, we do not observe any distinct dataset-based cluster.

A.2 Label Based Clustering

In Figure 4b, we run t-SNE on the discriminability parameters of a 5-dimensional 2PL model learned for the Dynasent datasets and color-code by dataset labels. We repeat the same visualizations using difficulty and discriminability parameters of a 3-dimensional 2PL model learned on Dynasent datasest (Figure 5b and 5d), a 3-dimensional 2PL model learned on NLI datasets (Figure 7b and 7d), and an 8-dimensional 2PL model learned on NLI datasets (Figure 6b and 6d). In all these experiments, we observe clearer clusters compared to Section A.1.

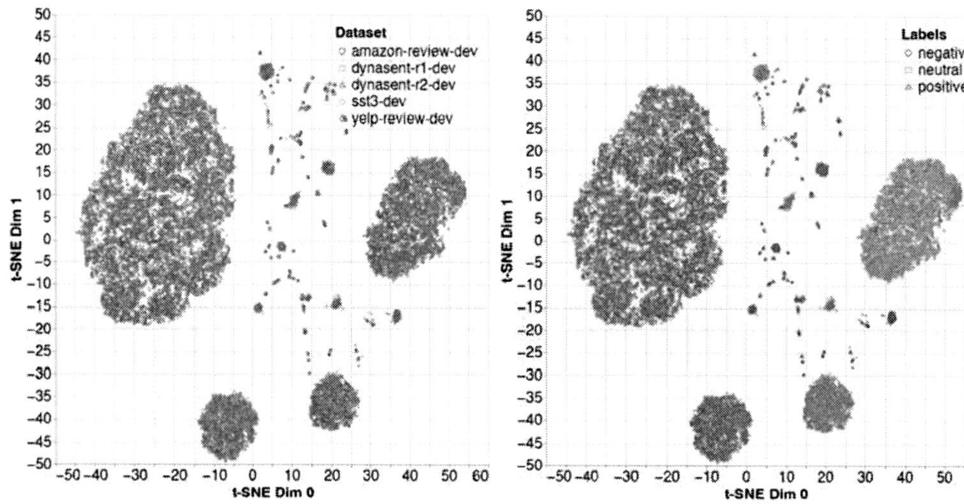

(a) (b)

Figure 4: T-SNE visualisation of the Dynasent datasets on the discriminability parameter of a 5-dimensional 2PL model: (a) marked by dataset, (b) marked by label.

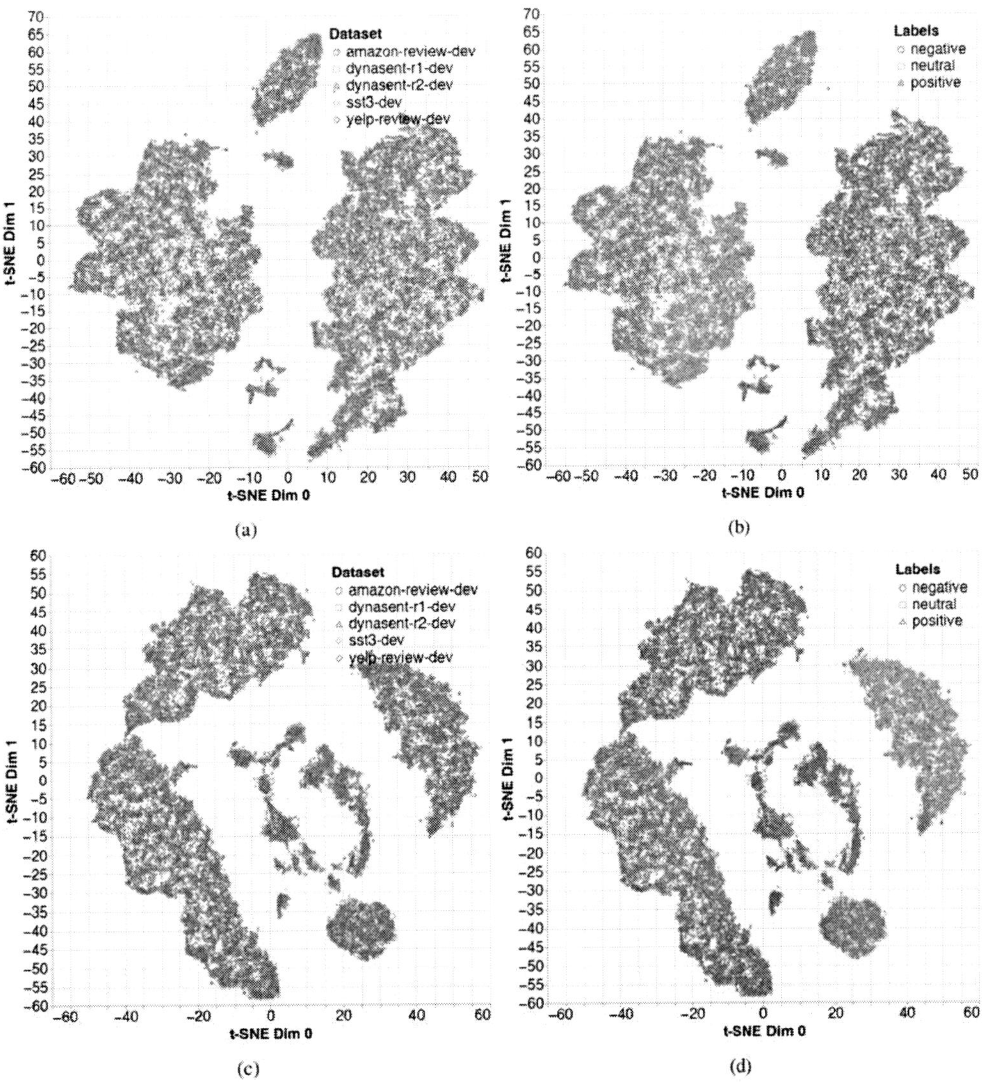

Figure 5: T-SNE visualisation of the Dynasent datasets on the parameters of a 3-dimensional 2PL model: (a) Difficulty marked by dataset, (b) Difficulty marked by label, (c) Discriminability marked by dataset, (d) Discriminability marked by label.

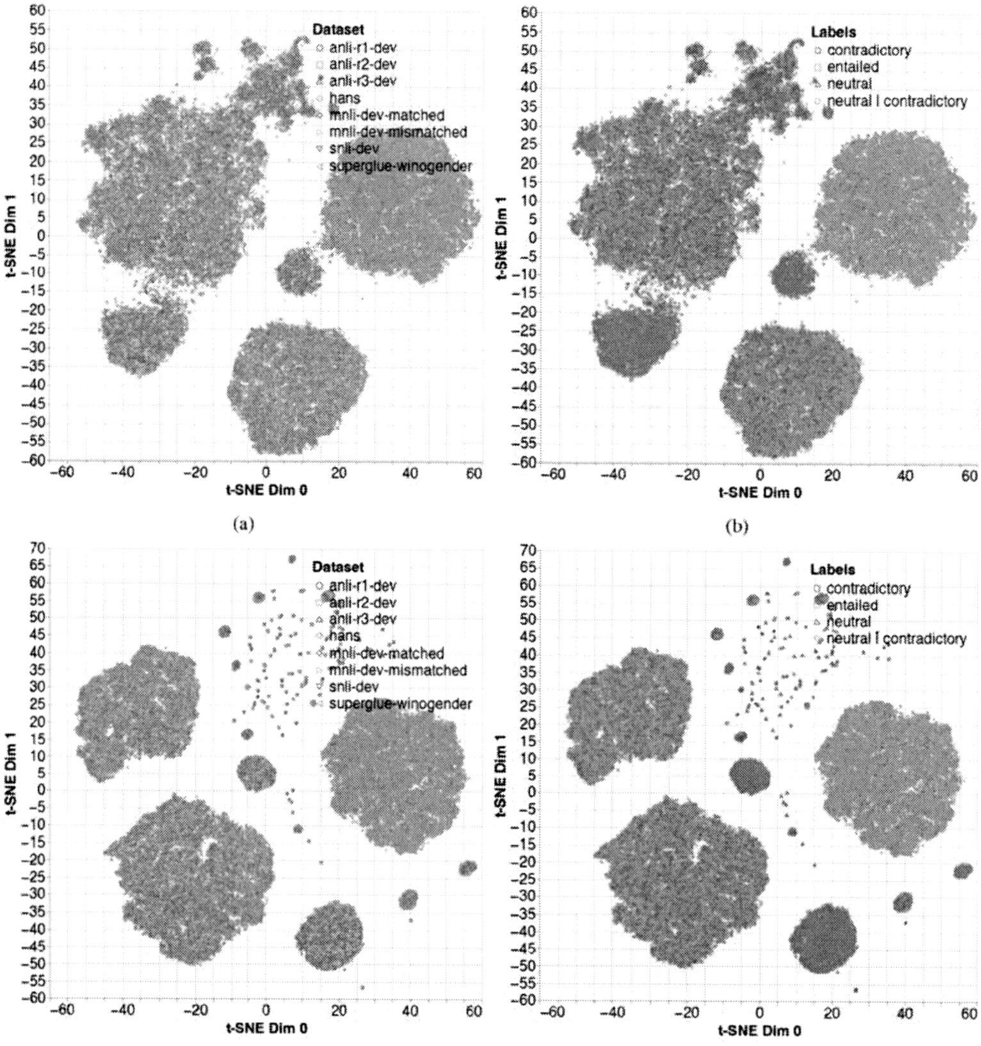

Figure 6: T-SNE visualisation of the NLI datasets on the parameters of a 8-dimensional 2PL model: (a) Difficulty marked by dataset, (b) Difficulty marked by label, (c) Discriminability marked by dataset, (d) Discriminability marked by label.

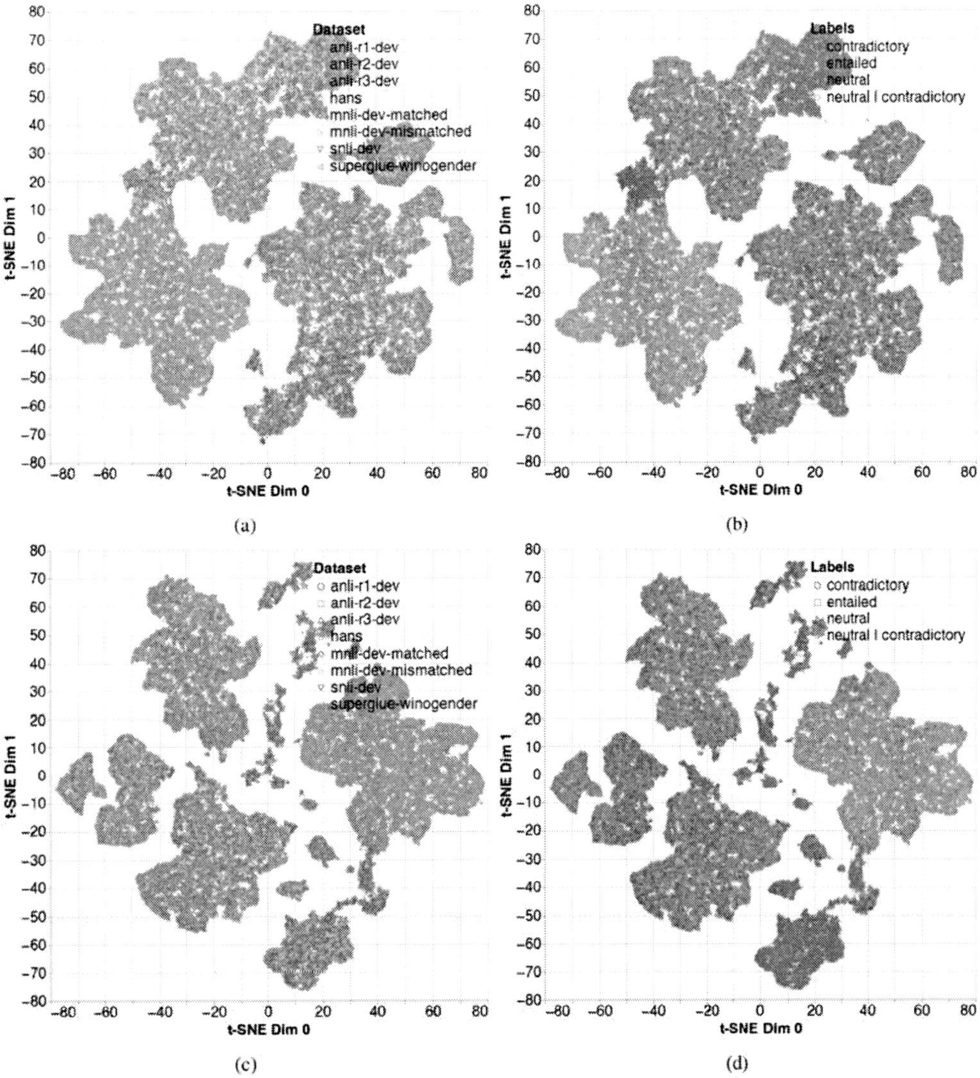

Figure 7: T-SNE visualisation of the NLI datasets on the parameters of a 3-dimensional 2PL model: (a) Difficulty marked by dataset, (b) Difficulty marked by label, (c) Discriminability marked by dataset, (d) Discriminability marked by label.

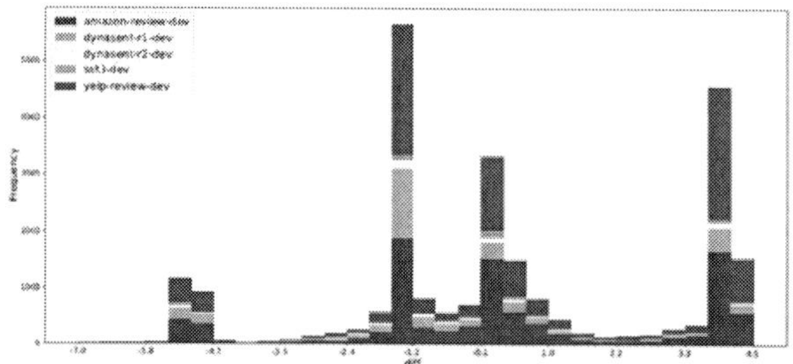

(a)

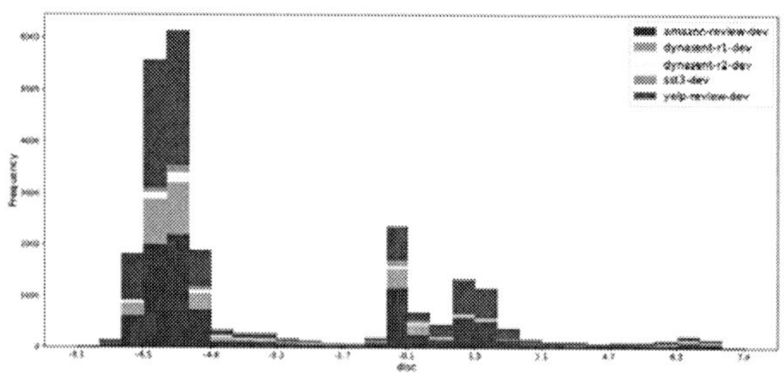

(b)

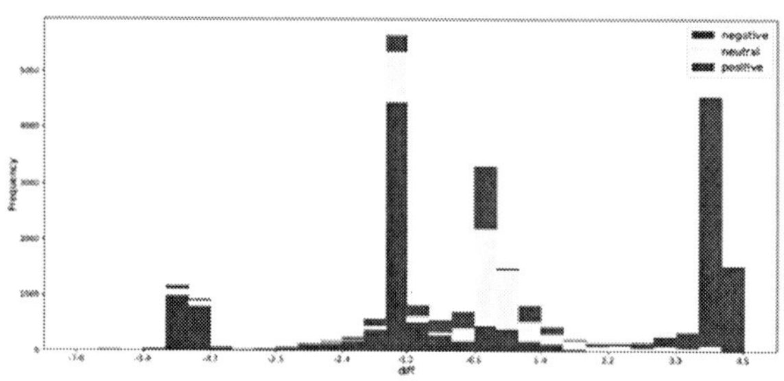

(c)

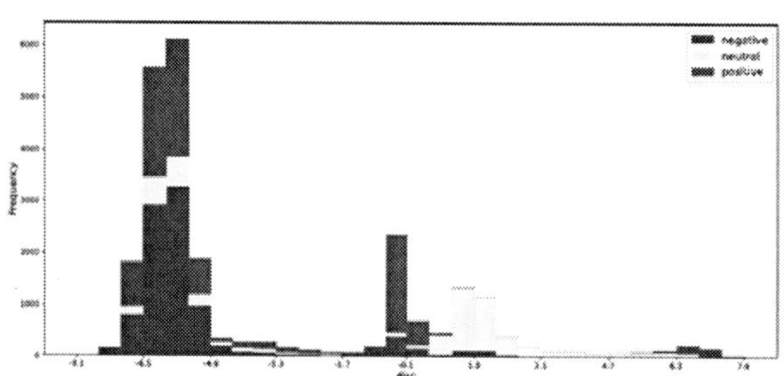

(d)

Figure 8: Distributions of examples for the sentiment datasets (3PL model): (a) Diff by dataset, (b) Disc by dataset, (c) Diff by label, (b) Disc by label.

On the Limits of Evaluating Embodied Agent Model Generalization Using Validation Sets

Hyounghun Kim[1] **Aishwarya Padmakumar**[2] **Di Jin**[2]
Mohit Bansal[1,2] **Dilek Hakkani-Tur**[2]
[1]UNC Chapel Hill [2]Amazon Alexa AI
{hyounghk, mbansal}@cs.unc.edu {padmakua, djinamzn, hakkanit}@amazon.com

Abstract

Natural language guided embodied task completion is a challenging problem since it requires understanding natural language instructions, aligning them with egocentric visual observations, and choosing appropriate actions to execute in the environment to produce desired changes. We experiment with augmenting a transformer model for this task with modules that effectively utilize a wider field of view and learn to choose whether the next step requires a navigation or manipulation action. We observed that the proposed modules resulted in improved, and in fact state-of-the-art performance on an unseen validation set of a popular benchmark dataset, ALFRED. However, our best model selected using the unseen validation set underperforms on the unseen test split of ALFRED, indicating that performance on the unseen validation set may not in itself be a sufficient indicator of whether model improvements generalize to unseen test sets. We highlight this result as we believe it may be a wider phenomenon in machine learning tasks but primarily noticeable only in benchmarks that limit evaluations on test splits, and highlights the need to modify benchmark design to better account for variance in model performance.

1 Introduction

Language guided embodied task completion is an important skill for embodied agents requiring them to follow natural language instructions to navigate in their environment and manipulate objects to complete tasks. Natural language is an easy medium for users to interact with embodied agents and effective use of natural language instructions can enable agents to navigate more easily in previously unexplored environments, and complete tasks involving novel combinations of object manipulations. Vision and language navigation benchmarks (Anderson et al., 2018; Thomason et al., 2019; Ku et al., 2020) provide an agent with natural language route instructions and evaluate their ability to follow these to navigate to a target location. It requires agents to have a deep understanding of natural language instructions, ground these in egocentric image observations and predict a sequence of actions in the environment. Other benchmarks study the manipulation and arrangement of objects (Bisk et al., 2016; Wang et al., 2016; Li et al., 2016; Bisk et al., 2018) - another crucial skill to complete many tasks that users may desire embodied agents to be able to complete. These tasks additionally require agents to reason about the states of objects and relations between them. Language guided embodied task completion benchmarks (Shridhar et al., 2020; Kim et al., 2020; Padmakumar et al., 2022) combine these skills – requiring agents to perform both navigation and object manipulation/arrangement following natural language instructions.

In this paper, we explore a challenging navigation and manipulation benchmark, ALFRED (Shridhar et al., 2020), where an agent has to learn to follow complex hierarchical natural language instructions to complete tasks by navigating in a virtual environment and manipulating objects to produce desired state changes. The ALFRED benchmark provides a training dataset of action trajectories taken by an embodied agent in a variety of simulated indoor rooms paired with hierarchical natural language instructions describing the task to be accomplished and the steps to be taken to do so. For validation and testing of models, there are two splits each - seen and unseen splits. The seen validation and testing splits consist of instructions set in the same rooms as those in the training set, while the unseen splits consist of instructions set in rooms the agent has never seen before, with rooms in the unseen test set being different from those in the train and unseen validation set. Performance on the unseen validation and test sets are considered to be the best indicators of whether a model can really solve the task as the agent must operate in

Proceedings of the Third Workshop on Insights from Negative Results in NLP, pages 113 - 118
May 26, 2022 ©2022 Association for Computational Linguistics

a completely novel floorplan, and cannot rely for example on memorized locations of large objects such as a fridge or a sink. Additionally, the ground truth action sequences are not publicly available for the seen and unseen test sets, and participants must submit prediction acted sequences on the test sets to an evaluation server where they are privately evaluated to obtain test performance. The evaluation server limits the number of submissions that can be made from an account to one per week to discourage directly tuning hyperparameters of a model on the test set. It is expected that following standard procedure in training machine learning models, one may use the validation sets to evaluate models trained with different hyperparameters, or ablating different components on the validation sets and only evaluate the best model on the test sets. Since ideally we would want a model to perform well on the unseen test set, it is reasonable to use success rate on the unseen validation set as a metric to choose which model is to be submitted for evaluation on the unseen test set.

One technique previously demonstrated to improve performance on ALFRED is the use of a multi-view setup (Nguyen et al., 2021; Kim et al., 2021) where an agent turns or moves its head in place at every time step to obtain additional views before deciding what action to take. In contrast to current models that simply concatenate features from each view, we use view-action matching - explicitly aligning embeddings of actions with embeddings of corresponding views - and using a score from fusing these aligned embeddings to select the next action to be taken. This is inspired by a dominant paradigm for modeling visual navigation tasks called viewpoint selection (Fried et al., 2018) where an agent predicts the next action by examining the resultant views each of those would produce and selecting the desired future view. Viewpoint selection is possible in some simulators such as R2R where the environment does not get altered by the agent's actions and the agent's movement is confined to a fixed grid. The ALFRED dataset uses the AI2-THOR simulator which supports a wider action space, physics modeling for movement and a more dynamic environment including irreversible actions. Hence, it is not possible to obtain the view that would result from an action without taking it, preventing direct application of viewpoint selection. Additionally, the agent must decide at each time step whether to perform navigation or manipulation actions. In contrast to prior work that uses a single classifier layer over all possible actions treating them equally, we propose a gate module which gives a higher weight to actions of a more relevant action type.

We follow standard experimental procedure training our modified models on the train split and using success rate on the unseen validation split to compare to baselines and perform ablation studies. On this set, the proposed model equipped with the aforementioned modules outperforms the state-of-the-art multi-view setup approaches and the ablation study shows each proposed module helps improve the model's performance.

However, we observe an unexpected and large performance gap between the unseen validation and test data splits. Our model outperforms state-of-the-art baseline models on the unseen validation split, but performs worse than them on the unseen test split. We hypothesize that it may be possible to overfit hyperparameters and design choices to one set of unseen environments (the unseen validation) and hence success on one such set of unseen environments is insufficient to guarantee that a model will generalize to another set of unseen environments (the unseen test). We report this finding as we believe this situation is likely more common during development on machine learning benchmarks, but such intermediate results are unlikely to be published. Instead after a poor result on a test set, it is likely that researchers continue further model modifications until a model setting is obtained that performs well on the test set. We believe that such models are likely overfitting to the test set of the benchmark and may not generalize well to a new test set.

2 Dataset & Environment

In this paper, we focus on improving models for the ALFRED (Shridhar et al., 2020) benchmark. ALFRED is built using the AI2-THOR simulator (Kolve et al., 2017) which consists of 120 indoor scenes across 4 types of rooms. Scenes also contain a diverse set of objects that are rearranged in different configurations for each trajectory in the dataset. In ALFRED, a agent is given a high level natural language goal statement (*"Put a chilled pan on the counter"*) as well as step by step natural language instructions corresponding to subgoals to be completed in order for achieving the goal (*"Turn around and cross the room and then go right and turn to the left to face the stove ... Put the pan down on the counter to the right of the toaster").* An agent has access to all these instructions at the start of the task and then has to iteratively predict navigation and manipulation actions in the environment based on egocentric image observations to complete subgoals in order. An agent must predict between a discrete set of possible navigation and manipulation actions, and predict a segmentation mask for the object to be manipulated if a manipulation action is predicted. The performance for an agent is evaluated by comparing the final states of the objects at the end of the action trajectory executed by the agent to the states of the objects at the end of the ground truth trajectory.

3 Model

We employ a vision-language transformer, LXMERT (Tan and Bansal, 2019) as the base architecture for our model. We encode the language input using a learned word embedding and transformer layer, and action history using a linear layer. Following Pashevich et al. (2021), we extract image features using a faster R-CNN (Ren et al., 2015) pretrained on images from the AI2-THOR simulator, and average-pool features of regions into a single vector. The visual and action features are first combined via a liner layer, and then fused with language features through a cross modal transformer layer.

View-Action Matching. We collect the multiple views (front, left, right, up, down) and go through the aforementioned process to obtain a feature V_i from the cross modal transformer for each view, and compute its matching score M_i with the corresponding action embedding A_i using a feedforward network.

Action-Type Gate. We additionally learn a gate vector using a linear layer over features of all views at the current time step to better distinguish between navigation and non-navigation actions. This layer is trained to predict high weights for actions of the same type as the ground truth action and low weights otherwise. The predicted weights are multiplied pointwise with match scores M_i and the action with the highest resultant score is selected. For example, if the ground truth action at a particular time step is `Move forward`, the gate will ensure that a prediction of `ToggleOff` which is a non-navigation action will receive a higher loss than a prediction of `Turn Right`, which is also an incorrect action but of the same type as the ground truth action (navigation).

	Model	Wide View	View-Act Matching	Act-Type Gate	Success Rate (%)
1	Base LXMERT Architecture	✗	✗	✗	4.7
2	VAM (Ours)	✓	✗	✗	9.3
3	VAM (Ours)	✓	✓	✗	11.8
4	VAM (Ours)	✓	✓	✓	13.8

Table 1: Performance improvement from wide view, view-action matching and action type gate modules on the ALFRED validation unseen split.

Loss. The model is trained via cross-entropy losses for action (teacher-forcing) and object type.

4 Experiments

Implementation & Training Details. We use 2 language and 2 cross-modal LXMERT layers for the model, and use 768 as the hidden size. We use AdamW (Loshchilov and Hutter, 2018) as the optimizer with the learning rate 1×10^{-5}. All of the experiments are run on AWS 'p3.16xlarge' EC2 instances running Ubuntu 18.04. We employ PyTorch (Paszke et al., 2017) to build our models.

Data Splits. Following Shridhar et al. (2020), we train our models on the train split and use success rate on the unseen validation split to perform model selection, and determine whether our model changes are likely to improve over existing state of the art models. We used the validation splits to evaluate the efficacy of variants of the transformer architecture, number of layers and number of epochs of training to use. We then submitted predictions from the best performing model on the unseen validation split to the evaluation server to obtain scores on the test sets.

Evaluation Metrics. We report two evaluation metrics from Shridhar et al. (2020) on validation and test splits. Success rate (SR) measures the fraction of episodes whether the predicted model trajectory results in all object state changes produced by the ground truth action trajectory. Goal Condition Success Rate (GC) measures the fraction of such desired state changes across all episodes that were accomplished by model-predicted trajectories.

Model Comparison. Recently, the best performing models on the ALFRED benchmark make use of semantic map representations of the environment (Blukis et al., 2021). However, these rely on pre-exploration of the environment to build a semantic map, rather than utilizing language instruc-

Subgoals	Wide View	(+) View-Act Matching	(+) Act-Type Gate
CleanObject	81.4	89.4	91.2
CoolObject	100.0	100.0	100.0
GotoLocation	62.0	66.2	67.1
HeatObject	100.0	100.0	98.5
PickupObject	69.2	68.5	68.5
PutObject	66.6	71.2	68.3
SliceObject	62.2	61.3	69.4
ToggleObject	51.4	42.2	41.6

Table 2: Success rate (%) of the sub-goal tasks on the ALFRED validation unseen split.

tions to directly navigate to target objects. Therefore, we focus on comparing our model with other multi-view setup models that are the state-of-the-art among non-SLAM models. LWIT (Nguyen et al., 2021) predicts an initial actions from an selected instruction alone and integrates the actions sequence with visual information to generate final actions to take. ABP (Kim et al., 2021) factorizes the model into interactive perception and action policy modules for adapting to two different tasks (the former needs a pixel-level and the latter requires a global information). However, although they employ multi-view setup, the information from each view collapses into one integrated feature. On the other hand, our model exploit each view directly to keep the useful clues without any loss.

5 Results

We first evaluate the utility of each modeling change on the unseen validation set of ALFRED. As shown Table 1, we gain 4.6% on success rate from adding a wider field of view, an additional 2.5% from view-action matching and a further 2% from action type gating. We observe a variance of 3% in success rate of the same type of model trained with different random seeds so we consider a 4.6% improvement to be sufficiently large to be unlikely from pure variance.

Sub-Goal Performance. Considering the proportion of GotoLocation to the total number of sub-goal tasks (i.e., 48%) and its role of bridging other sub-goal tasks, navigation is very crucial ability for a agent to successfully perform this challenging ALFRED task. As shown in Table 2, our full view-action matching (VAM) model improves the performance of GotoLocation task by 5.1% while also improves performance for some of other sub-goal tasks. This performance boost could attribute to the agent's ability to figure out where to go (View-Action Matching) and what to do (Action-Type Gate).

Validation-Test Performance Gap. When we compare to other baselines in Table 3, although our model outperforms other state-of-the-art models on the unseen validation split by a large margin, its performance on the unseen test split is poorer, whereas the reverse trend is seen with ABP (Kim et al., 2021). This suggests that good performance from a model on an unseen validation set may not be a good method to determine whether model changes are likely to generalize to another unseen test set.

This lack of generalization is more likely in current embodied learning tasks such as vision-and-language navigation or embodied task completion in comparison to other machine learning tasks due to the way unseen test sets are defined in embodied learning tasks. While ALFRED in particular does not introduce new object categories at test time, both validation and test unseen environments are visually different, by design from the training environment and from each other. When we compare models on the validation set, we hope that an increase in performance denotes a model that is more capable of generalizing to *any* unseen environment. However, it may only be the case that the model only generalizes better to the particular visual differences present in the unseen validation environment.

When the benchmark limits access to the test set, as in ALFRED, when dealing with a model that demonstrates variance when trained with different random seeds, hyperparameters and across training epochs, it is natural to choose the setting that results in the highest performance on the unseen validation set. However, a different setting may in fact be optimal for the unseen test set due to visual differences. While such a design is likely significantly more computationally expensive, it may be necessary to redesign benchmarks to take an average of performance from a few different variants of a model to reliably rank different modelling methods, instead of using scores from individual runs. We may also want to re-evaluate the value of keeping a test set private, as in the case of ALFRED that avoids prevents allowing models to overfit on the test set, but also makes it difficult to analyze the robustness of model performance between the validation and test sets. We would also like to encourage the reviewing community to enable the publication of modelling techniques whose performance is in the same ball-

Split	Model	Seen		Unseen	
		SR	GC	SR	GC
Val	LWIT	33.70	43.10	9.70	23.10
	ABP	42.93	50.45	12.55	25.19
	VAM (Ours)	40.9	47.9	13.8	28.1
Test	LWIT	29.16	38.82	8.37	19.13
	ABP	44.55	51.13	15.43	24.76
	VAM (Ours)	35.42	43.98	8.57	20.69

Table 3: Success rate (%) on the ALFRED evaluation splits (GC: Goal-Condition). Our model outperforms the state-of-the-art multi-view setup models on validation splits but not test splits.

park as existing state-of-the-art models, but novel in some way, as opposed to solely relying on a model achieving a top score on a leaderboard as a criterion for publication, as this limits the development that could be made using these alternative modeling approaches.

6 Conclusion

We attempted to improve a transformer model for embodied task completion by enabling it to effectively uses multiple views via view-action matching and action-type gating. Our view-action matching module computes a matching score between each a view and the embedding of the action used to generate it, and the gate module gives a higher weight to a more appropriate action type. While our model outperformed relevant baselines on the ALFRED unseen validation split, the trend was reversed on the unseen test split, suggesting that it may not be possible to over-utilize a validation split when making model selection choices so that the resultant model does not perform well on the test split. We choose to publish this result as we believe this phenomenon is likely more common than reported with machine learning benchmarks, but only noticeable to researchers when working on a benchmark with limited access to the test set. We additionally hope that our work encourages the publication of promising modelling approaches that do not work as reliably as expected, so that these can act as a guide to researchers to better inform their future directions.

Acknowledgments

We thank the reviewers for their helpful comments. This work was partially done while Hyounghun Kim was interning at Amazon Alexa AI and later extended at UNC, where it was supported by NSF Award 1840131 and DARPA KAIROS Grant FA8750-19-2-1004. The views contained in this article are those of the authors and not of the funding agency.

References

Peter Anderson, Qi Wu, Damien Teney, Jake Bruce, Mark Johnson, Niko Sünderhauf, Ian Reid, Stephen Gould, and Anton van den Hengel. 2018. Vision-and-language navigation: Interpreting visually-grounded navigation instructions in real environments. In *Proceedings of the IEEE Conference on Computer Vision and Pattern Recognition*, pages 3674–3683.

Yonatan Bisk, Daniel Marcu, and William Wong. 2016. Towards a dataset for human computer communication via grounded language acquisition. In *Workshops at the Thirtieth AAAI Conference on Artificial Intelligence*.

Yonatan Bisk, Kevin J Shih, Yejin Choi, and Daniel Marcu. 2018. Learning interpretable spatial operations in a rich 3d blocks world. In *Thirty-Second AAAI Conference on Artificial Intelligence*.

Valts Blukis, Chris Paxton, Dieter Fox, Animesh Garg, and Yoav Artzi. 2021. A persistent spatial semantic representation for high-level natural language instruction execution. In *5th Annual Conference on Robot Learning*.

Daniel Fried, Ronghang Hu, Volkan Cirik, Anna Rohrbach, Jacob Andreas, Louis-Philippe Morency, Taylor Berg-Kirkpatrick, Kate Saenko, Dan Klein, and Trevor Darrell. 2018. Speaker-follower models for vision-and-language navigation. In *NeurIPS*.

Byeonghwi Kim, Suvaansh Bhambri, Kunal Pratap Singh, Roozbeh Mottaghi, and Jonghyun Choi. 2021. Agent with the big picture: Perceiving surroundings for interactive instruction following. In *Embodied AI Workshop CVPR*.

Hyounghun Kim, Abhaysinh Zala, Graham Burri, Hao Tan, and Mohit Bansal. 2020. Arramon: A joint navigation-assembly instruction interpretation task in dynamic environments. In *Proceedings of the 2020 Conference on Empirical Methods in Natural Language Processing: Findings*, pages 3910–3927.

Eric Kolve, Roozbeh Mottaghi, Winson Han, Eli VanderBilt, Luca Weihs, Alvaro Herrasti, Daniel Gordon, Yuke Zhu, Abhinav Gupta, and Ali Farhadi. 2017. AI2-THOR: An Interactive 3D Environment for Visual AI. *arXiv*.

Alexander Ku, Peter Anderson, Roma Patel, Eugene Ie, and Jason Baldridge. 2020. Room-across-room: Multilingual vision-and-language navigation with dense spatiotemporal grounding. In *Proceedings of the 2020 Conference on Empirical Methods in Natural Language Processing (EMNLP)*, pages 4392–4412.

Shen Li, Rosario Scalise, Henny Admoni, Stephanie Rosenthal, and Siddhartha S Srinivasa. 2016. Spatial references and perspective in natural language instructions for collaborative manipulation. In *2016 25th IEEE International Symposium on Robot and Human Interactive Communication (RO-MAN)*, pages 44–51. IEEE.

Ilya Loshchilov and Frank Hutter. 2018. Decoupled weight decay regularization. In *International Conference on Learning Representations*.

Van-Quang Nguyen, Masanori Suganuma, and Takayuki Okatani. 2021. Look wide and interpret twice: Improving performance on interactive instruction-following tasks. *IJCAI*.

Aishwarya Padmakumar, Jesse Thomason, Ayush Shrivastava, Patrick Lange, Anjali Narayan-Chen, Spandana Gella, Robinson Piramuthu, Gokhan Tur, and Dilek Hakkani-Tur. 2022. Teach: Task-driven embodied agents that chat. *AAAI*.

Alexander Pashevich, Cordelia Schmid, and Chen Sun. 2021. Episodic Transformer for Vision-and-Language Navigation. In *ICCV*.

Adam Paszke, Sam Gross, Soumith Chintala, Gregory Chanan, Edward Yang, Zachary DeVito, Zeming Lin, Alban Desmaison, Luca Antiga, and Adam Lerer. 2017. Automatic differentiation in PyTorch. In *NIPS Autodiff Workshop*.

Shaoqing Ren, Kaiming He, Ross B Girshick, and Jian Sun. 2015. Faster r-cnn: Towards real-time object detection with region proposal networks. In *NIPS*.

Mohit Shridhar, Jesse Thomason, Daniel Gordon, Yonatan Bisk, Winson Han, Roozbeh Mottaghi, Luke Zettlemoyer, and Dieter Fox. 2020. ALFRED: A Benchmark for Interpreting Grounded Instructions for Everyday Tasks. In *The IEEE Conference on Computer Vision and Pattern Recognition (CVPR)*.

Hao Tan and Mohit Bansal. 2019. Lxmert: Learning cross-modality encoder representations from transformers. In *Proceedings of the 2019 Conference on Empirical Methods in Natural Language Processing*.

Jesse Thomason, Michael Murray, Maya Cakmak, and Luke Zettlemoyer. 2019. Vision-and-dialog navigation. In *Conference on Robot Learning (CoRL)*.

Sida I Wang, Percy Liang, and Christopher D Manning. 2016. Learning language games through interaction. In *Proceedings of the 54th Annual Meeting of the Association for Computational Linguistics (Volume 1: Long Papers)*, pages 2368–2378.

Do Data-based Curricula Work?

Maxim K. Surkov Vladislav D. Mosin Ivan P. Yamshchikov
LEYA Lab, Yandex, Higher School of Economics

Abstract

Current state-of-the-art NLP systems use large neural networks that require extensive computational resources for training. Inspired by human knowledge acquisition, researchers have proposed curriculum learning - sequencing tasks (task-based curricula) or ordering and sampling the datasets (data-based curricula) that facilitate training. This work investigates the benefits of data-based curriculum learning for large language models such as BERT and T5. We experiment with various curricula based on complexity measures and different sampling strategies. Extensive experiments on several NLP tasks show that curricula based on various complexity measures rarely have any benefits, while random sampling performs either as well or better than curricula.

1 Introduction

In the last years state-of-art results in natural language processing (NLP) are often obtained with Transformer-like architectures based on the self-attention mechanism (Vaswani et al., 2017) such as BERT (Devlin et al., 2019), GPT-3 (Brown et al., 2020), T5 (Raffel et al., 2020), which could have billions of parameters. Due to many parameters, these architectures require lots of time and hardware resources to be trained.

Curriculum learning (CL) is one of the popular methods to reduce training time and increase the resulting quality of the model. Inspired by the importance of adequately ordering information when teaching humans (Avrahami et al., 1997), curriculum learning increases the difficulty of training samples shown to the model over time (Elman, 1993). Previous studies have demonstrated that curriculum learning significantly impacts training time and quality in different machine learning domains, such as computer vision (Soviany, 2020) and reinforcement learning (Narvekar et al., 2020). In NLP, some results hint that CL might be beneficial (Platanios et al., 2019; Xu et al., 2020; Kocmi and Bojar, 2017); however, these results are not as optimistic as in reinforcement learning setup.

We suggest dividing recent research in curriculum learning into two main categories: *task-driven* curriculum and *data-driven* curriculum. The idea of the task-driven curriculum was inspired by human behavior. First, the model learns how to solve a simple task, and then the difficulty is gradually increased. This type of curriculum proposed by Bengio et al. (2009) is considered to be classical, and a majority of curriculum-related results are obtained in this framework. Alternatively to the task-driven curriculum, some curricula try to use some form of filtering or sorting of training data that could facilitate learning a model on a given task. We suggest calling these curricula *data-driven* and distinguishing them from the classical task-based approach.

This paper attempts to understand when data-driven curriculum learning works for transformer-based language models. Generally, data-driven curriculum learning is organized in two steps: first, estimating the complexity for the elements that comprise the dataset; second, designing a sampling strategy, thus forming a curriculum. In the first part of the paper, we list potentially useful natural language processing complexity measures. The second part discusses possible sampling strategies that might apply to corresponding complexity measures. We run extensive experiments with different metrics and sampling strategies on three classes of NLP tasks: unsupervised learning with masked language modeling, text classification, and machine translation. Our experiments show that data-driven curriculum learning does not give quality increase or time reduction on all metric-sampling strategy setups and often makes results even worse.

2 Metrics

The first important part of the curriculum learning pipeline is measuring the complexity of samples

Proceedings of the Third Workshop on Insights from Negative Results in NLP, pages 119 - 128
May 26, 2022 ©2022 Association for Computational Linguistics

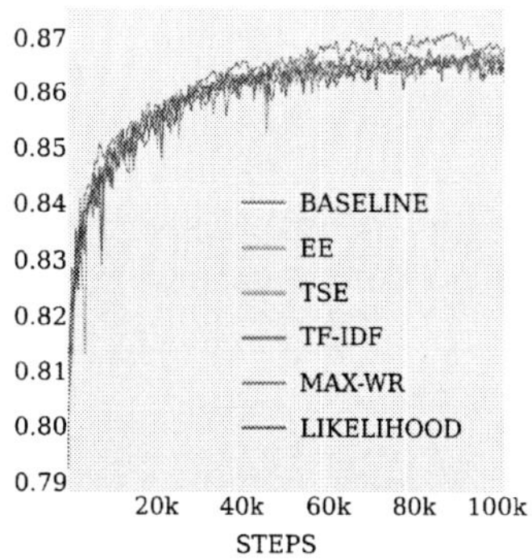

(a) Sentiment140 with sort-merge sampler for all complexity measures.

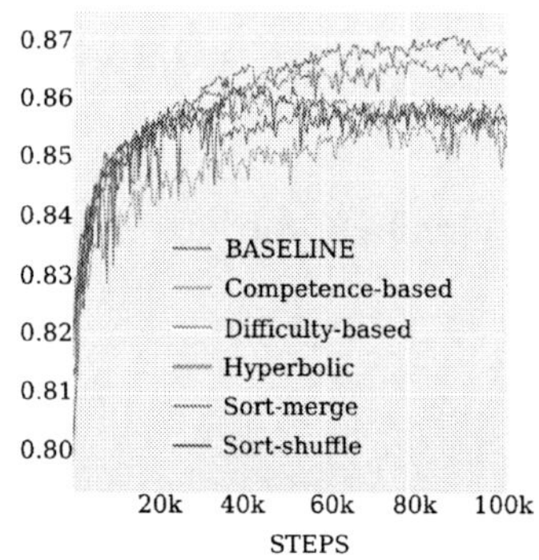

(b) Sentiment140 with max word rank complexity measure for all samplers.

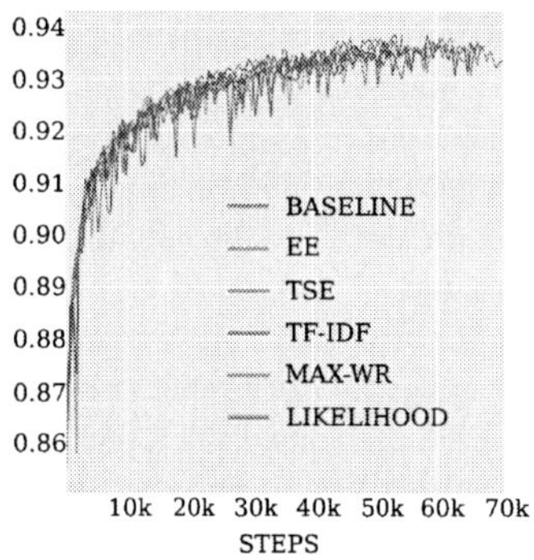

(c) Hyperpartisan News with sort-shuffle samples for all complexity measures

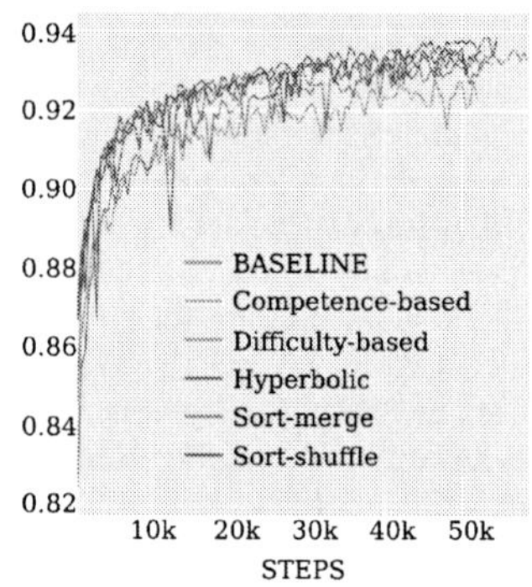

(d) Hyperpartisan News with max word rank complexity measure for all samplers.

Figure 1: Pre-trained BERT fine-tuned on Sentiment140 and Hyperpartisan News Detection datasets. Accuracy of the classifier as a function of the number of training steps.

for a given dataset. Texts could have a complex structure, and one can measure their complexity in different ways. A variety of heuristically motivated methods is accompanied by several metrics based on specific aspects of information theory. For a review of heuristic text complexity measures such as length of TF-IDF (Aizawa, 2003) we address the reader to Appendix A. In this paper, we also explore the metrics initially proposed by Ay et al. (2006) to measure the complexity of finite systems and try to see if one could apply these metrics to NLP tasks.

Ay et al. (2006) observes that for finite systems, a set of parts impacts the complexity of the system as well as inter-dependencies of the parts. In the context of NLP, this means that text is more than just a bag of words. The authors propose four different metrics to estimate the complexity of a system. However, one of these metrics maximizes on single-letter texts, such as "Aaaaaaaaa," while the second was created to measure cyclic sequences and does not apply to texts. Thus we experiment with two other metrics, namely, Tononi, Sporns, and Edelman (TSE) (Tononi et al., 1994) and excess entropy (EE), and adapt them to the complexity of texts. For the calculation of TSE and EE for NLP we address the reader to Appendix B.

3 Samplers

The second important part of curriculum learning is the sampling strategy (or sampler) - the algorithm deciding which samples should be shown to the model at which moment. Let us observe existing curricula and suggest some new ones.

Competence-based. CB
A competence-based curriculum, offered by Platanios et al. (2019), uniformly samples data from increasing dataset's prefix. Competence is a function $c(t)$, which defines the size of the dataset prefix.

$$c(t) = \min\left(1, \sqrt{t\frac{1-c_0^2}{T} + c_0^2}\right)$$

Where T - total number of steps, t - current step, c_0 - hyperparameter set to 0.01.

Hyperbolic. HYP

The main idea of this sampler is to increase average batch complexity through time. All samples are split by complexity into N sequential buckets with equal size. Training time is divided into N epochs and the probability of sampling the element from the j-th bucket on the i-th epoch is proportional to the distance between j and i.

$$Pr_i(j) = \frac{c}{|j - i|^{0.5}}$$

Where $Pr_i(j)$ - probability to sample from j-th bucket on the i-th epoch, c - constant to guarantee that sum of all probabilities equals to 1.

Difficulty-based. DB

This sampler is a reversed version of the competence-based one. A difficulty-based sampler takes elements from a linearly decreasing suffix instead of sampling from a gradually increasing prefix.

Sort-shuffle. SS

All previously described samplers do not guarantee that the model would see each element in the training data. Sort-shuffle samples each element exactly once, randomly splitting the data into batches and sorting by average complexity.

Sort-merge. SM

Many complexity estimates correlate with the length of the text. The main idea of a sort-merge sampler is to remove this correlation and train the model on stable length distribution. This algorithm consists of four main steps: sort dataset by length; sequentially split into buckets; sort each bucket by a complexity metric; form i-th batch from i-th elements from each bucket. Like a sequential one, the sort-merge sampler shows each element to the model exactly once.

Equipped with the list of metrics and curriculum samplers, we can discuss our experimental results.

4 Experiments

We perform our experiments on three NLP tasks: text classification, machine translation (NMT), and masked language modeling (MLM). Here we discuss the first task of classification in detail. The extensive results of the experiments are available in Appendix C. All the experiments are performed with the HuggingFace library (Wolf et al., 2020), which provides the models with their setups, such as hyperparameters and tokenizers. We did not change default parameters in our experiment unless specifically stated otherwise. Thus, the dataset and the model specify every experiment. We use the base version of the BERT model (Devlin et al., 2019) for MLM and classification, and the small version of the T5 model (Raffel et al., 2020) for machine translation. Experiments were performed on BooksCorpus[1] dataset for MLM, Sentiment140[2] and Hyperpartisan News Detection[3] for classification, and WMT16-en-de[4] for machine translation. To estimate the curriculum's convergence speed, we calculate the average number of steps to reach a threshold that is 10% lower than the resulting saturation quality metric for every problem.

4.1 Text Classification

Figure 1 summarizes the experiments with BERT for text classification. Neither different samplers nor complexity measures improve a BERT-based classifier's resulting accuracy.

4.2 Masked Language Modelling

Figure 2 shows the results of MLM pretraining of BERT on BooksCorpus. Irrespective of sampling, the complexity measures have similar ranking in terms of their performance on MLM: length, likelihood, TSE, EE, TF-IDF, maximum word rank. Since sorted sampler takes length into account by design, it is not included in the corresponding plots. Data-based curricula show inferior results in comparison with the baseline.

4.3 Neural Machine Translation

Table 1 shows the experiments with T5 model (Raffel et al., 2020) for machine translation and various curricula. We use the BLEU metric to estimate the quality of the resulting models. We calculate the average BLEU score over ten validations at saturation. Once again, curriculum learning does not give any notable benefits.

5 Discussion

We try to interpret obtained results cautiously. Though Platanios et al. (2019) report that

[1]https://huggingface.co/datasets/bookcorpus

[2]https://www.kaggle.com/kazanova/sentiment140

[3]https://huggingface.co/datasets/hyperpartisan_news_detection

[4]https://huggingface.co/datasets/wmt16

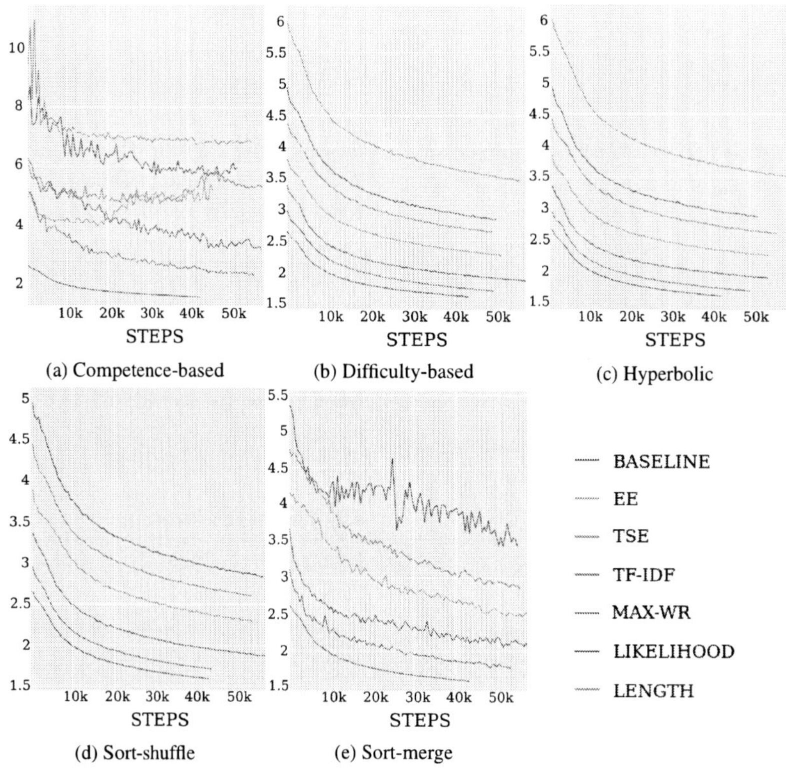

Figure 2: Loss function dependency on the number of training steps on MLM for BooksCorpus dataset during the first 40k steps of training. Every plot depicts results for six different complexity estimates combined with a specific sampler.

Table 1: The average BLEU score from 50k to 100k steps on WMT16 dataset. Results better than the baseline are highlighted. '-' denotes the cases when complexity measure and sampler are not compatible.

Metrics	Samplers				
	CB	DB	Hyp	SS	SM
baseline			18.3		
length	10.1	17.4	16.3	-	-
TSE	10.3	**18.4**	16.8	13.8	14.8
EE	10.2	18.2	16.9	13.3	15.0

competence-based sampling is beneficial for recurrent neural networks, we could not reproduce this result in transformer-based architectures. We also run experiments to check whether data-based curricula could work on non-transformer architectures. The results do not look encouraging; see Appendix C.2.

Curriculum learning depends on subtle factors, for example, a correct choice of hyperparameters. It is hard to check all possible values of hyperparameters, yet to the best of our capabilities, we address this issue in Appendix C.3. The results do not seem to depend on the learning rate, and once again, curriculum learning shows no benefits.

At this point, we can only conclusively say two things: (1) a deeper investigation of the underlying information theoretic principles that stand behind curriculum learning is badly needed; (2) until we better understand these principles, data-based curriculum learning is a gamble with very low odds to gain either speed or resulting performance.

6 Conclusion

In this work, we ran extensive experiments with curriculum learning for transformer-based architectures on three NLP tasks: masked language modeling, text classification, and machine translation. We demonstrate that curricula do not help in the standard training setting and sometimes even worsen results.

7 Acknowledgments

The publication was supported by the grant for research centers in the field of AI provided by the Analytical Center for the Government of the Russian Federation (ACRF) in accordance with the agreement on the provision of subsidies (identifier of the agreement 000000D730321P5Q0002) and the agreement with HSE University No. 70-2021-00139. This research was supported in part through computational resources of HPC facilities at HSE University (Kostenetskiy et al., 2021)

References

Akiko Aizawa. 2003. An information-theoretic perspective of tf–idf measures. *Information Processing & Management*, 39(1):45–65.

Judith Avrahami, Yaakov Kareev, Yonatan Bogot, Ruth Caspi, Salomka Dunaevsky, and Sharon Lerner. 1997. Teaching by examples: Implications for the process of category acquisition. *The Quarterly Journal of Experimental Psychology Section A*, 50(3):586–606.

Nihat Ay, Eckehard Olbrich, Nils Bertschinger, and Jürgen Jost. 2006. A unifying framework for complexity measures of finite systems. In *Proceedings of ECCS*, volume 6. Citeseer.

Yoshua Bengio, Jérôme Louradour, Ronan Collobert, and Jason Weston. 2009. Curriculum learning. In *Proceedings of the 26th annual international conference on machine learning*, pages 41–48.

Tom Brown, Benjamin Mann, Nick Ryder, Melanie Subbiah, Jared D Kaplan, Prafulla Dhariwal, Arvind Neelakantan, Pranav Shyam, Girish Sastry, Amanda Askell, Sandhini Agarwal, Ariel Herbert-Voss, Gretchen Krueger, Tom Henighan, Rewon Child, Aditya Ramesh, Daniel Ziegler, Jeffrey Wu, Clemens Winter, Chris Hesse, Mark Chen, Eric Sigler, Mateusz Litwin, Scott Gray, Benjamin Chess, Jack Clark, Christopher Berner, Sam McCandlish, Alec Radford, Ilya Sutskever, and Dario Amodei. 2020. Language models are few-shot learners. In *Advances in Neural Information Processing Systems*, volume 33, pages 1877–1901. Curran Associates, Inc.

Jacob Devlin, Ming-Wei Chang, Kenton Lee, and Kristina Toutanova. 2019. BERT: Pre-training of deep bidirectional transformers for language understanding. In *Proceedings of the 2019 Conference of the North American Chapter of the Association for Computational Linguistics: Human Language Technologies, Volume 1 (Long and Short Papers)*, pages 4171–4186, Minneapolis, Minnesota. Association for Computational Linguistics.

Jeffrey L Elman. 1993. Learning and development in neural networks: The importance of starting small. *Cognition*, 48(1):71–99.

Tom Kocmi and Ondřej Bojar. 2017. Curriculum learning and minibatch bucketing in neural machine translation. In *Proceedings of the International Conference Recent Advances in Natural Language Processing, RANLP 2017*, pages 379–386, Varna, Bulgaria. INCOMA Ltd.

PS Kostenetskiy, RA Chulkevich, and VI Kozyrev. 2021. Hpc resources of the higher school of economics. In *Journal of Physics: Conference Series*, volume 1740, page 012050. IOP Publishing.

Sanmit Narvekar, Bei Peng, Matteo Leonetti, Jivko Sinapov, Matthew E Taylor, and Peter Stone. 2020. Curriculum learning for reinforcement learning domains: A framework and survey. *Journal of Machine Learning Research*, 21(181):1–50.

Emmanouil Antonios Platanios, Otilia Stretcu, Graham Neubig, Barnabas Poczos, and Tom Mitchell. 2019. Competence-based curriculum learning for neural machine translation. In *Proceedings of the 2019 Conference of the North American Chapter of the Association for Computational Linguistics: Human Language Technologies, Volume 1 (Long and Short Papers)*, pages 1162–1172, Minneapolis, Minnesota. Association for Computational Linguistics.

Colin Raffel, Noam Shazeer, Adam Roberts, Katherine Lee, Sharan Narang, Michael Matena, Yanqi Zhou, Wei Li, and Peter J Liu. 2020. Exploring the limits of transfer learning with a unified text-to-text transformer. *Journal of Machine Learning Research*, 21:1–67.

Petru Soviany. 2020. Curriculum learning with diversity for supervised computer vision tasks. In *MRC@ECAI*.

Giulio Tononi, Olaf Sporns, and Gerald M Edelman. 1994. A measure for brain complexity: relating functional segregation and integration in the nervous system. *Proceedings of the National Academy of Sciences*, 91(11):5033–5037.

Frans van der Sluis and Egon L van den Broek. 2010. Using complexity measures in information retrieval. In *Proceedings of the third symposium on information interaction in context*, pages 383–388.

Ashish Vaswani, Noam Shazeer, Niki Parmar, Jakob Uszkoreit, Llion Jones, Aidan N Gomez, Ł ukasz Kaiser, and Illia Polosukhin. 2017. Attention is all you need. In *Advances in Neural Information Processing Systems*, volume 30. Curran Associates, Inc.

Thomas Wolf, Lysandre Debut, Victor Sanh, Julien Chaumond, Clement Delangue, Anthony Moi, Pierric Cistac, Tim Rault, Remi Louf, Morgan Funtowicz, Joe Davison, Sam Shleifer, Patrick von Platen, Clara Ma, Yacine Jernite, Julien Plu, Canwen Xu, Teven Le Scao, Sylvain Gugger, Mariama Drame, Quentin Lhoest, and Alexander Rush. 2020. Transformers: State-of-the-art natural language processing. In *Proceedings of the 2020 Conference on Empirical*

Methods in Natural Language Processing: System Demonstrations, pages 38–45, Online. Association for Computational Linguistics.

Benfeng Xu, Licheng Zhang, Zhendong Mao, Quan Wang, Hongtao Xie, and Yongdong Zhang. 2020. Curriculum learning for natural language understanding. In *Proceedings of the 58th Annual Meeting of the Association for Computational Linguistics*, pages 6095–6104.

Xuan Zhang, Gaurav Kumar, Huda Khayrallah, Kenton Murray, Jeremy Gwinnup, Marianna J Martindale, Paul McNamee, Kevin Duh, and Marine Carpuat. 2018. An empirical exploration of curriculum learning for neural machine translation. *arXiv preprint arXiv:1811.00739*.

A Heuristic Approaches to Text Complexity

The first idea is to determine the complexity of the text as its length. Despite its simplicity, this method is used in different works (Platanios et al., 2019; Kocmi and Bojar, 2017). The next family of approaches boils down to phonological, morphological, lexical, or syntactic metrics derived with some form of expert linguistic knowledge. However, van der Sluis and van den Broek (2010) used Wikipedia and Simple Wikipedia corpora to demonstrate that language-based metrics do not correlate with the common sense text complexity. The third class of methods treats text as a bag of words and builds metrics based on the frequency analysis. For example, every word gets a rank equal to its position in the dictionary sorted by the number of word appearances in a corpus. In this case, complexity may be measured as a maximum rank among the words in a bag (Kocmi and Bojar, 2017). This metric is called max frequency rank. Another possible metric is called likelihood. The metric calculates the probability of the text under the assumption that all tokens are independent, just by multiplying probabilities of all tokens in the text (Platanios et al., 2019). Another metric from this group is TF-IDF (Aizawa, 2003), which is widely used in search systems. Finally, the last array of methods is based on using different neural network losses as a complexity measure of a sample.

B Using Information Theory for Text Complexity

Let $X_V = (X_{v1}, X_{v2}, \ldots)$ be a sequence of random variables from set $V = (v1, v2, \ldots)$, and A is a subset of V, then X_A is a subsequence of X_V with elements from A. Let's determine $H(X_A)$ as entropy of sequence X_A. However, texts consist of words or tokens, not random variables. We propose the following procedure of transforming texts into random variable sequences. For each token in position i we compute the percentage of texts with this token on the same position and replace the original token with binary distribution with a probability of one equal to the calculated percentage. After transforming text into a sequence of random variables, we can compute its entropy.

$$\begin{aligned} H(X_V) &= H(X_{v1}) + H(X_{v2}|X_{v1}) \\ &+ H(X_{v3}|X_{v2}, X_{v1}) + \ldots \end{aligned}$$

If one wants to apply this formula, one must compute entropy for many different conditional distributions while these distributions depend on the order of tokens in a text. First, direct application of the formula would overfit a specific text since all texts are different in a corpus. Second, such computation could not be carried out in a reasonable time. The limit context for conditional distributions to the nearest neighbors one obtains the following formula

$$H(X_V) = H(X_{v1}) + \sum_{i=2}^{\#V} H(X_{v_i}|X_{v_{i-1}})$$

Using this approximation for entropy one can compute excess entropy (EE) and the complexity measure Tononi, Sporns and Edelman (TSE), (Tononi et al., 1994) as they are formulated by Ay et al. (2006)

$$EE(X_V) = \left[\sum_{v \in V} H(X_{V \setminus v})\right] - (n-1)H(X_V), \quad (1)$$

$$TSE(X_V) = \sum_{k=1}^{n-1} \frac{k}{n} C^{(k)}(X_V), \quad (2)$$

where n is a size of set V and

$$C^{(k)}(X_V) = \frac{n}{k\binom{n}{k}} \sum_{A \subseteq V, |A|=k} H(X_A) - H(X_V).$$

C Additional Experiments

C.1 Convergence Speed

Curriculum learning is often apprised for the speed-up of the model's convergence. The intuition here is to provide a curriculum that would help to achieve the same result faster, yet without a significant loss in quality. We carried out several experiments to see if data-based curricula could speed up the learning in transformer-based language models.

C.1.1 Classification

Tables 2 3 show average number of training steps needed to reach 90% of the resulting accuracy for the corresponding classification task. On Sentiment140 TF-IDF, TSE, and maximum word rank speed the convergence up to 3% with some samplers. However, other metrics or sampling strategies slow down the model's convergence speed, while on a bigger HND dataset, other curricula show results better than the baseline. One could conclusively say that length is the worse metric to organize curriculum in all experiment configurations. The one more important conclusion is that the model can not always estimate the complexity of the sample concerning its' internal state (MLM-loss does not speed up the training speed and drawdown the final model quality on the Sentiment140 dataset). This happens when the model is expressive enough, and all samples have equal complexity in model-based metrics.

C.1.2 Pretraining MLM

Figure 2 shows a significant slowdown in model convergence speed can be seen for all curricula compared to the baseline learning regime. One can also divide all metrics into two distinct groups. The first one consists of maximum word rank and TF-IDF. The second group includes EE, TSE, likelihood, and length. The metrics in the first group allow the model to converge to a lower loss value. However, the second group's metrics hinder the convergence and seem to have higher saturation loss. Hence, it isn't easy to find a universal threshold to reasonably compare all metrics and samplers. One should also note that only maximum word rank does not degrade the model quality compared to the baseline, while other curricula cause severe deterioration. Finally, the last main observation is that curriculum learning, unfortunately, does not allow us to run MLM faster. Moreover, the number of training steps needed to reach a given threshold could be several times higher in comparison with the baseline approach. Table 4 illustrates this fact.

C.2 Data-based Curricula for Other Architectures

It seems that data-based curriculum learning cannot increase quality or reduce training time for transformer-based models. Though Platanios et al. (2019) report that competence-based sampling is beneficial for recurrent neural networks, we could not reproduce this result in transformer-based architectures. While some curricula might be useful for smaller architectures on some tasks, they have no significant benefits for larger architectures. Let us double-check that with the recurrent neural network architecture to see if the negative result obtained above is associated with certain properties of attention-based architectures or could be reproduced with various artificial neural networks. We run our experiments on Sentiment 140 with 90% train and 10% test split. The curricula include Hyperbole, Difficulty-Based and Competence-Based samplers, and TSE and length difficulty metrics. Figure 3 shows that data-driven curricula do not have a significant influence on the results.

Comparing Figure 3 with Tables 3 – 2 one could see that data-based curricula are hardly beneficial even for smaller architectures. Rather, under certain conditions, one could get some improvement of convergence, yet on a different task, the same choice of complexity measure and sampling strategy would be on par with the baseline.

C.3 Data-based curricula and Hyperparameters

Extensive experiments on different NLP tasks show that data-based curriculum learning does not help to increase quality with default hyperparameters. Hyperparameters' importance for the curriculum is an open question. Some papers state that hyperparameters, especially learning rate, are essential for curriculum (Zhang et al., 2018). On the other hand, some papers propose methods that are not highly sensitive to hyperparameters (Platanios et al., 2019). It seems that hyperparameters choice is discussed mainly in the works addressing NMT, so we run additional experiments with our curricula and three different learning rates (10^{-3}, 10^{-4}, 10^{-5}) on NMT as well. Results demonstrate that models' behavior does not depend on the learning rate much, and for every learning rate, curricula do not give a significant quality increase. Results for excess entropy are presented in Figure 6.

Table 2: The average number of steps needed to reach given threshold for all configurations metric-sampler on text classification task on Hyperpartisan News Detections dataset. Maximal deviation for 3 runs is less than $3k$ steps. Results better than the baseline are highlighted. ∞ means that model did not reach the threshold, '-' denotes the cases when complexity measure and sampler are not compatible.

Metrics	Threshold	Accuracy	Samplers				
			CB	DB	Hyp	SS	SM
baseline	92.9%	93.8%			22k		
length	92.9%	93.7%	55k	23k	22.5k	-	-
TF-IDF	92.9%	93.5%	∞	**19.5k**	24k	23.5k	33k
TSE	92.9%	93.8%	56.5k	21k	23k	22k	31k
EE	92.9%	93.8%	71.5k	25.5k	22.5k	**19.5k**	32.5k
max wr	92.9%	93.6%	∞	22k	**20.5k**	22.5k	39k
likelihood	92.9%	93.8%	∞	**20k**	24k	**20k**	30k
MLM-loss	92.9%	**93.9%**	23.5k	**18k**	23k	24k	**20k**

Table 3: The average number of steps needed to reach given threshold for all configurations metric-sampler on text classification task on sentiment140 dataset. Maximal deviation for 3 runs is less than $3k$ steps. Results better than the baseline are highlighted. ∞ means that model did not reach the threshold, '-' denotes the cases when complexity measure and sampler are not compatible.

Metrics	Threshold	Accuracy	Samplers				
			CB	DB	Hyp	SS	SM
baseline	85.5%	**87%**			17.5k		
length	85.5%	86.2%	112.5k	20k	19k	-	-
TF-IDF	85.5%	86.7%	115.5k	21.5k	19.5k	**16.5k**	22k
TSE	85.5%	86.8%	95.5k	**16.5k**	20.5k	21.5k	18k
EE	85.5%	86.7%	59k	19.3k	23k	20k	19k
max wr	85.5%	86.7%	70k	18.5k	19.5k	**17k**	19k
likelihood	85.5%	86.7%	112k	17.5k	21.5k	17.5k	21.5k
MLM-loss	85.5%	86.1%	59.5k	21k	23.5k	19.5k	20k

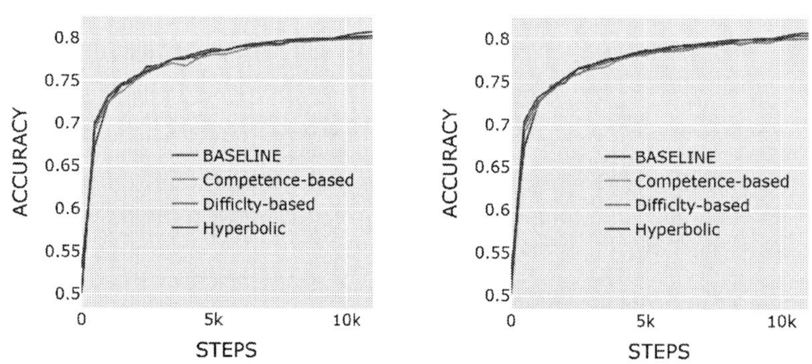

(a) Sentiment140 with length as complexity metric and three samplers.

(b) Sentiment140 with TSE as complexity metric and three samplers.

Figure 3: Test results with LSTM on Sentiment140 dataset. Accuracy of the classifier as a function of the number of training steps.

Table 4: The average number of steps needed to reach given threshold for all configurations metric-sampler on pretraining on BooksCorpus dataset. Maximal deviation for 3 runs is less than $3k$ steps. All complexity measures based curricula reach saturation at higher losses than the baseline thus we used an arbitrary threshold of 3.5 for them. Results better than the baseline are highlighted. ∞ means that model did not reach the threshold, '-' denotes the cases when complexity measure and sampler are not compatible.

Metrics	Threshold Loss	Saturation Loss	Samplers CB	DB	Hyp	SS	SM
baseline	2.00	**1.58**			9.5k		
max wr	2.00	**1.58**	∞	17.5k	16.5k	16.5k	27k
TF-IDF	2.00	1.84	∞	34k	35k	37.5k	∞
EE	3.50	2.25	∞	4k	**3.5k**	4.5k	9.5k
TSE	3.50	2.60	∞	9k	9k	8.5k	18k
likelihood	3.50	2.83	∞	13.5k	13.5k	15.5k	50k
length	3.50	3.45	∞	50.5k	∞	-	-

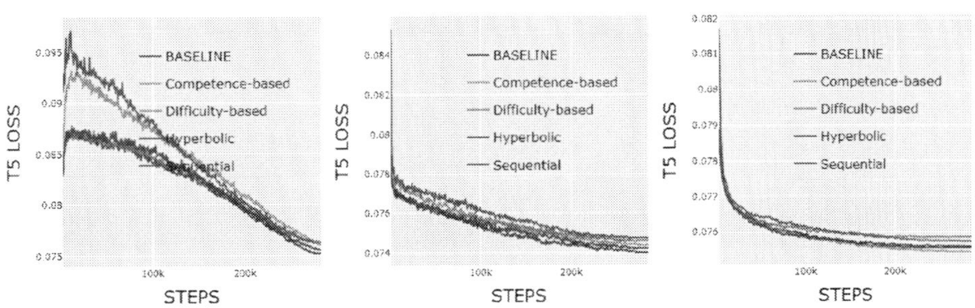

(a) learning rate 10^{-3} (b) learning rate 10^{-4} (c) learning rate 10^{-5}

Figure 4: Test results for NMT on WMT16 with different learning rates with excess entropy as a complexity measure

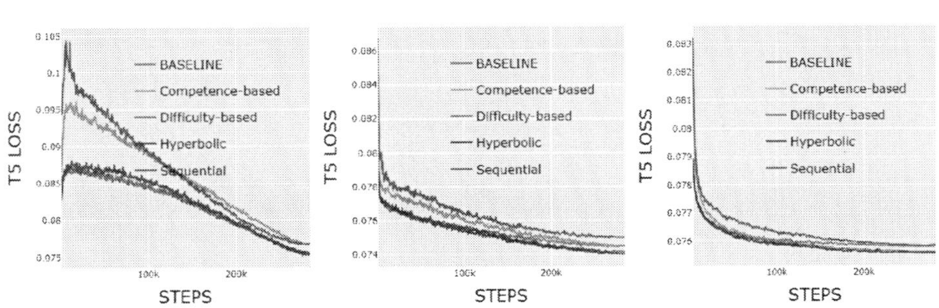

(a) learning rate 10^{-3} (b) learning rate 10^{-4} (c) learning rate 10^{-5}

Figure 5: Test results for NMT on WMT16 with different learning rates with TSE as a complexity measure

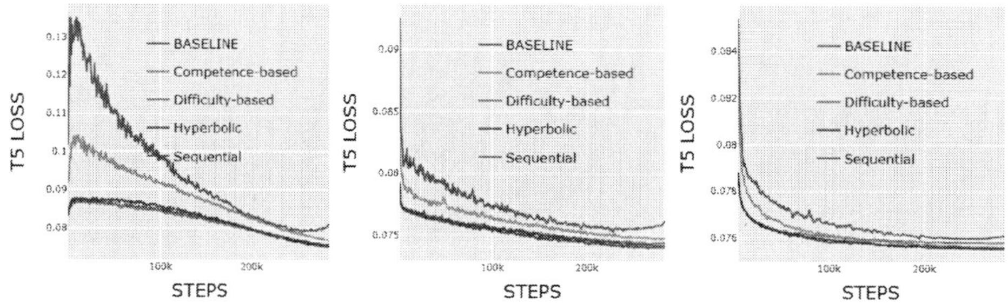

(a) learning rate 10^{-3}

(b) learning rate 10^{-4}

(c) learning rate 10^{-3}

Figure 6: Test results for NMT on WMT16 with different learning rates with length complexity measure

The Document Vectors Using Cosine Similarity Revisited

Zhang Bingyu[△] **Nikolay Arefyev**[◇,▽,△]

[△]National Research University Higher School of Economics / Moscow, Russia
[◇]Samsung Research Center Russia / Moscow, Russia
[▽]Lomonosov Moscow State University / Moscow, Russia
bchzhan_1@edu.hse.ru, nick.arefyev@gmail.com

Abstract

The current state-of-the-art test accuracy (97.42%) on the IMDB movie reviews dataset was reported by Thongtan and Phienthrakul (2019) and achieved by the logistic regression classifier trained on the Document Vectors using Cosine Similarity (DV-ngrams-cosine) proposed in their paper and the Bag-of-N-grams (BON) vectors scaled by Naive Bayesian weights. While large pre-trained Transformer-based models have shown SOTA results across many datasets and tasks, the aforementioned model has not been surpassed by them, despite being much simpler and pre-trained on the IMDB dataset only.

In this paper, we describe an error in the evaluation procedure of this model, which was found when we were trying to analyze its excellent performance on the IMDB dataset. We further show that the previously reported test accuracy of 97.42% is invalid and should be corrected to 93.68%. We also analyze the model performance with different amounts of training data (subsets of the IMDB dataset) and compare it to the Transformer-based RoBERTa model. The results show that while RoBERTa has a clear advantage for larger training sets, the DV-ngrams-cosine performs better than RoBERTa when the labelled training set is very small (10 or 20 documents). Finally, we introduce a sub-sampling scheme based on Naive Bayesian weights for the training process of the DV-ngrams-cosine, which leads to faster training and better quality.

1 Introduction

The word2vec algorithm originally published by Mikolov et al. (2013) is among the most famous methods to train vector representations of words. Soon after the emergence of word2vec, a similar method to build vector representations of documents was originally proposed by Le and Mikolov (2014) and further studied by Mesnil et al. (2015). It is known under different names, including Paragraph Vectors, Sentence Vectors, doc2vec, etc. This method jointly learns word embeddings and document embeddings such that a binary classifier can predict if a given word occurs in a particular document given only the corresponding embeddings. More formally, the following objective is minimized:

$$\sum_{d\in D}\sum_{w\in W_d}[-\log\sigma(v_d^T v_w)-\sum_{w'\sim V}\log\sigma(-v_d^T v_{w'})] \quad (1)$$

Here D denotes the set of documents, W_d is the list of words that make up the document d, w' is a word randomly sampled from the full vocabulary V, also known as a negative sample (Goldberg and Levy, 2014). Finally, v_d and v_w are the learnt embeddings of d and w. Intuitively, for each document, an embedding is learnt that has high similarity to the embeddings of those words that occur in this document and low similarity to the embeddings of some random words.

Later Li et al. (2015) switched from single words to n-grams and observed significant improvements. Building on that, Thongtan and Phienthrakul (2019) studied different objective functions. They have found that the cosine similarity outperforms the dot product, which led to a modified model called the Document Vectors using Cosine Similarity (we will call it **DV-ngrams-cosine** for short). The new objective is:

$$\begin{aligned}\sum_{d\in D}\sum_{u\in U_d}&[-\log\sigma(\alpha cos(v_d,v_u))\\ &-\sum_{u'\sim V}\log\sigma(-\alpha cos(v_d,v_{u'}))],\end{aligned} \quad (2)$$

where U_d denotes the set of all n-grams in d, v_u is the embedding of the n-gram u from d, $v_{u'}$ is the embedding of a randomly sampled n-gram, and α is a hyperparameter.

In the same paper, the authors proposed an ensemble consisting of the document embeddings from DV-ngrams-cosine and the Bag-of-N-grams

Proceedings of the Third Workshop on Insights from Negative Results in NLP, pages 129 - 133
May 26, 2022 ©2022 Association for Computational Linguistics

vectors scaled by Naive Bayesian weights (**NB-weighted BON** for short). They concatenated these two representations and trained the logistic regression classifier on top. The ensemble was reported to have very high test accuracy (97.42%) on the IMDB movie reviews dataset (Maas et al. (2011)). To the best of our knowledge, this accuracy remains the SOTA result on IMDB. Even large Transformer-based models pre-trained on a huge amount of texts, both in-domain and out-of-domain, have shown lower accuracy on this dataset (Yang et al., 2019; Suchin et al., 2020; Arefyev et al., 2021).

This extraordinary performance of such a simple model motivated us to thoroughly study the model and its implementation trying to understand the reasons behind its success. Unfortunately, during this study, we found a bug in the implementation of the evaluation procedure of the ensemble, which had made the estimation of the accuracy incorrect.

In our paper, we re-evaluate the ensemble as well as its individual components. We show that the originally reported test accuracy of the ensemble (97.42%) is incorrect and shall be corrected to 93.68%, which is only 0.55% higher than the accuracy on pure DV-ngrams-cosine embeddings.

Additionally, we analyze how the amount of training data affects the performance of the ensemble, as well as its individual components, and also the Transformer-based RoBERTa model (Liu et al., 2020), which has recently shown SOTA or near-SOTA results over a variety of tasks and datasets. Surprisingly, we have observed that DV-ngrams-cosine outperforms RoBERTa when the number of labelled training examples is small (10 or 20). We also ensemble RoBERTa with DV-ngrams-cosine, but only have achieved a marginal improvement. Finally, we propose a modification for the training process of DV-ngrams-cosine that results in faster training and better accuracy. The code reproducing our experiments is publicly available [1].

2 Re-evaluation of the ensemble

In the aforementioned ensemble proposed by Thongtan and Phienthrakul (2019), the NB-weighted BON and the DV-ngrams-cosine are concatenated and fed into the logistic regression classifier. However, we have found that in the original implementation the two vectors concatenated to obtain a single training or test example usually correspond to two different documents of the same class (see details in Appendix A). Specifically, the DV-ngrams-cosine vectors and the BON vectors are built from two different files having different orders of examples. As a result, after the concatenation, each input to the logistic regression corresponds to a combination of two examples. Due to the special structure of the files, those examples are guaranteed to belong to the same class and the same subset. For instance, a positive example from the test set is concatenated with another positive example from the test set.

In Appendix B.3 we provide an analysis that shows the reasons of high performance of this concatenation of two representations. From this analysis it follows that most examples from IMDB are correctly classified with high confidence (a large logit) using any of two representations, i.e. they are easy examples. Less than 10% of examples are classified incorrectly by each representation (hard examples), but they often obtain low confidence (a logit near zero). Hard examples are more often combined with easy examples just because of their dominance. In these cases, the logit from the easy example often outweigh the logit from the hard one resulting in the correct final prediction.

Thus, in both the training and the test sets, hard examples are often combined with simpler examples, making the classification task easier. In this process, the knowledge of the true labels is implicitly exploited to combine the examples this way, in both training and testing. This leads to an incorrect estimation of the classification accuracy for future examples.

After fixing this issue, we have observed that the combination of different representations of the same document leads to the test accuracy of 93.68% instead of 97.42% originally reported. Compared to the pure DV-ngrams-cosine embeddings, the ensemble improves the test accuracy by 0.55%, not 4.29% reported previously. This improvement also better agrees with the improvements of less than 1% observed by Li et al. (2015) for similar ensembles with the predecessor model DV-ngram. As a sanity check, Appendix B additionally reports the accuracy for different schemes of combining the two representations, showing that higher accuracy can be achieved only by those schemes that exploit the knowledge of the test labels.

[1] https://github.com/Bgzh/dv_cosine_revisited

3 Further analysis of performance

In his section we further analyze the performance of the ensemble described above, comparing it to its individual components as well as to the recently introduced Transformer-based RoBERTa model (Liu et al., 2020). We study the performance of these models depending on the number of labelled examples in the training set.

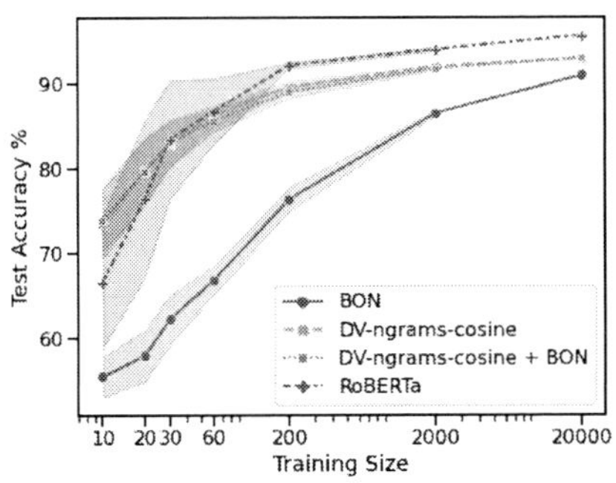

Figure 1: The performance of different models on training sets of different sizes. The mean values and standard deviations were calculated over 10 random subsets for RoBERTa and 30 random subsets for other models for each training set size. BON in the legend implies NB-weighted BON.

For a more fair comparison, the most important hyperparameters of each model were tuned on the validation set, employing the train/validation/test split of the IMDB dataset provided by (Suchin et al., 2020). Subsets of different sizes from 10 to 20000 examples were randomly sampled from the training set. The logistic regression classifier was trained on these subsets using the DV-ngram-cosine embeddings, the NB-weighted BON vectors, or their concatenation as its input representation.

We tuned the L2-regularization strength C of the classifier individually for each subset of the training set. Additionally, we multiplied the DV-ngram-cosine embeddings before concatenating them to the BON vectors in order to balance the magnitudes of the two representations, which may help the classifier to benefit from both representations. The scaling factor was also selected on the validation set.

The pre-trained RoBERTa base model[2] was fine-tuned on a part (10 out of 30) of the same subsets of the training set, using the validation set for early stopping. We used a batch size of 32, with a maximum learning rate of 1e-5, recommended by fairseq[3].

As shown in Fig. 1, the fine-tuned RoBERTa model usually achieves higher test accuracy. But when the number of labelled training examples is very small (10 or 20), the logistic regression on the DV-ngrams-cosine embeddings shows higher mean test accuracy and lower standard deviation. This result corroborated the notion that small models can be a better choice when the data are scarce.

On the other hand, logistic regression on the BON vectors performs significantly worse than all other models across all training set sizes. Finally, we don't observe any significant improvements from the ensembling when the training set size is less than 20k, as the difference is within one standard deviation.

It is important to notice that the DV-ngrams-cosine embeddings were pre-trained on the in-domain examples from the whole IMDB dataset, while RoBERTa was pre-trained on a huge but general-domain corpus. It is likely that the domain adaptation techniques (Suchin et al., 2020) will help RoBERTa when the number of labelled examples is small. However, for our study, we decided to compare the most standard approaches to training the corresponding models.

4 NB Sub-Sampling

In this section, we improve the training procedure of DV-ngrams-cosine by applying a sub-sampling procedure based on the Naive Bayesian weights of ngrams (**NB Sub-Sampling**) in order to make the model focus more on sentiment-related ngrams while building the document embeddings.

Inspired by the previous works (Wang and Manning (2012), Arefyev et al. (2021)), we trained a multinomial Naive Bayesian Classifier and exploited its weights to calculate the importance of each ngram f_i for the final classification task:

$$h_i = |\log p(f_i|y = 1) - \log p(f_i|y = 0)| \quad (3)$$

In each epoch we put an ngram into training with the probability

$$p(f_i) = min(\exp(h_i/n_a)/n_b, 1), \quad (4)$$

[2] `https://pytorch.org/hub/huggingface_pytorch-transformers/`

[3] `https://github.com/pytorch/fairseq/blob/main/examples/roberta/README.custom_classification.md`

Model	Test Accuracy %
Models trained on the original training set of IMDB (25K)	
NB-weighted BON	91.29
DV-ngrams-cosine	93.13
DV-ngrams-cosine + NB-weighted BON (Thongtan and Phienthrakul, 2019)	#97.42
DV-ngrams-cosine + NB-weighted BON (re-evaluated)	93.68
Models trained using the train/dev split from (Suchin et al., 2020) (20K/5K)	
DV-ngrams-cosine with NB sub-sampling	93.36
RoBERTa	95.79
DV-ngrams-cosine + RoBERTa	95.92
DV-ngrams-cosine with NB sub-sampling + RoBERTa	95.94

Table 1: Test results on the IMDB dataset. # indicates incorrect previously reported results.

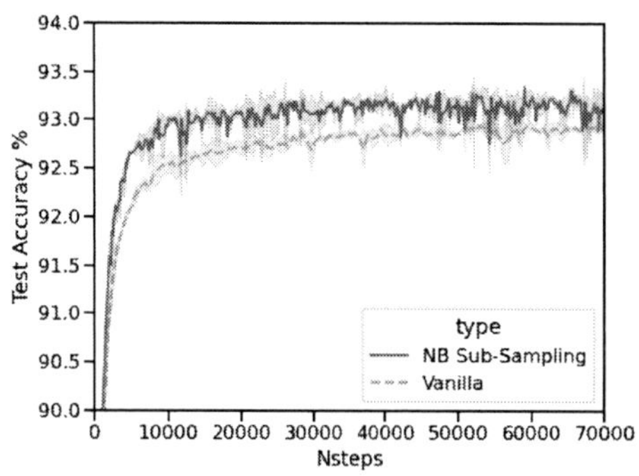

Figure 2: Training process with and without NB sub-sampling. The test accuracy of the logistic regression built on top of the document vectors is plotted. The mean values and standard deviations were calculated over 3 runs for each type.

where n_a and n_b are the hyperparameters. The choices are purely empirical. We tried different combinations of n_a and n_b and found 2 and 3 (respectively) to be the best in them.

The comparison of the training process with and without NB sub-sampling is shown in Fig. 2 (refer to Appendix C for details of the experiments and the accuracy on the validation set).

The runs with NB sub-sampling progress faster and show a distinct advantage after 2500 steps. After 30k steps, the runs with NB sub-sampling stagnated and kept fluctuating in a small region; the vanilla runs stagnated after 50k steps, in a lower area. It is also worth noticing that although the labels of the training set are used during pre-training for sub-sampling, we did not observe any significant overfitting due to that. Neither the validation score nor the test score showed a tendency to decay long after reaching the plateau, indicating that this sub-sampling scheme can be used as an add-on to the original model, boosting its performance while not creating additional overfitting trouble.

5 Ensemble DV-ngrams-cosine and RoBERTa

The ensemble proposed in (Thongtan and Phienthrakul (2019)) and described in Section 2 combines two different representations of documents, which are the DV-ngrams-cosine embeddings and the NB-weighted BON vectors. However, we have observed in Section 3 that the BON vectors are quite weak on their own, while RoBERTa outperforms all other models unless the number of examples is very small. Thus, it is interesting if DV-ngram-cosine can help RoBERTa. In this section, we combine the DV-ngrams-cosine (with or without NB sub-sampling) with the output of the last hidden layer of RoBERTa, and test on the IMDB dataset. Again, the train/validation/test splits by Suchin et al. (2020) were used. A scaling factor on the DV-ngrams-cosine and the hyperparameter C in the logistic regression were tuned on the validation set.
The results are shown in Table 1. Although RoBERTa is a much stronger model than DV-ngram-cosine, combining them has shown a small improvement of 0.13-0.15%.

6 Conclusion

The ensemble featuring the DV-ngrams-cosine reported by Thongtan and Phienthrakul (2019) was re-evaluated. The test accuracy of this ensemble on the IMDB dataset was corrected from 97.42% to 93.68%. The DV-ngrams-cosine embeddings with the logistic regression on top were compared with RoBERTa using different amounts of training data.

In this comparison, the DV-ngrams-cosine has surprisingly outperformed RoBERTa for a small number of training examples (10 or 20 documents). A sub-sampling scheme based on the Naive Bayesian weights was introduced to the training process of the DV-ngrams-cosine, resulting in faster training and better quality.

Acknowledgements

We are grateful to our anonymous reviewers. This research was partially supported by the Basic Research Program at the HSE University.

References

Nikolay Arefyev, Dmitry Kharchev, and Artem Shelmanov. 2021. Nb-mlm - efficient domain adaptation of masked language models for sentiment analysis. *EMNLP*, pages 9114–9124.

Yoav Goldberg and Omer Levy. 2014. word2vec explained: deriving mikolov et al.'s negative-sampling word-embedding method. *CoRR*.

V. Quoc Le and Tomas Mikolov. 2014. Distributed representations of sentences and documents. *ICML*, pages 1188–1196.

Bofang Li, Tao Liu, Xiaoyong Du, Deyuan Zhang, and Zhe Zhao. 2015. Learning document embeddings by predicting n-grams for sentiment classification of long movie reviews. *CoRR*.

Yinhan Liu, Myle Ott, Naman Goyal, Jingfei Du, Mandar Joshi, Danqi Chen, Omer Levy, Mike Lewis, Luke Zettlemoyer, and Veselin Stoyanov. 2020. Ro{bert}a: A robustly optimized {bert} pretraining approach.

Andrew L. Maas, Raymond E. Daly, Peter T. Pham, Dan Huang, Andrew Y. Ng, and Christopher Potts. 2011. Learning word vectors for sentiment analysis. In *Proceedings of the 49th Annual Meeting of the Association for Computational Linguistics: Human Language Technologies*, pages 142–150, Portland, Oregon, USA. Association for Computational Linguistics.

Grégoire Mesnil, Tomas Mikolov, Marc'Aurelio Ranzato, and Yoshua Bengio. 2015. Ensemble of generative and discriminative techniques for sentiment analysis of movie reviews. *international conference on learning representations*.

Tomas Mikolov, Kai Chen, Greg Corrado, and Jeffrey Dean. 2013. Efficient estimation of word representations in vector space. *CoRR*.

Gururangan Suchin, Marasović Ana, Swayamdipta Swabha, Lo Kyle, Beltagy Iz, Downey Doug, and Noah Smith A. 2020. Don't stop pretraining: Adapt language models to domains and tasks. *ACL*, pages 8342–8360.

Tan Thongtan and Tanasanee Phienthrakul. 2019. Sentiment classification using document embeddings trained with cosine similarity. In *Proceedings of the 57th Annual Meeting of the Association for Computational Linguistics: Student Research Workshop*, pages 407–414, Florence, Italy. Association for Computational Linguistics.

Sida Wang and Christopher Manning. 2012. Baselines and bigrams: Simple, good sentiment and topic classification. In *Proceedings of the 50th Annual Meeting of the Association for Computational Linguistics (Volume 2: Short Papers)*, pages 90–94, Jeju Island, Korea. Association for Computational Linguistics.

Zhilin Yang, Zihang Dai, Yiming Yang, G. Jaime Carbonell, Ruslan Salakhutdinov, and V. Quoc Le. 2019. Xlnet: Generalized autoregressive pretraining for language understanding. *ADVANCES IN NEURAL INFORMATION PROCESSING SYSTEMS 32 (NIPS 2019)*, pages 5754–5764.

Challenges in including extra-linguistic context in pre-trained language models

Ionut-Teodor Sorodoc[*] **Laura Aina**[*] **Gemma Boleda**[*†]

[*]Universitat Pompeu Fabra
[†]ICREA
Barcelona, Spain
{firstname.lastname}@upf.edu

Abstract

To successfully account for language, computational models need to take into account both the linguistic context (the content of the utterances) and the extra-linguistic context (for instance, the participants in a dialogue). We focus on a referential task that asks models to link entity mentions in a TV show to the corresponding characters, and design an architecture that attempts to account for both kinds of context. In particular, our architecture combines a previously proposed specialized module (an "entity library") for character representation with transfer learning from a pre-trained language model. We find that, although the model does improve linguistic contextualization, it fails to successfully integrate extra-linguistic information about the participants in the dialogue. Our work shows that it is very challenging to incorporate extra-linguistic information into pre-trained language models.

1 Introduction

Identifying the real-world entity an expression refers to is crucial for Natural Language Processing, since humans use language to talk about the world. This, however, requires models that represent the real world such that linguistic expressions can be mapped to them. For instance, in Figure 1, which is a snippet of a dialogue from the TV show *Friends*, we need to know that it is Joey Tribbiani who is speaking to be able to interpret the pronoun "I". State-of-the-art NLP models typically focus on linguistic context, not on extra-linguistic context such as who is speaking to whom. We aim at integrating extra-linguistic context, in particular information about participants in a dialogue; also, we aim at combining it with information coming from the linguistic context.

We focus on the character identification task of SemEval 2018 (Choi and Chen, 2018), aimed at classifying mentions from the dialogue scripts of the TV show *Friends* (see Figure 1). The model that

JOEY TRIBBIANI (183):
"*... see Ross, because I think you love her .*"
335 183 335 306

Figure 1: Example of the dataset. It shows the speaker (first line) of the utterance (second line) and the ids of the entities to which the target mentions (underlined) refer (last line).

won the SemEval competition (Aina et al., 2018) proposed an external module to encode entity information in a structured way (henceforth, "entity library"). This approach enabled the incorporation of extra-linguistic information, in particular speaker information, which allowed the model to learn patterns such as "*I* refers to the character that is speaking"; and, as a result, it worked comparatively well on rare entities. However, Aina et al. (2019) showed that the model's good performance was not correlated with meaningful entity representations. Moreover, the model performed poorly in expressions that require a good grasp of the linguistic context, like 3rd person pronouns and common nouns.

Aina et al.'s base model was an LSTM trained from scratch on the character identification task (with the exception of pre-trained non-contextualized word embeddings). We propose to instead add the entity library to a pre-trained language model: BERT (Devlin et al., 2019). Pre-trained language models (Peters et al., 2018; Devlin et al., 2019) have been shown to provide good contextual representations (Bai et al., 2021), and they have enabled advances also in referential tasks (Joshi et al., 2020; Zhou and Choi, 2018; Yang and Choi, 2019). We expected that combining BERT with the entity library would synthesize the benefits of both, encoding and exploiting both the extra-linguistic and linguistic information in the context. We also expected that, as a result of these improvements, this model would yield better entity representations.

Contrary to expectation, however, we do not

Proceedings of the Third Workshop on Insights from Negative Results in NLP, pages 134 - 138
May 26, 2022

improve on the state-of-the-art model of Aina et al. (2019). Through analysis, we show that our model does improve the performance for context-dependent expressions, such as third-person pronouns, suggesting that it is better at handling the linguistic context; however, it performs worse on expressions that depend on the extra-linguistic context, such as first- and second-person pronouns, which are much more frequent in the data. Moreover, the entity representations are only marginally improved. The problem, we argue, comes from the fact that integrating extra-linguistic information in pre-trained language models is far from trivial.

2 Method and main results

Task In order to have a comparable setup to previous studies, the dataset and the task are the same as the ones described in Choi and Chen (2018). The training and test data span the first two seasons of the sitcom *Friends*, and the task is to predict which character is referred to by each referring expression (see Figure 1).

Model In our model, the input tokens go through a pre-trained BERT. Then the speaker information (i.e., an embedding identifying the character who produced the utterance) is concatenated to the token representation. This representation is fed to a multi-layer perceptron (MLP). The output of this step is compared to the entity library (EntLib) proposed in Aina et al. (2018), via dot products with each character embedding in the EntLib, in order to produce the final prediction (softmax over the dot products). The entity library is a learnable matrix where each row is associated with one of the 401 characters from the dataset. As in the version in Aina et al. (2019), the parameters of the speaker embedding matrix and of the entity library are shared. The weights of BERT are tuned to the character identification task. Section A.2 in the Appendix reports model details.

The most notable differences of our architecture with that of Aina et al. (2018) and Aina et al. (2019) are the following: 1) We run the input text through a pre-trained language model; 2) our model processes the input token with its textual context before accessing the speaker information. By contrast, Aina et al.'s architecture directly passes the input token to the LSTM jointly with the speaker. This latter difference will be crucial in explaining the results, as we will see in the next section.

		all (78)		main (7)	
	models	F_1	Acc	F_1	Acc
random	-EntLib	40.4	63.6	70.6	69.4
	+EntLib	43.8	64.4	71.2	70.4
BERT	frozen-EntLib	31.6	64	72.5	72.8
	frozen+EntLib	35.3	63.8	70.9	71.1
	finet.-EntLib	38.6	62.2	68.9	69.1
	finet.+EntLib	**51.4**	*70.5*	*76.9*	*77.6*
LSTMEnt	+EntLib	49.6	**77.6**	**84.9**	**84.2**

Table 1: Model parameters and results on the character identification task. *finet*: fine-tuned.

We conduct ablation experiments to investigate the benefits of different components of our model:

- **random embeddings**: the BERT component is substituted by randomly initialized embeddings. Each token is linearly mapped to a vector, with no representation of sequences.
- **frozen BERT**: the BERT component of the model is not fine-tuned on the character identification task, and only the other components are updated during training.
- **-EntLib**: the model does not include the entity library. The output of the MLP is directly mapped to 401 dimensions to predict an entity.

Results The main results are presented in Table 1.[1] The newly proposed model does not improve over the best performing model from Aina et al. (2019): it is better on F1 score for all entities, and worse for the other three metrics. However, while Aina et al.'s model (henceforth, LSTMEnt) has the best overall results, it outperforms the proposed model (fine-tuned BERT +EntLib, henceforth BERTEnt) only on a few kinds of expressions, as shown in the analyses in Section 3.

Table 1 also shows that the entity library improves over all 3 model variations, confirming that dedicating a specialized component to entity representation is helpful for referential tasks. Among our variants, the complete model (BERTEnt) is the best, showing that all the components are beneficial for the task. The models initialized with random embeddings are comparable to the models with frozen BERT embeddings. This suggests that BERT representations are not directly applicable to the current task, without being adjusted through fine-tuning; that may be due to the differences between the data

[1]While the prediction is over 401 entities, "all entities" in Table 1 are only 78 because this is the number of entities appearing in the test data.

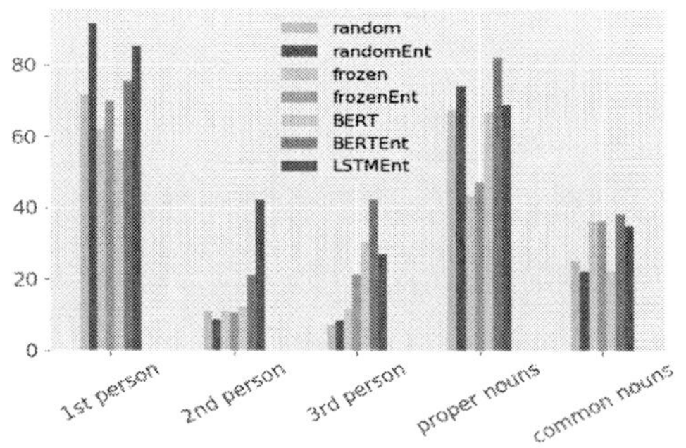

Figure 2: F1-score by type of referring expression (setup: all entities).

BERT was trained on (mostly narrative text) and the data we are deploying it on (dialogues from TV sitcoms).

3 Why does BertEnt not improve results?

Figure 2 presents the F1-score for the analyzed models for different types of referring expressions: first/second/third-person pronouns, proper nouns and common nouns. The graph shows results corresponding to all entities (column 'all' in Table 1). A graph focusing on the main entities is included in the Appendix.

As for first-person pronouns, recall that their interpretation depends on extra-linguistic information (who is speaking). Our models have speaker embeddings; to learn the right generalization, they should map the "I" token to the relevant speaker embedding. The entity library facilitates this process, and, accordingly, it is a beneficial component for first-person pronouns across all models.

Moreover, this is a type of referring expression that is easy for the models. The best strategy is actually to learn to treat the token representation for a first-person pronoun as a constant that functions simply as a prompt for the speaker embedding. This explains why the best results are actually obtained with random embeddings and entity library: The other models (including LSTMEnt) contextualize tokens, changing them depending on the content of the message. Since first-person pronouns do not depend on the linguistic context, but only on the extra-linguistic context, the other models have a harder time learning the right mechanism.

Second- and third-person pronouns are remarkably difficult for all models, and we find contrasting results between BERTEnt and LSTMEnt. BERTEnt is much worse than LSTMEnt at second-person pronouns, which again need extra-linguistic information (who the addresse is). As we explain in more detail later, in this case the problem is that in the current architecture speaker information is not contextualized together with the linguistic context. Instead, BERTEnt is better than LSTMEnt for third-person pronouns. This behaviour is expected given that third-person pronouns are tokens that require contextualization in the linguistic context (not the dialogue participants), and BERT specializes in contextualized representations.

Proper nouns are rigid designators, such that no contextual information is needed to predict which character "Ross" refers to (at least in the context of the sitcom) – neither linguistic nor extra-linguistic information. What is needed is to map the proper nouns to the corresponding characters, something that again is facilitated by the entity library. Most models are able to learn this mapping, with the exception of models with frozen BERT, which cannot adapt their proper noun representations to the context of the sitcom. BERTEnt is instead the most successful model for proper nouns, surpassing even LSTMEnt.

And the performance of BERTEnt is similar to that of LSTMEnt. This result is unexpected because common nouns bear resemblances to third-person pronouns (requiring contextualization, e.g. in the case of "woman") and to proper nouns (with some being more associated to a given character, like "paleontologist" with Ross), and BERTEnt outperforms LSTMEnt in both. However, common nouns are difficult for all the models. This can be traced back to two factors: 1) common nouns are rare in the training data; 2) the models are not learning good entity representations, which is necessary to learn the associations between nouns and characters (such as "paleontologist" with Ross). See Appendix A.5 for model biases that depend on training data distribution, and A.6 for the quality of entity representations.

Overall, the results show that BERTEnt and LSTMEnt have complementary strenghts: BERTEnt is better at accounting for linguistic context (with best results in third-person pronouns and proper nouns), and LSTMEnt at extra-linguistic context (with best results in first- an second-person pronouns). However, LSTMEnt achieves the best overall accuracy (Table 1) because of the data distribution: 44.4% of the datapoints are first-person pronouns, and 27.9% are second-person pronouns.

Thus, our proposed model succeeded in achieving better linguistic contextualization, but failed in incorporating extra-linguistic information, in particular information about the participants in the dialogue. We believe that the issue is that pre-trained language models like BERT do not have a "space" for extra-linguistic information; thus it is difficult to add it to current architectures. In particular, recall that, in our model, the speaker embedding is added at the output level: each token is processed by BERT, and then the speaker embedding is concatenated to the token. This means that the speaker embedding is not contextualized in the linguistic input, except via the MLP that further maps the concatenated token+speaker embeddings to the final decision. In LSTMEnt, instead, the token and the speaker embedding are processed jointly by the language model.

To understand the implications of this, consider the case of second-person pronouns: the entity we refer to when we use "you" is most probably an interlocutor who is the speaker of previous or future utterances. The current architecture doesn't have a straightforward way to access this information.

The way to go would be to include speaker information directly in the architecture of BERT. Since this entails all kinds of technical and conceptual issues, and in the spirit of "recycling" language models for referential tasks, we tried a middle-ground solution. We added a self-attention layer on top of the concatenation of the token and speaker information.[2] The self-attention layer operates on the whole sequence given as input: it compares the hidden representation at time step t with the hidden representations at all the other time steps. These comparisons are used to create a weighted representation. This layer should lead to incorporation of interlocutor information into the current representation. It however didn't work as expected: in our hyperparameter search, the best models did not use this component. This could be due to the component lacking a recency feature that encourages the model to focus more on the speakers surrounding the current token. For instance, for expressions like "you", the referent is usually a participant in the vicinity of the current utterance, such that it is harmful to consider all the spans considered in the BERT processing layer (more than 100 in the best instantiations of the model). Even though positional embeddings offer the possibility of focusing on more recent tokens, this information might not reach the output of BERT; thus the issue here could again be the fact that we include speaker information after BERT processing.

[2]We tried 1/2/4 attention heads and 1/2 layers of attention.

4 Conclusion

Our initial hypothesis was that the proposed model, BERTEnt, would attain the same performance as the previous state-of-the-art model (LSTMEnt) on mentions requiring extra-linguistic information, while improving linguistic contextualization and possibly the encoding of entity information. We instead find that the model does improve in linguistic contextualization (cf. higher performance in third-person pronouns), but instead fails to integrate extra-linguistic information about the participants in the dialogue (cf. lower performance in first- and second-person pronouns). Also, BERTEnt only slightly improves over LSTMEnt on entity representations (see Appendix A.6). The entity library does continue to be a valuable module, as in previous work (Aina et al., 2018, 2019), boosting performance across the board. Future work can focus on studying the benefits of the entity library in other pretrained models.

These results highlight requirements for successful architectures in situated Natural Language Processing. A model should be able to dynamically switch, depending on the input, between a strong sensitivity to the linguistic context and to the extra-linguistic context, to capture, e.g., that "I" points to the speaker, while "she" is to be disambiguated using the discourse context. This requires models to integrate the extra-linguistic context in their representations, a capacity that is severely underdeveloped at the moment. We have tackled the specific case of the participants in a dialogue, and have shown that it is very challenging to incorporate this kind of information in pre-trained language models. In order to address this issue, a possible approach for future research would be to develop a model which extends BERT to a multi-modal two-stream model, specialized on dialogue.

The *Friends* data that we have used is small for deep learning standards; one obvious way to go is to use more task-specific training data. Also, future work needs to conduct experiments on other dialogue-oriented tasks, in order to confirm our conclusion.

However, training data on any given "world", such as that of a particular TV show, or the environment in which an artificial assistant is typically deployed (think Siri or Alexa), is inherently limited, such that newer models will need to be able to do more with less.

Acknowledgments

We are grateful to the anonymous reviewers for their valuable comments. This project has received funding from the European Research Council (ERC) under the European Union's Horizon 2020 research and innovation programme (grant agreement No 715154). We are also grateful to the NVIDIA Corporation for the donation of GPUs used for this research. This paper reflects the authors' view only, and the EU is not responsible for any use that may be made of the information it contains.

References

Laura Aina, Carina Silberer, Ionut-Teodor Sorodoc, Matthijs Westera, and Gemma Boleda. 2018. AMORE-UPF at SemEval-2018 task 4: BiLSTM with entity library. In *Proceedings of The 12th International Workshop on Semantic Evaluation*, pages 65–69, New Orleans, Louisiana. Association for Computational Linguistics.

Laura Aina, Carina Silberer, Ionut-Teodor Sorodoc, Matthijs Westera, and Gemma Boleda. 2019. What do entity-centric models learn? insights from entity linking in multi-party dialogue. In *Proceedings of the 2019 Conference of the North American Chapter of the Association for Computational Linguistics: Human Language Technologies, Volume 1 (Long and Short Papers)*, pages 3772–3783, Minneapolis, Minnesota. Association for Computational Linguistics.

Jiaxin Bai, Hongming Zhang, Yangqiu Song, and Kun Xu. 2021. Joint coreference resolution and character linking for multiparty conversation. In *Proceedings of the 16th Conference of the European Chapter of the Association for Computational Linguistics: Main Volume*, pages 539–548, Online. Association for Computational Linguistics.

Jinho D. Choi and Henry Y. Chen. 2018. SemEval 2018 task 4: Character identification on multiparty dialogues. In *Proceedings of The 12th International Workshop on Semantic Evaluation*, pages 57–64, New Orleans, Louisiana. Association for Computational Linguistics.

Jacob Devlin, Ming-Wei Chang, Kenton Lee, and Kristina Toutanova. 2019. BERT: Pre-training of deep bidirectional transformers for language understanding. In *Proceedings of the 2019 Conference of the North American Chapter of the Association for Computational Linguistics: Human Language Technologies, Volume 1 (Long and Short Papers)*, pages 4171–4186, Minneapolis, Minnesota. Association for Computational Linguistics.

Mandar Joshi, Danqi Chen, Yinhan Liu, Daniel S. Weld, Luke Zettlemoyer, and Omer Levy. 2020. SpanBERT: Improving pre-training by representing and predicting spans. *Transactions of the Association for Computational Linguistics*, 8:64–77.

Matthew E. Peters, Mark Neumann, Mohit Iyyer, Matt Gardner, Christopher Clark, Kenton Lee, and Luke Zettlemoyer. 2018. Deep contextualized word representations. In *Proceedings of the 2018 Conference of the North American Chapter of the Association for Computational Linguistics: Human Language Technologies, Volume 1 (Long Papers)*, pages 2227–2237, New Orleans, Louisiana. Association for Computational Linguistics.

Zhengzhe Yang and Jinho D. Choi. 2019. FriendsQA: Open-domain question answering on TV show transcripts. In *Proceedings of the 20th Annual SIGdial Meeting on Discourse and Dialogue*, pages 188–197, Stockholm, Sweden. Association for Computational Linguistics.

Ethan Zhou and Jinho D. Choi. 2018. They exist! introducing plural mentions to coreference resolution and entity linking. In *Proceedings of the 27th International Conference on Computational Linguistics*, pages 24–34, Santa Fe, New Mexico, USA. Association for Computational Linguistics.

Label Errors in BANKING77

Cecilia Ying
Queen's University
Smith School of Business
y.ying@queensu.ca

Stephen Thomas
Queen's University
Smith School of Business
stephen.thomas@queensu.ca

Abstract

We investigate potential label errors present in the popular BANKING77 dataset and the associated negative impacts on intent classification methods. Motivated by our own negative results when constructing an intent classifier, we applied two automated approaches to identify potential label errors in the dataset. We found that over 1,400 (14%) of the 10,003 training utterances may have been incorrectly labelled. In a simple experiment, we found that by removing the utterances with potential errors, our intent classifier saw an increase of 4.5% and 8% for the F1-Score and Adjusted Rand Index, respectively, in supervised and unsupervised classification. This paper serves as a warning of the potential of noisy labels in popular NLP datasets. Further study is needed to fully identify the breadth and depth of label errors in BANKING77 and other datasets.

1 Introduction

NLP researchers and practitioners use standard benchmark datasets in the selection, development, and comparison of advanced NLP methods. The use of standard benchmarks enables an apples-to-apples comparison of competing methods, as well as an evaluation of a method under different business scenarios.

Recently, researchers have proposed three promising intent classification benchmark datasets that are large (>10,000 instances) and include more than 50 unique intents: BANKING77 (cas), HWU64 (Liu et al., 2019), and CLINC150 (lar).

The aforementioned datasets have been used to evaluate pretrained transformers (Zhang et al., 2021b), density-based models (gon), few-shot learning (luo), open intent detection (Zhang et al., 2021a), and intent discovery (cha).

These benchmark datasets are hand-labelled by humans and their categorization can be subjective in nature. In addition, humans may make mistakes in the labelling process. As such, it is important to assess the accuracy of the human-given labels (Northcutt et al., 2021a).

Our recent experience with BANKING77 suggested that several labeling errors were present in the dataset. Using confident learning (Northcutt et al., 2021b) and our own cosine similarity methodology (Section 3.2), we found that over 1,400 (14%) of the 10,003 training samples may have been incorrectly labelled. Table 1 shows representative examples.

Using noisy labels to train and evaluate an intent classifier could have disastrous consequences. First, the classifier could incorrectly classify new utterances. Second, any performance measures would be based on mislabelled truth and therefore be inaccurate. Finally, researchers and practitioners may make an incorrect recommendation or conclusion for the downstream task-oriented conversational system.

In this paper, we investigate the potential label errors present in BANKING77. First, we provide background on BANKING77 in Section 2. In Section 3, we describe our methodology for determining potential label errors. We first use Confident Learning (Northcutt et al., 2021a) and identify over 900 potential label errors. Next, we design a methodology based on cosine similarity and identify an additional 500 potential label errors. In Section 4, we quantify the potential impacts of errors on a downstream NLP task. Finally, in Section 5 we conclude and outline future work.

2 Background

BANKING77 was created in 2020 by researchers at PolyAI[1] as part of their study on a new intent classifier using pretrained dual sentence encoders based on fixed Universal Sentence Encoders (Cer et al., 2018) and ConveRT (Henderson et al., 2020). The dataset is a single-domain intent detection

[1] github.com/PolyAI-LDN/task-specific-datasets/tree/master/banking_data

Proceedings of the Third Workshop on Insights from Negative Results in NLP, pages 139 - 143
May 26, 2022 ©2022 Association for Computational Linguistics

Similar utterances with different labels	
Utterance	**Label**
"How long will it take for me to get my card?"	card_arrival
"Can you tell me how long it takes for a new card to come?"	card_delivery_estimate
"Can you tell me the status of my new card?"	lost_or_stolen_card
"how many days processing new card?"	contactless_not_working
"Can you tell me when my money transfer will go through"	pending_transfer
"How long am I to wait before the transfer gets to my account?"	transfer_timing
"How long before a bank transfer shows up in the account?"	balance_not_updated_after_bank_transfer
Dissimilar utterances with the same label	
Utterance	**Label**
"How do I check security settings using the app?"	card_not_working
"I cannot seem to use my card."	card_not_working
"Can I use app to reset PIN attempts?"	card_not_working
"How do I check security settings on my card?"	card_not_working
"HOW LONG TO TAKE THE TIME TO SOLVE"	card_not_working

Table 1: Examples of potential label errors. The top portion shows utterances with similar intents assigned to different labels. The bottom portion shows examples of utterances with different intents assigned to the same label.

dataset, containing 10,003 annotated customer service queries over 77 intents related only to banking.

Many of the previously available datasets only included a small number of labels and contained a small number of utterances from many distinct domains. The authors believe that BANKING77—given its single-domain focus yet large number of intents—makes the intent detection task more realistic and challenging.

The authors also acknowledged that there are partially overlapping intent categories, and therefore, the intent detection system cannot rely only on the semantics of individual words to correctly categorize the utterance. However, they did not provide any specifics regarding the extent and impact of such overlaps.

3 Identifying Potential Label Errors

While implementing our own intent classifier on BANKING77, we noticed unexpectedly poor performance in several intent categories. We found that our classifier was confusing many of the labels. For instance, we found that up to sixteen "truth" labels were predicted as a single intent by our classifier. Similarly, one predicted intent included up to twelve truth labels. (Table 1 shows examples of such confusion.) While some prediction errors are expected, we were quite surprised at the level of confusion. We performed a preliminary manual investigation of labels and found that many utterances seemed to have the wrong truth label assigned. Also, we found that labels related to *"card"* or *"top_up"* have high similarities, as shown in Figure 1, making it difficult to select a distinct and unique label.

To further understand the extend of these potential label errors, we applied and compared two automated approaches: the Confident Learning framework, and a Cosine Similarity approach.

3.1 Confident Learning Framework

We replicated the Confident Learning (CL) framework (Northcutt et al., 2021b)[2], which produces a *label noise estimation* to find potential label errors, identified through the joint distribution of the noisy (given) labels and latent (unknown) labels to characterize class-conditional label noise.

We trained a LightGBM classifier on SBERT (rei) MPNet (Song et al., 2020) sentence embeddings. We used 10-fold cross validation to obtain out-of-sample predictions to identify potential label errors.

We found that 965 utterances, representing 75 of the 77 labels, may have potential label errors. Table 2 summarizes the top five labels with the highest number of possible errors. It is interesting to point out that utterances related to *"transfers"* or *"top_up"* labels appear to be most problematic.

3.2 Cosine Similarity Approach

The CL approach excelled at finding utterances that were identified as noisy within the same label. However, in our manual investigation, we also noticed that many utterances were semantically identical (e.g., "*Why hasn't my transfer gone through*" and "*Why is my transfer still pending?*") but were assigned different labels.

[2]https://github.com/cleanlab/cleanlab

Label	Potential Errors
transfer_not_received _by_recipient	32
balance_not_updated _after_bank_transfer	31
top_up_failed	24
top_up_reverted	24
pending_top_up	23

Table 2: The top five labels with potential errors from the CL framework.

Label	Potential Errors
card_arrival	42
getting_virtual_card	37
declined_card_payment	33
pending_top_up	33
top_up_reverted	30

Table 3: The top five labels with potential errors from our Cosine Similarity approach.

We created a method to find such utterances as follows. First, we calculated the pairwise cosine similarity (based on SBERT MPNET embeddings). Next, we identified pair of utterances that had similarity score higher than δ =0.85 but were assigned different labels.

We found that 590 utterances, representing 49 of the 77 labels, may have potential label errors. Table 3 summarizes the top five labels with the most conflicting labels assigned to similar utterances. Utterances related to *"card_arrival"* have the largest number of label disagreements.

We also noticed that two labels related to *"top_up"* have been identified by both approaches, indicating further investigation related to these two labels is needed. 127 of the 10,003 utterances were identified as potential label errors by both approaches, of which only 80 shared the same suggested correct labels.

4 Experiment Results

To illustrate the negative impact of the noisy labels on the performance of an intent classifier, we designed an experiment as follows.

First, we considered two versions of the BANKING77 dataset. The **original**, unmodified version,

	Original	Trimmed
Unique labels	77	77
Utterances	10,003	8,575
Terms	4,518	4,230
Tokens	119,530	103,776
Tokens per utterance	11.9	12.1
Mean term occurrence	26.5	24.5

Table 4: Statistics of the original and trimmed versions of the BANKING77 dataset.

and a **trimmed** version whereby we removed all utterances with potential label errors identified by either the CL framework or cosine-similarity approach. Table 4 compares the statistics between the original and the trimmed version of the dataset.

Next, we built two intent classifiers, one supervised and one unsupervised, as follows. We obtained sentence embeddings for each dataset using SBERT and MPNet. We reduced the dimensionality of the embeddings using Uniform Manifold Approximation and Projection (UMAP) (McInnes et al., 2020) (n_components=20, n_neighbors=40).

In the supervised approach, we used LightGBM (n_estimators = 1000, learning_rate = 0.1, max_depth=4, num_leaves=15) to train two models. Using 5-fold cross validation, we measured each model's accuracy and F1-score.

For comparison, we used Agglomerative Clustering (n_clusters=77, affinity="euclidean", linkage="ward") as our unsupervised approach. We then measured five common clustering metrics: Adjusted Rand Index (ARI); Adjusted Mutual Information (AMI), Completeness, Fowlkes-Mallows, and Homogeneity.

Table 5 shows the results. We find that by removing utterances flagged as potential errors significantly improved the performance of the intent classifier according to all metrics. Notably, F1-score increased by **4.5%** in the supervised approach, and ARI increased by **8%** in the unsupervised approach.

5 Conclusion and Future Work

In this paper, we investigated potential label errors present in the popular BANKING77 benchmark dataset. We applied two automated techniques to identify potential label errors. First, we used the Confident Learning framework to find utterances based on class-conditional noise estimates. Sec-

Supervised Classifier			
LightGBM			
Metric	**Original**	**Trimmed**	**% Diff**
Accuracy	0.882	0.924	+4.5%
F1-Score	0.878	0.920	+4.5%
Unsupervised Classifier			
Agglomerative Clustering			
Metric	**Original**	**Trimmed**	**% Diff**
ARI	0.6344	0.6859	+8%
AMI	0.8333	0.8565	+3%
Completeness	0.8527	0.8735	+2%
Fowlkes-Mallows	0.6409	0.6909	+8%
Homogeneity	0.8392	0.8648	+3%

Table 5: Experiment results. We report various metrics on the original dataset, the trimmed dataset, and the difference between the two. ARI is the Adjusted Rand Index and AMI is the Adjusted Mutual Information.

ond, we developed our own cosine-similarity based technique to find utterances that are semantically similar but labeled differently. Together, these approaches identified over 1,400 utterances with potential label errors. A simple experiment showed that an intent classifier's performance can be improved by removing such utterances. F1-score increased by **4.5%** for the supervised classifier, and ARI increased by **8%** for the unsupervised classifier.

Given the importance of benchmark datasets in the development, evaluation, and selection of NLP techniques, it is important that the labels contain as few errors as possible. We would like to extend our work by developing an automated correction tool that can identify and fix label errors. We will also manually verify and correct errors in BANKING77, and it will serve as the ground truth for evaluating the performance of the automated correction tool. Furthermore, we will apply the methodology on other benchmark datasets such as CLINC150 and HWU64.

References

Density-Based Dynamic Curriculum Learning for Intent Detection. In *Proceedings of the 30th ACM International Conference on Information & Knowledge Management*, Virtual Event Queensland Australia.

Don't Miss the Labels: Label-semantic Augmented Meta-Learner for Few-Shot Text Classification. In *Findings of the Association for Computational Linguistics: ACL-IJCNLP 2021*, Online.

Efficient Intent Detection with Dual Sentence Encoders. In *Proceedings of the 2nd Workshop on Natural Language Processing for Conversational AI*, Online.

An Evaluation Dataset for Intent Classification and Out-of-Scope Prediction. In *Proceedings of the 2019 Conference on Empirical Methods in Natural Language Processing and the 9th International Joint Conference on Natural Language Processing (EMNLP-IJCNLP)*, Hong Kong, China.

Intent Mining from past conversations for Conversational Agent. In *Proceedings of the 28th International Conference on Computational Linguistics*, Barcelona, Spain (Online).

Sentence-BERT: Sentence Embeddings using Siamese BERT-Networks. In *Proceedings of the 2019 Conference on Empirical Methods in Natural Language Processing and the 9th International Joint Conference on Natural Language Processing (EMNLP-IJCNLP)*, Hong Kong, China.

Daniel Cer, Yinfei Yang, Sheng-yi Kong, Nan Hua, Nicole Limtiaco, Rhomni St John, Noah Constant, Mario Guajardo-Cespedes, Steve Yuan, Chris Tar, Yun-Hsuan Sung, Brian Strope, and Ray Kurzweil. 2018. Universal Sentence Encoder. *arXiv:1803.11175*.

Matthew Henderson, Iñigo Casanueva, Nikola Mrkšić, Pei-Hao Su, Tsung-Hsien Wen, and Ivan Vulić. 2020. ConveRT: Efficient and Accurate Conversational Representations from Transformers. *arXiv:1911.03688*.

Xingkun Liu, Arash Eshghi, Pawel Swietojanski, and Verena Rieser. 2019. Benchmarking Natural Language Understanding Services for building Conversational Agents. *arXiv:1903.05566*.

Leland McInnes, John Healy, and James Melville. 2020. UMAP: Uniform Manifold Approximation and Projection for Dimension Reduction. *arXiv:1802.03426*.

Curtis G. Northcutt, Anish Athalye, and Jonas Mueller. 2021a. Pervasive Label Errors in Test Sets Destabilize Machine Learning Benchmarks. *arXiv:2103.14749*.

Curtis G. Northcutt, Lu Jiang, and Isaac L. Chuang. 2021b. Confident Learning: Estimating Uncertainty in Dataset Labels. *arXiv:1911.00068*.

Kaitao Song, Xu Tan, Tao Qin, Jianfeng Lu, and Tie-Yan Liu. 2020. MPNet: Masked and Permuted Pre-training for Language Understanding. *arXiv:2004.09297*.

Hanlei Zhang, Hua Xu, and Ting-En Lin. 2021a. Deep Open Intent Classification with Adaptive Decision Boundary. *Proceedings of the AAAI Conference on Artificial Intelligence*, 35(16).

Jian-Guo Zhang, Kazuma Hashimoto, Yao Wan, Ye Liu, Caiming Xiong, and Philip S. Yu. 2021b. Are Pretrained Transformers Robust in Intent Classification? A Missing Ingredient in Evaluation of Out-of-Scope Intent Detection. *arXiv:2106.04564*.

A Appendix - Similarities between labels

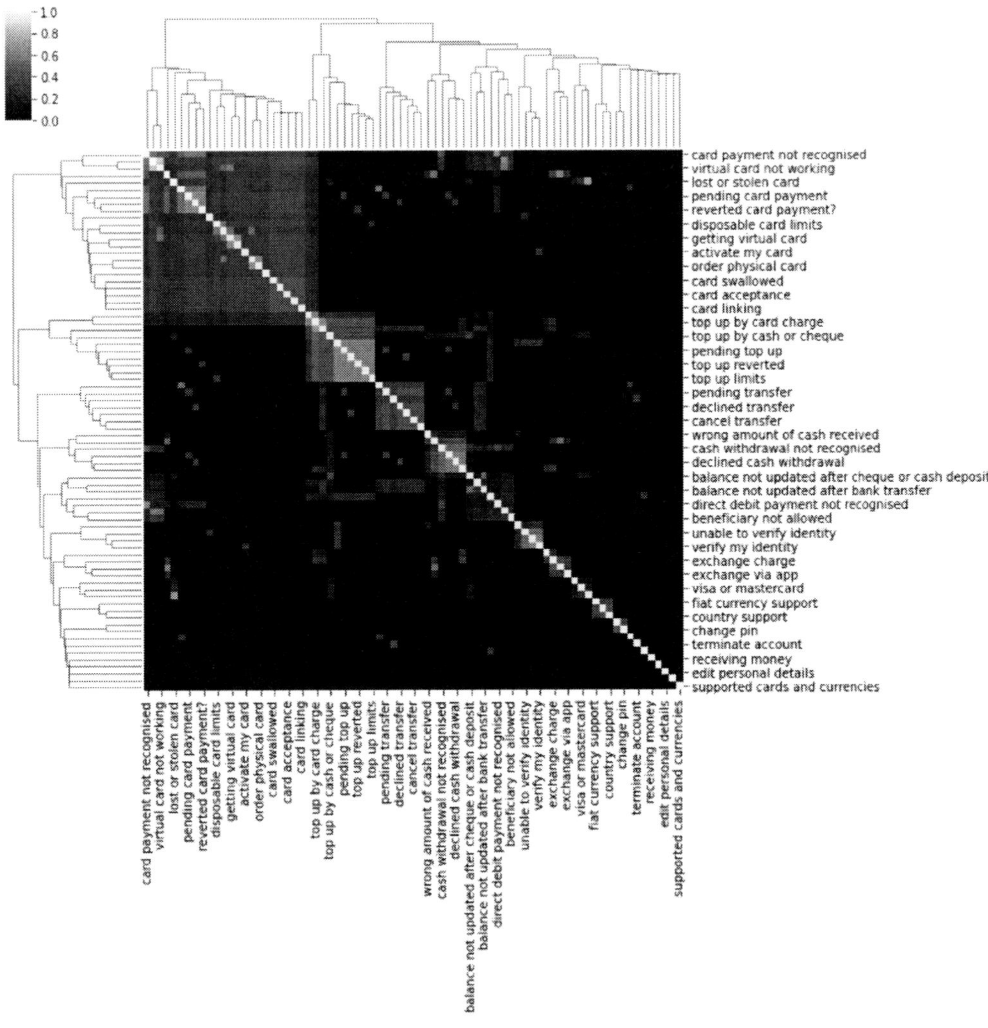

Figure 1: A heatmap of label similarities in the BANKING77 dataset, according to a simple word count. Labels are sorted based on their word count similarities. We see clusters of highly-similar labels, such as the top left corner with labels relating to *"card"*, and the middle cluster with labels relating tor *"top_up"*.

Pathologies of Pre-trained Language Models in Few-shot Fine-tuning

Hanjie Chen[1], **Guoqing Zheng**[2], **Ahmed Hassan Awadallah**[2], **Yangfeng Ji**[1]
[1]Department of Computer Science, University of Virginia, Charlottesville, VA, USA
[2]Microsoft Research
{hc9mx, yangfeng}@virginia.edu
{zheng, hassanam}@microsoft.com

Abstract

Although adapting pre-trained language models with few examples has shown promising performance on text classification, there is a lack of understanding of where the performance gain comes from. In this work, we propose to answer this question by interpreting the adaptation behavior using post-hoc explanations from model predictions. By modeling feature statistics of explanations, we discover that (1) without fine-tuning, pre-trained models (e.g. BERT and RoBERTa) show strong prediction bias across labels; (2) although few-shot fine-tuning can mitigate the prediction bias and demonstrate promising prediction performance, our analysis shows models gain performance improvement by capturing non-task-related features (e.g. stop words) or shallow data patterns (e.g. lexical overlaps). These observations alert that pursuing model performance with fewer examples may incur pathological prediction behavior, which requires further sanity check on model predictions and careful design in model evaluations in few-shot fine-tuning.

1 Introduction

Pre-trained language models (Brown et al., 2020; Liu et al., 2019; Devlin et al., 2019) have shown impressive adaptation ability to dowstream tasks, achieving considerable performance even with scarce task-specific training data, i.e., few-shot adaptation (Radford et al., 2019; Schick and Schütze, 2021a; Gao et al., 2021). Existing few-shot adaptation techniques broadly fall in fine-tuning and few-shot learning (Shin et al., 2020; Schick and Schütze, 2021b; Chen et al., 2021b). Specifically, fine-tuning includes directly tuning pre-trained language models with few task-specific examples or utilizing a natural-language prompt to transform downstream tasks to masked language modeling task for better mining knowledge from pre-trained models (Petroni et al., 2019; Jiang et al., 2020; Wang et al., 2021a). Few-shot learning leverages unlabeled data or auxiliary tasks to provide additional information for facilitating model training (Zheng et al., 2021; Wang et al., 2021b; Du et al., 2021a).

Although much success has been made in adapting pre-trained language models to dowstream tasks with few-shot examples, some issues have been reported. Utama et al. (2021) found that models obtained from few-shot prompt-based fine-tuning utilize inference heuristics to make predictions on sentence pair classification tasks. Zhao et al. (2021) discovered the instability of model performance towards different prompts in few-shot learning. These works mainly look at prompt-based fine-tuning and discover some problems.

This paper looks into direct fine-tuning and provides a different perspective on understanding model adaptation behavior via post-hoc explanations (Strumbelj and Kononenko, 2010; Sundararajan et al., 2017). Specifically, post-hoc explanations identify the important features (tokens) contribute to the model prediction per example. We model the statistics of important features over prediction labels via local mutual information (LMI) (Schuster et al., 2019; Du et al., 2021b). We track the change of feature statistics with the model adapting from pre-trained to fine-tuned and compare it with the statistics of few-shot training examples. This provides insights on understanding model adaptation behavior and the effect of training data in few-shot settings.

We evaluate two pre-trained language models, BERT (Devlin et al., 2019) and RoBERTa (Liu et al., 2019), on three tasks, including sentiment classification, natural language inference, and paraphrase identification. For each task, we test on both in-domain and out-of-domain datasets to evaluate the generalization of model adaptation performance. We discover some interesting observations, some of which may have been overlooked in prior work: (1) without fine-tuning, pre-trained mod-

Proceedings of the Third Workshop on Insights from Negative Results in NLP, pages 144 - 153
May 26, 2022 ©2022 Association for Computational Linguistics

els show strong prediction bias across labels; (2) fine-tuning with a few examples can mitigate the prediction bias, but the model prediction behavior may be pathological by focusing on non-task-related features (e.g. stop words); (3) models adjust their prediction behaviors on different labels asynchronously; (4) models can capture the shallow patterns of training data to make predictions. The insight drawn from the above observations is that pursuing model performance with fewer examples is dangerous and may cause pathologies in model prediction behavior. We argue that future research on few-shot fine-tuning or learning should do sanity check on model prediction behavior and ensure the performance gain is based on right reasons.

2 Setup

Tasks. We consider three tasks: sentiment classification, natural language inference, and paraphrase identification. Each task contains an in-domain/out-of-domain dataset pair: IMDB (Maas et al., 2011)/Yelp (Zhang et al., 2015) for sentiment classification, SNLI (Bowman et al., 2015)/MNLI (Williams et al., 2018) for natural language inference, and QQP (Iyer et al., 2017)/TwitterPPDB (TPPDB) (Lan et al., 2017) for paraphrase identification. The data statistics are in Table 4 in Appendix A.1.

Models. We evaluate two pre-trained language models, BERT (Devlin et al., 2019) and RoBERTa (Liu et al., 2019). For each task, we train the models on the in-domain training set with different ratio ($r\%, r \in [0, 1]$) of clean examples and then test them on in-domain and out-of-domain test sets.

Explanations. We explain model prediction behavior via post-hoc explanations which identify important features (tokens) in input texts that contribute to model predictions. We test four explanation methods: sampling Shapley (Strumbelj and Kononenko, 2010), integrated gradients (Sundararajan et al., 2017), attentions (Mullenbach et al., 2018), and individual word masks (Chen et al., 2021a). For each dataset, we randomly select 1000 test examples to generate explanations due to computational costs. We evaluate the faithfulness of these explanation methods via the AOPC metric (Nguyen, 2018; Chen et al., 2020). Table 6 in Appendix A.2 shows that the sampling Shapley generates more faithful explanations than other methods. In the following experiments, we adopt it to explain model predictions.

More details about the models, datasets and explanations are in Appendix A.

3 Experiments

We report the prediction results (averaged across 5 runs) of BERT and RoBERTa trained with different ratio ($r\% : 0 \sim 1\%$) of in-domain training examples on both in-domain and out-of-domain test sets in Table 2. Overall, training with more examples, BERT and RoBERTa achieve better prediction accuracy on both in-domain and out-of-domain test sets.

We look into the predictions of models from pre-trained to fine-tuned and analyze model prediction behavior change during adaptation via post-hoc explanations. In subsection 3.1, we observe that pre-trained models without fine-tuning show strong prediction bias across labels. The models fine-tuned with a few examples can quickly mitigate the prediction bias by capturing non-task-related features, leading to a plausible performance gain. In subsection 3.2, we further quantify the prediction behavior change by comparing the feature statistics of model explanations and training data. We discover that the models adjust their prediction behavior on minority labels first rather than learning information from all classes synchronously and can capture the shallow patterns of training data, which may result in pathologies in predictions.

3.1 Prediction bias in pre-trained models

In our pilot experiments, we find the predictions of pre-trained models without fine-tuning are biased across labels (see an example of confusion matrix in Figure 2 in Appendix B). Original pre-trained models tend to predict all examples with a specific label on each dataset. We denote the specific label as the majority label and the rest labels as minority labels. The results of majority labels are in Table 1.

We propose a metric, prediction bias (PB), to quantify the bias of model predictions across labels,

$$\text{PB} = \left| \frac{T_{i_1} - T_{i_2}}{T_{i_1} + T_{i_2}} - \frac{D_{i_1} - D_{i_2}}{D_{i_1} + D_{i_2}} \right|, \qquad (1)$$
$$i_1 = \underset{i \in \{1,\dots,C\}}{\text{argmax}}\,(T_i), i_2 = \underset{i \in \{1,\dots,C\}}{\text{argmin}}\,(T_i)$$

where i_1 and i_2 are the majority and most minority labels respectively. T_i and D_i denote the numbers of model predictions and test examples on label i respectively, and C is number of classes. The range

Models	IMDB	SNLI	QQP	Yelp	MNLI	TPPDB
BERT	Pos	Neu	Pa	Pos	Neu	Pa
RoBERTa	Pos	Con	Pa	Pos	Con	Pa

Table 1: The majority labels of original pre-trained models on different datasets. Pos: postive, Con: contradiction, Neu: neutral, Pa: paraphrases.

Model	r	In-domain						Out-of-domain					
		IMDB		SNLI		QQP		Yelp		MNLI		TPPDB	
		Acc	PB	Acc	PB	Acc	PB	Acc	PB	Acc	PB	Acc	PB
BERT	0	49.73	0.97	35.30	0.65	45.10	0.46	49.86	0.98	32.95	0.95	44.44	0.85
	0.01	-	-	48.45	0.20	65.33	0.45	-	-	34.77	0.92	80.25	0.35
	0.05	60.31	0.41	63.20	0.08	69.82	0.16	61.61	0.09	37.58	0.95	86.26	0.14
	0.1	70.76	0.13	69.13	0.12	73.65	0.04	67.11	0.41	38.27	0.93	86.69	0.07
	0.5	84.71	0.05	77.63	0.06	79.06	0.02	88.19	0.08	55.37	0.45	87.27	0.03
	1	85.46	0.05	80.33	0.06	80.16	0.05	89.09	0.03	58.81	0.34	85.22	0.07
RoBERTa	0	50.17	1.00	33.55	1.00	36.84	1.26	50.00	1.00	33.24	1.02	18.93	1.62
	0.01	-	-	36.27	0.61	66.26	0.54	-	-	32.48	1.00	81.07	0.38
	0.05	58.11	0.61	68.03	0.13	71.64	0.09	58.47	0.71	42.41	0.88	82.30	0.21
	0.1	78.58	0.10	77.04	0.07	76.82	0.04	76.59	0.37	54.72	0.75	83.54	0.21
	0.5	89.56	0.01	83.84	0.04	81.91	0.05	92.54	0.08	66.90	0.37	85.67	0.06
	1	90.34	0.01	85.43	0.03	83.19	0.05	93.76	0.01	70.47	0.20	85.78	0.08

Table 2: Prediction accuracy and bias of BERT and RoBERTa trained with different ratio ($r\%$) of in-domain training examples on both in-domain and out-of-domain test sets. Acc: accuracy (%), PB: prediction bias. For PB, darker pink color implies larger prediction bias. Note that we do not consider $r = 0.01$ for IMDB and Yelp datasets because the number of training examples is too small.

of PB is $[0, 2]$. PB takes 0 if the label distribtion of model predictions is consistent with that of data. For balanced dataset, the upper bound of PB is 1, that is all examples are predicted as one label. For imbalanced dataset, PB takes 2 in an extreme case, where the dataset only contains one label of examples, while the model wrongly predicts them as another label. We consider data bias because some datasets (e.g. QQP and TPPDB) have imbalanced label distributions.

The results in Table 2 show that both pre-trained BERT and RoBERTa have strong prediction bias on all of the datasets. The prediction bias decreases with models fine-tuned with more examples.

Models make biased predictions by focusing on non-task-related features. To understand which features are associated with model prediction labels, we follow Schuster et al. (2019); Du et al. (2021b) and analyze the statistics of model explanations via local mutual information (LMI). Specifically, we select top k important features in each explanation and get a set of important features ($E = \{e\}$) over all explanations. We empirically take $k = 10$ for the IMDB and Yelp datasets and $k = 6$ for other datasets based on their average sentence lengths. The LMI between a feature e and a particular label y is

$$\text{LMI}(e, y) = p(e, y) \cdot \log\left(\frac{p(y \mid e)}{p(y)}\right), \quad (2)$$

where $p(y \mid e) = \frac{count(e,y)}{count(e)}$, $p(y) = \frac{count(y)}{|E|}$, $p(e, y) = \frac{count(e,y)}{|E|}$, and $|E|$ is the number of occurrences of all features in E. Then we can get a distribution of LMI over all tokens in the vocabulary ($\{w\}$) built upon the dataset, i.e.

$$P_{\text{LMI}}(w, y) = \begin{cases} \text{LMI}(w, y) & \text{if token } w \in E \\ 0 & \text{else} \end{cases} \quad (3)$$

We normalize the LMI distribution by dividing each value with the sum of all values.

Figure 1 shows LMI distributions of BERT on the IMDB dataset with different r, where top 5 tokens are pointed in each plot (see Table 7 in Appendix B for more results on other datasets). When $r = 0$, we can see that BERT makes biased predictions on the positive label (in Table 1) by focusing on some non-task-related high-frequency tokens. The top features associated with the negative label include some relatively low-frequency tokens (e.g.

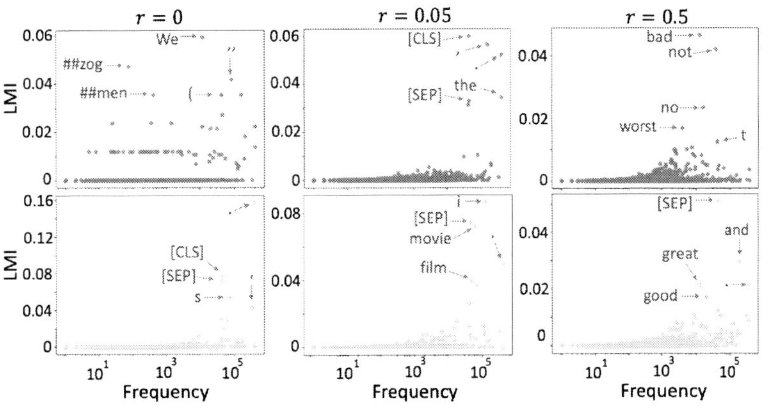

Figure 1: LMI distributions based on explanation statistics of BERT on the IMDB dataset with different r. The horizontal axis represents tokens in vocabulary in the ascending order of frequency. The upper and lower plots are on the negative and positive labels respectively. Top 5 tokens are pointed in each plot.

		In-domain																Out-of-domain													
		IMDB				SNLI						QQP				Yelp				MNLI						TPPDB			
Model	r	Ori		Data		Ori			Data			Ori		Data		Ori		Data		Ori			Data			Ori		Data	
		Neg	Pos	Neg	Pos	En	Con	Neu	En	Con	Neu	NPa	Pa	NPa	Pa	Neg	Pos	Neg	Pos	En	Con	Neu	En	Con	Neu	NPa	Pa	NPa	Pa
BERT	0.01	-	-	-	-	0.71	0.43	0.33	0.70	0.42	0.51	0.67	0.32	0.93	0.45	-	-	-	-	0.35	0.09	0.29	0.40	0.33	0.76	0.74	0.16	1.55	0.18
	0.05	2.26	0.45	0.90	0.63	0.58	0.60	0.47	0.31	0.17	0.16	0.49	0.14	0.23	0.22	2.20	0.69	0.66	0.43	0.43	0.45	0.41	0.76	0.27	0.63	0.87	0.02	0.58	0.03
	0.1	2.00	0.76	0.80	0.54	0.56	0.82	0.45	0.30	0.42	0.46	0.46	0.53	0.19	0.37	2.06	0.79	0.37	0.45	0.46	0.49	0.41	0.61	0.40	1.25	0.67	0.21	0.53	0.00
	0.5	1.39	0.80	1.16	0.52	0.70	1.51	0.94	0.14	0.54	0.46	0.31	0.67	0.08	0.21	1.61	0.93	0.73	0.52	0.92	1.70	0.78	0.82	0.91	1.02	0.93	0.09	0.37	0.04
	1	1.21	1.60	0.68	0.86	0.80	1.02	0.65	0.14	0.48	0.52	0.21	1.01	0.00	0.42	0.73	1.94	0.46	0.83	0.73	1.31	0.55	0.76	0.69	1.14	0.46	0.54	0.33	0.11
RoBERTa	0.01	-	-	-	-	-	0.96	-	0.76	0.52	0.56	-	0.08	0.54	0.36	-	-	-	-	-	0.95	-	0.33	0.84	0.95	-	0.00	1.55	0.00
	0.05	-	0.66	0.17	0.72	-	0.62	-	0.50	0.32	0.67	-	0.43	0.22	0.35	-	0.38	0.14	0.62	-	0.26	-	0.89	0.22	1.07	-	0.26	1.43	0.39
	0.1	-	1.03	0.69	0.71	-	1.05	-	0.22	0.57	0.45	-	1.27	0.17	0.59	-	0.96	0.30	0.47	-	0.18	-	1.05	0.10	0.62	-	0.39	0.72	0.36
	0.5	-	1.33	0.81	0.42	-	2.07	-	0.21	0.60	0.55	-	1.01	0.15	0.69	-	1.70	0.66	0.43	-	0.70	-	0.87	0.70	0.79	-	0.59	0.79	0.48
	1	-	1.41	0.86	0.62	-	0.30	-	0.17	0.32	0.23	-	0.42	0.27	0.23	-	1.91	0.65	0.78	-	0.18	-	0.72	0.66	0.51	-	0.64	0.95	0.47

Table 3: The KL divergence between LMI distributions. The columns of "Ori" and "Data" show the results with original pre-trained models' explanations or few-shot training data as the reference respectively. Neg: negative, Pos: postive, En: entailment, Con: contradiction, Neu: neutral, NPa: nonparaphrases, Pa: paraphrases. Darker color indicates larger KL divergence.

##men, ##zog) which may have been seen by the model during pre-training.

Models adjust prediction bias by capturing non-task-related features on minority labels. Fine-tuning BERT with a few examples ($r = 0.05$, exactly 9 examples) from IMDB can quickly mitigate the prediction bias along with a plausible improvement on prediction accuracy (in Table 2). However, Figure 1 (the middle upper plot) shows that the model captures non-task-related high-frequency tokens to make predictions on the minority label (negative), implying the performance gain is not reasonable. Only when the model is fine-tuned with more examples ($r = 0.5$), it starts capturing task-specific informative tokens, such as "bad", "good".

3.2 Quantifying model adaptation behavior

To quantify the model prediction behavior change (in Figure 1) during adaptation, we compute the Kullback–Leibler divergence (KLD) between the LMI distributions of the model without/with fine-tuning, i.e. $KL_y(P^0_{LMI}(w,y), P^r_{LMI}(w,y))$. The superscripts ("0" or "r") indicate the ratio of training examples used in fine-tuning. Besides, we also evaluate how much the model prediction behavior is learned from the patterns of training data. Specifically, we compute the LMI distribution of few-shot training examples via Equation 2 and Equation 3, except that E represents the set of features appearing in those examples. Then we use the LMI distribution of data as the reference and compute the KLD between it and the LMI distribution of model explanations.

Table 3 records the results of KLD with the LMI

distribution of original pre-trained model explanations as the reference (columns of "Ori") or that of training data as the reference (columns of "Data"). Note that we do not have the results of RoBERTa on some labels (e.g. "Neg") in "Ori" columns because the pre-trained RoBERTa does not make any predictions on those labels and we do not have the reference LMI distributions.

Models adjust their prediction behaviors on different labels asynchronously. In "Ori" columns, the KLDs on minority labels are larger than those on majority labels when r is small (e.g. 0.05). The changes of KLDs are discrepant across labels with r increasing. The results show that the models focus on adjusting their prediction behavior on minority labels first rather than learning from all classes synchronously in few-shot settings.

Models can capture the shallow patterns of training data. In "Data" columns, the KLDs on SNLI and QQP are overall smaller than those on IMDB, illustrating that it is easier for models to learn the patterns of datasets on sentence-pair classification tasks. With r increasing, the KLDs on the entailment label of SNLI are smaller than those on other labels, which validates the observations in previous work (Utama et al., 2021; Nie et al., 2019) that models can capture lexical overlaps to predict the entailment label. Another interesting observation is the KLDs on Yelp in "Data" columns are mostly smaller than those on IMDB. This indicates that models may rely on the shallow patterns of in-domain datasets to make predictions on out-of-domain datasets.

4 Conclusion

In this work, we take a closer look into the adaptation behavior of pre-trained language models in few-shot fine-tuning via post-hoc explanations. We discover many pathologies in model prediction behavior. The insight drawn from our observations is that promising model performance gain in few-shot learning could be misleading. Future research on few-shot fine-tuning or learning requires sanity check on model prediction behavior and some careful design in model evaluation and analysis.

Acknowledgments

We thank the anonymous reviewers for many valuable comments.

References

Samuel R. Bowman, Gabor Angeli, Christopher Potts, and Christopher D. Manning. 2015. A large annotated corpus for learning natural language inference. In *Proceedings of the 2015 Conference on Empirical Methods in Natural Language Processing*, pages 632–642, Lisbon, Portugal. Association for Computational Linguistics.

Tom Brown, Benjamin Mann, Nick Ryder, Melanie Subbiah, Jared D Kaplan, Prafulla Dhariwal, Arvind Neelakantan, Pranav Shyam, Girish Sastry, Amanda Askell, Sandhini Agarwal, Ariel Herbert-Voss, Gretchen Krueger, Tom Henighan, Rewon Child, Aditya Ramesh, Daniel Ziegler, Jeffrey Wu, Clemens Winter, Chris Hesse, Mark Chen, Eric Sigler, Mateusz Litwin, Scott Gray, Benjamin Chess, Jack Clark, Christopher Berner, Sam McCandlish, Alec Radford, Ilya Sutskever, and Dario Amodei. 2020. Language models are few-shot learners. In *Advances in Neural Information Processing Systems*, volume 33, pages 1877–1901. Curran Associates, Inc.

Hanjie Chen, Song Feng, Jatin Ganhotra, Hui Wan, Chulaka Gunasekara, Sachindra Joshi, and Yangfeng Ji. 2021a. Explaining neural network predictions on sentence pairs via learning word-group masks. In *Proceedings of the 2021 Conference of the North American Chapter of the Association for Computational Linguistics: Human Language Technologies*, pages 3917–3930, Online. Association for Computational Linguistics.

Hanjie Chen and Yangfeng Ji. 2020. Learning variational word masks to improve the interpretability of neural text classifiers. In *Proceedings of the 2020 Conference on Empirical Methods in Natural Language Processing (EMNLP)*, pages 4236–4251, Online. Association for Computational Linguistics.

Hanjie Chen, Guangtao Zheng, and Yangfeng Ji. 2020. Generating hierarchical explanations on text classification via feature interaction detection. In *Proceedings of the 58th Annual Meeting of the Association for Computational Linguistics*, pages 5578–5593, Online. Association for Computational Linguistics.

Yiming Chen, Yan Zhang, Chen Zhang, Grandee Lee, Ran Cheng, and Haizhou Li. 2021b. Revisiting self-training for few-shot learning of language model. In *Proceedings of the 2021 Conference on Empirical Methods in Natural Language Processing*, pages 9125–9135, Online and Punta Cana, Dominican Republic. Association for Computational Linguistics.

Jacob Devlin, Ming-Wei Chang, Kenton Lee, and Kristina Toutanova. 2019. BERT: Pre-training of deep bidirectional transformers for language understanding. In *Proceedings of the 2019 Conference of the North American Chapter of the Association for Computational Linguistics: Human Language Technologies, Volume 1 (Long and Short Papers)*, pages 4171–4186, Minneapolis, Minnesota. Association for Computational Linguistics.

Jingfei Du, Edouard Grave, Beliz Gunel, Vishrav Chaudhary, Onur Celebi, Michael Auli, Veselin Stoyanov, and Alexis Conneau. 2021a. Self-training improves pre-training for natural language understanding. In *Proceedings of the 2021 Conference of the North American Chapter of the Association for Computational Linguistics: Human Language Technologies*, pages 5408–5418, Online. Association for Computational Linguistics.

Mengnan Du, Varun Manjunatha, Rajiv Jain, Ruchi Deshpande, Franck Dernoncourt, Jiuxiang Gu, Tong Sun, and Xia Hu. 2021b. Towards interpreting and mitigating shortcut learning behavior of NLU models. In *Proceedings of the 2021 Conference of the North American Chapter of the Association for Computational Linguistics: Human Language Technologies*, pages 915–929, Online. Association for Computational Linguistics.

Tianyu Gao, Adam Fisch, and Danqi Chen. 2021. Making pre-trained language models better few-shot learners. In *Proceedings of the 59th Annual Meeting of the Association for Computational Linguistics and the 11th International Joint Conference on Natural Language Processing (Volume 1: Long Papers)*, pages 3816–3830, Online. Association for Computational Linguistics.

Shankar Iyer, Nikhil Dandekar, and Kornél Csernai. 2017. Quora question pairs.

Alon Jacovi and Yoav Goldberg. 2020. Towards faithfully interpretable NLP systems: How should we define and evaluate faithfulness? In *Proceedings of the 58th Annual Meeting of the Association for Computational Linguistics*, pages 4198–4205, Online. Association for Computational Linguistics.

Zhengbao Jiang, Frank F. Xu, Jun Araki, and Graham Neubig. 2020. How can we know what language models know? *Transactions of the Association for Computational Linguistics*, 8:423–438.

Wuwei Lan, Siyu Qiu, Hua He, and Wei Xu. 2017. A continuously growing dataset of sentential paraphrases. In *Proceedings of the 2017 Conference on Empirical Methods in Natural Language Processing*, pages 1224–1234, Copenhagen, Denmark. Association for Computational Linguistics.

Yinhan Liu, Myle Ott, Naman Goyal, Jingfei Du, Mandar Joshi, Danqi Chen, Omer Levy, Mike Lewis, Luke Zettlemoyer, and Veselin Stoyanov. 2019. Roberta: A robustly optimized bert pretraining approach. *arXiv preprint arXiv:1907.11692*.

Andrew Maas, Raymond E Daly, Peter T Pham, Dan Huang, Andrew Y Ng, and Christopher Potts. 2011. Learning word vectors for sentiment analysis. In *Proceedings of the 49th annual meeting of the association for computational linguistics: Human language technologies*, pages 142–150.

James Mullenbach, Sarah Wiegreffe, Jon Duke, Jimeng Sun, and Jacob Eisenstein. 2018. Explainable prediction of medical codes from clinical text. In *Proceedings of the 2018 Conference of the North American Chapter of the Association for Computational Linguistics: Human Language Technologies, Volume 1 (Long Papers)*, pages 1101–1111, New Orleans, Louisiana. Association for Computational Linguistics.

Dong Nguyen. 2018. Comparing automatic and human evaluation of local explanations for text classification. In *Proceedings of the 2018 Conference of the North American Chapter of the Association for Computational Linguistics: Human Language Technologies, Volume 1 (Long Papers)*, pages 1069–1078, New Orleans, Louisiana. Association for Computational Linguistics.

Yixin Nie, Yicheng Wang, and Mohit Bansal. 2019. Analyzing compositionality-sensitivity of nli models. *Proceedings of the AAAI Conference on Artificial Intelligence*, 33(01):6867–6874.

Fabio Petroni, Tim Rocktäschel, Sebastian Riedel, Patrick Lewis, Anton Bakhtin, Yuxiang Wu, and Alexander Miller. 2019. Language models as knowledge bases? In *Proceedings of the 2019 Conference on Empirical Methods in Natural Language Processing and the 9th International Joint Conference on Natural Language Processing (EMNLP-IJCNLP)*, pages 2463–2473, Hong Kong, China. Association for Computational Linguistics.

Alec Radford, Jeffrey Wu, Rewon Child, David Luan, Dario Amodei, Ilya Sutskever, et al. 2019. Language models are unsupervised multitask learners. *OpenAI blog*, 1(8):9.

Timo Schick and Hinrich Schütze. 2021a. Exploiting cloze-questions for few-shot text classification and natural language inference. In *Proceedings of the 16th Conference of the European Chapter of the Association for Computational Linguistics: Main Volume*, pages 255–269, Online. Association for Computational Linguistics.

Timo Schick and Hinrich Schütze. 2021b. It's not just size that matters: Small language models are also few-shot learners. In *Proceedings of the 2021 Conference of the North American Chapter of the Association for Computational Linguistics: Human Language Technologies*, pages 2339–2352, Online. Association for Computational Linguistics.

Tal Schuster, Darsh Shah, Yun Jie Serene Yeo, Daniel Roberto Filizzola Ortiz, Enrico Santus, and Regina Barzilay. 2019. Towards debiasing fact verification models. In *Proceedings of the 2019 Conference on Empirical Methods in Natural Language Processing and the 9th International Joint Conference on Natural Language Processing (EMNLP-IJCNLP)*, pages 3419–3425, Hong Kong, China. Association for Computational Linguistics.

Lloyd S Shapley. 1953. A value for n-person games. *Contributions to the Theory of Games*, 2(28).

Taylor Shin, Yasaman Razeghi, Robert L. Logan IV, Eric Wallace, and Sameer Singh. 2020. AutoPrompt: Eliciting Knowledge from Language Models with Automatically Generated Prompts. In *Proceedings of the 2020 Conference on Empirical Methods in Natural Language Processing (EMNLP)*, pages 4222–4235, Online. Association for Computational Linguistics.

Erik Strumbelj and Igor Kononenko. 2010. An efficient explanation of individual classifications using game theory. *The Journal of Machine Learning Research*, 11:1–18.

Mukund Sundararajan, Ankur Taly, and Qiqi Yan. 2017. Axiomatic attribution for deep networks. In *International Conference on Machine Learning*, pages 3319–3328. PMLR.

Prasetya Ajie Utama, Nafise Sadat Moosavi, Victor Sanh, and Iryna Gurevych. 2021. Avoiding inference heuristics in few-shot prompt-based finetuning. *arXiv preprint arXiv:2109.04144*.

Chengyu Wang, Jianing Wang, Minghui Qiu, Jun Huang, and Ming Gao. 2021a. TransPrompt: Towards an automatic transferable prompting framework for few-shot text classification. In *Proceedings of the 2021 Conference on Empirical Methods in Natural Language Processing*, pages 2792–2802, Online and Punta Cana, Dominican Republic. Association for Computational Linguistics.

Yaqing Wang, Subhabrata Mukherjee, Haoda Chu, Yuancheng Tu, Ming Wu, Jing Gao, and Ahmed Hassan Awadallah. 2021b. Meta self-training for few-shot neural sequence labeling. In *Proceedings of the 27th ACM SIGKDD Conference on Knowledge Discovery & Data Mining*, pages 1737–1747.

Adina Williams, Nikita Nangia, and Samuel Bowman. 2018. A broad-coverage challenge corpus for sentence understanding through inference. In *Proceedings of the 2018 Conference of the North American Chapter of the Association for Computational Linguistics: Human Language Technologies, Volume 1 (Long Papers)*, pages 1112–1122, New Orleans, Louisiana. Association for Computational Linguistics.

Xiang Zhang, Junbo Zhao, and Yann LeCun. 2015. Character-level convolutional networks for text classification. *Advances in neural information processing systems*, 28:649–657.

Tony Z Zhao, Eric Wallace, Shi Feng, Dan Klein, and Sameer Singh. 2021. Calibrate before use: Improving few-shot performance of language models. *arXiv preprint arXiv:2102.09690*.

Guoqing Zheng, Ahmed Hassan Awadallah, and Susan Dumais. 2021. Meta label correction for noisy label learning. In *Proceedings of the 35th AAAI Conference on Artificial Intelligence*.

A Supplement of Setup

A.1 Models and Datasets

We adopt the pretrained BERT-base and RoBERTa-base models from Hugging Face[1]. For sentiment classification, we utilize movie reviews IMDB (Maas et al., 2011) as the in-domain dataset and Yelp reviews (Zhang et al., 2015) as the out-of-domain dataset. For natural language inference, the task is to predict the semantic relationship between a premise and a hypothesis as entailment, contradiction, or neutral. The Stanford Natural Language Inference (SNLI) corpus (Bowman et al., 2015) and Multi-Genre Natural Language Inference (MNLI) (Williams et al., 2018) are used as the in-domain and out-of-domain datasets respectively. The task of paraphrase identification is to judge whether two input texts are semantically equivalent or not. We adopt the Quora Question Pairs (QQP) (Iyer et al., 2017) as the in-domain dataset, while using the TwitterPPDB (TPPDB) (Lan et al., 2017) as the out-of-domain dataset. Table 4 shows the statistics of the datasets.

We implement the models in PyTorch 3.6. We set hyperparameters as: learning rate is $1e-5$, maximum sequence length is 256, maximum gradient norm is 1, and batch size is 8. All experiments were performed on a single NVidia GTX 1080 GPU. We report the time for training each model on each in-domain dataset (with full training examples) in Table 5.

A.2 Explanations

We adopt four explanation methods:

- sampling Shapley (SS) (Strumbelj and Kononenko, 2010): computing feature attributions via sampling-based Shapley value (Shapley, 1953);
- integrated gradients (IG) (Sundararajan et al., 2017): computing feature attributions by integrating gradients of points along a path from a baseline to the input;
- attentions (Attn) (Mullenbach et al., 2018): attention weights in the last hidden layer as feature attributions;
- individual word masks (IMASK) (Chen et al., 2021a): learning feature attributions via variational word masks (Chen and Ji, 2020).

[1] https://github.com/huggingface/pytorch-transformers

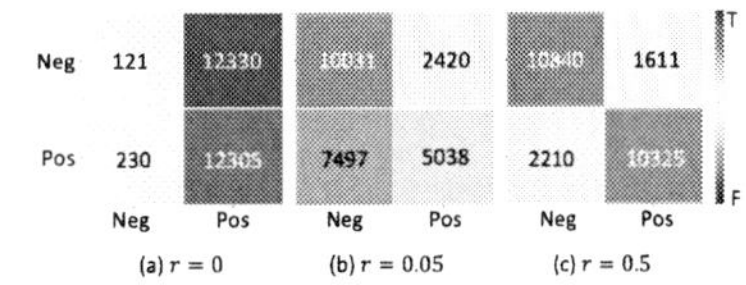

Figure 2: Confusion matrix of BERT (with different r) on the IMDB dataset. "Neg" and "Pos" represent negative and positive labels respectively. Vertical and horizontal dimensions show ground-truth and predicted labels respectively. Green and pink colors represent true or false predictions respectively. Darker color indicates larger number.

Explanation faithfulness. An important criterion for evaluating explanations is their faithfulness to model predictions (Jacovi and Goldberg, 2020). We evaluate the faithfulness of the four explanation methods via the AOPC metric (Nguyen, 2018; Chen et al., 2020). AOPC calculates the average change of prediction probability on the predicted class over all examples by removing top $1 \dots u$ words identified by explanations.

$$\text{AOPC} = \frac{1}{U+1} \langle \sum_{u=1}^{U} p(y|\boldsymbol{x}) - p(y|\boldsymbol{x}_{\backslash 1 \dots u}) \rangle_{\boldsymbol{x}}, \tag{4}$$

where $p(y|\boldsymbol{x}_{\backslash 1 \dots u})$ is the probability for the predicted class when words $1 \dots u$ are removed and $\langle \cdot \rangle_{\boldsymbol{x}}$ denotes the average over all test examples. Higher AOPC score indicates better explanations.

We test the BERT and RoBERTa trained with 1% in-domain training examples on each task. For each dataset, we randomly select 1000 test examples to generate explanations due to computational costs. We report the results of AOPC scores when U = 10 in Table 6. Sampling Shapley consistently outperforms other three explanation methods in explaining different models on both in-domain and out-of-domain datasets.

B Supplement of Experiments

Datasets	*C*	*L*	*#train*	*#dev*	*#test*	Label distribution
IMDB	2	268	19992	4997	24986	Positive: *train*(10036), *dev*(2414), *test*(12535) Negative: *train*(9956), *dev*(2583), *test*(12451)
Yelp	2	138	500000	60000	38000	Positive: *train*(250169), *dev*(29831), *test*(19000) Negative: *train*(249831), *dev*(30169), *test*(19000)
SNLI	3	14	549367	4921	4921	Entailment: *train*(183416), *dev*(1680), *test*(1649) Contradiction: *train*(183187), *dev*(1627), *test*(1651) Neutral: *train*(182764), *dev*(1614), *test*(1651)
MNLI	3	22	391176	4772	4907	Entailment: *train*(130416), *dev*(1736), *test*(1695) Contradiction: *train*(130381); *dev*(1535), *test*(1631) Neutral: *train*(130379), *dev*(1501), *test*(1581)
QQP	2	11	363178	20207	20215	Paraphrases: *train*(134141), *dev*(7435), *test*(7447) Nonparaphrases: *train*(229037), *dev*(12772), *test*(12768)
TPPDB	2	15	42200	4685	4649	Paraphrases: *train*(11167), *dev*(941), *test*(880) Nonparaphrases: *train*(31033), *dev*(3744), *test*(3769)

Table 4: Summary statistics of the datasets, where C is the number of classes, L is average sentence length, and # counts the number of examples in the *train/dev/test* sets. For label distribution, the number of examples with the same label in *train/dev/test* is noted in bracket.

Models	IMDB	SNLI	QQP
BERT	856.43	25402.52	17452.12
RoBERTa	912.47	256513.98	17514.80

Table 5: The average runtime (s/epoch) of each model on each in-domain dataset.

		In-domain			Out-of-domain		
Model	*r*	IMDB	SNLI	QQP	Yelp	MNLI	TPPDB
BERT	SS	0.41	0.82	0.61	0.53	0.77	0.40
	IG	0.08	0.34	0.19	0.12	0.31	0.10
	Attn	0.07	0.35	0.28	0.12	0.26	0.14
	IMASK	0.09	0.28	0.25	0.09	0.25	0.08
RoBERTa	SS	0.25	0.86	0.53	0.28	0.84	0.28
	IG	0.02	0.36	0.21	0.04	0.38	0.09
	Attn	0.02	0.33	0.26	0.03	0.23	0.09
	IMASK	0.02	0.18	0.18	0.03	0.17	0.05

Table 6: AOPC scores of different explanation methods in explaining different models.

Datasets	r	Labels	Top Features
IMDB	0	Neg	we ##zog " ##men (' [SEP] capitalism lynch hell
		Pos	. [CLS] [SEP] s , t movie film plot)
	0.5	Neg	bad not no worst t off terrible nothing stupid boring
		Pos	[SEP] and great . good [CLS] love , film characters
Yelp	0	Neg	. they majestic adds state owners loud dirty priced thai
		Pos	. [CLS] [SEP] , s t for i you m
	0.5	Neg	not no bad t worst never off rude over nothing
		Pos	[SEP] great and good . [CLS] amazing love friendly experience
SNLI	0	En	a [SEP] man the woman dog sitting sits his fire
		Con	[SEP] [CLS] is the a , are in of there
		Neu	. people woman girl are playing looking [CLS] group boy
	0.5	En	[SEP] . [CLS] and is a man there woman people
		Con	the a in [SEP] at sitting with man on playing
		Neu	[SEP] are for . man [CLS] is the a girl
MNLI	0	En	the [SEP] ##ists israel ' recession ata consultants discusses attacked
		Con	[SEP] [CLS] , s to of in . the not
		Neu	. [CLS] they we you people about it really i
	0.5	En	. [CLS] and is [SEP] there are , was of
		Con	the ' . not no t [CLS] don to didn
		Neu	[SEP] [CLS] the for to all when . you it
QQP	0	NPa	? is the a ' what india does quo why
		Pa	[SEP] [CLS] ? in i , of . best s
	0.5	NPa	? what [CLS] is how , why a the .
		Pa	[SEP] quo [CLS] best trump ##ra india life your sex
TPPDB	0	NPa	trump ' the obama " we is russia a says
		Pa	[SEP] . [CLS] , s of in to ##t t
	0.5	NPa	. , [CLS] ? '@ ; - a is
		Pa	[SEP] trump [CLS] inauguration obama russia repeal ##care cia senate

Table 7: Top 10 important tokens for BERT predictions on different labels. Neg: negative, Pos: postive, En: entailment, Con: contradiction, Neu: neutral, NPa: nonparaphrases, Pa: paraphrases.

An Empirical study to understand the Compositional Prowess of Neural Dialog Models

Vinayshekhar Bannihatti Kumar*
Applied Scientist AWS AI
vinayshk@amazon.com

Vaibhav Kumar*
Applied Scientist Alexa AI
kvabh@amazon.com

Mukul Bhutani
Carnegie Mellon University
mukul.bhutani93@gmail.com

Alexander Rudnicky
Carnegie Mellon University
air@cmu.edu

Abstract

In this work, we examine the problems associated with neural dialog models under the common theme of compositionality. Specifically, we investigate three manifestations of compositionality: (1) Productivity, (2) Substitutivity, and (3) Systematicity. These manifestations shed light on the generalization, syntactic robustness, and semantic capabilities of neural dialog models. We design probing experiments by perturbing the training data to study the above phenomenon. We make informative observations based on automated metrics and hope that this work increases research interest in understanding the capacity of these models.

1 Introduction

Fully data-driven and end-to-end approaches to dialog response generation (Vinyals and Le, 2015; Serban et al., 2016; Bordes et al., 2016; Serban et al., 2017; Zhao et al., 2017) within the sequence-to-sequence (seq2seq) (Hochreiter and Schmidhuber, 1997; Sutskever et al., 2014; Bahdanau et al., 2014; Vaswani et al., 2017) framework have become ubiquitous and now produce competitive results.

Recently, there have been a few attempts to explore the capabilities of such models. A well known problem in seq2seq modeling is the tendency to generate short and meaningless replies in conversation (Li et al., 2015; Mou et al., 2016). By drawing a parallel between machine translation and dialog generation, Wei et al. (2019) suggest that such models encounter a severe mis-alignment problem i.e a given input utterance can have many plausible replies.

Sankar et al. (2019) empirically investigate the information captured in seq2seq models by synthetically perturbing the test set during inference. They demonstrate an inability of seq2seq models to use all the information that is presented. They also present their study as a "diagnostic tool" to evaluate dialog models.

Although they provide useful insights, such studies fail to systematically demonstrate the compositional features of seq2seq dialog models. Further, their "diagnostic tool" is only helpful for evaluating syntactic robustness of models at *test time*. In this work, we carefully design experiments to investigate and evaluate the compositional generalizability of neural dialog models.

Compositionality has been well studied for Neural Machine Translation (Cho et al., 2014; Lake and Baroni, 2017) as well as some other tasks. In these works, for a system to be compositional, it should be able to generalize beyond its observations. For example, Kaiser and Sutskever (2015) observe that Neural GPUs are able to generalize addition and multiplication to larger sequences than what they are trained on. However, one should carefully note that such a definition of compositionality is peripheral and represents only a part of what it truly means.

To provide a complete picture, Hupkes et al. (2019) collect the different manifestations of compositionality and translate them into a series of theoretically-grounded tests. By adapting (and modifying) some of these tests, the experiments in this paper aim to quantitatively elucidate the compositional nature of seq2seq based neural dialog models. Below, we provide a motivation and description for each of the adapted tests:

Productivity - Upon taking part in a number of reasonable length conversations, it might not be difficult for humans to carry conversations consisting of a larger number of turns. Based on this intuition, we test the ability of a dialog system to **extend its prediction** beyond the length of the observed conversational history.

Substitutivity - There is a many-to-many correspondence between utterances and their possible responses. Given the responses of a particular con-

* equal contribution, Work done while students at CMU

Proceedings of the Third Workshop on Insights from Negative Results in NLP, pages 154 - 158
May 26, 2022 ©2022 Association for Computational Linguistics

Dataset	Baseline	DS-0.75	DS-0.5	DS-0.25	DNS-0.75	DNS-0.5	DNS-0.25	BT-Russian
				Transformer				
dailydialog	$33.2_{[0.7]}$	$140.6_{[11.6]}$	$56.3_{[2.0]}$	$41.1_{[1.3]}$	$131.6_{[2.6]}$	$63.4_{[1.0]}$	$42.9_{[0.4]}$	$117.2_{[7.9]}$
MutualFriends	$12.5_{[0.1]}$	$30.1_{[3.0]}$	$18.1_{[1.2]}$	$15.0_{[0.3]}$	$39.6_{[1.1]}$	$21.3_{[0.8]}$	$17.1_{[0.3]}$	$150.8_{[16.8]}$
Babi	$1.0_{[0.0]}$	$19.8_{[0.7]}$	$6.3_{[0.4]}$	$3.5_{[0.2]}$	$16.1_{[1.6]}$	$3.3_{[0.1]}$	$2.1_{[0.1]}$	$6.4_{[1.2]}$
				S2S				
dailydialog	$29.4_{[0.3]}$	$104.8_{[2.4]}$	$47.1_{[0.6]}$	$35.6_{[0.2]}$	$150.9_{[5.4]}$	$61.9_{[1.3]}$	$39.4_{[0.5]}$	$192.9_{[14.3]}$
MutualFriends	$13.3_{[0.1]}$	$25.4_{[0.2]}$	$17.2_{[0.2]}$	$15.2_{[0.3]}$	$50.1_{[2.1]}$	$24.3_{[0.5]}$	$18.3_{[0.3]}$	$227.1_{[8.6]}$
Babi	$1.2_{[0.0]}$	$3759.0_{[1994.7]}$	$52.6_{[13.2]}$	$8.2_{[1.4]}$	$121.0_{[24.4]}$	$7.9_{[1.8]}$	$3.0_{[0.1]}$	$59.3_{[14.9]}$
				S2SA				
dailydialog	$26.9_{[0.2]}$	$94.7_{[4.0]}$	$45.5_{[0.2]}$	$32.6_{[0.3]}$	$130.2_{[5.3]}$	$58.6_{[1.1]}$	$37.3_{[0.7]}$	$173.0_{[16.5]}$
MutualFriends	$10.2_{[0.1]}$	$20.1_{[0.3]}$	$13.6_{[0.1]}$	$11.8_{[0.2]}$	$40.5_{[1.4]}$	$19.0_{[0.2]}$	$14.1_{[0.2]}$	$216.4_{[18.4]}$
Babi	$1.0_{[0.0]}$	$961.0_{[421.5]}$	$68.2_{[22.5]}$	$8.1_{[2.2]}$	$118.8_{[43.4]}$	$7.5_{[1.2]}$	$2.8_{[0.2]}$	$630.8_{[136.1]}$

Table 1: Performance of the models based on perplexity. The second column represents the baseline scores of the models on different datasets. Columns 3-5 shows the effect of dropping stop words at a certain rate. Columns 6-8 shows the effect of dropping non stop words at a certain rate. Column 9 shows the difference in perplexity of the model when the test set is changed by back translation and evaluated using the baseline model. All experiments are repeated 5 times and the mean(μ) and std deviations(σ) are reported in every cell. For all experiment runs and other metrics refer to A.1.

versation, if we encounter a semantically equivalent conversation, we can easily produce the same set of responses to this new conversation. Based on this, we attempt to observe if dialog models are also capable of such reasoning. This property of compositionality accounts for the **semantic expressiveness** of neural models.

Systematicity - Humans can understand how to fill in missing pieces of information, or to introduce additional words which can make an utterance in a conversation more fluent. This makes humans capable of recombining known fragments and rules. Without the presence of topic-inducing words, it might become difficult for humans to make sense of a conversation. Based on this intuition, we test the ability of the model to recombine known fragments and rules. This property of compositionality accounts for the **syntactic robustness** of neural models.

The contributions of this paper are threefold: **(i)** We observe that neural dialog models don't generalize well to dialogs with longer turns when they are trained on dialogs with shorter number of turns. **(ii)** Neural dialog models pay less attention to the topic inducing "content words" of the dialog. In fact, we observe that they are highly sensitive to the stop words (a type of "function word") present in utterances. **(iii)** We also observe that the neural dialog models don't perform well when the same utterance is presented to the model in a semantically similar but syntactically different fashion i.e they are not robust to syntactic variations. The code for reproducing results is released along with this paper [1].

2 Datasets

Following Sankar et al. (2019), we experiment with using an open domain, a closed domain, and a synthetically generated dataset. The details of the dataset are presented below:

DailyDialog: An open domain, manually labelled dataset (Li et al., 2017) consisting of conversations on multiple topics which can occur on a daily basis. There are 13,118 total dialogs with an average of 7.9 turns per dialog.

Mutual Friends: A task-oriented dataset (He et al., 2017) that encourages open-ended dialog acts. It has a total of 11,157 dialogs with an average length of 11.4 utterances per dialog.

Babi: A synthetic dataset created by Bordes et al. (2016). We use task 5 of this dataset which requires the prediction of the text of the entire dialog and not just dialog acts. Each dialog in this task has an average of 13 utterances and there is a total of 1,000 dialogs.

3 Experiments and Results

We investigate using Seq2Seq(**S2S**) (Sutskever et al., 2014), Seq2Seq-Attention(**S2SA**) (Luong et al., 2015) and Transformer models (Vaswani

[1] https://github.com/vinayshekharcmu/ComposionalityOfDialogModels

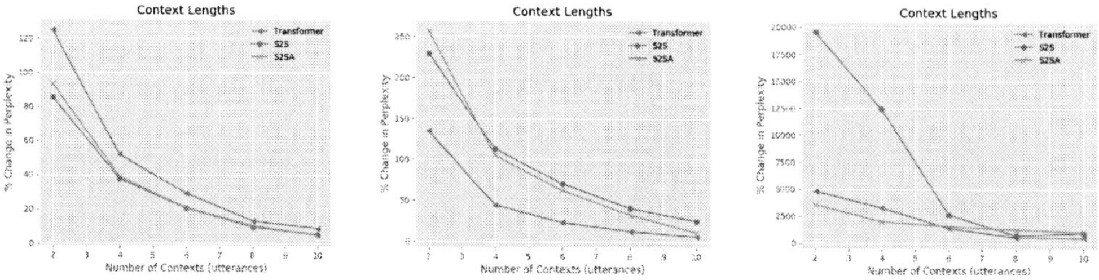

(a) Daily Dialog (b) Mutual Friends (c) Babi - Task 5

Figure 1: Results of the model on the test of productivity. We see that all the models don't learn to generalize from dialogs with fewer utterances to dialogs with more utterances.

et al., 2017). The behaviour of these models is examined using the three standard datasets described in Section 2.

Both S2S and S2SA utilise a two-layer LSTM for the encoder and the decoder. Each layer has 128 hidden units with a dropout of 0.1. On the other hand, the transformer utilises a 300 dimensional embedding with 2 layers and 2 attention heads. Perplexity has been shown to correlate well with **human judgement** for Dialog Systems (Adiwardana et al., 2020) making it a suitable metric for our study. By choosing perplexity we also remain consistent with the previous study conducted by Sankar et al. (2019). Note that we do not aim to achieve state-of-the-art results, but rather, our aim is to observe and characterize the behaviour of the models based on different aspects of compositionality. Hence we pick three seminal models that tackles the problem of language generation and probe them to understand their manifestations.

The upcoming subsections first provides a brief description of the experimental setup employed for measuring the compositional capabilities of the various models, and then later discusses the results.

3.1 Productivity

This experiment aims to test whether neural dialog models can learn from meaningful dialogs consisting of fewer utterances and then generalize to dialogs consisting of a larger number of utterances than what they had observed during training time.

In order to test this capability, we train the models with trimmed context. For each dialog in the training set, we restrict the context utilised by the models to the previous k utterances, where $k \in \{2, 4, 6, 8, 10\}$. However, at test time the models utilise all the available context. We compare the performance of the models trained on different context lengths to that of the baseline model which is trained by utilising the entire context.

The results are displayed in Figures 1a, 1b, 1c. These figures show the % increase in perplexity of the models from their baseline perplexity as a function of number of utterances in the dialog. It is quite clear from the figures that the model are incapable of generalizing from shorter dialogs to longer dialogs.

The average number of utterances within the dialogs is ~ 8 for all the three datasets. Based on the results we see that even when models use previous 8 utterances, their performance is still significantly lower than that of the baseline. This experiment questions the generalizing ability of the model beyond what was observed during train time.

3.2 Systematicity

Two different experiments were performed to understand the semantic robustness of these models. The first experiment was done to understand the importance of stop words. A comparison between model's sensitivity to dropping of stop words (**DS**) and dropping of content words (**DNS**) sheds light on the relevance of stop words in dialogs. We drop stop words and content words at the rate of 0.75, 0.5 and 0.25 and observe the effect on models' performance. When the rate of stop words removal is 1, all the stop words are removed and when it is 0.25, 25% are removed, etc.

In second experiment we drop words based on their rank in the corpus. Six different conditions are used in this experiment. We first drop words from the top ranks such that only 10% of the total number of words are removed in the corpus. We then repeat this by using the mid ranked words. Ideally, the models should be affected equally in

Rank Range	Transformer	S2S	S2SA
	DailyDialog		
0-1	$49.4_{[0.6]}$	$49.1_{[7.1]}$	$42.4_{[1.3]}$
1-3	$59.6_{[0.9]}$	$59.5_{[2.1]}$	$55.4_{[1.6]}$
0-3	$92.7_{[1.9]}$	$92.5_{[1.3]}$	$88.7_{[4.2]}$
500-1000	$52.6_{[1.1]}$	$59.6_{[1.1]}$	$52.3_{[1.2]}$
1000-1500	$39.4_{[0.7]}$	$42.0_{[1.1]}$	$38.8_{[0.4]}$
500-1500	$59.5_{[0.9]}$	$76.3_{[3.6]}$	$72.5_{[1.8]}$
	MutualFriends		
0-1	$14.9_{[0.2]}$	$16.7_{[0.5]}$	$12.9_{[0.5]}$
1-3	$17.6_{[0.4]}$	$20.5_{[0.4]}$	$15.0_{[0.3]}$
0-3	$19.9_{[0.4]}$	$23.0_{[0.5]}$	$18.0_{[0.8]}$
300-600	$13.9_{[0.2]}$	$15.1_{[0.2]}$	$12.0_{[0.8]}$
600-1000	$14.3_{[0.3]}$	$15.1_{[0.2]}$	$11.8_{[0.3]}$
300-1000	$16.0_{[0.5]}$	$17.8_{[0.2]}$	$13.8_{[0.2]}$
	Babi		
0-1	$2.0_{[0.1]}$	$3.9_{[0.5]}$	$4.8_{[0.7]}$
0-2	$3.7_{[0.2]}$	$11.2_{[1.4]}$	$11.0_{[1.6]}$
36-44	$1.5_{[0.0]}$	$2.1_{[0.1]}$	$2.0_{[0.1]}$
36-55	$1.5_{[0.0]}$	$2.2_{[0.1]}$	$2.1_{[0.1]}$

Table 2: The first column represents the range of ranks based on which the words were removed from the dataset. We chose to experiment with the top and the mid ranking words. We dropped words from both sections such that it accounts for $\approx 10\%$ of the words in its respective corpus. We see that the model is very sensitive to the top ranked words (which are stop-words most of the time). The effect of dropping 1000, 700 and 20 "content words" from the middle section is equivalent to dropping 3,3,2 stop words for dailydialog, mutualfriends and babi respectively.

both these settings, as, in each setting we end up removing 10% of the words in the training data. In fact, it should be affected more in the latter case as the mid-rank words are majorly responsible for inducing the topic of the dialog and it should be difficult to continue a conversation without knowing the topic. Note that, for both these experiments, we do not remove any word during test time.

Table 1 shows the result of the first experiment. We see that each of model's performance increases as the rate of dropping stop words decreases. This observation suggests the high sensitivty of the models towards stop words. Even dropping 25% of the stop words affects the models adversely. While dropping of the content words also affects models performance, we observe that all the models perform just slightly worse when content words are dropped as compared to stop words. However, it is interesting to see that the transformer's performance is stable across different drop rates whereas the LSTM based sequence to sequence models suffer when the drop rate is high.

The results for the second experiment are provided in Table 2. It is clear that removal of higher ranked words leads to a greater drop in the model performance when compared to the drop caused by the removal of middle ranked words, even though in both the cases we remove the same percentage of words. This provides two insights: (1) Models don't focus on the mid ranking words (which are mostly topic inducing) and (2) Models have an over-reliance on top ranking words (which are mostly stop words).

3.3 Substitutivity

Given that we (humans) know the answer to a particular question, we will not have any difficulty in answering it even if it is asked in various different ways. This experiment aims to test if neural dialog models are also capable of this ability.

In order to do this, we evaluate the baseline models on the backtranslated (**BT**) version of the test set. Basically, back translation provides a paraphrased version of individual utterances (Wieting et al., 2017), which brings in syntactic variations while keeping the semantics intact.

We back translate the test set from both German and Russian back into English. Since the BLEU scores when translating from German were considerably lower than that of Russian, we decided to test the models based on Russian Backtranslations. The final backtranslations have a BLEU score of 35.91, 10.12, 43.49 on Daily Dialog, Mutual Friends and Babi respectively.

The results for the experiment are provided in Table 1. It is clear that the models are adversely affected when presented with back translated (paraphrased) utterances. One would expect the models to have similar perplexities when utterances are paraphrased, however we see that there is a significant increase in perplexity. This observation is consistent across the three different models. We also observe that the transformer is slightly more robust to syntactic variation than others.

4 Conclusion

This work interprets the behaviour of seq2seq based Neural Dialog Models under the general umbrella of compositionality. We observe that such models lack the ability to reason and produce response based on surface level information. The results provided in this paper motivate the need for better modelling approaches.

References

Daniel Adiwardana, Minh-Thang Luong, David R So, Jamie Hall, Noah Fiedel, Romal Thoppilan, Zi Yang, Apoorv Kulshreshtha, Gaurav Nemade, Yifeng Lu, et al. 2020. Towards a human-like open-domain chatbot. *arXiv preprint arXiv:2001.09977*.

Dzmitry Bahdanau, Kyunghyun Cho, and Yoshua Bengio. 2014. Neural machine translation by jointly learning to align and translate. *arXiv preprint arXiv:1409.0473*.

Antoine Bordes, Y-Lan Boureau, and Jason Weston. 2016. Learning end-to-end goal-oriented dialog. *arXiv preprint arXiv:1605.07683*.

Kyunghyun Cho, Bart Van Merriënboer, Dzmitry Bahdanau, and Yoshua Bengio. 2014. On the properties of neural machine translation: Encoder-decoder approaches. *arXiv preprint arXiv:1409.1259*.

He He, Anusha Balakrishnan, Mihail Eric, and Percy Liang. 2017. Learning symmetric collaborative dialogue agents with dynamic knowledge graph embeddings. *arXiv preprint arXiv:1704.07130*.

Sepp Hochreiter and Jürgen Schmidhuber. 1997. Long short-term memory. *Neural computation*, 9(8):1735–1780.

Dieuwke Hupkes, Verna Dankers, Mathijs Mul, and Elia Bruni. 2019. The compositionality of neural networks: integrating symbolism and connectionism. *arXiv preprint arXiv:1908.08351*.

Łukasz Kaiser and Ilya Sutskever. 2015. Neural gpus learn algorithms. *arXiv preprint arXiv:1511.08228*.

Brenden M Lake and Marco Baroni. 2017. Still not systematic after all these years: On the compositional skills of sequence-to-sequence recurrent networks. *arXiv preprint arXiv:1711.00350*.

Jiwei Li, Michel Galley, Chris Brockett, Jianfeng Gao, and Bill Dolan. 2015. A diversity-promoting objective function for neural conversation models. *arXiv preprint arXiv:1510.03055*.

Yanran Li, Hui Su, Xiaoyu Shen, Wenjie Li, Ziqiang Cao, and Shuzi Niu. 2017. Dailydialog: A manually labelled multi-turn dialogue dataset. *arXiv preprint arXiv:1710.03957*.

Minh-Thang Luong, Hieu Pham, and Christopher D Manning. 2015. Effective approaches to attention-based neural machine translation. *arXiv preprint arXiv:1508.04025*.

Lili Mou, Yiping Song, Rui Yan, Ge Li, Lu Zhang, and Zhi Jin. 2016. Sequence to backward and forward sequences: A content-introducing approach to generative short-text conversation. *arXiv preprint arXiv:1607.00970*.

Chinnadhurai Sankar, Sandeep Subramanian, Christopher Pal, Sarath Chandar, and Yoshua Bengio. 2019. Do neural dialog systems use the conversation history effectively? an empirical study. *arXiv preprint arXiv:1906.01603*.

Iulian V Serban, Chinnadhurai Sankar, Mathieu Germain, Saizheng Zhang, Zhouhan Lin, Sandeep Subramanian, Taesup Kim, Michael Pieper, Sarath Chandar, Nan Rosemary Ke, et al. 2017. A deep reinforcement learning chatbot. *arXiv preprint arXiv:1709.02349*.

Iulian V Serban, Alessandro Sordoni, Yoshua Bengio, Aaron Courville, and Joelle Pineau. 2016. Building end-to-end dialogue systems using generative hierarchical neural network models. In *Thirtieth AAAI Conference on Artificial Intelligence*.

I Sutskever, O Vinyals, and QV Le. 2014. Sequence to sequence learning with neural networks. *Advances in NIPS*.

Ashish Vaswani, Noam Shazeer, Niki Parmar, Jakob Uszkoreit, Llion Jones, Aidan N Gomez, Łukasz Kaiser, and Illia Polosukhin. 2017. Attention is all you need. In *Advances in neural information processing systems*, pages 5998–6008.

Oriol Vinyals and Quoc Le. 2015. A neural conversational model. *arXiv preprint arXiv:1506.05869*.

Bolin Wei, Shuai Lu, Lili Mou, Hao Zhou, Pascal Poupart, Ge Li, and Zhi Jin. 2019. Why do neural dialog systems generate short and meaningless replies? a comparison between dialog and translation. In *ICASSP 2019-2019 IEEE International Conference on Acoustics, Speech and Signal Processing (ICASSP)*, pages 7290–7294. IEEE.

John Wieting, Jonathan Mallinson, and Kevin Gimpel. 2017. Learning paraphrastic sentence embeddings from back-translated bitext. *arXiv preprint arXiv:1706.01847*.

Tiancheng Zhao, Allen Lu, Kyusong Lee, and Maxine Eskenazi. 2017. Generative encoder-decoder models for task-oriented spoken dialog systems with chatting capability. *arXiv preprint arXiv:1706.08476*.

Combining Extraction and Generation for Constructing Belief-Consequence Causal Links

Maria Alexeeva
Department of Linguistics
University of Arizona
Tucson, AZ
alexeeva@email.arizona.edu

Allegra A. Beal Cohen
Agricultural and Biological Engineering Department
University of Florida
Gainesville, FL
aa.cohen@ufl.edu

Mihai Surdeanu
Computer Science Department
University of Arizona
Tucson, AZ
surdeanu@email.arizona.edu

Abstract

In this paper, we introduce and justify a new task—causal link extraction based on beliefs—and do a qualitative analysis of the ability of a large language model—InstructGPT-3—to generate implicit consequences of beliefs. With the language model-generated consequences being promising, but not consistent, we propose directions of future work, including data collection, explicit consequence extraction using rule-based and language modeling-based approaches, and using explicitly stated consequences of beliefs to fine-tune or prompt the language model to produce outputs suitable for the task.

1 Introduction

Natural language processing can successfully capture the causal dynamics present in many complex systems. This type of automated extraction is particularly useful for computational modelers, who may be faced with a large and complex domain literature that cannot be easily summarized by humans. Information extraction systems like Eidos (Sharp et al., 2019) can help modelers build skeleton models of causes and effects present in systems by extracting causal links that exist between entities and processes.

While many causal dynamics are mechanistic, such as water level driving crop yield, other dynamics are driven by subjective factors, such as the political beliefs of a population driving their decisions to wear masks. Extracting these dynamics comes with two challenges: Extracting the beliefs and consequences present in the text, and inferring implicit consequences of beliefs. For example, the following sentence contains both a belief and an explicit consequence:

1. *Peanut and maize are generally sown after a few big rains when farmers believe that the rainy season has really started.*

The above sentence can be represented by a binary, directed causal link, where the first node is the belief about the rainy season and the second node is the consequence of the belief (crop sowing). However, the consequences of beliefs are frequently implied, such as in the following sentence:

2. *Also use of chemicals and machinery on their paddy field is often considered undesirable.*

To a human, the obvious consequence is that the farmers will not use chemicals, but the text does not explicitly state this. A modeler wants to generate causal belief-consequence pairs from a large literature without annotating every implicit consequence; thus, methods of automating belief extraction ought to account for implicit consequences.

In this paper, we address the problem of extraction of beliefs and their consequences with a novel extraction + generation approach. We first extract beliefs using an event extraction grammar; and we then use text generation with large language models (LM) to generate possible consequences of the extracted beliefs when no consequence is stated in text. We expect that given a belief and its context, there is only a limited number of possible consequences humans can infer. For the consequence generation approach to be considered successful, we want machine-generated consequences to match those produced by humans—that would be an indicator that generated beliefs are indeed relevant for the model.

With this work, we make the following contributions:

- We define a new task—causal link extraction based on beliefs—which can be used to enrich models with subjective beliefs of local populations.
- We conduct a qualitative analysis of automatic consequence generation. We find that InstructGPT-3 model (Ouyang et al., 2022),

Proceedings of the Third Workshop on Insights from Negative Results in NLP, pages 159 - 164
May 26, 2022 ©2022 Association for Computational Linguistics

which we use, is able to produce consequences relevant to beliefs, but does not seem to make consistently relevant predictions.

- We propose the next steps for this project, which include collecting and annotating data for the task, explicit consequence extraction, and using explicitly stated consequences for fine-tuning or prompting language models to make their outputs consistently relevant for the task.

2 Related Work

2.1 Modeling causality.

Causality modeling is a popular area of investigation thanks to its usefulness for multiple applications, e.g., question answering (Sharp et al., 2016). Both rule-based approaches (e.g., Sharp et al., 2019) and deep learning approaches (Li et al., 2021) have been proposed. We are not aware of any other work that investigates causal links rooted in beliefs.

2.2 Rule-based extraction.

Rule-based approaches have been shown to be powerful and robust, e.g., by Valenzuela-Escárcega et al. (2015) with their rule-based information extraction framework Odin. The framework allows for both surface and syntactic dependency-based rules and has been successfully used for extracting information in several projects, including protein interaction extraction (Valenzuela-Escárcega et al., 2018) and causal events extraction (Sharp et al., 2019).

2.3 Automatic text generation

Most recently, OpenAI released models that were trained to allow for human-augmented text generation, in which the user can provide the model with prompts either defining the task or providing examples to the model to demonstrate the task in a few shot setting (Ouyang et al., 2022). We use this model in our experiments.

3 Procedure

We automatically extracted beliefs from a collection of documents—scientific publications and reports—related to agriculture and social norms of Senegal. We then double-annotated fifty of those beliefs with whether or not their consequences were explicitly stated in one-sentence and one-paragraph

```
- name: belief-rule
  label: Belief
  type: dependency
  pattern: |
    trigger = [lemma=/consider/]
    believer:Agent = /nsubj/
    belief:Proposition = /xcomp/
```

Figure 1: A sample rule for extracting beliefs implemented using the Odin information extraction framework (Valenzuela-Escárcega et al., 2015)

context windows. When there was no explicit consequence stated, the annotators provided the consequences they believed to be fitting based on the belief and one paragraph-long context. We also compared human-generated implicit consequences with those generated by the InstructGPT-3 model (*text-davinci-001* in the API) (Ouyang et al., 2022).

3.1 Belief and Explicit Consequence Extraction

For extracting beliefs, we converted PDF files to text files using the pdfminer.six package and used the Odin rule-based information extraction framework (Valenzuela-Escárcega et al., 2015) for extraction. Using the framework, we wrote a grammar based on a set of triggers indicating beliefs, e.g., *think*, *believe*, *consider*, etc, and extracted events with believer (optional) and belief arguments. A sample rule is in Figure 1. We excluded beliefs of the author of the documents and only extracted reported beliefs (Prabhakaran et al., 2015)—in our case those are the beliefs of the local population.

Explicitly-stated consequences can be extracted using a rule-based approach like we do with beliefs. While the rule-based framework that we use supports same sentence extraction with cross-sentence coreference resolution, to extract consequences across sentences, the framework will need to be expanded. We leave the task of extracting explicit consequences to future work.

3.2 Implicit Consequence Generation

For the beliefs that are not accompanied by explicit consequences, we generated consequences using the InstructGPT-3 model (Ouyang et al., 2022). We primed the model with six few-shot examples with the following structure: "Belief: <text of belief extraction> Consequence: <text of a possible consequence>", e.g.:

3. **Belief:** *Rice grown in the dry season produced higher yields and was perceived to have lower risks.*
Consequence: *Farmers may not need to buy insurance for rice grown during the dry season.*

For creating the prompts, we used beliefs that were automatically extracted from text. The consequences in the prompts were either taken directly from text or were created by the authors to match the task. Both beliefs and consequences taken directly from text were edited slightly for clarity. Additionally, we experimented with providing the model with fewer examples (two and four in addition to six as discussed above) and also prompting the model to generate a consequence by using a discourse marker *That's why* without including any belief-consequence pairs as examples. We did not do any prompt tuning.

3.3 Evaluation

We do a qualitative analysis of human and machine-generated implicit consequences. For every belief, we manually inspect the two consequences produced by the human annotators and judge them to be the same if there is an overlap in context even if the form—the exact wording—is different. For automatically-generated vs. human-generated comparison, we consider the generation successful if at least one out of three automatically-generated consequences overlaps with at least one of the human-generated consequences.

Additionally, we evaluate the quality of automatically-generated consequences in terms of their relevance to the belief prompt, regardless of their similarity to human-generated consequences.

4 Results and Discussion

Based on the comparison of two sets of annotations, we see that a large number of beliefs do not have associated explicitly-stated consequences: the two annotators judged an average of 72% of the 50 beliefs annotated to not have consequences explicitly stated within the same sentence and an average of 49% to not have them within the one paragraph context window. These results indicate that both extraction and generation have to be included in the approach.

Analyzing the 18 beliefs that both annotators agreed did not have explicitly stated consequences, we see that, as expected, annotators tend to agree on possible consequences of beliefs: for 72% of beliefs, human annotators produced potential consequences with similar content (Table 1). We also see that there is promise for generating consequences using large language models: the GPT-3 model can produce consequences that match those produced by human annotators:

Condition	Overlap
two annotators	13 (72%)
GPT-3 and one annotator	12 (66%)
GPT-3 and both annotators	9 (50%)

Table 1: Overlap in content between different consequences produced (based on 18 beliefs with no consequences explicitly stated in text).

4. **Belief:** *Planners and technicians feel that the development of irrigation systems could offer a solution to the crisis in food production in Africa.*
Annotator 1: *Planners and officials will invest more in the development of irrigation systems.*
Annotator 2: *They should develop irrigation systems.*
GPT-3: *Planners and technicians focus on the development of irrigation systems.*

However, while producing some consequences that overlap with those produced by human annotators (Table 1), GPT-3 also generates text that, while thematically relevant to the prompt, does not constitute a successful consequence generation. To evaluate consequence generation independently from that done by human annotators, we analyze 54 GPT-3-generated consequences (three per each of the 18 beliefs with no explicit consequences) for whether or not they are appropriate for the corresponding beliefs. We judge 40 of the GPT-3-generated consequences (74%) to be possible consequences for the given belief prompt.

The quality of several consequences generated for each belief is not necessarily consistent. As seen from Table 2, for a given belief, all, some, or none of the three generated consequences can be appropriate. This poses a potential issue for downstream tasks in how there is no way to verify that a correct prediction was generated or selected from several generated predictions. We see several ways in how this could be addressed. First, we believe that with additional training using a dedicated data

Condition	Count
all correct	8
a mix of correct and incorrect	7
all incorrect	3

Table 2: Counts of beliefs for which all three generated consequences were correct, some were correct, or none were correct.

set, consequences of beliefs can be generated more consistently. Second, following Lu et al. (2021), we could apply logical or lexical constraints on the decoding side. Third, with several consequences generated, we may be able to assign higher weights to consequences that overlap in content with the other consequences generated for the same belief. Finally, this approach can be used for augmentation, not automation of some human efforts, e.g., modeling, in which case the domain expert will be able to evaluate produced belief-consequence pairs before using them.

Some of the error types observed among the 54 consequences generated by the GPT-3 model in a few-shot setting and example sentences to illustrate the error types are in Table 3. The counts of the error types are in Table 4. We note that for this analysis, not all error types necessarily disqualify a prediction from being a possible consequence. For instance, in the following example, while the specific dollar values make us judge the generated text to be too specific, a budget increase is indeed a possible consequence of a decision to rehabilitate the land:

5. **Belief:** *[...] personnel believe that up to an additional 60,000 ha could be rehabilitated.*
   Consequence: *They recommend an increase in the annual budget for rehabilitating degraded lands from $10 million to $15 million.*

In our experiments, we also see that providing examples to the model is crucial. In a zero-shot setting (i.e., with no belief-consequence examples provided to the model), the model did generate some propositions that could be seen as appropriate consequences for given beliefs. However, in this setting, in most cases the model also continued generating text until the word limit was reached. This was not the case for the majority of consequences generated in the few-shot setting: following the format of the provided examples, the model stopped generating after one sentence. Moreover, without explicit examples provided to the model, the generated text tended to contain information that was too specific to count as a successfully generated consequence. This included people's or company names, hot political topics (see example 6), or conversation markers (see example 7).

6. **Belief with a prompt:** *[...] centers are often considered the best private family planning clinics. That's why*
   Consequence: *the Trump administration's proposed rule to cut $300 million in Title X family planning funding is so alarming. Title X*

7. **Belief with a prompt:** *people believe that their hard work in the rice paddies is part of a covenant with their supreme deity. That's why*
   Consequence: *they work so hard." "I see. So their hard work is a form of worship." "Exactly*

We do not observe major differences between providing two vs. four vs. six examples to the model.

5 Future Work

To address the issues with GPT-3 generations discussed in the paper, in future work, we want to explore the possibility of using explicitly stated consequences as data to improve explicit consequence generation by large language models, both for fine-tuning and as few-shot examples.

For extracting explicit consequences, we will be exploring expanding the current rule-based framework to cross-sentence extractions as well as using GPT-3 text generation for event extraction. With the latter, the task can be framed in the following way: given a belief and its context, the model should produce the text that matches the text span that indicates the consequence of the belief.

For both these directions, we need to have a corpus of belief-consequence annotations, which means we will be conducting an annotation exercise. This will also help us support our findings regarding distributions of explicit and implicit consequences as well as the ability of human annotators to infer implicit consequences based on the belief and its context.

	Belief	Consequence	Error Type
1.	women unanimously believe their work to be profitable and well worth pursuing.	Women continue to engage in embroidery work.	too specific
2.	Mothers also believe that a child does not need to eat solid food before 8 months.	Breastfeeding rates are low in the study area.	contradiction
3.	farmers strongly feel that increased bird pressure intensity with resulting higher bird damages are the main reason for these lower yields in 2006.	Farmers stop growing rice.	wrong focus
4.	gifts, financial support, and physical attention are themselves considered important demonstrations of romantic love.	Men in this culture often give gifts, offer financial support, and provide physical attention to more than one woman at a time.	unsubstantiated consequence
5.	personnel believe that up to an additional 60,000 ha could be rehabilitated.	The additional 60,000 ha will not be rehabilitated.	wrong polarity
6.	use of chemicals and machinery on their paddy field is often considered undesirable.	Use of chemicals and machinery on their paddy field is often considered undesirable.	restatement

Table 3: Some of the error types observed in belief consequences generated by GPT-3.

Error Type	Count
too specific	9
contradiction	3
wrong focus	2
unsubstantiated consequence	1
wrong polarity	1
restatement	1

Table 4: Some of the error types and their counts observed observed in the 54 consequences generated by GPT-3 for the 18 beliefs (three consequences generated per belief).

Finally, we want to use belief-consequence pairs to build cognitive models of decision-making, e.g., modeling how a belief about rains causing crop damage might cause the believer to harvest early.

6 Conclusion

In this paper, we introduce the task of causal link extraction based on beliefs. We propose an approach for the task that combines extraction and generation, and provide a small-scale, qualitative analysis of a large language model performance on the task. Additionally, we outline directions of future work.

Acknowledgements

The authors thank the anonymous reviewers for helpful discussion and Andrew Zupon for help with annotation.

This work was supported by the Defense Advanced Research Projects Agency (DARPA) under the Habitus program. Maria Alexeeva and Mihai Surdeanu declare a financial interest in lum.ai. This interest has been properly disclosed to the University of Arizona Institutional Review Committee and is managed in accordance with its conflict of interest policies.

References

Zhongyang Li, Xiao Ding, Kuo Liao, Bing Qin, and Ting Liu. 2021. Causalbert: Injecting causal knowledge into pre-trained models with minimal supervision. *arXiv preprint arXiv:2107.09852*.

Ximing Lu, Peter West, Rowan Zellers, Ronan Le Bras, Chandra Bhagavatula, and Yejin Choi. 2021. NeuroLogic decoding: (un)supervised neural text generation with predicate logic constraints. In *Proceedings of the 2021 Conference of the North American Chapter of the Association for Computational Linguistics: Human Language Technologies*, pages 4288–4299, Online. Association for Computational Linguistics.

Long Ouyang, Jeff Wu, Xu Jiang, Diogo Almeida, Carroll L Wainwright, Pamela Mishkin, Chong Zhang, Sandhini Agarwal, Katarina Slama, Alex Ray, et al. 2022. Training language models to follow instructions with human feedback. *Preprint.*

Vinodkumar Prabhakaran, Tomas By, Julia Hirschberg, Owen Rambow, Samira Shaikh, Tomek Strzalkowski, Jennifer Tracey, Michael Arrigo, Rupayan Basu, Micah Clark, Adam Dalton, Mona Diab, Louise Guthrie, Anna Prokofieva, Stephanie Strassel, Gregory Werner, Yorick Wilks, and Janyce Wiebe. 2015. A new dataset and evaluation for belief/factuality. In *Proceedings of the Fourth Joint Conference on Lexical and Computational Semantics*, pages 82–91, Denver, Colorado. Association for Computational Linguistics.

Rebecca Sharp, Adarsh Pyarelal, Benjamin Gyori, Keith Alcock, Egoitz Laparra, Marco A. Valenzuela-Escárcega, Ajay Nagesh, Vikas Yadav, John Bachman, Zheng Tang, Heather Lent, Fan Luo, Mithun Paul, Steven Bethard, Kobus Barnard, Clayton Morrison, and Mihai Surdeanu. 2019. Eidos, INDRA, & delphi: From free text to executable causal models. In *Proceedings of the 2019 Conference of the North American Chapter of the Association for Computational Linguistics (Demonstrations)*, pages 42–47, Minneapolis, Minnesota. Association for Computational Linguistics.

Rebecca Sharp, Mihai Surdeanu, Peter Jansen, Peter Clark, and Michael Hammond. 2016. Creating causal embeddings for question answering with minimal supervision. In *Proceedings of the 2016 Conference on Empirical Methods in Natural Language Processing*, pages 138–148, Austin, Texas. Association for Computational Linguistics.

Marco A Valenzuela-Escárcega, Özgün Babur, Gus Hahn-Powell, Dane Bell, Thomas Hicks, Enrique Noriega-Atala, Xia Wang, Mihai Surdeanu, Emek Demir, and Clayton T Morrison. 2018. Large-scale automated machine reading discovers new cancer-driving mechanisms. *Database*, 2018.

Marco A. Valenzuela-Escárcega, Gus Hahn-Powell, Mihai Surdeanu, and Thomas Hicks. 2015. A domain-independent rule-based framework for event extraction. In *Proceedings of ACL-IJCNLP 2015 System Demonstrations*, pages 127–132, Beijing, China. Association for Computational Linguistics and The Asian Federation of Natural Language Processing.

Replicability under Near-Perfect Conditions – A Case-Study from Automatic Summarization

Margot Mieskes
University of Applied Sciences Darmstadt
Germany
margot.mieskes@h-da.de

Abstract

Replication of research results has become more and more important in Natural Language Processing. Nevertheless, we still rely on results reported in the literature for comparison. Additionally, elements of an experimental setup are not always completely reported. This includes, but is not limited to reporting specific parameters used or omitting an implementational detail. In our experiments based on two frequently used data sets from the domain of automatic summarization and the seemingly full disclosure of research artifacts, we examine how well results reported are replicable and what elements influence the success or failure of replication. Our results indicate that publishing research artifacts is far from sufficient, and that publishing all relevant parameters in all possible detail is crucial, but often neglected, making the situation in automatic summarization only near-perfect.

1 Introduction

Replicability is gaining more and more attention in the NLP world with dedicated workshops[1], replication checklists[2] etc. While this improves the situation considerably, and the availability of research artifacts is improving, there is still the question if replicability is possible if all artifacts necessary are available. Additionally, often results from the literature are cited, but it is far from clear whether the reported results are obtained experimentally (by re-implementing or re-running a particular method) or also cited. One domain where the availability of research artifacts is almost perfect, is Automatic Summarization. Standard benchmark data sets published in the course of various shared tasks are available, the evaluation method is well known, its implementation is available and resulting data submitted to shared tasks have also been made available by the organizers. Therefore, it should be straightforward to replicate results reported by the organizers of the shared task, as well as results reported in the literature.

This would hardly be a submission to a workshop on insights from negative results if things were that easy. Normally, successfully replicating previous results would just appear as one or more number in a table used for comparison. But our results indicate that despite this near-perfect conditions, reporting and replicating results is far from straightforward. Based on a literature review and experiments in replicating results we show the discrepancies that occur both in cited results, as well as when experiments are replicated.

Our contributions are therefore a closer look and comparison of reported results from the domain of automatic summarization and results from replicated experiments and factor benefitting or hindering complete replication.

2 Replication in NLP

Experiments in reproducing results in the NLP domain such as those presented by Fokkens et al. (2013) are still quite rare. One reason is, that when undertaking such projects, "sometimes conflicting results are obtained by repeating a study"[3].

Fokkens et al. (2013) report, that their experiments on two tasks in NLP are difficult to carry out and to obtain meaningful results. Preprocessing, experimental setup, versioning, system output, and system variation cause experimental variation according to the authors.

The 4Real workshop[4] focuses on the "the topic of the reproducibility of research results and the citation of resources, and its impact on research

[1] examples are https://lrec2020.lrec-conf.org/en/reprolang2020/ and https://reprogen.github.io

[2] https://2021.naacl.org/calls/reproducibility-checklist/

[3] https://sciencebasedmedicine.org/science-based-medicine-101-/

[4] http://4real.di.fc.ul.pt/

Proceedings of the Third Workshop on Insights from Negative Results in NLP, pages 165 - 171
May 26, 2022

integrity". Their call for papers asks for submissions of "actual replication exercises of previous published results" (Branco et al., 2016). Results from this workshop suggest that reproducing experiments gives additional insights, and is therefore beneficial for the researchers as well as for the community (Cohen et al., 2016).

Horsmann and Zesch (2017) present a study on the replication of results in the context of Part-of-Speech tagging and whether LSTMs really work as well as the literature suggests. The results are mixed and show that the replicability depends on parameters such as tagset complexity.

Crane (2018) looks into the area of Question Answering and finds that "Source code without a reproducible environment does not mean anything". The author presents a set of experiments to show, that different parameters can lead to different results, similar in magnitude to those reported in the literature.

Dror et al. (2017) give a more general overview on this issue, as they perform a replicability study on various NLP tasks. They find that the increasing amount of evaluation data sets is a two-edged sword and only beneficial if the data reflects a variety of linguistic phenomena and are heterogeneous at least with respect to language or domain. Otherwise, showing that results are valid on one data set is probably sufficient.

Other authors look into the availability of research artifacts (i.e. (Mieskes, 2017; Wieling et al., 2018) who found that a large proportion of research artifacts are not available. A recent study by Belz et al. (2021) systematically looked into the replicability of various publications from the NLP domain, finding, that only approx. 14 % of the examined publications were replicable.

3 Automatic Summarization

Fokkens et al. (2013), Crane (2018) and others observe that re-implementation does not guarantee the reproducibility of the reported results, but rather a range of parameters cause differences between reported results and replicated results. Therefore, we focus on available data, systems and differences due to the evaluation method.[5]

The **DUC 2002** data set is used for an evaluation on Single-Document Summarization (SDS). It contains over 500 documents from 59 thematic clusters. The target length of the summaries is 100 words. The **DUC 2004** data set is used for the evaluation on the Multi-Document Summarization (MDS) task. It contains 500 documents from 50 thematic clusters. The length restriction was set to 665 bytes, which, for English, also results in a length of 100 words.

For both data sets the organizers of the shared task published reference summaries as well as submitted summaries. Furthermore, the evaluation results are available as well. Lin (2004) introduced an automatic evaluation metric, which became the standard both for subsequent shared tasks, as well as for automatic summarization in general. ROUGE has a range of parameters, which have to be set prior to running the evaluation. Several of these parameters are not binary, which results in a extensive parameter space. Graham (2015) gives details on these parameters and the resulting issues.

Both data sets that have been widely used in the past 15 to 20 years and therefore provide a reasonable basis for our analysis, which contains three parts: First, we will look into results reported in the literature and we aim to replicate those reported results. Second, we use available summarization methods out of the box or retrain them and evaluate the results. Third, we use a data set published by Hong et al. (2014) to replicate their results.

In our experiments, we stick as close as possible to the description offered in the cited publications and cite the results given.

3.1 Single Document Summarization (SDS)

Table 1 lists the ranking for DUC 2002 both based on the officially released results[6], as well as three examples from the literature: Lloret and Palomar (2010); Mihalcea and Tarau (2004) and Barrera and Verma (2011). Table 2 additionally shows results reported in these three papers. We experiment with various settings for ROUGE, relying on parameters reported in the literature.

We specifically focus on the stopword and stemming parameters, as we observe that they result huge differences in the results – marked as "Stopwords" and "Stemmed" in the table. "Both" indicates that stopwords were filtered and stemming was applied. Both tables (1 and 2) show that there is quite some discrepancy between the rankings

[5]Please note, that we do not report all publications that cite the same results, but rather highlight the differences.

[6]S19 and S27 are very close together and the error bars as published in `https://www-nlpir.nist.gov/projects/duc/pubs/2002slides/overview.02.pdf` do not allow for an exact distinction between the two.

reported officially and those in the literature. The comparison between the official results and the results in the literature might not be quite appropriate, as the official evaluation has not been done using ROUGE and while ROUGE has shown high correlation with human judgements, the ranking does not necessarily match exactly. The situation is somewhat different for the three reported rankings, which have all been done using ROUGE, as can be seen in Table 2.

Loret	Barrera	Mihalcea	official
S28	S28	S27	S19
S21	S19	S31	S27
S19*	S21*	S28	S28
–	S29*	S21	S21
–	S23*	S29*	S31

Table 1: Ranking as listed in the literature; * did not beat the baseline according to the source paper.

Some systems (i.e. S31) do not even occur in all three reported rankings. A closer look at the reported and replicated ROUGE-scores show that they vary considerably. We also observe that applying stopword filtering gives the worst results, while applying stemming gives the highest results, which are also similar to results reported by Mihalcea and Tarau (2004, 2005) and Barrera and Verma (2011). Applying both stopword filtering and stemming gives results that are in a similar range to those reported by Lloret and Palomar (2010). It is interesting to note, that in all four papers the baseline is reported differently: 0.4779 (Barrera and Verma, 2011), 0.4599 (Mihalcea and Tarau, 2004), 0.4799 (Mihalcea and Tarau, 2005) and 0.4113 (Lloret and Palomar, 2010). As only Lloret and Palomar (2010) note the parameters for the evaluation[7] this is the only experiment we could replicate in detail. But differences remain. It is interesting to see that while Mihalcea and Tarau (2004) also experimented with stemming and stopword filtering, they report the best results when using the basic settings, while our results are highest when stemming is applied, whereas stopword filtering gives the worst results.

3.2 Multi-Document Summarization (MDS)

For the MDS scenario the situation is somewhat better as ROUGE has been used in the official evaluation as well. The best system was identified as S65 and there is no discrepancy we could find in the literature regarding this.

[7]-n 2 -m 2 4 -u -c 95 -r 1000 -f A -p 0.5 -t 0 -l 100 -d

Citation	S28	S21	S19
Mihalcea and Tarau (2004)	0.4703	0.4683	na
stemmed	0.4890	0.4869	na
stemmed/no stopwords	0.4346	0.4222	na
Mihalcea and Tarau (2005)	0.4890	0.4869	na
Lloret and Palomar (2010)	0.4278	0.4149	0.4082
Barrera and Verma (2011)	0.4781	0.4754	0.4552
Stemmed	0.473	0.467	0.452
Stopwords	0.395	0.380	0.379
Both	0.421	0.406	0.404

Table 2: Evaluation results for systems in DUC 2002 based on reports from the literature and based on our own replication with various parameter settings.

basic	Stemmed	Stopwords	Both
0.35909	0.38317	0.27068	0.30595

Table 3: Results for various preprocessing parameters for the output for S65 from DUC 2004.

Table 3 presents our results for evaluating S65 with various preprocessing parameters. As with the DUC 2002 data, stemming the resulting summaries give the best results, while the basic parameters only give the second best results.

Citation	ROUGE-1
Original	0.38224
Yih et al. (2007)†	0.305
Alguliev et al. (2012)	0.3822
Ryang and Abekawa (2012)	0.3827
Manna et al. (2012)†	0.3913
Rioux et al. (2014)†	0.3828
Ren et al. (2016)†	0.3788
Wang et al. (2017)†	0.3762

Table 4: Results on S65 as reported by the organizers (Original) and in various publications ever since. † indicates that parameters have been reported in the publication.

Table 3 presents the results for S65 as officially reported and various results found in the literature, which show a considerable range. When running ROUGE on the available data with various parameter settings we observe that the results also vary considerably, similar to the SDS scenario. Comparing the results in Table 3 to those officially published and reported in the literature (Table 4) we observe that applying stemming gives results close to what has been officially reported. Applying both stemming and stopword filtering our results are close to those reported by Yih et al. (2007). As indicated, most of the cited papers also report the evaluation parameters. A closer look at these parameters shows that although there are some differences, the parameters affecting ROUGE-1 are the same, except for Rioux et al. (2014), where `-l 250` was used. This allows summaries to be longer than 100 words, which could have a considerable effect on the ROUGE scores. Ren et al. (2016) do not set any length parameter, which means that the summaries are evaluated in their full length. Ren et al. (2016) presents a summarization method that ensures a final length of 100 words. And in all cases, stemming was applied, but no stopword filtering. Taking this into account, our results are similar to those originally reported, but also to those reported by Alguliev et al. (2012), Ryang and Abekawa (2012) and Rioux et al. (2014), where longer summaries were considered.

3.3 Re-run Summarization Methods

For the 2004 MDS data we perform two additional experiments. First, we use MEAD which has successfully participated in various shared tasks on automatic summarization. Second, we follow instructions to retrain and run an SVM-based summarization method and compare our evaluation with the reported results.

MEAD can be downloaded[8] and used for summarization. Therefore, we use the code as is to summarize the DUC 2004 data. Table 5 shows the results found in the literature. Preprocessing has a considerable influence on the results, as with no preprocessing we only achieve R-1 = 0.31 and the best result is R-1 = 0.349. This is still lower than the reported results, which are considerably higher and as with previous experiments, vary considerably. Unfortunately, only Hong et al. (2014) report the parameters used, but nevertheless, our results are considerably different.

Citation	Result
Erkan and Radev (2004a) (added features)	0.38304
Erkan and Radev (2004b)	0.3758
Alguliev et al. (2012)	0.3673
Hong et al. (2014)[†]	0.3641
re-run	0.3494

Table 5: Results for MEAD on DUC 2004 (MDS) data. [†] indicates that parameters have been reported in the publication.

SVM We retrain the SVM introduced by Sipos et al. (2012), following the guidelines provided[9]. This included all relevant packages and detailed instructions on how to train the SVM model, which data has been used and how the resulting model was applied to the data. Table 6 shows our results and the result reported in the original publication. We observe that the results are similar to each other and the confidence interval (CI) indicates, that the results do not significantly differ.

Sipos et al. (2012)	re-train & eval (95% CI)
0.4066	0.3995 (0.3883–0.4117)

Table 6: Results for Sipos et al. (2012) re-evaluation on DUC 2004 data.

Summary Data The final experiment builds on data introduced by Hong et al. (2014), which contains summaries for a range of methods.[10] The authors give the parameters used for evaluation and results for R-1, but also for ROUGE-2 (R-2) and ROUGE-4 (R-4). Table 7 shows the results as originally reported (O) and as replicated (R).[11] Comparing the results, we can see some differences and out of 36 values 22 do not match exactly (marked in italics). Out of these 22 only 8 differ by more than 0.01 points (marked in bold). For CLASSY 04 we see a difference of 0.04 in R-1 and for KL we see a difference of 0.03 in R-2.

System	R-1	R-2	R-4
LexRank (O)	35.95	7.47	0.82
LexRank (R)	**35.97**	**7.49**	0.82
Centroid (O)	36.41	7.97	1.21
Centroid (R)	36.41	*7.98*	1.21
FreqSum (O)	35.30	8.11	1.00
FreqSum (R)	35.30	*8.10*	*0.99*
TsSum (O)	35.88	8.15	1.03
TsSum (R)	*35.89*	8.15	1.03
KL (O)	37.98	8.53	1.26
KL (R)	**38.00**	**8.56**	1.26
CLASSY 04 (O)	37.62	8.96	1.51
CLASSY 04 (R)	**37.66**	*8.97*	1.51
CLASSY 11 (O)	37.22	9.20	1.48
CLASSY 11 (R)	**37.20**	*9.21*	1.48
Submodular (O)	39.18	9.35	1.39
Submodular (R)	*39.17*	*9.34*	*1.38*
DPP (O)	39.79	9.62	1.57
DPP (R)	**39.81**	*9.63*	*1.58*
RegSum (O)	38.57	9.75	1.60
RegSum (R)	*38.56*	9.75	*1.61*
OCCAMS_V (O)	38.50	9.76	1.33
OCCAMS_V (R)	38.50	9.76	*1.32*
ICSISumm (O)	38.41	9.78	1.73
ICSISumm (R)	38.41	**9.80**	1.73

Table 7: Original (O) and replicated (R) results for the data set published by (Hong et al., 2014).

[8] `http://www.summarization.com/mead/`

[9] Unfortunately, the link given in the original publication is not functional anymore.

[10] The link given in the original publication is still functional and provides the data set, as well as the recommended evaluation settings.

[11] Please note that for better comparison we adopt their notation.

4 Discussion

We looked into the question of whether the fact that all necessary research artifacts are available for specific benchmark data sets in automatic summarization allow for a straightforward evaluation and replication. We also looked into results reported in the literature, as often results are cited in subsequent works as baselines or for comparison.

We observed quite severe differences not only in the exact values obtained by running the evaluation, but also in the conclusions drawn from these with respect to the ranking of the system outputs.

We also observed that the results highly depend on the parameters used for evaluation. If **evaluation parameters** and **system output** results are given, results are reproducible, as we were able to show with the data and results presented by Hong et al. (2014). Using their data and the evaluation parameters, our results were almost identical to those reported in the original publication. As only some results differed, it remains open if the observed differences are due to changes on the hardware and/or software level. Also, not all three evaluation metrics differed. As most values were in the range of ± 0.1 one assumption is, that this is due to differences in rounding. In order to evaluate this, a more detailed analysis of individual results is required. If the **method used to produce** the summaries has been described in enough detail, it is possible to achieve similar results as we did with work by Sipos et al. (2012).

Despite the seemingly ideal circumstances, we failed to reproduce the results for System 65 in DUC 2004. For the DUC 2002 task we were only partially able to replicate or reproduce results reported in the literature, despite similar circumstances. We could not reproduce results reported in the literature. Also our experiments with MEAD were not conclusive. They showed that depending on the parameters used for evaluation, the results can vary considerably, sometimes even significantly, even though the system implementation is available and the evaluation metric is known.

A closer look at the publications analyzed for this study, we found that only about 40% report the full set of evaluation parameters. Almost 50% of the publications did not mention the evaluation parameters at all.[12] Replicating or even reproducing results for these publications is therefore unnecessarily complicated and involves testing all possible combinations of parameters. As the correct parameter set is unknown in these cases, comparisons are as not as valuable as they could be. Additionally, re-implementations such as py-rouge[13] do not offer all the parameters ROUGE originally offered, making comparisons even harder. Therefore, one of our next steps is to re-evaluate the presented experiments using py-rouge.

More analysis, also in other areas of NLP would be beneficial to strengthen the results of this study. While ROUGE has quite an extensive parameter range, it is negligible compared to modern machine learning approaches and as has been pointed out by Crane (2018) they "often go unreported". Nevertheless, our results highlight a problem that will become more severe the more complicated the methods developed in NLP become: Disclosing all parameters used for creating and evaluating a specific system is crucial. Publishing the algorithms and the resulting data is not enough to ensure replicable results. And even having details about the evaluation procedure (including relevant parameters) does not ensure that results can be replicated and conclusions in line with previous work can be drawn. While this might sound trivial, our results indicate that this is not being done in enough detail to ensure replicability and reproducibility of results.

Acknowledgements

This work was supported by the research center for Digital Communication and Media Innovation (DKMI) of the University of Applied Sciences, Darmstadt.

References

Rasim M. Alguliev, Ramiz M. Aliguliyev, and Makrufa S. Hajirahimova. 2012. Gendocsum + mclr: Generic document summarization based on maximum coverage and less redundancy. *Expert Systems with Applications*, 39:12460–12473.

Araly Barrera and Rakesh Verma. 2011. Automated extractive single-document summarization: Beating the baselines with a new approach. In *Proceedings of the 2011 ACM Symposium on Applied Computing (SAC '11)*, pages 268–269, TaiChung, Taiwan.

Anya Belz, Shubham Agarwal, Anastasia Shimorina, and Ehud Reiter. 2021. A systematic review of re-

[12]A detailed analysis of this would allow a more reliable quantification of this issue, not only in the context of automatic summarization.

[13]`https://github.com/andersjo/pyrouge`

producibility research in natural language processing. In *Proceedings of the 16th Conference of the European Chapter of the Association for Computational Linguistics: Main Volume*, pages 381–393, Online. Association for Computational Linguistics.

António Branco, Nicoletta Calzolari, and Khalid Choukri, editors. 2016. *4REAL Workshop: Workshop on Research Results Reproducibility and Resources Citation in Science and Technology of Language*. An LREC 2016 Workshop, Portorož, Slovenia.

Kevin Cohen, Jingbo Xia, Christophe Roeder, and Lawrence Hunter. 2016. Reproducibility in Natural Language Processing: A Case Study of two R Libraries for Mining PubMed/MEDLINE. In *4REAL Workshop: Workshop on Research Results Reproducibility and Resources Citation in Science and Technology of Language*, pages 6–12, Portorož, Slovenia. An LREC 2016 Workshop.

Matt Crane. 2018. Questionable answers in question answering research: Reproducibility and variability of published results. *Transactions of the Association for Computational Linguistics*, 6:241–252.

Rotem Dror, Gili Baumer, Marina Bogomolov, and Roi Reichart. 2017. Replicability Analysis for Natural Language Processing: Testing Significance with Multiple Datasets. *Transactions of the Association for Computational Linguistics*, 5:471–486.

Günes Erkan and Dragomir R. Radev. 2004a. Lexpagerank: Prestige in multi-document text summarization. In *Proceedings of the 2004 Conference on Empirical Methods in Natural Language Processing*, Barcelona, Spain.

Günes Erkan and Dragomir R. Radev. 2004b. Lexrank: Graph-based lexical centrality as salience in text summarization. *Journal of Artificial Intelligence Research*, 22:457–479.

Antske Fokkens, Marieke van Erp, Marten Postma, Ted Pedersen, Piek Vossen, and Nuno Freire. 2013. Offspring from Reproduction Problems: What Replication Failure Teaches Us. In *Proceedings of the 51st Annual Meeting of the Association for Computational Linguistics (Volume 1: Long Papers)*, pages 1691–1701, Sofia, Bulgaria. Association for Computational Linguistics.

Yvette Graham. 2015. Re-evaluating Automatic Summarization with BLEU and 192 Shades of ROUGE. In *Proceedings of the 2015 Conference on Empirical Methods in Natural Language Processing*, pages 128–137, Lisbon, Portugal. Association for Computational Linguistics.

Kai Hong, John M. Conroy, Benoit Favre, Alex Kulesza, Hui Lin, and Ani Nenkova. 2014. A repository of state of the art and competitive baseline summaries for generic news summarization. In *Proceedings of the Ninth International Conference on Language Resources and Evaluation (LREC'14),* Reykjavik, Iceland, 26–31 May 2014, pages 1608–1616. European Language Resources Association (ELRA).

Tobias Horsmann and Torsten Zesch. 2017. Do lstms really work so well for pos tagging? – a replication study. In *Proceedings of the 2017 Conference on Empirical Methods in Natural Language Processing,* Copenhagen, Denmark, 7–11 September 2017, pages 738–747. Association for Computational Linguistics.

Chin-Yew Lin. 2004. ROUGE: A package for automatic evaluation of summaries. In *Proceedings of the Workshop on Text Summarization Branches Out,* Barcelona, Spain, 2004, pages 74–81.

Elena Lloret and Manuel Palomar. 2010. Challenging issues of automatic summarization: Relevance detection and quality-based evaluation. *Informatica*, 34:29–35.

Sukanya Manna, Byron J. Gao, and Reed Coke. 2012. A subjective logic framework for multi-document summarization. In *Proceedings of the 24th International Conference on Computational Linguistics,* Mumbay, India, December 2012, pages 797–808.

Margot Mieskes. 2017. A quantative study of data in the nlp community. In *Proceedings of the First ACL Workshop on Ethics in Natural Language Processing*, pages 23–29, Valencia, Spain. Association for Computational Linguistics.

Rada Mihalcea and Paul Tarau. 2004. Textrank: Bringing order into texts. In *Proceedings of the 2004 Conference on Empirical Methods in Natural Language Processing* Barcelona, Spain, 25–26 July 2004.

Rada Mihalcea and Paul Tarau. 2005. A language independent algorithm for single and multiple document summarization. In *The Second International Joint Conference on Natural Language Processing (IJCNLP-05)*, pages 19–24, Jeju Island, Korea.

Pengjie Ren, Furu Wei, Zhumin Chen, Jun Ma, and Ming Zhou. 2016. A redundancy-aware sentence regression framework for extractive summarization. In *Proceedings of the 26th International Conference on Computational Linguistics: Technical Papers*, pages 33–43, Osaka, Japan.

Cody Rioux, Sadid A. Hasan, and Yllias Chali. 2014. Fear the reaper: A system for automatic multi-document summarization with reinforcement learning. In *Proceedings of the 2014 Conference on Empirical Methods in Natural Language Processing, October 25-29, 2014, Doha, Qatar*, pages 681–690.

Seonggi Ryang and Takeshi Abekawa. 2012. Framework of automatic text summarization using reinforcement learning. In *Proceedings of the 2012 Joint Conference on Empirical Methods in Natural Language Processing and Computational Natural Language Learning,* Jeju Island, Korea, 12–14 July 2012, pages 256–265.

Ruben Sipos, Pannaga Shivaswamy, and Thorsten Joachims. 2012. Large-margin learning of submodular summarization models. In *Proceedings of the*

13th Conference of the European Chapter of the Association for Computational Linguistics, Avignon, France, April 23–27, 2012, pages 224–233.

Kexiang Wang, Tianyu Liu, Zhifang Sui, and Baobao Chang. 2017. Affinity-preserving random walk for multi-document summarization. In *Proceedings of the 2017 Conference on Empirical Methods in Natural Language Processing,* Copenhagen, Denmark, 7–11 September 2017, pages 210–220. Association for Computational Linguistics.

Martijn Wieling, Josine Rawee, and Gertjan van Noord. 2018. Squib: Reproducibility in computational linguistics: Are we willing to share? *Computational Linguistics*, 44(4):641–649.

Wen-Tau Yih, Joshua Goodman, Lucy Vanderwende, and Hisami Suzuki. 2007. Multi-Document Summarization by Maximizing Informative Content-Words. In *Proceedings of the Twentieth International Joint Conference on Artificial Intelligence* Hyderabad, India, 6–12 January, 2007, pages 1776–1782.

BPE beyond Word Boundary: How NOT to use Multi Word Expressions in Neural Machine Translation

Dipesh Kumar*
Indian Institute of Technology (BHU) / Varanasi
dipesh.kumar.cse17@iitbhu.ac.in

Avijit Thawani*
University of Southern California / Los Angeles
Information Sciences Institute / Marina del Rey
thawani@usc.edu

Abstract

BPE tokenization merges characters into longer tokens by finding frequently occurring **contiguous** patterns **within** the word boundary. An intuitive relaxation would be to extend a BPE vocabulary with multi-word expressions (MWEs): bigrams (in_a), trigrams (out_of_the), and skip-grams ($he{\cdot}his$). In the context of Neural Machine Translation (NMT), we replace the least frequent subword/whole-word tokens with the most frequent MWEs. We find that these modifications to BPE end up hurting the model, resulting in a net drop of BLEU and chrF scores across two language pairs. We observe that naively extending BPE beyond word boundaries results in incoherent tokens which are themselves better represented as individual words. Moreover, we find that Pointwise Mutual Information (PMI) instead of frequency finds better MWEs (e.g., New_York, $Statue\_of\_Liberty$, $neither{\cdot}nor$) which consistently improves translation performance. We release all code at `https://github.com/pegasus-lynx/mwe-bpe`.

1 Introduction

Subword tokenization algorithms like Byte Pair Encoding (BPE) (Sennrich et al., 2016) group together frequently occurring patterns, such as *-ing* or *-ly*, into individual tokens. The success of subword tokenization points to the benefit in modeling longer patterns, even though any given text can be represented simply as a sequence of characters. This paper stretches the motivation further by allowing BPE to cross word boundaries. In the context of NMT, we find that the straightforward way to find MWEs by BPE (sorted by frequency) hurts performance whereas sorting by PMI scores improves scores. We hypothesize and discuss a reason for these observations and provide further recommendations on using MWEs with BPE.

N-gram tokens have been used in traditional NLP for a long time and with much success. For example (Table 1), the bigram *New York* can be a concise yet useful feature in a Named Entity Recognition task. Similarly, a Spanish-English Machine Translation (MT) model might benefit from having the bigram *te amo* or its trigram translation *I love you* in its vocabulary. Finally, a model's vocabulary could even extend to non-contiguous tokens or k-skip-n-grams such as *neither · nor*. This token reappears in several contexts e.g. *neither tea nor coffee* and *neither here nor there* (underlined words replace the · skip).

Raw	He lives in New York .
Tok	He_ lives_ in_ New_York_ ._
Raw	I love the Statue of Liberty!
Tok	I_ love_ the_ Statue_of_Liberty_ !_
Raw	She lost her bag .
Tok	She_ · her_ lost_ <SKIP> bag_ ._

Table 1: Example tokenizations of MWEs (bigrams, trigrams, skip-grams) in our implementation. Raw = original sentence, Tok = tokenized form. Typical BPE tokens are colored yellow and MWEs are colored green.

This paper experiments with two ways to expand BPE with MWEs for the task of NMT. Concretely, we promise the following contributions:

1. We find, counter-intuitively, that the straightforward frequency-based BPE, when applied beyond words, performs worse than baseline on NMT across two language pairs (§3).

2. We hypothesize that this negative result is caused by the constituents of such high frequency MWEs (e.g. in_the) combining in many diverse ways, rendering such tokens incoherent (§4.1).

3. We show that PMI-based BPE for MWEs reverses the drop and improves BLEU scores. We offer more recommendations on where and how to use MWEs with BPE (§4.2).

* Equal Contribution.

Proceedings of the Third Workshop on Insights from Negative Results in NLP, pages 172 - 179
May 26, 2022 ©2022 Association for Computational Linguistics

Lang. Pair	Hi → En				De → En			
Split	Dev		Test		Dev		Test	
Metric	sacre BLEU	chrF $\beta = 2$	sacre BLEU	chrF $\beta = 2$	sacre BLEU	chrF $\beta = 2$	sacre BLEU	chrF $\beta = 2$
Baseline	20.8	49.5	22.0	52.3	39.1	**62.4**	35.6	59.1
Unigram	19.5	49.0	21.2	51.5	36.5	60.3	32.4	56.8
BPE+ngms	19.5	49.0	21.2	51.6	38.7	62.2	35.3	58.9
BPE+n/sgms	18.4	48.1	20.7	51.3	38.4	62.1	35.2	58.9
PMI methods								
Bigrams	20.6	49.2	**22.2**	**52.6**	**39.1**	**62.4**	35.8	**59.3**
Trigrams	20.7	49.5	22.0	52.3	39.0	62.2	35.7	59.0
N-grams	**21.2**	**50.0**	22.1	**52.6**	38.9	62.3	35.8	59.1
Skip-grams	20.6	49.9	22.1	52.4	38.7	62.1	**35.9**	59.2

Table 2: Different methods of adding MWEs to a BPE vocabulary on NMT across two language pairs.

2 Methods

MWEs have been commonly used in traditional NLP but rarely in the age of transformers and subword vocabularies. Here we describe two kinds of ways to add MWEs to a BPE vocabulary.

2.1 BPE beyond words

Our baseline is the vanilla BPE tokenization scheme which starts from characters and iteratively adds the most frequent subwords to vocabulary. An intuitive extension to BPE is **BPE+ngms**, i.e., allowing BPE to choose between not just adding subwords but also frequently occurring n-grams (e.g., of_the appears at 163rd position in vocabulary). This paper limits n-grams to bigrams and trigrams.

Besides continuous multi-word expressions, we also experiment with discontinuous MWEs, i.e., k-skip-n-grams, which we refer to concisely as skip-grams. In particular, we focus on 1-skip-3-grams, e.g., *neither · nor*, *I · you*. We replace a 1-skip-3-gram ($w_1 \cdot w_2$) occurrence with (w_{12} · `<SKIP>`) where w_{12} is a new token representing the occurrence of this specific 1-skip-3-gram, and `<SKIP>` is another new token but shared by all skip-grams to indicate that the skip-gram ends here. The last row of Table 1 shows an example tokenization with skip-grams. In **BPE+n/sgms**, we allow frequent skip-grams (e.g., (·); neither · nor) to also be part of the vocabulary.

2.2 Adding MWEs with PMI

As hinted in Section 1, the intuitive extension to BPE does not work well in practice. Instead of raw frequency, here we find MWEs using a common technique of finding word collocations: Pointwise Mutual Information (PMI), which is a measure of the association between two word types in text. We calculate PMI of n-grams as:

$$PMI(a_1, ..., a_n) = \log(\frac{P(a_1, ..., a_n)}{\prod_{i=1}^{n} P(a_i)})$$

where a_i are unigrams (words) from the corpus; $P(a_i)$ denote their independent probabilities; and $P(a_i, ...a_n)$ denotes joint probability of n-grams. In this paper, we report experiments with only **Bigrams** ($n = 2$), **Trigrams** ($n = 3$), and their combination **N-grams**.

We also experiment with **Skip-grams** or 1-skip-3-grams ($w_1 \cdot w_2$) from our corpus in the same way as bigrams ($w_1 w_2$), ordered by PMI. We identify candidate word pairs separated by one word (which we depict by ·) and sort them based on PMI scores, some of which are deemed good enough to replace the least frequent subwords in the BPE vocabulary.

We find that the skip-grams obtained by simply ordering by PMI are often better suited to be trigrams, e.g., the · in *Statue · Liberty*, a high-ranked candidate skip-gram, is almost always *of*. To disentangle such skip-grams, we filter out candidates where the middle (skipped) word has a spread-out distribution: the skipped word in *I · you* could be replaced with several words like *love*, *hate*, or *miss*. In practice, we filter these by enforcing (1) a lower limit (15) on the number of unique words which replace the · token, and (2) an upper limit on the probability (10%) of the most frequently occurring skipped token for the particular skip-gram.

3 Datasets

We use the IIT Bombay Hindi-English parallel corpus v3.0 (Kunchukuttan et al., 2018), tokenized using IndicNLPLibrary (Kunchukuttan, 2020) and Moses Tokenizer (Koehn et al., 2007) respectively. The Train : Dev : Test splits have $1.6M$: $0.5K$: $2.3K$ sentences respectively.

For German-English, the datasets are retreived from the News Translation task of WMT2019 (Barrault et al., 2019). The Train : Dev : Test splits have $4.5M$: $3K$: $2K$ sentences respectively.

While we use the originally mentioned training set for our main results in Table 2, we found several noisy sentence pairs in the training dataset (the dev and test set were clean). Some such sentences had English characters (latin alphabet) in the source (Hindi) side and others had non-English characters on the target (English) side. We filtered out 250K sentence pairs where either the source side had non-Hindi characters or the target side had non-English characters, wherein we count the following near-universal symbols as part of either language: $.,()[]!:-"';<>?\&\breve{}@$

4 Experiments

While MWEs can augment the subword vocabulary of any NLP model, this short paper focuses on the task of NMT. Following Gowda and May (2020), we fix the transformer architecture (Vaswani et al., 2017) and train models with different vocabularies from scratch.

Our baseline vocabulary is BPE with 8K subword tokens for Hi-En and 16K for De-En. Each of our methods maintains the same vocabulary size, replacing the least frequently occurring subwords with corresponding n-grams or skip-grams. We show representative MWEs learned from corpora in Table 4 alongside the coverage of (PMI) MWEs across language pairs.

We also compare with a Unigram (Kudo, 2018) SentencePiece vocabulary of 8K tokens each on source and target sides, with *split_by_whitespace* flag set to `false` (Kudo and Richardson, 2018). This allows the Unigram method to go beyond the word boundary and add n-grams to its vocabulary.

Our NMT model is a 6 layer transformer encoder-decoder (Vaswani et al., 2017) that has 8 attention heads, 512 hidden vector units, and a feed forward intermediate size of 2048, with GELU activation. We use label smoothing at 0.1, and a dropout rate of 0.1. We use the Adam optimizer with a controlled learning rate that warms up for 16K steps followed by a decay rate recommended for training transformer models. We trim longer sequences to a maximum of 512 tokens after BPE. Each model is trained from scratch, and the hyperparameters (per language pair) are chosen by grid search to optimize the baseline validation BLEU.

We train all models for up to $100K$ steps (batch size = $24K$ tokens) and report sacreBLEU (Post, 2018) and chrF ($\beta = 2$) scores (Popović, 2015).

The number of tokens replaced in the original BPE vocabulary with a corresponding MWE ordered by PMI, is also a hyperparameter optimized by grid search between 1.25% to 10% of the vocabulary size (Hi-En models performing best when 1.25% tokens were replaced and De-En models performing best at 2.5% for Bigrams/Trigrams and 5% for Skipgrams). We make sure to not replace any rare base characters like Q or @.

For ablations (Section 5.2) with limited compute budget, we train Hi-En models for up to 200K steps.We apply a patience of 10 validations, each 1000 update steps apart. To decode, we average the best 3 checkpoints, and use a beam size of 4 with length penalty of 0.6. We use NLCodec and RTG libraries (Gowda et al., 2021) and contribute our extensions to them as well.

5 Results and Discussion

Table 2 shows our main results. We find that naively extending BPE beyond words harms the model, and Unigram likewise fails to consistently outperform the baseline. On the other hand, adding MWEs using PMI gives the best performance across language pairs and metrics.

Moreover, since the methods of extracting MWEs is purely emprirical and is language agnostic, the results and observations can be extended for different language pairs.

We now attempt to reason why BPE fails beyond word boundaries in its vanilla form, and why switching to PMI solves the problem. We also study where does it help the most to add MWEs. Unless noted otherwise, the analysis is reported on the Hi-En dataset.

5.1 Words combine in Diverse ways

Empirically, we observe (Table 2) that BPE with high frequency MWE tokens sees a drop in performance whereas the PMI counterpart as well as the original baseline (within word boundary) performs

	Train	Dev	Test
Hi-En	IITB-Training (1.3M)	IITB-Dev (0.5K)	IITB-Test (2.5K)
De-En	Europarl v10 (1.8M) WMT13CommonCrawl (2.4M) NewsCommentary v14 (0.3M)	NewsTest18 (3K)	NewsTest19 (2K)

Table 3: Training, validation and testing datasets along with sentence count in each set.

	from Hi-En to De-En	from De-En to Hi-En
Bi	1.55%	1.30%
Tri	0.30%	0.40%
Skip	**13.34%**	**13.45%**

Bigrams	Trigrams	Skip-Grams	Freq
per cent	New York City	the · of	of the
New York	European Central Bank	a · of	do not
Prime Minister	Italian Prime Minister	(·)	they are
Middle East	behind closed doors	was · to	as well as
United Nations	former Prime Minister	not · to	one of the

Table 4: **Left**: Coverage of the top 5 most frequent English MWEs (PMI-based), extracted from the first language pair and (coverage) evaluated over the second. Coverage of a token is defined as the fraction of target (English) sentences containing the token. **Right**: The top five MWEs of each type (PMI except when labelled Freq).

well. What then happens at the word boundary that the BPE algorithm stops working? We hypothesize that this is the result of words combining in more diverse ways than subwords.

BPE beyond word boundary adds frequently occurring n-grams to its vocabulary such as in_the which occurs in over a tenth of all test sentences. Despite adding it as a separate token to the vocabulary, the average BLEU on this subset of test sentences drops compared to the baseline (20.0 vs 21.8)! One factor for this result could be that the constituents of in_the combine in more ways than one. The word in appears as the ending of over 30 n-grams ($that\_in$, was_in, ...) and the word the appears as the beginning of 200 other n-grams (the_people, the_first, ...) - all of which combine to a total of over another tenth of the test set, more than the frequency of in_the itself.

Such versatile combinatorics is rarely observed at the subword level. Suffixes like ing almost never appear as prefixes whereas prefixes like de almost never appear as suffixes. When such subwords combine to form longer tokens, they generally retain a coherent meaning, unlike n-grams like in_the. Finally, this hypothesis may explain why MWEs ordered by PMI help improve MT scores – they are by definition units that co-occur as a coherent unit. Indeed, the MWEs thus found (e.g. New_York, per_cent) include constituents which exclusively form only these tokens.

To summarize, we argue that BPE stops working at word boundaries because word pairs rarely, unlike subwords, combine into meaningful units that deserve a unique representation. We find convincing arguments from sentence-level BLEU scores and the number of different ways the constituents of different tokens occur, more of which are reported in supplementary materials.

5.2 Where do MWEs help NMT?

Here, we conduct ablations for the PMI method (on a smaller batch size of 1K tokens, on the Hi-En dataset) to determine whether MWEs help more for machine translation on the source side (Hi), on the target side (En), or both? Table 2 reports on the 'both' setting but here we revisit this design choice. Table 5 reports BLEU scores with each such variant. Bold-faced cells indicate the best performing (on dev set) variant for every row. We observe that continuous MWEs (bigrams and trigrams) benefit more on the source-side whereas discontinuous MWEs (skip-grams) help the most when applied to both source and target side. Note that, since De-En has been usually used in a triple shared vocabulary setting, we followed the same and thereby it must always follow the 'both' model.

Finally, we show in Figure 1 some representative examples of sentences with MWEs (particularly, the skip-grams) from the PMI-BPE Hi-En model's vocabulary. The first two rows show examples where the skip-gram indeed occurred in the reference, hence it helped the model. The last row shows how the model overuses the skip-gram, i.e. using skip-gram instead of separate tokens, and gets a

Source	Reference	Baseline	Skip-Gram	Helps/ Hurts?
यह परियोजना पूरे यूरोपीय महाद्वीप की ऊर्जा सुरक्षा का एक मुख्य तत्व है।	**This** project **is** a key element of energy security of the whole European continent.	The project is a major element of the energy security of the entire European continent.	**This** project **is** the main element of energy security of the entire European continent.	Helps
यह पुरस्कार व्यापक रूप से ...	**This** award **is** widely considered the ...	The award is widely recognized as the ...	**This** award **is** widely regarded as the ...	Helps
यह क्षेत्र एक ... से भरा हुआ है, ...	The area is filled with ...	The region is filled with a ...	**This** area **is** full of ...	Hurts

Figure 1: Qualitative error analysis over Hi-En test set, showing examples comparing the Baseline and the Skip-Gram augmented model, where the skip-gram **(This · is)** occurs in the latter's predictions.

	Target (En)	Source (Hi)	Both
Bi	14.4 / 14.8	**15.9 / 16.0**	15.8 / 15.3
Tri	14.7 / 15.4	**15.5 / 15.5**	15.4 / 15.2
Skip	15.3 / 15.2	15.1 / 15.1	**15.5 / 15.0**

Table 5: Do MWEs help more when added to the source-side, the target-side or both? Each cell reports Dev/Test BLEU scores over Hi-En dataset only. Baseline scores without MWEs are 15.6 / 14.4 respectively.

translation wrong thus hurting the score as the reference sentence does not use the skip-gram. We note that BLEU itself relies only on the presence or absence of contiguous n-grams, and may unfairly penalize paraphrased outputs such as these.

6 Related Work

Attempts at merging NMT with MWEs typically include pairing up the network with a phrase based SMT system (Wang et al., 2017; Park and Tsvetkov, 2019; Lample et al., 2018) and hierarchical phrases are expressive enough to cover discontinuous MWEs (Chiang, 2007). Zaninello and Birch (2020) add manually annotated MWEs aligned across the source and target language (En-It). However, this might not work for low resource languages, hence we extract MWEs automatically with PMI. They count discontinuous MWEs, one of our main contributions, among future work.

Multi-word tokens have a proven track record in NLP. Skip-gram tokens, for instance, have already been used in phrase-based machine translation (Lample et al., 2018; Park and Tsvetkov, 2019; Wang et al., 2017) to tackle cases where certain phrases in a source language (*duonianlai* in Chinese) are better represented as skip-grams in a target language (*over the last · years* in English) (Chiang, 2007). Our work revisits these ideas and adapts them to a transformer-based NLP model relying on subword segmentation. There also exists prior work on defining, counting, and evaluating k-skip-n-grams (Guthrie et al., 2006; Pickhardt et al., 2014; Ptaszynski et al., 2014), although unrelated to the task of NMT. Finally, readers interested in other applications of extracting MWEs via PMI scores may refer to Levine et al. (2021) where similar techniques are used to efficiently mask tokens while pretraining BERT (Devlin et al., 2019).

7 Conclusion

This paper systematically studies the impact of extending a BPE vocabulary with multi-word expressions for neural machine translation. Our results point to the vast unexplored scope of different granularities of tokenization that can be exploited by NLP systems. Notably, our methods extend to not only longer contiguous tokens like n-grams but also skip-grams, which have been relatively unexplored with transformer-based NLP.

In future work, we intend to compare our PMI-based methods to human-annotated MWEs as well as to recent workarounds to interfering tokenization schemes such as subword regularization or BPE dropout (Provilkov et al., 2020). We also wish to extend experiments to NLP tasks beyond NMT, and the scope of our tokens to, say, variable-skip-grams which allow for any number of skips.

References

Loïc Barrault, Ondřej Bojar, Marta R. Costa-jussà, Christian Federmann, Mark Fishel, Yvette Graham, Barry Haddow, Matthias Huck, Philipp Koehn, Shervin Malmasi, Christof Monz, Mathias Müller, Santanu Pal, Matt Post, and Marcos Zampieri. 2019. Findings of the 2019 conference on machine translation (WMT19). In *Proceedings of the Fourth Con-*

ference on Machine Translation (Volume 2: Shared Task Papers, Day 1)*, pages 1–61, Florence, Italy. Association for Computational Linguistics.

Jan A. Botha and Phil Blunsom. 2013. Adaptor Grammars for learning non-concatenative morphology. In *Proceedings of the 2013 Conference on Empirical Methods in Natural Language Processing*, pages 345–356, Seattle, Washington, USA. Association for Computational Linguistics.

David Chiang. 2007. Hierarchical phrase-based translation. *Computational Linguistics*, 33(2):201–228.

Jacob Devlin, Ming-Wei Chang, Kenton Lee, and Kristina Toutanova. 2019. BERT: Pre-training of deep bidirectional transformers for language understanding. In *Proceedings of the 2019 Conference of the North American Chapter of the Association for Computational Linguistics: Human Language Technologies, Volume 1 (Long and Short Papers)*, pages 4171–4186, Minneapolis, Minnesota. Association for Computational Linguistics.

Thamme Gowda and Jonathan May. 2020. Finding the optimal vocabulary size for neural machine translation. In *Findings of the Association for Computational Linguistics: EMNLP 2020*, pages 3955–3964, Online. Association for Computational Linguistics.

Thamme Gowda, Zhao Zhang, Chris A Mattmann, and Jonathan May. 2021. Many-to-english machine translation tools, data, and pretrained models.

David Guthrie, Ben Allison, Wei Liu, Louise Guthrie, and Yorick Wilks. 2006. A closer look at skip-gram modelling. In *Proceedings of the Fifth International Conference on Language Resources and Evaluation (LREC'06)*, Genoa, Italy. European Language Resources Association (ELRA).

Philipp Koehn, Hieu Hoang, Alexandra Birch, Chris Callison-Burch, Marcello Federico, Nicola Bertoldi, Brooke Cowan, Wade Shen, Christine Moran, Richard Zens, Chris Dyer, Ondřej Bojar, Alexandra Constantin, and Evan Herbst. 2007. Moses: Open source toolkit for statistical machine translation. In *Proceedings of the 45th Annual Meeting of the Association for Computational Linguistics Companion Volume Proceedings of the Demo and Poster Sessions*, pages 177–180, Prague, Czech Republic. Association for Computational Linguistics.

Taku Kudo. 2018. Subword regularization: Improving neural network translation models with multiple subword candidates. In *Proceedings of the 56th Annual Meeting of the Association for Computational Linguistics (Volume 1: Long Papers)*, pages 66–75, Melbourne, Australia. Association for Computational Linguistics.

Taku Kudo and John Richardson. 2018. SentencePiece: A simple and language independent subword tokenizer and detokenizer for neural text processing. In *Proceedings of the 2018 Conference on Empirical Methods in Natural Language Processing: System Demonstrations*, pages 66–71, Brussels, Belgium. Association for Computational Linguistics.

Anoop Kunchukuttan. 2020. The IndicNLP Library. `https://github.com/anoopkunchukuttan/indic_nlp_library/blob/master/docs/indicnlp.pdf`.

Anoop Kunchukuttan, Pratik Mehta, and Pushpak Bhattacharyya. 2018. The IIT Bombay English-Hindi parallel corpus. In *Proceedings of the Eleventh International Conference on Language Resources and Evaluation (LREC 2018)*, Miyazaki, Japan. European Language Resources Association (ELRA).

Guillaume Lample, Myle Ott, Alexis Conneau, Ludovic Denoyer, and Marc'Aurelio Ranzato. 2018. Phrase-based & neural unsupervised machine translation. In *Proceedings of the 2018 Conference on Empirical Methods in Natural Language Processing*, pages 5039–5049, Brussels, Belgium. Association for Computational Linguistics.

Yoav Levine, Barak Lenz, Opher Lieber, Omri Abend, Kevin Leyton-Brown, Moshe Tennenholtz, and Yoav Shoham. 2021. {PMI}-masking: Principled masking of correlated spans. In *International Conference on Learning Representations*.

Chan Young Park and Yulia Tsvetkov. 2019. Learning to generate word- and phrase-embeddings for efficient phrase-based neural machine translation. In *Proceedings of the 3rd Workshop on Neural Generation and Translation*, pages 241–248, Hong Kong. Association for Computational Linguistics.

Rene Pickhardt, Thomas Gottron, Martin Körner, Paul Georg Wagner, Till Speicher, and Steffen Staab. 2014. A generalized language model as the combination of skipped n-grams and modified Kneser Ney smoothing. In *Proceedings of the 52nd Annual Meeting of the Association for Computational Linguistics (Volume 1: Long Papers)*, pages 1145–1154, Baltimore, Maryland. Association for Computational Linguistics.

Maja Popović. 2015. chrF: character n-gram F-score for automatic MT evaluation. In *Proceedings of the Tenth Workshop on Statistical Machine Translation*, pages 392–395, Lisbon, Portugal. Association for Computational Linguistics.

Matt Post. 2018. A call for clarity in reporting BLEU scores. In *Proceedings of the Third Conference on Machine Translation: Research Papers*, pages 186–191, Brussels, Belgium. Association for Computational Linguistics.

Ivan Provilkov, Dmitrii Emelianenko, and Elena Voita. 2020. BPE-dropout: Simple and effective subword regularization. In *Proceedings of the 58th Annual Meeting of the Association for Computational Linguistics*, pages 1882–1892, Online. Association for Computational Linguistics.

Michal Ptaszynski, Fumito Masui, Rafal Rzepka, and Kenji Araki. 2014. First glance on pattern-based language modeling. *Language Acquisition and Understanding Research Group Technical Reports*.

Michal Ptaszynski, Rafal Rzepka, and Yoshio Momouchi. 2011. Language combinatorics: A sentence pattern extraction architecture based on combinatorial explosion. *International Journal of Computational Linguistics*, 2(1):24–36.

Rico Sennrich, Barry Haddow, and Alexandra Birch. 2016. Neural machine translation of rare words with subword units. In *Proceedings of the 54th Annual Meeting of the Association for Computational Linguistics (Volume 1: Long Papers)*, pages 1715–1725, Berlin, Germany. Association for Computational Linguistics.

Ashish Vaswani, Noam Shazeer, Niki Parmar, Jakob Uszkoreit, Llion Jones, Aidan N Gomez, Łukasz Kaiser, and Illia Polosukhin. 2017. Attention is all you need. In *Advances in neural information processing systems*, pages 5998–6008.

Xing Wang, Zhaopeng Tu, Deyi Xiong, and Min Zhang. 2017. Translating phrases in neural machine translation. In *Proceedings of the 2017 Conference on Empirical Methods in Natural Language Processing*, pages 1421–1431, Copenhagen, Denmark. Association for Computational Linguistics.

Andrea Zaninello and Alexandra Birch. 2020. Multiword expression aware neural machine translation. In *Proceedings of the 12th Language Resources and Evaluation Conference*, pages 3816–3825, Marseille, France. European Language Resources Association.

A Visualizing the top-scoring MWEs

We already report highest scoring English MWEs throughout the paper, particularly in Table 4. In Figure 2, we enumerate similarly the highest scoring bigrams, trigrams, and skip-grams from the other two languages: German and Hindi.

B Scope of MWEs

As the name suggests, MWEs include only word level expressions i.e., *each constituent should be a whole word.* This is a less expressive but more intuitive approach to going beyond word boundaries with BPE. For example, our implementation does not allow for tokens that combine the ending of one word and the beginning of another.

Note that our implementation also allows for variable length skip-grams (Ptaszynski et al., 2011), represented as $(w_1 * w_2)$. Instead of skipping a single token, we can allow skipping any number of tokens and still map to the same skip-gram, e.g., *neither ∗ nor → neither do I drink nor do I smoke.* Such tokens would be much more expressive but also much computationally expensive to find, and would require some simplifying assumptions such as disallowing nested skip-grams. We leave such experiments to future work.

Note that we do not merge bigrams, trigrams, and skip-grams. PMI scores across n-grams and skip-grams are not comparable, hence they can not be combined in a straightforward way. Such an amalgamation may indeed give an even bigger boost but requires grid search over multiple hyperparameters corresponding to the fraction of each kind of MWE to be included. Such experiments warrant an extensive compute budget, so we leave this to future work.

We wish to implement even newer forms of tokenization, particularly extending skip-gram tokens. While this paper limits skip-grams to only act at the word level, one could also imagine character or subword level skip-grams, such as *r-n* serving as a skip-gram common to both *run* and *ran*. Finally, k-skip-n-gram tokens need not be limited to a fixed k, allowing for a variable number of tokens to be skipped, similar to a hierarchical phrase translation system (Chiang, 2007). Such variable length skips can also be useful at the character level, e.g., *k-t-b* as a skip-gram for both *kitaab* and *kutub* (Botha and Blunsom, 2013).

German			Hindi		
Bi/Tri Grams (Freq)	Bi/Tri Grams (PMI)	Skip-Grams	Bi/Tri Grams (Freq)	Bi/Tri grams (PMI)	Skip-Grams
in der	Vereinten Nationen	die • des	के लिए	मोबाइल फोन	का • किया
zu den	ums Leben	bis • Prozent	नहीं किया	क्रेडिट कार्ड	कोई • नहीं
in Bezug auf	kurze Zeit später	Zwischen • und	जिन लोगों ने	सुभाष चन्द्र बोस	इस • में

Figure 2: Top scoring multi-word expressions extracted from the training corpora.

Pre-trained language models evaluating themselves - A comparative study

Philipp Koch♣ **Matthias Aßenmacher**♠ **Christian Heumann**♠

Department of Statistics
Ludwig-Maximilians-Universität
Ludwigstr. 33, D-80539 Munich, Germany
♣P.Koch@campus.lmu.de, ♠{matthias,chris}@stat.uni-muenchen.de

Abstract

Evaluating generated text received new attention with the introduction of model-based metrics in recent years. These new metrics have a higher correlation with human judgments and seemingly overcome many issues of previous n-gram based metrics from the symbolic age. In this work, we examine the recently introduced metrics BERTScore, BLEURT, NUBIA, MoverScore, and Mark-Evaluate (Petersen). We investigate their sensitivity to different types of semantic deterioration (part of speech drop and negation), word order perturbations, word drop, and the common problem of repetition. No metric showed appropriate behaviour for negation, and further none of them was overall sensitive to the other issues mentioned above.

1 Introduction

Alongside with the current developments in Natural Language Generation (NLG), evaluating the quality of artificially generated text is an equally important (and ever harder) task in the field. N-gram based metrics, like BLEU (Papineni et al., 2002) or ROUGE (Lin, 2004), come with severe drawbacks (Belz and Reiter, 2006; Reiter and Belz, 2009) and given the increasing versatility of modern NLG systems, they are assumed to struggle even more (Zhang et al., 2020; Sellam et al., 2020). Architectures based on the Transformer (Vaswani et al., 2017), like BERT (Devlin et al., 2019) or the complete GPT series (Radford et al., 2018, 2019; Brown et al., 2020), have increased the quality of artificially generated text to an extent that even humans tend to struggle distinguishing natural from artificial texts (Clark et al., 2021). Based on these models, new metrics have been introduced, such as BERTScore (Zhang et al., 2020), BLEURT (Sellam et al., 2020), NUBIA (Kane et al., 2020), MoverScore (Zhao et al., 2019), or Mark-Evaluate (Mordido and Meinel, 2020), claiming to increase correlation with human judgment. We examine the latter introduced metrics using synthetic data. The examination will include several practical problems commonly observed in NLG systems. The code to reproduce our experiments is publicly available on GitHub.[1]

2 Related work

Caglayan et al. (2020) compared different metrics, including BERTScore, regarding their sensitivity to specific impairments. Their experiment (related, but not similar to ours) indicated that BERTScore is more sensitive to the semantic integrity than n-gram based metrics. Another analysis by Kaster et al. (2021) provides an evaluation of model-based metrics based on linguistic properties of their input. They showed that even model-based metrics tend to behave differently regarding specific modifications to their input. Some metrics showed a higher sensitivity to semantics, while others showed higher sensitivity to syntactic issues. Eventually, ensembling methods were proposed to combine the strengths of metrics. Based on the CheckList library (Ribeiro et al., 2020), Sai et al. (2021) introduced a library for assessing NLG metrics via different perturbations to the input data. Multiple metrics, including model-based ones, were assessed, and neither of them did show a proper *overall* sensitivity to *all* modifications. The most severe issue was found in an overall insensitivity to negation. In contrast to Sai et al. (2021), our work focuses on examining different degrees of perturbations and how metrics reflect these modifications towards maximal impairment. Sai et al. (2021) further underline the criticism of evaluating metrics according to their correlation with human judgments, which was already criticized in an in-depth analysis by Mathur et al. (2020) about applying correlation as an evaluation measure. Furthermore, our work does not focus on correlation but solely on the scores which

[1] https://github.com/LazerLambda/MetricsComparison

Proceedings of the Third Workshop on Insights from Negative Results in NLP, pages 180 - 187
May 26, 2022 ©2022 Association for Computational Linguistics

the different metrics report when confronted with specific impairments to various degrees, how metrics behave in contrast to BLEU when a particular part of speech is dropped, and how these metrics react to negated sentences.

3 Materials and Methods

The metrics examined in this work are BERTScore (Zhang et al., 2020), BLEURT (Sellam et al., 2020), NUBIA (Kane et al., 2020), Mark-Evaluate Petersen (ME-P) (Mordido and Meinel, 2020), and MoverScore (Zhao et al., 2019). As a baseline, the BLEU score is always computed as well. The examined metrics can be subdivided into model-based metrics and metrics as trained models. NUBIA and BLEURT are trained models for evaluating generated text, while the other metrics are computed using specific formulas incorporating language models. Detailed descriptions of the metrics are provided in Appendix A. Additionally to describing the respective metric, an exact specification of the setup and model-specific details are reported in Appendix B.

4 Experiments

For all our experiments we used the CNN/Daily Mail data set (Hermann et al., 2015) from `huggingface.datasets` as a reference corpus. Since it represents a corpus of high-quality news articles, it is ideally suited to use the scores of its original sentences as an upper bound for the evaluated metrics. The data set is in English entirely, i.e. all our findings do not necessarily transfer to other languages. We randomly sampled 2000 texts from this corpus for all of the models, except for NUBIA and ME-P.[2] Resulting scores from artificial impairments of different degrees can subsequently be compared to this upper bound. The modifications[3] include the following different commonly observed flaws in NLG systems and the underlying language models:

Word Swap Random word pairs are chosen and swapped. The higher the intensity, the more random the sequence of tokens becomes, such that the original sequence should not be recognizable anymore. This approach was inspired by Mordido and Meinel (2020) and Semeniuta et al. (2019).

[2]NUBIA and ME-P are not optimized for use with GPUs, which is why we resorted to only using 50 of the 2000 texts.

[3]Examples for each of the different modifications are provided in Appendix C.

Word Drop A random drop of words mimics general quality deterioration. The larger the intensity, the larger the drop probability gets. At the highest level, only a few tokens are left. Similar to word swap, this task was inspired by Mordido and Meinel (2020) and Semeniuta et al. (2019).

Repetition As shown by Fu et al. (2021), repetition remains a problem in text generated by NLG systems. A sequence at the end of the sentence is chosen and repeatedly added to the sentence to mimic this issue. With increasing intensity, the chosen sequence is repeated more often and the overall sentence becomes longer. At the maximum degree, the sequence is repeated as many times as there are tokens in the reference sentence.

Negation Sentences were negated to change the semantics severely. A simple syntactic change of the sentence has the power to shift the semantics in an entirely different direction. The CheckList library's (Ribeiro et al., 2020) experimental[4] negation function was utilized to apply this change. Specifically, the root of the dependency grammar tree is negated. This task was also used in the work of Sai et al. (2021).

POS-Drop Words with different part-of-speech (POS) tags were dropped to examine how the metrics behave when different kinds of words are removed. We assume for our experiment that some part-of-speech units like determiners have less influence over the semantic integrity than the removal of verbs, nouns, or adjectives. SpaCy (Honnibal et al., 2020) and NLTK (Bird et al., 2009) were used to execute the different POS drops. The semantic-invariant and n-gram-based BLEU score is computed for each impairment, which we then use for displaying the changes relative to modern metrics. (cf. Fig. 2).

5 Results

We expected to see a strict monotonous decrease for the impairments with increasing degree of severity. For Negation we expected a sharp drop due to the deterioration of semantic meaning. In the case of POS-Drop, the loss of rather unimportant POS (DET) should intuitively not lead to more damage to the semantic integrity than the drop of important POS (NOUN, VERB, ADJ), which is expected to be reported by the metrics as well. Furthermore,

[4]See the respective notebook on GitHub.

Figure 1: Development of the different metrics with increasing degrees of impairment

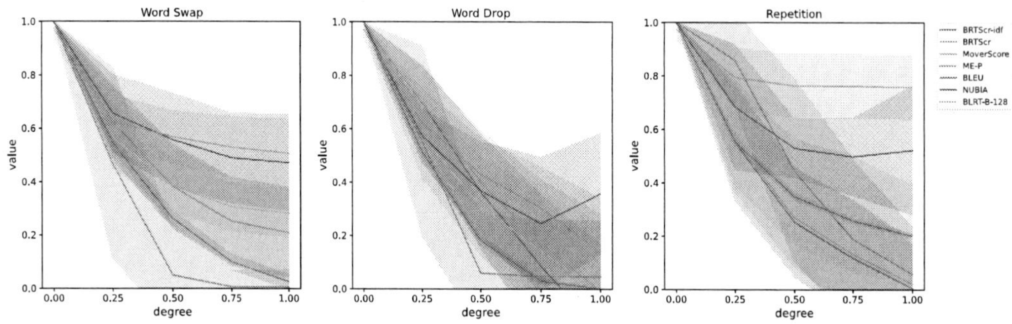

the loss of different words should be reasonably comparable to BLEU.

Results for continuous impairments (word drop, word swap and repetition) are displayed in Figure 1, while negation and POS drop are shown in Figure 2. For each type of impairment, we will report the most striking observations.

Word Swap While BLEU exhibits, as expected, a steady drop to almost zero, some metrics tend to report higher values even when all words are swapped and the order is essentially random. NUBIA and BLEURT both have minimum values above 0.4, while MoverScore and BERTScore yield values above 0.2 for the highest degree of impairment. In contrast to this behavior, ME Petersen is most sensitive to word order perturbation and shows a sharp decline. It already drops to 0.47 at the first level of word order perturbation and reports a score of 0.01 for the random permutation.

Word Drop In this task, BLEU, MoverScore, BERTScore, and ME-P drop continuously until they eventually all (nearly) reach zero. ME-P again drops the fastest, similar to the Word Swap but stops at 0.05. A different behavior, however, can be observed for BLEURT and NUBIA, which again exhibit higher values compared to the rest. BLEURT eventually drops to 0.14, and NUBIA even increases from its lowest value at the third level of impairment of 0.24 to 0.36 at the last level.

Repetition A less uniform behavior is observed for the repetition impairment, where the values strongly diverge at the highest level. Both BERTScore metrics monotonically decrease until they eventually reach zero, ME-P also finally drops to a value near zero (0.06). However, it does not monotonically decrease, but drops sharply after the first level. BLEU and MoverScore both monotonically decrease strictly but end up way above zero at around 0.2. BLEURT and NUBIA behave entirely different, such that BLEURT seems to converge to 0.76 from the second level onward and does not show proper sensitivity to this issue, while NUBIA again increases after the third level from 0.5 to 0.52.

POS-Drop The most exceptional deviation from BLEU is observed in the removal of determiners (cf. Fig. 2). Most metrics (BERTScore, ME-P, BLEURT, and NUBIA) deviate positively from the reference, implying that the loss of determiner is less critical for the score, as expected. Adjectives, nouns, and verbs did affect metrics in different directions. Furthermore, BERTScore consistently reported higher values than BLEU.

Negation Since negation is a severe impairment to semantics, a significant drop in reported values was expected. However, the lowest reported score was observed in NUBIA, which dropped to an average of 0.65. BLEURT scores the second-lowest at an average of 0.77. All other metrics report an average between 0.81 and 0.86, including BLEU.

6 Discussion

Regarding word order perturbation, repetition, and word drop, it was expected to see a strict monotonous decline in the reported scores, which was not met by a single metric in every task (although ME-P came close to meeting the expectations). However, at least one metric dropped to a value of zero or close to zero for every task. A crucial result is a metric-dependent sensitivity to word order perturbations and repetition. Especially for NUBIA and BLEURT, two trained metrics, the

Figure 2: Average Deviations (incl. Standard deviations) for all metrics relative to BLEU (for POS-Drop) and Boxplots for the impact of Negation on all metrics.

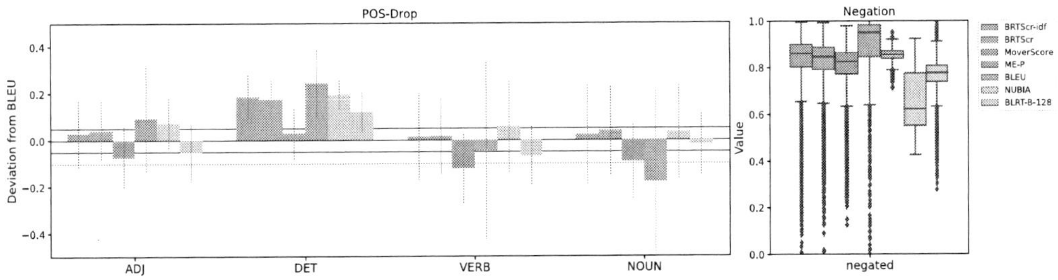

observed behavior is alarming. A further investigation of why both architectures behave differently from other representation-only-based metrics is thus needed in the future.

Our POS-drop task showed that some tokens influence scores more than others. Notably, the removal of determiners, which was expected not to influence the semantic integrity, did not lower the scores of most metrics compared to BLEU. However, the syntactic integrity is affected, which must be considered when interpreting respective metrics. Semantic-focused behavior like this was also shown in Kaster et al. (2021) and was indicated by Caglayan et al. (2020) regarding BERTScore. No uniform behavior in most metrics was seen for removing verbs, nouns, and adjectives. However, sensitivity to semantic integrity is bound by the underlying model's capabilities, as observed in our negation task. No metric reported a proper value for the severe semantic modification of negation, which aligns with Sai et al. (2021). The work of Kassner and Schütze (2020) and Ettinger (2020) already examined BERT regarding its understanding of negation, and they showed a general lack of understanding of the concept of negation.

The most significant limitation of this work is the lack of expected ideal behavior when metrics are confronted with modified samples. It should be suspected that metrics show a higher drop in quality over more severe modifications, though it is unclear how humans would evaluate these specific cases. This issue is especially crucial in the task of negation since on the one hand side, it is not clear how severe the metrics are intended to reflect the impaired input, and on the other hand side it is also unclear how humans would rate negated sentences compared to the original sample. Consequently, the lack of human evaluation has to be considered when interpreting the results of this work. The same issue must be stated for POS-Drop tasks, in which human evaluation also becomes crucial. Further, it has to be taken into consideration that we use a feature described as experimental by its creators[5] for negating the sentences. Another arising issue, in this case, might be the rather long and detailed sentence structure of news article sentences, where the algorithm might be prone to negate only parts of the sentences. This issue might also arise for the POS-Drop case, since some POS units might occur more often in this data set than in other text.

7 Conclusion & Future work

Our results additionally underline that model-based metrics should be used with caution. The most severe drawback is the lack of sensitivity to negation, for which no metric reported a proper value. Hence further research in natural language understanding is necessary to overcome this issue. Furthermore, state-of-the-art metrics like BLEURT and NUBIA lacked sensitivity to repetition, which is a severe issue in NLG. Although many metrics deviated from the expected behavior, some others did not. Thus, we endorse the proposal of Kaster et al. (2021) to ensemble metrics, since some showed strengths where others showed weaknesses, and validate against the perturbation checklist package Sai et al. (2021).

[5]See the respective notebook on GitHub.

References

Anja Belz and Ehud Reiter. 2006. Comparing automatic and human evaluation of NLG systems. In *11th Conference of the European Chapter of the Association for Computational Linguistics*, Trento, Italy. Association for Computational Linguistics.

Steven Bird, Ewan Klein, and Edward Loper. 2009. *Natural language processing with Python: analyzing text with the natural language toolkit.* " O'Reilly Media, Inc.".

Tom B. Brown, Benjamin Mann, Nick Ryder, Melanie Subbiah, Jared Kaplan, Prafulla Dhariwal, Arvind Neelakantan, Pranav Shyam, Girish Sastry, Amanda Askell, Sandhini Agarwal, Ariel Herbert-Voss, Gretchen Krueger, Tom Henighan, Rewon Child, Aditya Ramesh, Daniel M. Ziegler, Jeffrey Wu, Clemens Winter, Christopher Hesse, Mark Chen, Eric Sigler, Mateusz Litwin, Scott Gray, Benjamin Chess, Jack Clark, Christopher Berner, Sam McCandlish, Alec Radford, Ilya Sutskever, and Dario Amodei. 2020. Language models are few-shot learners.

Ozan Caglayan, Pranava Madhyastha, and Lucia Specia. 2020. Curious case of language generation evaluation metrics: A cautionary tale. In *Proceedings of the 28th International Conference on Computational Linguistics*, pages 2322–2328, Barcelona, Spain (Online). International Committee on Computational Linguistics.

Daniel Cer, Mona Diab, Eneko Agirre, Iñigo Lopez-Gazpio, and Lucia Specia. 2017. SemEval-2017 task 1: Semantic textual similarity multilingual and crosslingual focused evaluation. In *Proceedings of the 11th International Workshop on Semantic Evaluation (SemEval-2017)*, pages 1–14, Vancouver, Canada. Association for Computational Linguistics.

Hyung Won Chung, Thibault Févry, Henry Tsai, Melvin Johnson, and Sebastian Ruder. 2020. Rethinking embedding coupling in pre-trained language models.

Elizabeth Clark, Tal August, Sofia Serrano, Nikita Haduong, Suchin Gururangan, and Noah A. Smith. 2021. All that's 'human' is not gold: Evaluating human evaluation of generated text. In *Proceedings of the 59th Annual Meeting of the Association for Computational Linguistics and the 11th International Joint Conference on Natural Language Processing (Volume 1: Long Papers)*, pages 7282–7296, Online. Association for Computational Linguistics.

Jacob Devlin, Ming-Wei Chang, Kenton Lee, and Kristina Toutanova. 2019. BERT: Pre-training of deep bidirectional transformers for language understanding. In *Proceedings of the 2019 Conference of the North American Chapter of the Association for Computational Linguistics: Human Language Technologies, Volume 1 (Long and Short Papers)*, pages 4171–4186, Minneapolis, Minnesota. Association for Computational Linguistics.

Allyson Ettinger. 2020. What BERT is not: Lessons from a new suite of psycholinguistic diagnostics for language models. *Transactions of the Association for Computational Linguistics*, 8:34–48.

Zihao Fu, Wai Lam, Anthony Man-Cho So, and Bei Shi. 2021. A theoretical analysis of the repetition problem in text generation.

Karl Moritz Hermann, Tomás Kociský, Edward Grefenstette, Lasse Espeholt, Will Kay, Mustafa Suleyman, and Phil Blunsom. 2015. Teaching machines to read and comprehend. In *NIPS*, pages 1693–1701.

Matthew Honnibal, Ines Montani, Sofie Van Landeghem, and Adriane Boyd. 2020. spaCy: Industrial-strength Natural Language Processing in Python.

Hassan Kane, Muhammed Yusuf Kocyigit, Ali Abdalla, Pelkins Ajanoh, and Mohamed Coulibali. 2020. NUBIA: NeUral based interchangeability assessor for text generation. In *Proceedings of the 1st Workshop on Evaluating NLG Evaluation*, pages 28–37, Online (Dublin, Ireland). Association for Computational Linguistics.

Nora Kassner and Hinrich Schütze. 2020. Negated and misprimed probes for pretrained language models: Birds can talk, but cannot fly. In *Proceedings of the 58th Annual Meeting of the Association for Computational Linguistics*, pages 7811–7818, Online. Association for Computational Linguistics.

Marvin Kaster, Wei Zhao, and Steffen Eger. 2021. Global explainability of BERT-based evaluation metrics by disentangling along linguistic factors. In *Proceedings of the 2021 Conference on Empirical Methods in Natural Language Processing*, pages 8912–8925, Online and Punta Cana, Dominican Republic. Association for Computational Linguistics.

Matt J. Kusner, Yu Sun, Nicholas I. Kolkin, and Kilian Q. Weinberger. 2015. From word embeddings to document distances. In *Proceedings of the 32nd International Conference on International Conference on Machine Learning - Volume 37*, ICML'15, page 957–966. JMLR.org.

Chin-Yew Lin. 2004. ROUGE: A package for automatic evaluation of summaries. In *Text Summarization Branches Out*, pages 74–81, Barcelona, Spain. Association for Computational Linguistics.

Yinhan Liu, Myle Ott, Naman Goyal, Jingfei Du, Mandar Joshi, Danqi Chen, Omer Levy, Mike Lewis, Luke Zettlemoyer, and Veselin Stoyanov. 2019. Roberta: A robustly optimized bert pretraining approach.

Nitika Mathur, Timothy Baldwin, and Trevor Cohn. 2020. Tangled up in BLEU: Reevaluating the evaluation of automatic machine translation evaluation metrics. In *Proceedings of the 58th Annual Meeting of the Association for Computational Linguistics*, pages 4984–4997, Online. Association for Computational Linguistics.

Gonçalo Mordido and Christoph Meinel. 2020. Mark-evaluate: Assessing language generation using population estimation methods. In *Proceedings of the 28th International Conference on Computational Linguistics*, pages 1963–1977, Barcelona, Spain (Online). International Committee on Computational Linguistics.

Kishore Papineni, Salim Roukos, Todd Ward, and Wei-Jing Zhu. 2002. Bleu: a method for automatic evaluation of machine translation. In *Proceedings of the 40th Annual Meeting of the Association for Computational Linguistics*, pages 311–318, Philadelphia, Pennsylvania, USA. Association for Computational Linguistics.

Alec Radford, Karthik Narasimhan, Tim Salimans, and Ilya Sutskever. 2018. Improving language understanding by generative pre-training.

Alec Radford, Jeff Wu, Rewon Child, David Luan, Dario Amodei, and Ilya Sutskever. 2019. Language models are unsupervised multitask learners.

Ehud Reiter and Anja Belz. 2009. An investigation into the validity of some metrics for automatically evaluating natural language generation systems. *Computational Linguistics*, 35(4):529–558.

Marco Tulio Ribeiro, Tongshuang Wu, Carlos Guestrin, and Sameer Singh. 2020. Beyond accuracy: Behavioral testing of NLP models with CheckList. In *Proceedings of the 58th Annual Meeting of the Association for Computational Linguistics*, pages 4902–4912, Online. Association for Computational Linguistics.

William Edwin Ricker. 1975. Computation and interpretation of biological statistics of fish populations. *Bull. Fish. Res. Bd. Can.*, 191:1–382.

Yossi Rubner, Carlo Tomasi, and Leonidas Guibas. 2000. The earth mover's distance as a metric for image retrieval. *International Journal of Computer Vision*, 40:99–121.

Ananya B. Sai, Tanay Dixit, Dev Yashpal Sheth, Sreyas Mohan, and Mitesh M. Khapra. 2021. Perturbation CheckLists for evaluating NLG evaluation metrics. In *Proceedings of the 2021 Conference on Empirical Methods in Natural Language Processing*, pages 7219–7234, Online and Punta Cana, Dominican Republic. Association for Computational Linguistics.

Victor Sanh, Lysandre Debut, Julien Chaumond, and Thomas Wolf. 2020. Distilbert, a distilled version of bert: smaller, faster, cheaper and lighter.

Thibault Sellam, Dipanjan Das, and Ankur Parikh. 2020. BLEURT: Learning robust metrics for text generation. In *Proceedings of the 58th Annual Meeting of the Association for Computational Linguistics*, pages 7881–7892, Online. Association for Computational Linguistics.

Stanislau Semeniuta, Aliaksei Severyn, and Sylvain Gelly. 2019. On accurate evaluation of gans for language generation.

Ashish Vaswani, Noam Shazeer, Niki Parmar, Jakob Uszkoreit, Llion Jones, Aidan N Gomez, Ł ukasz Kaiser, and Illia Polosukhin. 2017. Attention is all you need. In *Advances in Neural Information Processing Systems*, volume 30. Curran Associates, Inc.

Adina Williams, Nikita Nangia, and Samuel Bowman. 2018. A broad-coverage challenge corpus for sentence understanding through inference. In *Proceedings of the 2018 Conference of the North American Chapter of the Association for Computational Linguistics: Human Language Technologies, Volume 1 (Long Papers)*, pages 1112–1122, New Orleans, Louisiana. Association for Computational Linguistics.

Tianyi Zhang, Varsha Kishore, Felix Wu, Kilian Q. Weinberger, and Yoav Artzi. 2020. Bertscore: Evaluating text generation with BERT. In *8th International Conference on Learning Representations, ICLR 2020, Addis Ababa, Ethiopia, April 26-30, 2020.*

Wei Zhao, Maxime Peyrard, Fei Liu, Yang Gao, Christian M. Meyer, and Steffen Eger. 2019. MoverScore: Text generation evaluating with contextualized embeddings and earth mover distance. In *Proceedings of the 2019 Conference on Empirical Methods in Natural Language Processing and the 9th International Joint Conference on Natural Language Processing (EMNLP-IJCNLP)*, pages 563–578, Hong Kong, China. Association for Computational Linguistics.

Appendix

A Metrics

BERTScore is a cosine-similarity based metric for which the input is encoded using RoBERTa embeddings (Liu et al., 2019). Recall and Precision are computed by summing over tokens and computing maximum similarity to each token from the other sentence. The result is averaged by the sentence length. For Precision, the sentence summed over is the reference sentence, and vice versa for Recall. F1 measure is the harmonic mean of the former two. Furthermore, inverse-document-frequency (idf) weighting can be applied to each maximal similarity in reference and precision, which is computed from the reference corpus. We use both a configuration without and with idf-weighting in our experiments.

MoverScore (MS) is based on the Word Mover's Distance (Kusner et al., 2015), an instance of Earth Mover's Distance (Rubner et al., 2000). It computes the minimal transportation cost necessary to transform one sentence into the other based on the distance between n-gram representations, additionally considering relative idf-weights. Representations are extracted from the last five layers of a DistilBERT model (Sanh et al., 2020).

Mark-Evaluate Petersen (ME-P, Mordido and Meinel, 2020) utilizes population estimators (Ricker, 1975) to score the quality of candidate-reference pairs. Since the population size is known prior to the estimate, the capture mechanism is based on whether a vector is inside the k-nearest-neighborhood of the opposite embedding set. The assumption that each sample is uniformly likely to be captured is intentionally violated. The deviation between known and estimated population size is computed to obtain the final score of the metric.

BLEURT (Sellam et al., 2020), in contrast to previous models, is a BERT model (RemBERT , Chung et al., 2020) specifically trained for evaluation. For adapting the model to the evaluation task, an additional training step is introduced in which artificially altered sentences are fed to the model alongside with the original ones to augment the evaluation process. Modification include dropping words from sentences, back-translating them or replacing random words with BERT predictions. A quality score can be computed based on different signals stemming from these alterations. These signals include metrics like BLEU, BERTScore and ROUGE, back-translation likelihood, a binary back-translation flag as well as entailment-flags. Further, the model is also fine-tuned on human ratings.

NUBIA (NeUral Based InterchangeAbility, Kane et al., 2020) is an ensemble metric consisting of three transformer-based models focussing on different aspects of the assessment: A pre-trained RoBERTa model, finetuned on STS-B (Cer et al., 2017), another pre-trained RoBERTa model, fine-tuned on MNLI (Williams et al., 2018), and a pre-trained GPT-2 model (Radford et al., 2019). The results are combined in an aggregator module and subsequently calibrated to fit in $[0, 1]$.

B Technical Setup

Table 1: Overview on the technical setup of the evaluated metrics.
♡ Available on GitHub
◇ As recommended in the official implementation

Metric	Underlying Model	Remarks
BERTScore (+ idf)	`microsoft/deberta-xlarge-mnli`	rescaled, hug_trns = 4.14.1, vers. = 0.3.11
BLEURT	`BLEURT-20`	finetuned RemBERT
Mark-Evaluate	`BERT-Base-MNLI`♡	k = 1 (kNN)
MoverScore	`distilbert-base-uncased`◇	n = 1 (n-gram)
	`roberta-sts`	
NUBIA	`roberta-mnli`	
	`gpt-2`	sequences are clipped to max 1024 tokens

C Perturbation Examples

Table 2: Examples of the different deteriorations. All other necessary details needed to reproduce our experiments can be found in the GitHub repository.

	Output
Original	`He's quick, he's a very complete player and in great form.`
Negation	`He's quick, he's not a very complete player and in great form.`
Repetition	`He 's quick, he 's a very complete player and in great form and in great form and in great form and in great form and in great form and in great form and in great form and in great form and in great form and in great form and in great form and in great form and in great form and in great form and in great form and in great form and in great form.`
Word Swap	`very complete a, he 's quick He 's and player great in form.`
Word Drop	`, player.`
Part of Speech Drop (ADJ)	`He's he's a very player and in form.`

Author Index

Association for Computational Linguistics
209 N. Eighth Street
Stroudsburg, Pennsylvania 18360

ISBN 978-1-7138-6741-8

CURRAN ASSOCIATES INC.
proceedings.com